Robert Gordon Latham

Russian and Turk

From a geographical, ethnological, and historical point of view

Robert Gordon Latham

Russian and Turk
From a geographical, ethnological, and historical point of view

ISBN/EAN: 9783337299354

Printed in Europe, USA, Canada, Australia, Japan

Cover: Foto ©ninafisch / pixelio.de

More available books at **www.hansebooks.com**

RUSSIAN AND TURK,

FROM

A GEOGRAPHICAL, ETHNOLOGICAL,

AND

HISTORICAL POINT OF VIEW.

BY

R. G. LATHAM, M.A., M.D., ETC.,

LATE FELLOW OF KING'S COLLEGE, CAMBRIDGE,
LATE PROFESSOR OF ENGLISH IN UNIVERSITY COLLEGE, LONDON;
AUTHOR OF "THE VARIETIES OF MAN"; "THE NATIONALITIES OF EUROPE";
"THE ENGLISH LANGUAGE," ETC.

LONDON:

WILLIAM H. ALLEN AND CO.,

13 WATERLOO PLACE, PALL MALL, S.W.

1878.

PREFACE.

THE present work is, to a certain extent, a republication of an earlier one, "The Nationalities of Europe," published fifteen years ago; this being preceded by one on a closely allied subject "The Native Races of the Russian Empire."

The reader is apprised of this in order that he may understand that the forthcoming pages have by no means been extemporized on the strength of the late war and the events connected with it. On the contrary, for many years an adequate amount of investigation has been applied to the subject.

In neither of these earlier works was there much political speculation; but of the little that there was there is nothing that has been falsified by the subsequent events. Of the first, the two Empires, here under notice, formed about half; but, as the object was almost wholly ethnological, a great proportion of it was devoted to the description of numerous petty populations of little national importance. This has been replaced by matter of a more appropriate character.   Still, the analysis of the complex and various elements of the two vast Empires, rather than the history of either of them as a whole, has been the main subject of the work.   Neither Turkey nor Russia, when reduced to its component parts, is exactly what it is, when considered as a unity. Hence the heterogeneous elements of which the two opposing powers consist, are exhibited in detail rather than in their action upon one another as masses.   In neither of them is an analysis of this kind superfluous; and in one of them it is most especially called for.

It is not necessary that a work of this kind should be written in the spirit of a partizan.   Neither is it very safe to prophecy as to the future; or to speculate as to what would have been the present result if something else had been done instead of what was done.

Nor yet is much to be got out of the doctrine of race; and not much more from reflections upon the relative merits or demerits of the combatants as exhibited in their previous history.   What really wants looking to is the actual amount of vice and suffering, which has its root in unjust government; and which by better government may be abated.

In respect to this it has been determined by England there is more to be done by forcing reforms upon the weaker of the two parties than by trusting, or pretending to trust in the moderation, or the promises of the stronger; that it is better to direct the Sultan, than to run the risk of being misled by the Czar.   It is not, however, argued that the best line of action is one upon which there can be no second opinion. In the eyes, however, of the present writer, England has much for which she may be both proud and thankful. There is no doubt that she has risked the chance of a very serious war; but by the decision with which she made known her views, and the steadiness with which she declared her resolution to act upon them if necessary, peace has ensued; and that at a time when there was but little encouragement and no alliances. May the continuation of our interposition be conformable to the beginning of it.

CONTENTS.

CHAPTER I.

Page.

Othman. Orkhan. Crosses the Bosphorus and establishes himself in
Europe. Amurath 1. Interregnum. Mahomet I. Bajazet I.
Amurath II. Mahomet II. Conquers Constantinople. Bajazet II.
Selim, his Conquests. Solyman I. First Siege of Vienna. Con-
quest of Rhodes. Selim II. First recorded War with Russia.
Amurath III. Mahomet III. Othman I. and Mustapha II. Amu-
rath IV. Ibrahim. Mahomet IV. The Kiuprili Viziers. Solyman
II. Achmet II. Mustapha II. Battle of Zenta. War with Russia
under Peter the Great. Treaty of Carlowitz   .   .   .   1

CHAPTER II.

Treaty of Carlowitz. Of the Pruth. Of Passarowitz. Of Belgrade. Of
Kainardji. Of Yassi. Of Bukarest. Of Akkerman. Of Adrianople.
Of Unkiar Skelessi. Of Paris   .   .   .   36

CHAPTER III.

Religious Creeds and Sects of the Ottoman Empire. General View.
Sunnite and Shiite Mahometanism. The Wahabis. Judaism, Judean
and Samaritan. Three forms of Syrian Christianity: Nestorian,
Eutychian, Romanist   51

CHAPTER IV.

Page

Religious Creeds and Sects of the Ottoman Empire. Haranites and Mendeans. Druzes. Ismaeli. Nasarieh, Nosrani, or Ansari. Mutuali   70

CHAPTER V.

Bulgaria and the Bulgarians. Their Ethnological Elements. Their early
History. Latin and Paulician Elements in the Bulgarian Creed.
Rumelia. Bosnia. Croatia. Herzegovina .   .   . 129

CHAPTER VI.

Macedonia, Thessaly, and Greece. Descent of the Modern Greeks. Slavonic, Vallachian, and other Elements. Bosnia and Herzegovina . 145

CHAPTER VII.

Turks other than Ottoman. The Sultan and the Czar. General Character 156

CHAPTER VIII.

The Turks other than Ottoman. Their Area. The Alani. The Huns.
The Avars. The Khazars. The Petshinegs. The Uz. The Cumanians. The Tshuvash 166

CHAPTER IX.

Non-Ottoman Turks. The Mongol Conquest. The Kiptshak. The Four
Khanates. The present Population of them. The Nogays, Bashkirs,
Meshtsheriaks, Tyeptyars, Kirghis, Barabinski, Karagass, Koibals,
Yakuts. Karakalpaks. Doubtful Turks, the Tshuvash .   . 224

CHAPTER X.

Page.

The Fin or Ugrian Family. Ugrians or Fins in Cúrland, Livonia, Estonia, the Governments of St. Petersburg, Novogorod. Finlanders of the Duchy of Finland. Tavastrian, Karelian, and Quain. Their early Christianity. Their present Popular Poetry. The Kalevala. The Laps 244

CHAPTER XI.

The Permians and Zirianians. The Votiaks. The Volga Fins, the Tsherimis and Mordvins. The Voguls and Ostiaks. The Samoyeds 304

CHAPTER XII.

Lithuania and the Lithuanic Family. Prussians. Yatshvings. Lithuanians Proper. Letts 320

CHAPTER XIII.

The Lithuanians Proper. Their Poetry. Their Fairy Tales . 337

CHAPTER XIV.

The Letts. The Baltic, or German Provinces of Russia : Estonia, Livonia, Cúrland 347

CHAPTER XV.

Populations neither Turk nor Fin. Of Northern Asia. Mongols. Tungusians. Yeniseians. Jukahiri. Koriaks and Kamtshatkans. Aino or Kurilians Islanders. Aleutians. The Independent Tshutshi. The Eskimo. Caucasus and Transcaucasia. Shamil . 358

CHAPTER XVI.

Page.

Rise and progress of the Russian Empire. Early piracy. Probable Russians. The name Rôs. The early historical period. Conquests of Vladimir the Great, and his successors, in the direction of the Baltic. Conquests of Ivan IV. the Terrible. Peter the Great. The Czarinas Anne and Catherine. Conquest of the Crimea. Incorporation of Lithuania. Conquest of Finland. The Treaty of Vienna . 373

CHAPTER XVII.

The Decline of the Ottoman Empire. After Mahomet II. too large for practical Administration. Mahomet II.'s Conquest of the Crimea. Selim I.'s Conquests in Armenia, Persia, Syria, Egypt. Soliman I., the Barbary Regencies. No permanent Impression made on Germany. Injurious Effects of the Ottoman Attacks upon Persia. Natural Antagonism on the part of Russia. Peter the Great as an Enemy; and less formidable than Anne or Catherine. Value of Sweden as an Element in the Balance of Power of Poland. Decline of the Influence of both. The subsequent conditional integrity of the Ottoman Empire. Retrospect . . . 395

RUSSIAN AND TURK.

CHAPTER I.

THE OTTOMAN TURKS. From A.D. 1288 to A.D. 1699.

Othman.—Orkhan.—Crosses the Bosporus and establishes himself in Europe.
—Amurath I.—Interregnum.—Mahomet I.—Bajazet I.—Amurath II.—
Mahomet II.—Conquers Constantinople.—Bajazet II.—Selim, his Con-
quests.—Solyman I.—First Siege of Vienna.—Conquest of Rhodes.—
Selim II.—First recorded War with Russia.—Amurath III.—Mahomet
III.—Othman I. and Mustapha II.—Amurath IV.—Ibrahim.—Mahomet
IV.—The Kiuprili Viziers.—Solyman II.—Achmet II.—Mustapha II.—
Battle of Zenta.—War with Russia under Peter the Great.—Treaty of
Carlowitz.

OF Turkish kingdoms there have been many, and some of
them may claim the more ambitious title of Empire. But the
Turkish Empire of the present day is that of the Osmanlis, or
Ottoman, Turks. And the distinction is important. At the
present moment the Sultan in Constantinople is an Ottoman in
every sense of the word ; but the Khedive in Egypt is scarcely
an Ottoman in any sense ; neither are his subjects Turks. Indeed, the term "Turk" is one of inordinate generality and
extent. More than a third of Central Asia is Turk, and in
Russian, Chinese, and Independent Turkestan, the name
presents itself ; while the great majority of Tatars are merely
Turks under another name. Further northwards we find Turks
in Siberia ; and, in the far east, along the banks of the Lena,
a Turk dialect is spoken as far as, and beyond, the Arctic Circle.

1

Then there are the Turcomans of the parts between the Caspian and the western extremity of the Himalayas. In every one of these instances the Turk occupancy is continuous; the Turks are the dominant population; and, except in certain districts on the Persian frontier, the Turkish is the vernacular language. There are Turks along the coast of the Arctic Sea, and there are Turks within the western boundaries of China.

Neither is the name *Ottoman* an old one, though the name *Turk* occurs as far back as the sixth century, when the ruler of the Turks sent an embassy to the Emperor Justinian; these being the Turks of the parts to the east and north of Lake Aral. It is not, however, in these parts that we must look for any such names as Ottoman; neither, except as the proper name of an individual, do we hear of either Ottomans or Osmanlis until after the Fourth Crusade, and the conquest of Constantinople by the Franks. The Osman, or Othman, that gave to his dynasty its name, died no earlier than A.D. 1326. This is what we know about the name and the bearer of it. But the father of Othman was Ertogrul, and the father of Ertogrul was Solyman Shah, and higher than this we have no continuous genealogy; nor is the exact personality of Solyman beyond a doubt.

The history of Ertogrul, of his brother Dundar, and of his son Othman, is as follows :—At some time subsequent to the Mongol invasion of Asia Minor, and apparently not far from the middle of the thirteenth century, and on some spot somewhere between the Armenian frontier and the Egean, an armed force of four hundred and forty-four horsemen under the captaincy of Ertogrul, or the Right-hearted man, as they were moving westwards, came in sight of a battle-field, in which one of the two armies was manifestly the weaker one. This was enough for Ertogrul, who immediately led his followers in defence of it, and so won the battle for no less a potentate than Alaeddin, the Sultan of Iconium, and against an enemy no less formidable than the Mongols. A grant of land—we may call it a fief— was Ertogrul's reward, and, as he was an efficient captain on other occasions afterwards, other fiefs were added to it; and with these Ertogrul was contented. He was simply the vassal and lieutenant of the Sultan.

Othman, his son, is this and something more. The nucleus of his territory is the classical range of Mount Olympus, and its chief town is Brusa. This he had won from the Greeks, against whom he fought his first regular battle in 1301. This was the battle of Baphæum, near Nicomedia. Here he was victorious. The Greeks, however, held the towns which were of primary importance—Brusa, Nicomedia, and Nicæa. For these Othman was content to wait patiently. His son Orkhan promised to be, like his father, a conqueror; and, of the three great cities, it was the first (Brusa) that was taken during Othman's lifetime. Othman bore himself as an independent prince—probably as an Emir of an Emirate—rather than as a mere officer of the Sultan. It is manifest that if Constantinople is to be conquered from Asia, the Bithynian Emirate of Othman is just the district from which the conquerors are to be expected.

Orkhan, like his father, is an Emir—not a Sultan. In the first year of his reign he takes Nicomedia, and four years afterwards Nicæa; both in Bithynia, both won from the Greeks.

Pergamus, with Mysia, is won, six years later, from a Turkish Prince. This is in Asia—what Orkhan did in Europe was but little; still, it was in Orkhan's reign that the first steps were taken towards Constantinople, and they were taken in the near neighbourhood of the capital itself. Cantacuzen, a usurper, in spite of the difference of religion, was his father-in-law; for Orkhan had married his daughter, and had assisted him against the legitimate Palæologi in return. This was one alliance. On the other hand the Genoese had the suburb of Galata, and the Venetians that of Pera; but the Venetians were the allies of Cantacuzen, the Genoese of Orkhan. With complications like this, with ambition, with opportunity, with nothing against them but the weak tie of relationship by marriage, the friendship between Cantacuzen and Orkhan came to an end: indeed John Palæologus, like Orkhan himself, was a son-in-law of Cantacuzen. In a Genoese bark, Soliman, the son of Orkhan,

1 *

crossed the Bosphorus and surprised Tzympe. Instead of recovering it, Cantacuzen asked the aid of Orkhan. This was
administered by Orkhan, and the forces of Palæologus routed.
Money was offered by Cantacuzen for Tzympe, but before it was
paid circumstances had changed, and Gallipoli was taken and
fortified.

It was with Orkhan's son and successor, Amurath I., that the
career of ambitious, systematic, and continuous conquest began.
He it was who reduced Adrianople, and made it, until the
taking of Constantinople, the Ottoman capital. He it was, too,
who first fought against enemies more formidable than the
degenerate Greeks, viz., the Bulgarians and Servians. Of these
the former had been, upon the whole, the more inveterate
enemies of the Empire; for they were the first of the barbarians
who threatened the walls of Constantinople, and for nearly nine
hundred years their name had been formidable. The Servians,
as a separate nation, had not been known by name so long;
but, with varying relations to Bulgaria, Wallachia, and Albania,
they, also, had long been formidable. Under their great king,
Stephen Dushan, in the thirteenth century, they held, for a short
time, a wider dominion than the Bulgarians. These were the
first Slavonians that were conquered by the Ottomans, and
Servia and Bulgaria are the oldest of the Ottoman provinces.
There are two battles of Kossova, and the first was the one
which Amurath I. won against the Servians; and it was on the
field of Kossova, and while the battle was going on, that Amurath I. was stabbed by a Servian noble who presented himself
to him as a deserter. He died on the field.

Under Bajazet I. Wallachia was constrained to pay tribute,
and the wars against Bosnia and Hungary commenced. It
was not until this latter kingdom was threatened that, in the
eyes of the Popes and the Crusaders, the difference between
Christianity and Mahometanism seems to have been recognised.
The heretics of Servia and Bulgaria found no sympathy among
the Franks; but the attack on a Romanist kingdom like Hungary was answered by a voice from the Vatican, and Pope
Boniface IX. proclaimed a crusade. The heretic Servians re-

mained faithful to their conquerors, and, for the first time on European ground, the flower of European chivalry was ignominiously defeated at the great battle of Nicopolis.

Bajazet I. died A.D. 1403, the year after his defeat near Angora, and in 1405 died his conqueror Timor. This was the time when, in spite of its conquests in Europe, the Ottoman Empire was in greater peril than it has ever been before or since. For eleven years there was an interregnum : and, after that, Mahomet I. reigned till 1421, and Amurath II., who succeeded him, till the middle of the century. It was Amurath II. who first laid siege to Constantinople, A.D. 1422. We know that he did not complete it, but there is no exact explanation of the motives that led him to abandon it. There is the belief that the Panagia, or Holy Virgin, came down from Heaven for the protection of the sacred maidens of Constantinople ; and there is the belief that counter-movements and conspiracies elsewhere called the Sultan into Asia Minor, and that, as he could afford to let the capital stand over for a future day, he chose to abandon it rather than neglect a civil war. This he soon extinguished ; but he did not renew the siege. Other cities, however, were surrendered, and an annual tribute was paid to him by the Emperor. Under Amurath II. the war against the Christians took a more serious form than it had done hitherto. It was an easy matter to fight against the Greek and the Imperial soldiers, and it was not very difficult to overrun such countries as Bulgaria, Servia, and Bosnia, all three of which were separate kingdoms, and by no means friendly to one another. But with states like Hungary, Poland, and Venice it was no light matter to enter into conflict. They always presented a solid resistance ; and when, in addition to the *vis inertiæ* of their mass, there was the *vis viva* of skilful and adventurous generals, there was much to retard the progress of even warriors like Amurath. This means that his days were also the days of a great general and of an unrivalled party warrior—Huniades and Scanderbeg, the former for Hungary and Wallachia, the latter for his native land, Albania. Of these it is safe to say that, at the very least, they gave the Turks much trouble; that they foreshadowed for them the difficulties that would attend any over-ambitious attempt against Western Europe, and, above all, delayed the final capture of Constantinople. Both fought obstinately and with varied success, and both made their names pre-eminently formidable to their common enemy, and both pass for one of the few great heroes of their respective countries. Before the death of Amurath, Huniades was beaten in the second battle of Kossova; and before the death of Mahomet II., Albania became a Turkish province.

Amurath II. was the father of Mahomet II.

On the 29th of May 1453, Mahomet II. took possession of Constantinople; in other words, the reduction of the capital of the eastern empire was the first of his conquests. Like his father he reigned thirty years, and during the whole of that period he either effected fresh conquests or completed and consolidated those of his predecessors. "Mahomet II.," writes Sir Edward Creasy, "was but twenty-three years of age when he took Constantinople, being one year older than Alexander was when he fought the battle of the Granicus, and three years less than the age of Napoleon, when he commanded at Lodi. The succession of wars and victories which filled the thirty years of Mahomet's reign, might, perhaps, bear comparison with the exploits of the other two imperial conquerors whom we have mentioned. The fragments of the Greek empire, which had lingered for a while unconnected with the central power of the emperor, were speedily subdued by the new ruler of Constantinople. The Peloponnesus was conquered in 1454, and Trebizond in the following year." The same writer when describing the Institutes of Mahomet, for he was a legislator as well as a conqueror, compared the military tenures which were granted to his followers in the countries they had conquered with the feudal system of Western Europe; and added that, like the barons of the time alluded to, they, the grantees of the Ziamets and Timars, aggrandized themselves, as in mediæval Christianity, at the expense of both the monarchy and the commonalty. How this began, we have seen in the notice of Othman, and the state, in his time, of Asia Minor. How long it lasted we shall see

when we come to the history of the present century; for it was
not until lately that the power of the descendants of these feudal
nobles, the Deri Beys, or Lords of the Valleys, were put down;
and, even at the present time, their power, whether for good
or for evil, is still but incompletely abolished. On the Turkish
ground, then, it was natural; and, in Greece, which is now especially under notice, though it was not aboriginal, it had been
thoroughly acclimatized; for the Franks, and the descendants
of the fourth campaign, had made Greece as feudal as England
was in the eleventh and twelfth centuries. It is difficult to
believe that the following extract from Finlay applies, not to
the soil of Spain, France, or Italy, but to that of Greece, as it
was in the fourteenth century.

During the period the duchy of Athens was possessed by the Sicilian branch
of the house of Aragon, the Catalans were engaged in wars with all their
neighbours. * * * * The lieutenants general of the dukes, who arrived
from Sicily, were always compelled to bring with them fresh supplies of
mercenary troops. The lieutenants of the Sicilian dukes mentioned in history
are, Berenger d'Estañot, and Alphonso, the natural son of King Frederic II.,
who governed in succession during the life of Manfred. Roger de Lauria, son
of the renowned admiral, represented Frederic of Randazyo. Afterwards,
Frances George, Marquis of Boudonitza, Philip of Dalmas, and Roger and
Antonia de Lauria, sons of the preceding Roger, ruled the duchy. During the
government of Roger and Antonio de Lauria, Louis, Count of Salon, son of the
Regent Alphonso, died, leaving an only daughter as his heiress. Louis was
proprietor of a very large portion of the duchy, and the disputes that arose
concerning the marriage of his daughter, caused the ruin of Catalan power,
and the conquest of Athens by Nerio Acciaiuoli, the Governor of Corinth.
The Catalans were the constant rivals of the Franks of Achaia, and, as
Nerio Acciaiuoli, as Governor of Corinth, was the guardian of the principality
against their hostile projects, the marriage of the young Countess of Salona
involved the two parties in war. The mother of the bride was a Greek lady;
she betrothed her daughter to Simeon, son of the Prince of Vallachian
Thessaly; and the Catalans, with the two Laurias at their head, supported
this arrangement. But the bozans of Achaia, headed by Nerio Acciaiuoli,
pretended that the feudal suzerain of Athens and Achaia was entitled to dis-
pose of the hand of the Countess, though the race of Baldwin II. was extinct;
for Jacques de Baux, the last titular Emperor of Romania, died before the war
between the Catalans and the Governor of Corinth commenced. Nerio was
nevertheless determined to bestow the young Countess, with all her immense
possessions, on a relation of the Acciaiuoli family, named Peter Sarrasin. The
wars concerning the Countess of Salona and her heritage appears to have

commenced about the year 1386. The Catalans were defeated, and Nerio gained possession of Athens, Thebes, and Livadea; but a few of the Spanish proprietors, and the remains of the military force attached to the viceroys, continued for some years to offer a most determined resistance in other parts of the duchy, and rallied round them a body of Navarrese troops in the service of the last Spanish governors.

Again—it was much the same in the islands. They suited the Venetians better than a territory on the mainland; and it is in the hands of a Venetian that we find them; although the transaction which put him in possession of them is obscure or unknown. Mark Sanudo was the first Duke of Naxos and of those islands of the Archipelago to which it was the political centre, viz.: Paros, Antiparos, Ios, Sikinos, Polykandros, Kimolos, Melos, Amorgos, Thera or Santorin, and Anaphe.

Of these, Melos plays a part of some importance; whilst Ios commands notice from the fact of its having been depopulated by an invasion of the Turks to such an extent as to lose the bulk, if not the whole, of its Greek population, which was made good by a colony from Albania; so that, at the present moment, Ios, like so many districts on the continent, is an actual Albanian occupancy.

A principle, not unlike the one upon which our Indian empire was allowed to develop itself in the hands of a private company of merchant adventurers, was adopted by the Venetians in respect to its territory in the islands. Private individuals were allowed to reduce certain islands, archipelagoes, or parts of islands, on condition of holding them as fiefs under the Republic. In this way Marco Dandolo and Jacomo Viaro occupied Gallipoli.

Marino Dandolo . . .	Andros.
The Ghisi family . . .	Tenos Mykone, Skyros, Skiathos, and Skopelos.
The Justiniani and Michieli .	Keos.
The Navigajosas . . .	Lemnos.
The Quirini	Astypalæa.

But Mark Sanudo was more powerful than all the rest put together; and the Naxian archipelago was the true representative of Venice in the Ægean. The *first* onslaught, however, made on

Greece was by Bajazet, and, in the parts north of the Morea, it was an effective one. Mahomet II. reduced the Morea, and partitioned into fiefs—Ziamets and Timars—the whole country, not only on the mainland, but in Labæa, and the Ionian islands, and Albania. This he divided into Sandjaks.

	Ziamets.	Timars.
The Sandjak of the Morea . . .	109	342
———— Negropont . . .	12	188
———— Thessaly	60	344
———— Epakto (*Naupactus*) . .	13	287
———— Karlili (*Ionian islands*) .	11	119
———— Yanina (*Albania*) . .	62	345
	267	1625

The tribute of children (one-fifth of the males) he instituted as the means of recruiting his army.

Immediately after his conquest of Greece, Mahomet turns his arms against Trebizond, a pretensious empire, famous in romance rather than in real history. Until the discovery by Fallermayer of the books of Cardinal Bessarion preserved at Venice, of the Chronicle of Michael Panaretos, the little that was known of the details of the history of Trebizond was collected from the works of the Constantinopolitan writers; who could scarcely have been either accurately informed or impartial. The voids which they left exercised the critical acumen of Ducange and stimulated the curiosity of Gibbon. They are now, to a great degree, filled up. They tell us much worth knowing. They leave, however, the Trebizond of history far below the Trebizond of romance.

When Asia Minor, Anatolia, or Roum, became Turk, Trebizond remained Imperial; Imperial and, to a great extent, Greek. Whilst Constantinople was in the hands of the Crusaders, Trebizond remained what may by courtesy be called Roman. But the town itself was but a small part of the Trapezuntine remnant. To take the measure of this we must extend Asia Minor, and carry it into Georgia, as far as Imereti, as far, perhaps, as Suaneti—at any rate beyond the Phasis. We must include the Lazic district of the wars under Justinian. We must include the ancient and mythic Colchis. We must include a portion both of Georgia and Armenia.

Whilst under the Byzantine Empire the Trapezuntines were connected with an important name, and one suggestive of more speculation than can be indulged in; for the theme to which Trebizond belonged was the theme Chaldia, and its Dukes were the Dukes of Chaldia.

The Trapezuntine wars were alliances chiefly with the Turks, under the Sultan of Iconium or Konieh, the Empire, and the Turcomans; and, when the Sultans were strong and the Trapezuntine Emperors weak, the former took the supremacy of suzerain, whilst the latter yielded the homage of the vassal.

Other political relations were with the Khans of Khawerezm, or Transoxiana, with the Temudzhinian Mongols, and with the Genoese of Kaffa, who, upon the whole, were their most formidable enemies. In spite, however, of the dangers of its environment, Trebizond flourished; was never reconquered by the Emperors; and lasted as an independent State from 1204 to 1461, when it was reduced by Mahomet II.

The retribution that followed the tyranny of Andronicus I. showed the weakness of the Emperor, and disorganized the empire; and, in doing this, suggested ideas of independence to the more distant themes. Trebizond was one of these, and a scion of the Comnenian family, on the male side, who had fair grounds for looking upon the ruling Emperor as a usurper, declared himself independent and something more. He denominated himself Emperor, and considered Trebizond to be the true capital of the Eastern Empire. As far as he was concerned he removed, in his own ambitious fancy, Constantinople to Trebizond. His title was The Faithful (Orthodox) King and Autocrat of all the East (Anatolia), the Iberians, the Perateia, and the Great (Grand) Comnenus—Perateia meaning a portion of the Crimea and Cherson, in which the Gothic district of Gothia was German.

Trebizond itself was Greek; Greek, at least in language, for the purposes of commerce, literature, and diplomacy. But the mass of the country, on the eastern side at least, was Georgian, and on the south Armenian, and, perhaps, Kurd. Add to this the likelihood of certain Turcomans having been included within its boundaries.

Alexios I. held his own, and transmitted his sceptre to his sons and his sons' sons, Georges, Johns, Manuels, Michaels, Basils, and Andronici, as Kings; Irenes and Theodoras, as Queens. These names are given on the strength of their truly Byzantine character, and as contrasts to the French and Italian names of Greece and the Archipelago.

As a town, or as a province, Trebizond flourished. As an empire, it was but a small and pretentious affair. The dynasty was legitimate, and, as far as it was Greek, native. The men who formed its armies and manned its fleets were neither Italians nor French ; neither Genoese nor Catalans. They were, on the contrary, essentially Asiatics—more so than even the most Asiatic portion of the true empire.

We have seen that Wallachia is already a tributary. But, where Wallachia ends, the territory of the Tatars of the Crimea begins, and it extends from the Pruth to the Cuban. To reduce these is to become master of the Black Sea, and this is a position of no slight importance; for, though the Tatars were the lords of the land, it was the Genoese who had the commerce—we may almost say the monopoly—of the Euxine. Their great port or emporium was Kaffa, and as the Venetian fleet was dominant in the Ægean, so was that of Genoa in the Euxine. There seems to have been nothing arbitrary in the order of Mahomet's conquests. This naturally followed that of Trebizond, but it was not made by Mahomet in person, and, what is rare in the early Ottoman history, there was a pretext for it. Whether it were not one of Mahomet's own concoction is another question. A ruler is either deposed or conspired against by his brothers, and appeals to Cæsar, and Cæsar deposes both him and his unbrotherly brethren. Three hundred years later there is the same conquest and the same pretext. The Khan of the same Crimeans, A.D. 1770, is conspired against, and, unread in the history of his predecessors, appeals to a

Cæsar of a different sex ; and the Tatar principality in the fifteenth century passes from its legitimate rulers to Mahomet, passes from their descendants to the Czarina Catherine.

Ahmed Keduk, Admiral and Grand Vizier, was the conqueror of the Crimea. Kaffa was pillaged, and, next to Constantinople, it was the wealthiest city in the Empire. Thousands of its inhabitants were transplanted to Constantinople, and 15,000 young Genoese were enlisted in the armies of the conquerors as Janissaries. Such was the blow struck against one of the great trading republics between whom the commerce of Constantinople was monopolised. Such, too, the blow at their maritime prerogative in one of the great Eastern seas.

The rival of Genoa was Venice, and what Genoa was in the Euxine such was Venice in the Ægean. But in the Black Sea there was one great emporium ; in the Ægean there were islands and islands. Selection in the order of the conquest of them was needed here, and it was made judiciously. Lesbos and Lemnos were the nearest to the Dardanelles, Eubæa to Greece, Cephalonia to Italy, and these Mahomet reduced himself; the others he left to his successors. Of the predecessors the most notable action of the Turkish navy was that of the boat which took Orkhan across the Bosphorus, and the fleet that followed with the soldiers of Amurath I.

Towards the end of Mahomet's reign his activity was as it was at the beginning, and his ambition, so far, at least, as it was manifested in action, greater. Bosnia he already conquered, but Albania was ably defended by its great hero George Castriotes, or Scanderbeg. Towards the end of his life, however, Albania was completely reduced, and then began the collision of the most inveterate, and, upon the whole, the most effective opponent of the Porte—the great Republic of the Adriatic. In 1477 an Ottoman army entered the territory of Friuli, and returned loaded with booty. The city was left intact, for a treaty was concluded which (according to one Italian historian) " contained a stipulation by which the Republic was to aid the Sultan, if attacked, with a fleet of 100 galleys, and the Sultan was, in case of necessity, to send 100,000 Turkish cavalry against the enemies of Venice."* This I believe to be the first instance of an amicable treaty between the Ottoman and any Christian power. There had been truces, one of which was disgracefully broken by the Christians, and there had been a temporary recognition of the great Scanderbeg as an independent prince in Albania; but the treaty, if real, is the nearest approach to European warfare that I have met with. It was, probably, meant to ensure the neutrality of Venice in the attempts of the last of Mahomet's expeditions, which shortly afterwards followed.

The conquest that the Sultan meditated was that of Italy, and, subsidiary to this, that of Rhodes, now in possession of the Knights of St. John. This attack was heroically repulsed under the Grandmastership of Pierre d'Aubrisson. The second, of which Lisle Adam was the first of many heroes, will be noticed hereafter. But the first siege of Rhodes was the one in which Mahomet II. failed.

On the same day that the Ottomans retreated from Rhodes, Ahmed Keduk, the conqueror of the Crimea, marched against Otranto, which he stormed 11 August 1480. On the 3rd of May of the following year, Mahomet II. suddenly died in the midst of the army. It was collected on the Asiatic side of the Bosphorus, but no one but the Sultan knew its destination. "His maxim was that secrecy in design and celerity in execution are the great elements of success in war. Once, when at the commencement of a campaign, one of his chief officers asked him what were the main objects of his operations, Mahomet answered sharply, 'If a hair of my beard knew them, I would pluck it out and cast it into the fire.'"

The reign of Mahomet's successor, Bajazet II., was by far the most inglorious of those of the early Sultans, or the Sultans of the rise and progress of the Empire. Indeed, the history reads as if it belonged to its decline and fall. The first event in it, and it may be looked upon as the first retrograde movement in Turkish history, was the recall from Italy of the able and successful Ahmed Keduk. His successor in the govern-

* Sir Edward Creasy, History of the Ottoman Turks, p. 91, ed. 1877.

ment of Otranto was subsequently driven out of Italy by the Prince of Calabria, and so ended the first and last Ottoman occupation of the soil of Italy.   Then there was a chronic state of warfare all along the debatable frontiers of Hungary, Venice, and Poland; for the conquest of the Crimea had brought the Tatar and the Kosak districts in contact with one another, and in the direction of Bratislav and Podolia there was always, until the time of the partitions, either alliances or wars between Poland and the Porte.   There were in Asia Minor rebellions of irrepressible Caramanians, and in the same districts there were outbreaks of the Shiite heresy.   Lastly there were aggressions on the part of the Marmelukes of Egypt upon the southern districts of Anatolia.   But it is not these that form the main subjects in the history of Bajazet's unhappy reign.   There were internecine fraternal feuds; there was the sad history of the Sultan's unhappy brother Djem; and, finally, there was the rebellion of Selim against his father, and the forced abdication of Bajazet, the weakest, but not the wickedest, of the early Sultans.

It is in the reign of Bajazet that we first find the Sultan appealed to as the representative potentate of the Mahometan world, and the protector of the creed of the Faithful; and this is not unconnected with another fact, the rapid development of the Ottoman navy.   Kemal Reis, in 1483, is sent to ravage the coast of Spain, in consequence of the entreaty of the Moors of Grenada to the Sultan of Constantinople, the "lord of the two seas and the two continents," for succour against the Christians.   After this we find him either victorious, or skilfully fighting against superior forces, in the naval wars against Italy, Venice, and Spain.

As the name of Spain first appears in Turkish history during this reign, so does that of Russia.   In A.D. 1492, Ivan III. proposed diplomatic relations between the two empires.   Three years later an ambassador appeared at Constantinople, with special injunctions to allow precedence to no other ambassador, and not to bow the knee to the Sultan.   He seems to have obeyed,—perhaps, to have overstepped his injunctions, and to have done his best to behave arrogantly.   Bajazet merely de-

clined to send an ambassador in return. Under none of his predecessors would the Russian ambassador himself have returned.

We are scarcely prepared by the notice of the reign of
Bajazet II. to expect that in that of his son and successor the
extent of the Ottoman empire will be nearly doubled. But such
is the case; and, what is more remarkable, it is not at the
expense of the Christian kingdoms of Europe that such an
inordinate aggrandizement will be made. In this direction as
much has been done as is feasible. It is not, however, difficult
to see the quarters in which desperate struggles are likely to
take place; viz., the parts to the east and south of Asia Minor,
Persia, and Armenia, Syria, and Egypt. Indeed, the coming
events have already cast their shadows before them. There are
two great Mahometan kingdoms, Persia and Egypt, and both are
seen during the reign of Bajazet at enmity with the Sultan.
The Persians are, in the eyes of the orthodox Sunnites—and
this is what the Turks are in general—heretics and Shiites; and,
if not into Asia Minor, Shiite doctrines in their worst form, had
even before the time of the Crusades, found their way into Syria.
Doctrines, too, of the same kind had at a still later period developed
themselves in Egypt; indeed, in both Egypt and Persia, they
seem to have been indigenous. Now Selim was a persecutor,
and not the less so because he was a man of more than ordinary
culture: and we have seen that, before he came to the throne,
there was a Shiite insurrection in Asia Minor. Again, the Mameluk inroads, on the side of Egypt, in the Turkish districts of
the Syrian frontier, had led even the peaceful Bajazet into a war
in which he won little renown. Between the two we get the
important fact that Selim is the champion in a war of religion,
and that Mahometanism is divided against itself. And as Selim
was of the Sunnite Sultans, so was his adversary, Ismail of Persia,
one of the ablest and the most earnest of the Shiite Shahs. We
have already said that Selim nearly doubled the extent of the
empire bequeathed to him by his grandfather; but had the wars
taken a different turn he might have forfeited the half of it.

The Persian campaign was the first of the two, and thus he
makes himself master of the capital, Tabriz. Here he halts,

and, thence, marches into the more impracticable districts of Armenia, so far, indeed, that his troops refuse to follow him. He fails, then, to conquer Persia ; but the Armenian and the Kurd districts about Diabekir he reduces. In the Egyptian campaign he reduces and retains Cairo, and subsequently all Egypt and Syria. This last conquest makes him not only the Sultan of Egypt, but the Calif of Sunnite Mahometanism. As a persecutor he can best be compared with Charles IX. of France. As the organizer of the administration of Egypt, he appears to deserve praise.

Solyman I., the Magnificent, reigned when the great kingdoms of Europe had become consolidated ; when Charles V. ruled in Spain, and Francis I. in France. With the latter he contracted alliances.

In 1526, Hungary was conquered on the bloody field of Mohacz, Buda being taken   Louis, the king, died childless, and the archduke of Austria, Ferdinand, claimed the Hungarian crown, as brother-in-law to the late king. The Hungarians would recognize none but a native; and Zapolya, one of the nobles, was their spokesman and champion. Worsted by Ferdinand, he betook himself to Solyman, and became a native king of Hungary under a suzerain. The wars with Austria arose out of the first siege of Vienna ; where Solyman was repulsed. He was also unsuccessful against Malta ; but Mesopotamia, part of Arabia, and the Barbary States, he reduced ; Candia, Cyprus, Georgia, and Caucasus, being all he left for his successors.

But the great conquest of Solyman's reign was one which, though the smallest in the matter of territorial acquisition, was in its moral effects greater than any which had been made since the taking of Constantinople. It was made in the face of civilized Europe, which looked on and did nothing to retard it ; and it was against the oldest and most formidable enemy to Mahometanism that it was effected. The Knights of St. John were something more than mere enemies of the Ottoman Empire. Long before it existed, when the distant ancestors of Ottoman were but rude soldiers, or, at best, but subordinate captains, they constituted the working force of the Crusades, so discreditable to the pilgrim warriors of Europe, so glorious to the permanent occupants of either Acre or Jerusalem. The Island of Rhodes, under the Knights of St. John, had foiled the vast fleet and army of Mahomet II., fresh from victories in every part of the Levant; and their grand master D'Aubusson had been succeded by men in whom his spirit glowed with equal intensity. It was against greater odds that Lisle Adam had to contend. The actual numbers in all wars, except those of modern times, are unattainable; and the tendency is always to exaggerate differences where notable differences exist.

At the election, however, of Fabricius Caretto in 1513, the list of the suffragan knights was as follows :—

Of the French		language	100
„	Provençal	—	90
„	Castilian and Portuguese	—	88
„	Auvergnat	—	34
„	Arragonese	—	66
„	Italian	—	60
„	English	—	38
„	German	—	5
			453

This favours the accuracy of the number of knights and men-at-arms found in the garrison when Lisle Adam, expecting that the dawn of the next day would bring the Turkish fleet in sight, made his inspection : viz.—

Of Men-at-arms	.	.	.	4500
„ Knights	.	.	.	600
				5100

To this may be added the companies formed by the Rhodians themselves, the crews of the vessels in the harbour, and the force of the country people; who were made available as pioneers. Against this is given to the army of Solyman :—

Soldiers .	.	.	.	140,000
Pioneers, &c. .	.	.	.	60,000
				200,000

On the 26th of June, 1522, it was signalled that the Turkish fleet was in sight. The procession of the Feast of St. John was going on, and it was finished with its usual solemnity. Mass was then said : when the grand-master having walked towards the altar

2

elevated the Host, and prayed to the Most High for his succour in the struggle that was impending. After this each man betook himself to his post: the French, the Provençals, the English. the Spaniards, and the Italians, to the five bastions bearing the name of their several languages.

There was some real, some imputed treachery. There was a Turkish slave who attempted to fire the city; a female. There was a Jew physician. There was a suspected knight. The guilt, —of which the historian* here followed acquits him,—of the unhappy D'Amaral is doubtful. His position was such as to have warranted him in contesting the grand-mastership against even Lisle Adam; and he bore his defeat suspiciously. Distrusted from the first, he was accused by one of his followers, who was found on one of the bastions with a bow in his hand; the arrow during the siege being the chief means by which communications were effected. He accused his master, who was condemned, disgraced, beheaded; a brave knight, and lost to the defence when no single hand could be spared.

The mounds by which the Turks tried to command the town rose higher and higher, until they overlooked the Spanish and Auvergnat bastions: and on the English bastion the storm beat stronger still. A few minutes longer and it would have been taken. When the alarm reached the chapel of St. Mary of Victory, the words—

"Deus in adjutorium meum intende."

were being intoned: and the grand-master accepted the augury— " Come, my brethren, let us exchange the sacrifice of our prayers and praises for that of our lives; and let us die, if God so will it, in defence of our religion." The storm of the unfaithful was rolled back. On the 13th of September the Italian, on the 17th the English, bastion was attempted; and on the 24th those of Spain, Italy, and Auvergne, were simultaneously attacked; but September and October passed before signs of surrender showed themselves. By the knights they were spurned to the last; but the citizens sent deputations, and the bishop supported them. The brave and skilful engineer, Martinigo, to whom, after the grand-master, the siege owes the glory which alone rewarded

* Porter ; History of the Knights of Malta.

its resistance, gave a solemn and responsible opinion that the works were no longer in a condition to be held. The voice of the knights was that they would be buried under their ruins.

November wore through; and the 6th of December came before a white flag, waving from the top of one of the churches, was answered by another from one of the Turkish positions. The terms of capitulation followed. The knights, and such citizens as chose, were free to leave the town, with their personal property. Those who remained were to be free from tribute for five years. The churches, and all property, public and private, were to be respected. The other alternative was, the worst that a victorious army, and that army a Turkish one, could do.

After the terms had been accepted, the Sultan took certain exceptions to the form; and for eleven days longer hostilities continued; after which, terms essentially the same were agreed to. Nor were they violated. "There has been nothing so well lost in the world as Rhodes," was the remark of Charles V. when he heard of its fall.

Under Selim began the first war with Russia, an unsuccessful one on the part of Turkey; the field of battle being the parts between Astrakan and the Caucasus.

The conquest of the islands (with the exception of the Lesbian group, reduced by Mahomet II.) still stands over.

Chios was a Genoese dependency administered by the Maona, an analogue to our own East India Company; a joint-stock adventure in which the Justiniani were the great hereditary directors. The good it did is measured by the material prosperity of the island. The bad lay in the encouragement of piracy and the slave-trade. It was, indeed, pre-eminently infamous as a slave depôt. Reduced by Piali, it suffered less than any other island during its transfer; indeed, until the year 1821 Chios was the favoured spot in the Archipelago.

The same year saw the reduction of Naxos. The Greeks offered to betray the Duke, John VI., on condition that the farming of the revenues might be made over to them. The Duke was betrayed; but the collection of the revenues was given to a Portuguese Jew, who sent a Romanist Spaniard as his deputy. Mahometan sovereignty, Hebrew finance, and Castilian toleration were the rewards of the greedy Naxiots.

2 *

Cyprus was wrested by Richard Cœur de Lion in the second crusade from the Pasha of Egypt, under the rule of the Seldzhukian Turks, long before the founder of the Ottomans was born : so that it was in no respect a portion of the modern Turkish Empire. When the Holy City was lost to the Crusaders the title of King of Jerusalem accompanied that of the King of Cyprus. The Lusignan family gave the dynasty—a dynasty, like that of the Emperors of Trebizond, more prominent in romance and heraldry than in real history. It now became Turk.

Connected with Maina as ancient *Crete* was with Sparta, the Venetian corsairs of Candia had always abetted the indestructible Mainot spirit of insubordination. They ran their cargoes into the harbours of Cape Matapan and shared their booty with the mountaineers ; always in rebellions, often put down. Finlay is probably right in stating that the Ottoman government was intermediate in character to that of the Genoese of Chios and the oligarchy of Venice ; more tyrannical than the commercial, less oppressive than the aristocratic, rule. " If," writes Paul Sarpi, " the gentlemen of these colonies do tyrannize over the villages of their dominion, it is best not to let them see it, that there may be no kindness between them and their subjects ; but if they offend in anything else 'twill be well to chastise them severely, that they may not brag of their privileges more than others."

A single detail, the murder of an accepted son-in-law, who was a despised Greek, by the father of the bride who had gone to church to marry her, along with the local insurrection that arose out of it, an abortive Sicilian Vespers, gives us a concrete instance of the pride, dissimulation, and cruelty of the dominant class. Other details convey a notion of the extent of the piracy which, between the Knights from Malta and the Venetians from Crete, rivalled that of the Barbary States. And in this piracy the Spaniards and Italians joined—Catalans from so respectable a kingdom as Arragon, Italians from such Republics as Pisa, Lucca, and Florence. Out of these grew the war which cost Venice Candia ; the last important conquest of the Ottomans.

The preparations were made as if against Malta ; but the storm (not unexpected) broke on Crete, which was harassed or blockaded for twenty-three years. The Greeks favoured the Turks, and were plundered and killed by the Venetians for their want of patriotism. In 1666 the Grand—we may say the Great—Vizier Kiuprili took the command himself, and, after a protracted resistance, the keys of Candia were given up to him by Morosini in '69.

The interval between the conquest of Candia and the beginning of the Venetian war in the Morea was one of sixteen years; and they were years in which the arrogance of the Porte displayed itself at the expense of almost every Government in Europe—more, however, by haughtiness of language, by the contemptuous rejection of just complaints, and by the barbarous treatment of ambassadors, than by any acts of aggressive warfare on a great scale. Of border forays there were many: forays by the Kosaks from Poland; forays by the Morlaks from Dalmatia; piracies on the part of the Uskoks at the head of the Adriatic; piracies on the part of the Knights of Malta. The proper redress for these injuries should have been found in appeal to Venice as a maritime Power, to Austria and Poland as great Powers by land. But such appeals were disregarded to an extent which seems to have been amply sufficient to put the Christian Powers in the wrong. They trifled and prevaricated. They would and they would not. Half Hungary was already under the suzerainty of the Sultan, and the Austrian half was governed on purely Austrian principles. What these are now they were in the days between the conquest of Candia and the second siege of Vienna. One man alone, without respect to either prudential fears or diplomatic considerations, was purely and simply inveterate and unswerving in his hostility to the name of Turk and Infidel; the great Polish warrior and king, John Sobieski. His relief of Vienna has been noticed elsewhere.

Scarcely his rival as a soldier, but incomparably above him as a politician and an administrator, Morosini, still alive and in his sixty-sixth year, was called by the republic to retrieve the loss of Candia; though it was Morosini himself who had surrendered it. Neglected, if not disgraced, after doing all that skill or courage could do, for not prolonging the tenure of an untenable fortress, he was now entrusted with the command of the Republic, which had determined on a war against Turkey.

The capture of Santa Maura was followed by that of Prevesa;

and the conquest of the Morea was inaugurated by the reduction of Coron. Relying (on certain occasions too much) on the discontent of the Greeks, especially that of the fickle Mainots, Morosini landed his forces, and, during the campaign of '55, the strong and central fortress of Patras was reduced. After the Morea, with the exceptions of Misitra and Monemvasia, was evacuated, Athens became a Venetian possession. The Turks, who held out until the city was no longer tenable, were allowed, on their capitulation, to embark with their families; and about two thousand five hundred individuals sailed for Smyrna. About thirty remained and were baptized. That Athens, defended by a Turkish garrison, always brave, and, when behind stone walls, of more than ordinary obstinacy, should be taken without damage to the beautiful remains of its ancient architecture, was not to be hoped. It was in the front of the Propylæa that the Turks had constructed their chief batteries, and it was in the Parthenon that they stowed the bulk of their movable property and some of their gunpowder. Both the Parthenon and the Propylæa were battered and burnt. One of the mosques became a Catholic, another a Lutheran, chapel. The last act of Morosini, when, driven out by the plague, he quitted Athens, was to take away, among other discreditable trophies which he was less successful in getting to Venice, the four lions which still guard the Venetian arsenal. For ten years Morosini, either as general or Doge, directed this war; in which, besides the temporary occupancy of Athens, Eubœa was unsuccessfully attempted, Chios taken, and several strongholds in Northern Greece surrendered. Still, towards the end of the campaign, the war languished, and when peace was made between the Emperor, the King of Poland, the Republic, and the Porte, Venice retained, besides its conquests in Dalmatia, and besides Ægina, the whole of the Morea. The tribute exacted by the Sultan for Zante was also given up. Prevesa, on the other hand, and Lepanto were surrendered to the Porte after the destruction of their fortresses.

The conquest of Belgrade preceded that of Rhodes; the great battle of Mohacz followed it. In this died Louis IV., the last King of Hungary. But it was not the intention of Solyman to make Hungary a Turkish province. He preferred to nominate and hold in vassalage its sovereign. After marching along the Danube to the Austrian frontier, and ravaging the whole country, he was recalled by disturbances in Asia, so that it was not till 1529 that he returned to Hungary. Here he considered it his mission to regulate the succession to the throne, inasmuch as Louis had died without issue, and his brother-in-law, the Archduke Ferdinand, the brother of the Emperor Charles V., claimed it; whereas the Hungarians held that no one could be King of Hungary unless he were a native Magyar. This led to the election of one of the most powerful of the nobles, Zapolya, and when he was ignored by the Emperor he applied to Solyman. It is easy to anticipate the result of this. There is, on the part of Solyman, the invasion of Austria, and the *first* siege of Vienna, from which his army, baffled and disappointed, retired on the 14th of October 1529.

With the first siege of Vienna begins the long period of hostilities between Turkey and Austria—Austria as opposed to Hungary, a period beginning with the humiliation of the Emperors, but destined to terminate in their triumph. For there is another siege of Vienna to come. But, at present, there is no retaliation on the part of Austria, and Solyman is free to turn his arms in other directions. Accordingly, he increases his conquests in Persia, and greatly strengthens his power on the Mediterranean. We have seen that as early as the reign of Bajazet II., and when the naval power of the Ottomans was in its infancy, the Mahometans of Grenada had sued for the protection of the Turkish fleet, and the first of the great Turkish admirals, Kemal Reis, was sent to their aid. Under Solyman the naval power is at its height; for it is the time of Barbarossa, of Dragut, of Piali, and others of scarcely less note—the time when the alliance of the Sultan is sought by so Christian a king as Francis I. In one attempt, however, it is destined to fail.

We have already seen how Rhodes has been twice attacked, firstly by Mahomet II., under the grandmastership of Pierre d'Aubuisson, and, secondly, by Solyman himself, where the heroic resistance of Adam de Lisle, though eventually unsuccessful, was more glorious than many victories. After the evacuation of Rhodes the Order re-established itself in Malta, which was granted to them by the Emperor Charles V. Here they took an accurate value of the natural defences of the

island, and with equal skill and rapidity availed themselves of
it. The island was strongly fortified, and the naval force increased, and this, of course, during the reign of Solyman
himself. In the last year of his reign he resolved upon either
the destruction or the dissolution of the Order; nor, independent
of other motives, can it be denied that he had good reasons
for taking offence. It was a time in which piracy was organised
and almost licensed, and on the high seas the conduct of the
Knights had been, in many instances, piratical rather than
chivalrous. Beyond all doubt it was the bounden business of
the Sultan to coerce the knights if he could. Solyman had
ejected them from Rhodes, and he now prepared to eliminate
them from the Mediterranean altogether. A fleet of a hundred
and eighty sail was despatched from Constantinople under
Mustapha, the Vizier, and the more formidable Piali, and it
was to be joined by another under Dragut and Ouloudj Ali.
These met the fleet before Malta, somewhat behind their time,
so that the first steps in the conduct of the attack were not
made under the direction or with the counsel of Dragut. He
demurred to them, but not to the extent of withholding his co-
operation. Against these there is simply the garrison of the
island and such naval help as may be collected from either the
vessels afloat elsewhere or such assistance as any Christian
naval power might send them. On the 16th of June Dragut
ordered a general assault. On the 11th of September the
Grandmaster could only muster six hundred men fit for service.
But it would have been the same if he could have mustered
six thousand. The handful he had about him had done their
work, and the Ottoman fleet had withdrawn. Though less
protracted than that of Rhodes, the defence of Malta was as
obstinate. Subsequently to the attack of the 16th of June, a
fleet from Algiers, under the son of the great Barbarossa, joined
in the siege, and the best admirals of the Porte were engaged
in it. On the other hand it was known to the Turks that the
Viceroy of Sicily had despatched a fleet in aid of the Christians.
Its magnitude seems to have been exaggerated; but, at any
rate, the siege was abandoned, and the Sultan was for a second
time foiled and mortified.

It was in the last year of their lives that both Mahomet II. and Solyman II. failed in their efforts against the order of St. John; and the persistency with which the policy of the conqueror of Constantinople was followed up more than half a century after his death is a measure of the impression of Frank valour which, partly on the soil of Syria and partly in the two insular fastnesses, was left upon the minds of the Paynim. The two great Sultans under notice both failed twice, and, throughout their long series of campaigns, only twice. Both fought against the Knights and both against Belgrade, against which Mahomet failed. Concurrently with this there is another invasion of Hungary, and during this the great conqueror and lawgiver died in his tent before Szigeth. He died more than seven weeks before the end of the campaign, and, until the fall of Szigeth, his death, whether known to few or many, was not known to the army at large.

Selim II., from 1566 to 1574.—It is during the reign of Selim II., the son and successor of Solyman, that the first war between Turkey and Russia breaks out, and the date of it is an epoch of importance in the history of both empires. It is the beginning of the decline of Turkey and of the rise of Russia. In the opinion of the present writer a great deal too much has been written about the misery and degradation of Russia under what is called the tyranny of the Mongols; for the notion that from the thirteenth to the sixteenth century Russia was in a state of comparative bondage is certainly a common one. That she was under vassalage of some kind to the so-called representative of Tshingis-Khan, and that it paid tribute to a power called "*Mongol*," is true enough; but whether the lord was much stronger than the vassal, or whether the *Mongol* was not as little of a *Mongolian* as the Great *Mogul* was in India, is by no means certain. That the so-called Mongol Empire of the Kiptshak was at a very early period more Turkish than Mongolian is beyond doubt.

But, be this as it may, the Russians, in the time of Selim II., are not only emancipated but actual and aspiring conquerors. They are the masters of two out of the three Khanates on their frontier, viz., Kazan and Astrakan; and the boundary of the latter is not only on the mouth of the Volga and the coast of the Caspian, but on the eastern frontier of the Tatars of the Crimea. These, as we have seen, were reduced to a state of vassalage in the reign of Mahomet II., and, upon the whole, had been faithful in their allegiance to the Porte. It was not a matter for the Sultan to complain of if they extended their frontier at the expense of their neighbours, and not unnatural that reprisals should be made in return. Long before the time of Selim II. there had been complaints on the side of Russia, and, probably, just ones. We have seen that in the unwarlike time of Bajazet II. a Russian ambassador was sent to Constantinople, and, doubtless, it was matters connected with Crim Tatary that he was sent about. In the present instance there was something more than the mere aggressions of two neighbouring enemies. To a great extent the movement of Sokolli was *in odium tertii*. It was suggested that there was an easier way of invading Turkey and Armenia than by the way of Asia Minor. The Black Sea led to the Don, and the Don and the Volga at one point were within thirty miles of each other. The Volga, then, led to the Caspian, and, with a navy on the Caspian, the whole seaboard of Persia lay open to an invasion from the Crimea.

Now this notion of attacking Persia through the Don, the Volga, and the Caspian Sea was no novelty in the time of Selim, and his Vizier Sokolli might have got the idea from an Arabic writer whom he was likely to have read. Masudi writes, " At the beginning of the fourth century of the Hejira (about A.D. 912), came about five hundred ships of *Russians,* each carrying a hundred men, and ran into the arm of the Nit (the Sea of Azov), which is connected with the Khazar river (another reading is the Khazar Sea, *i.e.,* Lake). When these ships of the Russians had got up to the outworks of the Khazars on the mouth of the river (Don), they sent to the King of the Khazars asking leave to pass through his land, to sail down his river (the Volga) into the Khazar Sea (the Caspian, which is the sea of Georgia and Taberistan and other Persian districts), in which case they promised to give him on their return half the booty they might bring back."* They succeed in their ex-

---

* Zeuss, Die Deutschen und Die Nachbarstämme, p. 550.

pedition and return; and, *inter alia,* there is the remarkable statement that they find their way from the Caspian to the Black Sea by a *"canal."*

This is as much as need be said at present in respect to the geography of the contemplated road to Persia. The passage from which the previous statement has been taken is a long one, and, as it bears upon the origin and early import of the name Ρῶς, or *Russ,* it will be submitted to criticism in another place. I am not inclined to think that Sokolli was the first Ottoman who suggested the idea, any more than to believe that his suggestion of a similar communication between the Red Sea and the Mediterranean was a novelty. He might, indeed, have been, under other circumstances, a great engineer; he was certainly an able vizier. What he excogitated in respect to the junction of the Don and the Volga, he tried to put into execution by a canal through the isthmus of Suez, but was interrupted or anticipated by an opposition movement on the part of Arabia.

What follows is, perhaps, an explanation of the importance which a few weeks ago was so much attached by the Grand Duke Nicholas to the fact of his not having dined with the Sultan, and I am not aware that any previous exclusion from the Sultan's dinner-table was alluded to. I suggest that the late omission of a similar invitation had something to do with it. Trifles of this kind, if anything in diplomatic etiquette can be branded as trifling, are long remembered in Russia. It was not by accident that the day for the signing of the treaty of Kanairdji, so humiliating to the Sultan, took place on the anniversary of that of the Pruth, so humiliating to the Czar.

The Czar Ivan had, in 1490, sent an ambassador named Nossolitof to Constantinople, to complain of the Turkish attack on Astrakan, and to propose that there should be peace, friendship, and alliance between the two empires. Nossolitof, in addressing the Viziers, dwelt much on the toleration which his master showed to Mahometans in his dominion, as a proof that the Czar was no enemy to the faith of Islam. The Russian ambassador was favourably received at the Sublime Porte, and no further hostilities between the Turks and Russians took

place for nearly a century. But the Ottoman pride and contempt for Russia were shown by the Sultan omitting to make
the customary inquiry of Nossolitof respecting his royal
master's health, and by the Czar's representative not receiving
the invitation to a dinner before audience, which was usually
sent to ambassadors.*

So much in respect to the minor details of this war against
Russia and the Khan of the Crimea and his suzerain. The
continuation was as follows:—The work of the pioneers was
interrupted by the Janissaries, but the Janissaries were dispersed, and it was on this occasion that the first trophies from
the Ottomans were won by the Muscovites. As for the Tatars
in general, they were on the side of Russia rather than the Porte,
while those that fought for the Turks were defeated. So the
Sultan sailed homewards. The end, however, so far as we
know anything more about it, was that A.D. 1571 the Khan of
the Crimea took Moscow by storm and sacked the city.

Towards the end of his reign the Ottomans reduced Cyprus,
a conquest which was followed by the battle of Lepanto, a
battle more important from its moral than its material results.
Don John of Austria was the hero of Europe, and his fame
still survives. But the political results of his glorious victory
were wholly incommensurate with the splendour of the action.
He also took Tunis, but Tunis was retaken within two years,
and Cyprus remained in possession of the Ottomans.

However much Turkey may fail in its wars against the
Empire, she always seems able to make inroads upon Persia.
Amurath III. is a weak prince; yet he can not only conquer a
great part of Persia, but adds so important a kingdom as Georgia
to the empire. In the wars that are about to follow between
the Porte and the new enemy Russia, a lodgment in the Caucasian districts thus effected is of importance. With Georgia
on the south and the Crimean Tatars on the north, the im-
passable character of the Caucasian mountains is greatly abated.
The fleet, too, is still efficient, and the measure of its re-
spectability may be taken from the fact that no less a sovereign
than Elizabeth of England should have addressed more than

* Sir E. Creasy, History of the Ottoman Turks, p. 126, ed. 1877.

one request to Amurath for assistance on the sea against the Armada. She allows herself to be called, in the appeal made to him, "the unconquered and most puissant defender of the true faith against the idolaters who falsely profess the name of Christ;" and her advocate suggests that if the two countries join in a maritime war, "the proud Spaniard and the lying Pope will be struck down."* Besides his unimpaired navy he still retained the service of the able vizier Sokolli; for now the time is coming when, instead of able Sultans and nominal Viziers, there will be able Viziers and degenerate Sultans.

Amurath III. is succeeded by Mahomet III., who reigns from 1595 to 1603. Two years before his accession another war with Austria has begun. In this, as in all the previous wars, the great battle of the campaign is won by the Ottomans. It was fought October 23rd 1596, on the River Cerestes, an affluent of the Theiss. For the first two days of the fighting the Christians had the advantage, but on the third they were hopelessly routed. This, however, was the last of their continuous victories. Then there is an insurrection in Asia Minor, and a war in Persia.

In the third year of the reign, and in the seventeenth of the age, of Achmed I., the protracted hostilities between Austria and the Porte were brought to an end, and the treaty of Sitvatorok was concluded. It is not important on account of the material changes that it effected, but it is very important in the alteration it shows in the language and demeanour of the Sultans. It is no longer of that imperious and insulting character which even powerful states and high-spirited individuals had to put up with. The terms were no longer those which a superior seems to dictate to an inferior. The negotiators were no longer men of inadequate rank, and intentionally rude bearing. The titles were no longer disparaging or uncourteous. The commissioners gave the Emperor the title of "*Padishah*"; hitherto he had been the "*King of Vienna.*" Since the withdrawal of Solyman I. from the walls of Vienna, an annual payment of thirty thousand ducats had been made by Austria. It was called a present, but it was very

Peace of Sitvatorok, Nov. 1606.

* Sir E. Creasy, History of the Ottoman Turks, p. 227, ed. 1877.

like a tribute, and beyond all doubt one of the conditions of peace. Presents at Sitvatorok were, undoubtedly, made; but they were made on both sides, and there was a mutual inter-change of friendly expressions. Moreover, a definite point of etiquette was established, viz., that no ambassador under the rank of a Sandjak Bey should be sent to Vienna.

It is difficult to give the exact position of Transylvania at this time. It is important, however, to know that to the treaty of Sitvatorok the Prince was admitted as a party. This is ten years before the elevation to that dignity of the famous Bethlehen Gabor, or Gabriel Bethlen. Of him and of his prin-cipality during the first half of the sixteenth century we know a good deal. He was certainly independent of the Emperor, except so far as he was Duke of Ratibor and of Oppeln; and he certainly was not bound very closely to the Sultan. The title he gave himself was " *Prince of the Sacred Roman Empire, Lord of some parts of Hungary, and Duke of Oppeln and Ratibor,*" in Silesia.

Sultan Achmet dies A.D. 1617, and up to his time the trans-mission of the Empire had been from father to son for fourteen generations. Achmet, however, was succeeded by his brother Mustapha, though he left behind him seven sons, of which three reigned after him; but only after a break. Up to the time of Mustapha the succession had been from father to son; and that uninterruptedly. During the reigns of the three successors of Achmet the mere state of Turkey is a secondary consideration. Under anything like pressure from any powerful state she must have collapsed, or have existed only on sufferance. But the rest of Europe was either like England and France, friendly or indifferent, or, like Spain, declining in power, or, like Germany and Russia, convulsed by civil war. There was nothing more formidable than Venice, Poland, and Persia.

Mustapha, the brother of Achmet, succeeds him, but in less than three months is deposed as either an idiot or a lunatic, and is succeeded by Othman his nephew, Achmet's son, who reigns till 1622, when he is deposed and strangled, and Mustapha, who had been deposed before him, is restored. In 1623, however, he is again deposed, and Amurath IV., the eldest surviving brother of Othman, rules in his stead—from 1623 to 1640.

Amurath IV. was little better than a savage in his reckless-ness for human life and human suffering; yet he was resolute, courageous, and capable, when in action, of abstemiousness. But he had to deal with rebellious Janissaries and insurgent provinces. In this he was successful, and in the fifteenth year of his reign recovered Bagdad from the Persians.

Of Ibrahim we must write as of Caligula, or some similar tyrant whose sanity is doubtful. During the reign of Amurath he had lived the life of a possible rival of his brother, a prisoner in the palace, and in daily expectation of his death. He was slow to believe that the Sultanship was really vacant, and took those who announced his succession for his executioners. Except in his suspicion and vindictiveness against those whom he considered his enemies or his rivals, his Vizier Kara Mus-tapha was not without high merits. He was just and tolerant to the Christians, and, to his peril and disgrace, very plain spoken to the Sultan. But not with impunity; he was strangled, having resisted the men who were sent to murder him to the last. A true servant of the Sultan should have met his doom with apathy and resignation. His successor, as we anticipate, encourages his master in all his vices, and these were many—sensuality in the gratification of every appetite, natural or unnatural; acts of cruelty, as an exercise when done by him-self, as a spectacle when committed by others; extravagance in every form, all the more lavish at first, because there were the well-stored coffers of Amurath to draw upon. Afterwards there was oppression, undue taxation of every kind, unjust confiscations, and the necessary end. His eldest son was only seven years old, but it was decided by the conspirators that the rule of a minor was better than that of a madman. Ibrahim was deposed and put to death, and Mahomet IV. succeeded.

Mahomet IV. reigns forty-seven years. Under Mahomet IV. began the vizierate of the first Kiuprili, the founder of a dynasty of ministers, that raised Turkey, in spite of the de-ficiency of her princes, once more to comparative power, and prosperity, and glory, and who long retarded, if they could not avert, the ultimate decline of the Ottoman Empire.

As Mahomet IV. grew up he grew into neither a general nor an administrator. He was a mighty hunter rather than aught else. In one respect, however, he was better than a better man.

The simple fact of the successes of the Ottomans having been for more than two hundred years regulated by the personal character of the rulers to an extent beyond that of the other European kingdoms, condemns either the institutions or the character of the people. Yet such was the case from Orkhan to Solyman; and when Mahomet IV. succeeded Ibrahim, it was the viziers of the family of Kiuprili who did the work of the early Sultans; and it was by leaving matters in stronger hands than his own that Mahomet IV. did well at all. For his reign was the time when great warriors like Montecuculi and Sobieski appear on the field. On the 1st of August 1664, the great battle of St. Gothard, on the Raab, was fought and won by Montecuculi, the first in which the Christians were conquerors. It was followed by a truce for twenty years; but the peace that followed was short and precarious.

Then came a war of equal magnitude and more complex in its relations. It was between the Porte and Russia and Poland, rather than one against Russia singly. Moreover it was a *Cossack* and not a Tatar war.

There are two Cossack districts in Russia, that of the Cossacks on the Don and that of the Cossacks of the Dnieper. The former touch the frontier of the Crimean Tatars, and it is difficult to say exactly how far this extended in the direction of the Dnieper. The Dnieper Cossacks were evidently on the boundary of Russia and Poland, for they were the Marchmen or men of the Ukraine. They were Russian in language, wonderfully heterogeneous in blood, not committed by any strong feeling of nationality to either of the neighbouring powers, probably more Polish in feeling than Muscovite, and probably more Lithuanic than Polish. The three great names in their history are Daskievitsh, who first organized the federation; Bogdan, the most notable of their fighting men; and, lastly,

Doroscenski, who is the hero of the campaigns under notice. The points of most importance in our geography are the districts where Podolia, Bessarabia, and Lodomiria (the eastern or Ruthenian part of Gallicia) join, and Khoczin, Kamenice, and Lemberg (in Gallicia), the chief town; the last a strong and noted fortress. The line of the Jagellons in Poland has come to an end, and Stephen Bathory is the first elected King of Poland. The fourth is Michael Koribut, a weak and unpopular Lithuanian. He has a great captain under him, and one who is destined to supersede him as King—John Sobieski. The Grand Vizier in Turkey is the second of the Kiuprilis.

Bogdan, the Cossack, died in 1667, and his son succeeded him in one-half of the Ukraine. The other was held by a rival chief. The son of Bogdan did homage to the Czar, his rival to the Republic; so that when the war began each of these powers were mixed up in it. In the background, however, were the Tatars, and behind these the Turks. The result was, as far as such a contradiction in terms is possible, a triangular duel. Against these Cossacks Sobieski was sent; and it was Sobieski whom, under their Hetman Dorescensko, they bravely resisted—bravely but ineffectually. Neither could they defend themselves through the assistance of the Tatars of their frontier. So that it was to the Porte direct that they applied. Their Hetman, who presented himself in person at Constantinople, was nominated Bey of the Ukraine; and the Ukraine was enrolled as a Turkish province. The Khan of the Crimea was ordered to protect it, and six thousand Turkish troops were marched into the district. Against these high-handed proceedings the Poles protested strongly; and not only the Poles but the Czar as well. An Ottoman protectorate of any portion of the Cossack district was a contingency against which either power had an equal interest in protecting itself. The contempt with which the Porte treated their joint remonstrance, along with the high language in which it is couched, astonishes the reader of the present time. "Such is Islam that the union of the Russians and the Poles matters not to us. Our empire has increased since its origin; nor have all the Christian kings who have ranged against us been able to pluck one hair from our beard. With God's grace it shall ever be so, and our empire shall continue till the day of judgment." Kiuprili, by no means one of the most boastful of the viziers, but, on the contrary, a cool and cautious calculator, used similar language. "If a free people places itself under our protection it shall be protected, and the sword by which Islam has triumphed for more than a thousand years, shall decide between us and our opponents."

The first brunt of the war fell upon Podolia, and the first acts of the Grand Vizier justified his arrogant language. The important fortress of Kaminiec fell after a nine days' siege. A fortnight after Lemburg did the same. Peace was made. Podolia was ceded. An annual tribute was imposed upon Poland. The King of Poland, Michael Koribut, made the treaty. The nobles reserved their acceptance of it; in other words, they determined to repudiate it. And they were in a position to do so, for they had among them their future king, Sobieski. Koribut was set aside, and he bore his degradation with patience, not to say satisfaction. Such were the conditions under which the new campaign began. It was fought on the same ground as the previous one, but with a difference, and the events were reversed. Sobieski won a great victory at Khoczim, and a greater at Lemberg, which had previously been taken by siege; and the fighting continued during the whole of 1644. But the Turkish general, Ibrahim Scheitan (the Devil), reduced Podolia, and attacked Gallicia. Poland, however, was in a distracted state, and Sobieski was constrained, after a battle at Zurawna, to make peace. By this the Porte gained Kaminiec and the whole of Podolia, and, with a few specified exceptions, the suzerainty of the Ukraine, a dangerous dominion ; for, if there was one point in which Poland and Russia agreed, it was that the Ukraine should be neither Tatar nor Turk.

Peace of Zurawna, A.D. 1676.

Of the Kiuprili family, Mohammed was the first Grand Vizier, and Ahmed Kiuprili the second. But he dies soon after the peace of Zurawna, and the pre-eminently bad Vizier, Kara Mustapha, succeeds him. His evil deeds are matters of notoriety. It was he who encouraged a war with Russia, and directed it unsuccessfully. It was he who brought on the war with Austria, which led to the *second* siege of Vienna ; and how disgracefully this was carried—how the whole host of the Ottomans was scattered by a mere handful of Poles under Sobieski, are matters that read like romance rather than history. All this was due to Kara Mustapha, and when this had been done Mahomet IV. was deposed.

Solyman II., from 1687 to 1691 : Ahmed II., from 1691 to 1695 : Mustapha II., from 1695 to 1703.—Another of the family of Kiuprili, Kiuprili-zade-Mustapha, is now made Vizier, and the Ottoman history is no longer a simple succession of disasters and disgraces. There are occasional gleams of success, but there is insurrection within, and wars against both Austria and Russia abroad, and, except in the characters of the Sultan and his Vizier, there are but few elements of regeneration. But Kiuprili, who was a soldier as well as an administrator, is killed in the battle of Salankeman, near Peterwaradein ; and Ahmet II. succeeds Solyman, and Mustapha II. Ahmet. The best generals in Europe are now steadily engaged in the recovery of Hungary; and sometimes, even against these, they have partial success. Salankeman is fought and won by Louis of Baden in 1691, and in 1696 the great battle of Zenta (on the Theiss) is won by Eugene of Savoy. Again there is a vizier (Husein) of the family of Kiuprili. But an enemy more formidable is now at hand and in action, and Azof has been taken by Peter the Great of Russia.

However, on the 26th of January 1699, was signed the treaty of Carlowitz, and, from this time forwards, it is by its treaties rather than its battles that we must measure the weakness of the Porte.

CHAPTER II.

From A.D. 1699 to A.D. 1841.

Treaty of Carlowitz.—Of the Pruth.—Of Passarowitz.—Of Belgrade.—Of Kainardji.—Of Yassi.—Of Bukarest.—Of Akkerman.—Of Adrianople.—Of Unkiar Skelessi.--Of Paris.

THE result of the battle of the Zenta was the treaty of Carlowitz. The Sultan retired to Temesvar, and then to Constantinople; and another of the family of the Kiuprilis was made Grand Vizier. He was too wise a man to wish any continuation of the war, but careful to prepare for it if renewed. One fleet he sent into the Mediterranean, where the Venetians were still active, and another into the Black Sea, against a more formidable opponent, the Czar of Muscovy, Peter the Great. He had already taken Azof; and, besides this, the Ottomans had ceded the Morea to the Venetians, Podolia to the Poles, and more than half of Hungary to the Austrians. Heavy as these losses were, they are scarcely the most significant parts of the treaty. Neither England nor Holland were parties to the war; yet, in the congress that preceded the peace, each was represented. In this we see the recognition of the intervention of non-belligerents. In the treaty, too, of Carlowitz, Russia, for the first time, in a congress of like generality, took a part. Russia, however, though not a member of the Polish, Austrian, and Venetian alliance, was a belligerent; and the peace which Russia made was a separate, independent, and partial one. It was, indeed, merely an armistice for two years; but in 1700 it was changed into one for thirty. In this it was stipulated that the fortifications of four of the towns captured by the Czar should be demolished; and that, as a border-land, there should be a Ukrain, or March, of twelve leagues between Perekop and Azof. The seventh article added to the city of Azof, which was now Russian, a district in the direction of the Kuban; and connected with this were the names of the Nogay Tatars and the Circassians. Neither should the Crimean Tatars make inroads upon the Russian territory.

Much stress is laid upon the fact of two non-belligerents having been parties to the treaty of Carlowitz, and to those being England and Holland. They are freely taken as a measure of the extent to which the Ottoman Empire had become a declining power, and the recognition of the necessity of supporting it as such. There is, doubtless, much in this. It was through the mediation of England that the peace was brought about; and the Sultan was so gratified by the part taken by the English, that he cordially thanked the British Ambassador after its conclusion. On the other hand, the Czar warned him against both powers. They were, he said, "intent on commercial interests only, and were not to be trusted." But, practically, the two were one; inasmuch as, at the time of the mediation, it was William III. who was King of Great Britain. The time, moreover, was one in which the "Balance of Power" was almost a bye-word in diplomacy. The presence of the two representatives, no doubt, represents something in the way of the Porte's decline; but, upon the whole, it is a sign of the times as much as aught else.

In 1702 the Vizier, Kiuprili, died. In 1703 the Sultan, Mustapha II., abdicated. Meanwhile the conditions of the peace had been but indifferently kept by the Czar, and of this Achmet III., soon after his accession, complained in a letter to him. The Sultan, however, was not inclined to make war. The events that led to the treaty of the Pruth, the next in order to it, and only twelve years later than that of Carlowitz, are mainly the history of two kings—kings, however, of no commonplace character. In 1709 was fought the decisive battle o. Pultowa, in which Charles XII. of Sweden was defeated, and constrained to take refuge on Turkish soil, having first retreated to Oczakof and then to Bender. Both these fortresses were in

the territory of the Khan of Crimea; and before the battle of
Pultowa (8th July 1709), he had received indirect assurances
that, in case of his invading the Russian districts on his frontier,
the Khan would send an army to his assistance. The Sultan
himself, if he did not diapprove of these proceedings, abstained
from sanctioning them. But when the Czar demanded the ex-
tradition of the defeated king, and insisted more strongly upon
that of the Hetman Mazeppa; the Sultan, despite of both threats
and entreaties, persevered in his refusal. And, in doing this,
he did no more than what has been systematically done by
both his predecessors and his successors. There is no point
upon which Turkish honour is more to be relied on than in
their reception of fugitives. The Russians, however, crossed
the frontier, and surprised and carried off as prisoners a body
of Swedes. It was their intention to kidnap the king. Charles
himself asked for an army supplied by the Sultan to escort him
through Poland to his own dominions, a request which was
simply a challenge to the Czar. The Grand Vizier, however,
was unwilling to offend Russia, so that, by a compromise, an
article was added to a previous treaty with Russia that the
King of Sweden should be at liberty to return to his country
by any road he chose.

It was in vain that the Sultan pressed his royal fugitive to
withdraw. We know how obstinate he was in his refusals, and
how thankless he showed himself to his protector. One of the
effects of his obstinacy was the disgrace of the Vizier who had
failed to persuade him. Tshuli Ali was superseded, and his
successor was another of the family of Kiuprili, Kiuprili
Nonouman. Under him fresh offence was given, and aggressions increased. We expect to find the Khan of Crimea
a complainant, who, besides his real grievances, had committed
himself to the support of Charles. The Czar had more than
enough on his hands in Livonia, and he was, probably forced
into a declaration of war. Be this as it may, he loses by it;
for Azof was surrendered, and Taganrog and Kamienski were
dismantled, and the ordnance and military stores at the latter
were given up. The Czar was to abstain from interference
with either the Tatars or the Cossacks, who were dependent on

the Khans of the Crimea. There was to be freedom of commerce, but no Russiam ambassador was to reside in Constantinople; all slaves and prisoners were to be liberated, whether enslaved or captured before or after the commencement of hostilities. The King of Sweden should have a free and safe passage to his own kingdom without molestation or hindrance, and that it was recommended that, if they could, the two enemies should make peace with one another. The stipulations, for they did not, in the first instance, amount to a treaty, were made on the spot, and it was nearly four years before they took their full form. In the Treaty of the Pruth, 1711, the Porte and Russia only, and no non-belligerents, took part. It could not but wound the pride of the Czar. In Constantinople it was thought that the conqueror, who was also the Grand Vizier, had made much too little use of his advantage. There was discontent in the hearts of the Ottomans, and there was somewhat less than the fulfilment of his engagements on the part of the Czar. Neither party was thoroughly at peace. Charles, too, compromised his protector, and before he left the country of the Crimean Khan, had resisted the forces which the Sultan had sent to eject him.

But this was not all. The great Venetian Morosini, whose misfortune it was to have made the surrender of Candia, ten years after that disgrace, effected the conquest of the Morea. This the Ottomans now reconquered, and, more than this, they deprived the Venetians of all their islands on the Greek coast except Corfu. When this was attacked, the Emperor Charles VI. entered into an alliance with Venice, no matter with what motive. He did nothing to get back the Morea for his allies, but forced the Porte into another war with Austria. In this, Temesvar, the last remnant of the Turkish dominion in Hungary, was won back. Then Belgrade was taken, and, again, the great general of the Austrians was Eugene of Savoy. Now, also, was a treaty in which, as at Carlowitz, England and Holland, non-belligerents, took part. But, although the principals began the war in alliance with Venice, no attempt was made by Austria to recover the Morea. There have been many betrayals of a weak confederate, and this of Venice by

Austria is one of the most disgraceful. The result of the

The Treaty of
Passarowitz,
July 21st, A.D. 1718.

treaty was that the city of Temesvar, the last possession of the Ottomans in Hungary, was made over to Austria; and now every acre of Hungary was Austrian. Belgrade and other cities on Servian ground were also surrendered to her, and so was Little Wallachia. The Czar, too, made peace with the Sultan, and in 1723 the Sultan and the Czar are such firm friends as to arrange between themselves the partition of Persia; the Czar taking Asterabad, Mazenderan, Gilan, with parts of Shirvan and Lesgistan; the Sultan the greater part of Kurdistan and Aderbijan. If the Shah would recognize the mutilation he might retain the remainder of his kingdom; largely diminished, on the east, by the independence and encroachments of the Afghans. This strengthened the Turks in Caucasus; though, at the same time, it engendered complications with Russia. As the Persians were Shiites, the Turks were justified in what they did. Their punishment, however, grew out of their crime. It was in defence of the integrity of the Persian empire that the notorious Kuli Khan first emerged from the obscurity of a slave and a robber to become the most formidable conqueror of his age and country—or, by a change of name, the famous Nadir Shah, King of Persia, conqueror of Georgia, devastator of Northern India.

Peter the Great was not the worst enemy to the Porte. As long as he lived he never revenged the capitulation of the Pruth, though he collected the materials for the use of his successors; and, under Anne and Elizabeth, they were either applied to war against Persia or left to accumulate. But a more unscrupulous spirit, and, possibly, a more commanding one, than even his own was now the directress of Russian policy—that of the famous, or infamous, Catherine. There were details as to the suzerainty over parts of Caucasus, which had been crossed by the troops of the Khan of the Crimea during the Persian war; details, too, as to the suzerainty over some Caucasian districts. But, more than that, there was the interference of Russia in the affairs of Poland; and Poland, notwithstanding its championship of Christianity, under Ladislas and Sobieski, was, in the main, the friend rather than the enemy of the Porte. Then began, on the side of Russia, the campaign against the Crimea. Whilst this was going on, the Emperor of Austria formed an alliance with the Czarina; but not with a Eugene as its commander. It ends with the battle of Krotza. The Austrians fell back upon Belgrade, and Belgrade was recovered by the Ottomans. On the first of September it was agreed in the preliminary articles that that fortress was to be restored, and along with it all the districts in Bosnia, Servia, and Wallachia which had been ceded to Austria. Hence, as between the Porte and Austria, such was the Treaty of Belgrade. With Russia it was agreed that the city of Azof and the district around it was to be a border-land; that Taganrok was not to be rebuilt, but that Russia might construct a fortress on the Kuban; that she should have a fleet in either the Sea of Azof or the Black Sea, and that she should acknowledge the independence of the Kabardas. A boundary was to be fixed between the two empires, and by this Russia gained some ground in the Ukraine districts; but her conquests in Moldavia and Bessarabia were restored.

The Treaty of Belgrade, A.D. 1739.

Up to the Treaty of Belgrade there has always been some sign of recovery on the part of the Ottomans; but with that of Kanardji, the downfall is conspicuous. There are gleams, in the sequel, of her former greatness; but the whole series of treaties are those of an empire under pressure which seems to be irresistible. Nor is this a mere general view. In every subsequent treaty there is loss, not merely of prestige, but of territory; and that not only by foreign conquest but by the falling-off of provinces; and even in these there is always either the assistance or the instigation of the old enemy.

The interval between the two treaties which we have thus contrasted with one another is thirty-five years, of which the first twenty-nine are years of comparative tranquillity. Nor is it difficult to see why they should be this. The times are those of the Austrian war of succession, and, after that, of the Seven Years War; and in these, though neither Russia nor Turkey were directly concerned, there were numerous points in which they were interested. There was the rise of a new power—the Prussia of Frederick II.—and, with this, there were alliances and counter-alliances, and manœuvres and intrigues to an extent almost unprecedented. But, what was of more importance to the Porte, there was the great diversion in the direction of Poland on the parts of Russia, Austria, and Prussia.

Of these thirty-five years, the first fifteen belong to the reign of Mahmoud I., which began in 1730 and lasted till 1754.

The next three are those of that of Mahmoud's son— Othman II.

Then follows Mustapha III., and he reigns from 1757 to 1773 ; and it is not till 1768 that between Turkey and Russia any serious hostilities have been entered on. The last years, however, of Mustapha's reign are the prelude to the Treaty of Kainairdji.

How at this time the affairs of Poland were such as led to the First Partition, and how they eventually forced Turkey into a war with Russia, belongs to Polish history. Sultan Mustapha declared war against the Czarina Catherine; and at no time, either before or after, did the Khan of the Crimea more honestly and more effectively serve his suzerain. This Ghirai, however, died shortly after an expedition against Russia ; and the suspicion was that he was poisoned at the instigation of the Prince of Wallachia. Be this as it may, his successor, Dewlet Girai, was one of the last Khans of the Crimea. The last ruler who paid homage to the Porte was Selim Ghirai. Shahin Girai

The Treaty of   was the vassal of the Czarina. It was *before* the
Kainairdji,   Treaty of Kainairdji that the Crimea was made
July 17, 1774. independent of Turkey. It was a few years *after*
that treaty that it was definitely annexed to Russia.

The time between the Treaty of Kainardji and of Yassi is still that of Catherine in Russia, of Frederick the Great in Prussia; but it is also that of the Revolution in France, and of the Partitions in Poland. France has much to look to nearer home; but neither Austria nor Russia are so wholly absorbed with the dismemberment of Poland as to be unable to ally themselves in an attack upon Turkey. Austria gains but little by her alliance, but Russia has the foremost of its many great generals, Suvaroff. It is his campaign in Bessarabia

Treaty of
Yassi,
A.D. 1792.
which leads to the Treaty of Yassi; and it is with
the Treaty of Yassi that the relations between Russia
and Roumania, which are now invested with such
importance, may be said to begin. They are, in some points,
of older standing; but it is with the Treaty of Yassi that the
Russian frontier begins gradually to extend itself in the
direction of Bessarabia, itself being Roumanian, though Roumanian with both Slavonic and Tatar elements. When the
Treaty of Kainardji was signed, Kilburn, on the left bank of
the Dnieper, was Russian, whilst, on the right, Oczakof was
Turkish, as we have seen. We may see, if we look at the
debates in the English Parliament of the time, that the Oczakof
question was one which was warmly debated, and that then,
as now, it was the Tories who distrusted, and the Liberals,
with Fox among the foremost of them, who confided in and
lauded Russia. We have seen, however, that not only was
Oczakof ceded to Russia, but, along with it, the district between
the Bog and the Dniester. According to the maps of the time,
it seems to be neither Russian nor Roumanian, but Turk, or,
more specifically, Tatar. North of Bender lie, with conspicuous capitals, the Tatars of Oczakof; west of these, and
also north of Bender on the Dniester, the Tatars of Budziak;
then, on the Upper Bog, in the government of Braczlaw, the
Human Cossacks; and, fourthly, between the Pruth and Dniester,
the Lipka Tatars. This tells how close to the Polish frontier
lay the western boundary of the Tatars of the Crimea, and how
the Tatar and the Cossack lay in contact with one another.

The Treaty of Yassi was followed by the death of the Empress
Catherine, and never was the integrity of the Ottoman Empire
more seriously imperilled than it was at this very moment.
Her plans were matured, her army and her navy were ready;
the affairs of Poland were brought to a conclusion. There was
on the side of the Turks some military skill, some adminis-
trative ability, and, what never is wanting, undaunted and
desperate bravery. Neither was the Sultan, Selim III., unworthy of his position. He saw the necessity of sweeping and
fundamental reforms; he partially succeeded in introducing

them, but they cost him his life. In 1807 he is deposed and put to death by the Janissaries, and Mustapha IV. succeeded him; but Mustapha is deposed by Bairactar.

The last two years of the century introduce a new influence; one which, upon the whole, has been friendly to Turkey, but which at the beginning was very much the reverse. There is Napoleon in Italy, and there is Egypt *nimium vicina Cremonæ;* and we know how, from this time till the year 1815, a very twisted skein in the history of war and diplomacy lies before the general historian. The present writer, however, limits himself to the practical loss of two provinces, Egypt and Servia; a loss, at present, only inchoate, and still not absolutely complete. There is war on the part of Turkey with France; but there is no surety against Napoleon becoming an ally of the Sultan; and, if so, no improbability in England being allied with Russia. Such combinations, we know, were real; but we also know that they were ephemeral, and that, with the exception of England, every one of his foes had been at one time his friend, and *vice versâ.*

It was in 1798 that Napoleon landed an army of 30,000 men in Egypt, and takes possession of Alexandria. It was the Mamelukes—the Egyptian analogues of the Janissaries—who were the real rulers of the country; and it was on the strength of this that Napoleon could represent himself as a friend and saviour. It was, he said, against the tyranny of the Mamelukes that he came to protect the natives; and it was as an ally of the Sultan's that he had to defeat an imperial army. Alexandria he had taken by storm in the first instance. The Mamelukes he defeated at the Pyramids. Before the end of July Cairo had submitted, and, on the first of August, was fought the battle of the Nile. The result was an alliance against France between Turkey, Russia, and England. The details of this lead us on to Syria; this being the time of Napoleon's repulse at Acre, a repulse followed by his return to France, leaving Kleber in his place. Kleber wins the great battle of Heliopolis, but by this time the French are well out of Egypt.

Concurrent with the occupation and evacuation of Egypt by the French, runs the history for ten years of the Ionian Islands

and the districts along the opposite coast of Albania. Of the
Ionian Islands the whole belonged to Venice, and, on the mainland, some half-dozen ports and fortresses—Previsa, Butrinto,
Parga, Vonitza, and Gomenitza. But, after the Treaty of
Campo Formio, the Republic of Venice, by its sister Republic
of France, was eliminated from the community of common-
wealths, and it became French, and, with it, its dependencies.
But France was now engaged elsewhere, and the Porte had an
opportunity for recovering them. Here, then, begins the career
of the notorious Albanian Pasha Ali. He recovered, with the
exception of Parga, the whole of the main-land, nominally for
the Porte, virtually for himself; but the islands he did not
recover. Neither did France keep them. There is an alliance
now between the Porte and Russia, and, through their joint
action, the islands are recovered. They are, moreover, to be
occupied and administered by the Turks and Russians conjointly. An arrangement like this cannot well be permanent.
The Russians were preferred by the islanders to the Turks; so
that it was the Russians who held the archipelago until they
were ejected by the French, and the French till they are superseded by the English. This, however, is not till after the
Treaty of Vienna.

In the same year the Sultan gave another instance of his
goodwill towards the Czar. The gainers by this were the
Danubian Hospodariats, Wallachia and Moldavia. Nor was
Russia a loser. The reigning Hospodars were not to be removed without reference to Russia; nor were any Turkish
officials or soldiers to enter either. This was in 1802. The
joint occupation of the Ionian Islands took place in 1800; and
between this and the arrangements in Wallachia and Moldavia
(1801) the Treaty of Amiens was effected. By a concurrent
treaty between France and Egypt, the suzerainty of the Porte
over Egypt was acknowledged by France; and for a time there
was an armistice—little more. Indeed, in respect to Turkey,
it was only a respite from attacks on the side of Russia and the
other external powers. The Wahabite insurrection continued
to run its course in Arabia. In Syria, Djezzar Pasha continued
his insubordination until his death in 1804; and, in Egypt, the

Mamelukes remained as antagonistic and as intractable as before. As for Ali Pasha, in Albania, he was in open rebellion. The Servian insurrection had begun, and, with Ali Viditsh on the west, in Bosnia, and with Paswan Oglou, the Pasha of Bulgaria, half the Empire was in rebellion against the Porte. In Servia, however, the revolt had the merit of being one of the people, and not one of either their Beys or their Pashas. Of the Greek rebellion the seeds were only germinating. It was to Russia that Servia looked for sympathy, and as much aid as could be given without umbrage to the Porte. This was not an easy matter; for the Sultan had yielded more to Russia as an ally than either his subjects approved or circumstances appeared to justify. The passage of the Dardanelles had been conceded to her, and she knew how to use it. She had enlisted soldiers from Albania, and she had strengthened her positions in the Caucasian districts. In 1805 Turkey was required to join in an alliance with Russia against France, with whom the Porte was not only at peace, but on close terms of friendship. This was the time when Russia demanded the protectorate of Greek Christians of the Ottoman Empire, wheresoever they might be. This proposal the Porte took time to consider, and, in the meantime, became open to overtures from the French. This was successful on the part of France, but it brought Russia and England into an alliance against Turkey. It was in this war that the English fleet, under Sir John Duckworth, forced the passage of the Dardanelles, and returned without attacking Constantinople. Nor was an attack upon Egypt more successful. The war, along with the alliance, lasted six years, and, in 1812, was signed the Treaty of Bucharest. But, before this was effected, Selim III. had been succeeded by Mustapha IV., and Mustapha IV. by Mahmoud IV.

We may now look upon the domestic history of the Porte. Selim is deposed, and Mustapha IV. succeeds. He is raised to the Sultanship by the Janissaries; and when Selim, his cousin, and Mahmoud, his own brother, shall have been put to death, the only surviving descendant of Othman will be Mustapha. When this is the case we know what to expect, whether in a novel or a history. A great crime will be attempted; but only one-half of it will be accomplished. This is the case. On May 29, 1807, Mustapha begins to reign. Then, on the July of the following year (on the 20th), Selim is murdered, and Mahmoud is just saved from a like fate. Mustapha is deposed, and, after a time (March 17, 1809), put to death. Such is the external history of the deposition and death of two Sultans within the year; but the state of affairs that led to it is one that requires a fuller exposition. Selim III. was a reformer, an honest and not an incompetent one. He might have effected less than he did, and yet have been a courageous and able ruler. But, in 1807, the Mufti, who, in his religious capacity, had most especially supported him, died; while the Ulema as a body were his opponents, and, in conjunction with the Ulema, the Janissaries. Thirdly, there was the individual traitor, Moussa Pasha, who had the full confidence of the Pasha, and who betrayed him. The deposition of Selim is committed to the Janissaries, and sanctioned by the Ulema. Nor is it, in the first instance, accompanied by bloodshed. Mustapha, the eldest son of Abdul Hamid, is made Sultan, and Selim lives a prisoner in the palace; but only for a while. Mustapha Bairactar, the Pasha of Rustshuk, marches upon Constantinople on the same day that Selim is murdered and of Mahmoud's escape, and deposes Mustapha. Bairactar then becomes Mahmoud's Vizier, and lives long enough to punish the traitor Moussa Pasha, but not long enough to put down the Janissaries. They have opposed his innovations by a general revolt, in which the palace of the Vizier was set fire to. Bairactar escaped to a stone tower, and defended himself bravely; but the tower was blown up, and Bairactar was buried in the ruins. Mahmoud II. was fain to make terms with the Janissaries; but, by 1826, he will have destroyed them root and branch. By remembering this we can fix our attention exclusively on the external relations of the Porte, and we know how various these are, and how shifting and uncertain. The Porte, indeed, is at this time the least part of itself; it neither knows exactly what belongs to it in the way of revolted and revolting provinces, nor, in the way of alliances and hostilities, has any certainty that it will keep either a friend or an enemy twelve months. And all this is

her misfortune rather than her fault; for the whole of Europe is well nigh in the same predicament. It is a time when no alliance is worth two years' purchase; and when no one knows who is to be ally or who his enemy twelve months after the signature of a treaty. But the treaties themselves, though ephemeral, are important; and the changes which they effect are of more than ordinary magnitude. For the times are those of the great battles of Austerlitz, of Jena, of Eylau, and of Friedland, the battles of which the compact of Tilsit (1809) is the result. And then comes the secret agreement that the Emperor and the Czar shall divide Europe between them; a secret which is no better kept than secrets in general. Austria gets knowledge of it. The Porte gets knowledge of it. England thinks that her alliance with Russia against Turkey is a mistake. But the power of Austria is again broken by the campaign of Wagram; and England concludes with Turkey the treaty of the Dardanelles, A.D. 1809. With Russia, however, the war continues; and so does the Servian rebellion under Kara George. But the friendship between the Czar and Napoleon is growing colder and colder, and the march to Moscow is approaching. This is an opportunity for both Turkey and Russia; for the Emperor is desirous of an alliance with the Porte, and Russia can ill afford to do much more for Servia. The original demands of the Czar were Wallachia, Moldavia, and Bessarabia. He now relinquishes the demand for the first two, but remains in possession of Bessarabia. Something, too, is done for Servia. An amnesty is granted, and, with it, a moderate amount of self-government. The imports are no longer to be farmed, but to be paid directly to the Porte. On the other hand, the fortresses are to be garrisoned by Turks. The Servians

The Treaty of Bucharest, May 28, 1812. considered that there was little in this for which they should be thankful. Such, however, was the Treaty of Bucharest.

Soon after this came the downfall and death of their great leader Kara George, and the rise of the Obrenovitsh family, of which the present Prince is the representative.

What follows is the fall of Napoleon, the Treaty of Vienna, the redistribution of the territories that he had either annexed to France or reduced in their dimensions, the precarious pacification of Western Europe under the influence of the Holy Alliance, and the continuation of the numerous revolts in the several Ottoman provinces.

Servia continues under the jurisdiction of Micael Obrenovitsh as the administrator of the Sultan ; practically autonomous, but with no definite *status*. There are no great international wars. On the other hand, however, there is revolt in most of the provinces of the Ottoman Empire. These need only to be alluded to. The three most important are those of the Danubian Principalities, of Albania under Ali Pasha, and of Greece.

The chief event in the domestic history of the Porte is the massacre of the Janissaries, under the direction of Mahmoud II., in 1826. It was preceded by—indeed it was a copy of—that by Mehemet Ali of the Mamelukes in Egypt. Both were acts of monstrous and abominable cruelty—perfidious and cold-blooded. But the existence of either of the bodies was incompatible with the safety of the states to which they were a danger and a disgrace.

The massacre of the Janissaries took place only a few months after the death of the Czar, Alexander I. His successor Nicolas was less unsympathetic than his father with the revolutionary movement that pervaded every province of the Porte. Under him the liberation of Servia reached its penultimate stage, and that of Greece was completed. In the first instance, Nicolas insisted, *inter alia,* on the confirmation of the rights of the Servians, which were left in a very indefinite form by the Treaty of Bucharest. In short, he forced upon the Porte the Treaty of Akkerman. The Wallachians and Moldavians were also restored to the condition in which they were before their rebellion in 1821.

The Treaty of
Akkerman,
Oct. 7, 1826.

In the July of the next year was signed, by England, France, and Russia, the Treaty of London, in favour of Greece. This the Porte resisted, and the battle of Navarino was the result. It certainly liberated Greece ; but whether anyone but the Czar was a gainer by the destruction of the Turkish fleet is another question. At any rate, Russia continued the war on her own account ; for there was a question still pending about the

4

cession of some fortress in Asia. With an enemy of whom it was said that "the Sultan had destroyed his army, and his allies had destroyed his fleet," the quarrel seemed to be a safe one. But the defence of Turkey was one that well displayed the inherent bravery of the national spirit, and the unconquerable courage of Mahmoud II., the greatest, under adversity, of all the Sultans. There were two campaigns; one in Europe and one in Asia. The whole war lasted nearly two years.

This secondary war, as it began in 1828 on the European side of the Bosphorus, was by no means discreditable to the Turks, nor were the gains on the side of Russia important. "If we consider the enormous sacrifices that the war cost the Russians in 1828, it is difficult to say whether they or the Turks won or lost it." Such was the opinion of Baron Moltke.

In Asia events were less favourable, and in 1829 both campaigns were almost fatal. Concurrently with the fluctuating warfare on the European continent, Paskievitsh had effected definite conquest on the frontiers of Georgia and Armenia, by which Kars, Akhalkhaliki, and other fortresses, were lost to the Turks. Kars was subsequently recovered, and has twice been fought for since; but Akhalkhaliki remained and remains in the hands of Russia. Along with Akhaltzikh, it constituted an important addition to the Empire. The Georgian fortress, then known as Gumri, changed its name and became Alexopol; and how important this ground has since been we know from the history of the parts about Kars and Erzeroum during both the Crimean war and the present one. Anapa, too, in Apkhazi country, and on the Bosphorus, was captured.

Still more damaging was the famous campaign of Marshal Diebitsch in Bulgaria. The Turks attempt to recover Pravadi, Shumla being the base of their operations; but are opposed by the Russians under Roth and Rudiger. Meanwhile Diebitsch is besieging Silistria. With a part of his forces he places himself between Pravadi and Shumla, joins Ruth and Rudiger, and, on June 11, fights and wins the decisive battle of Kulevtsha. The Turkish general judges that the siege of Shumla will be continued, and, with the view of relieving it, weakens the army that was defending the passes of the Balkans. Of this error

Diebitsch takes the full advantages, and in nine days crosses the Balkans. " He," writes Moltke, " besieged one fortress and fought one battle; but this brought him into the very heart of the hostile Empire. He arrived there, followed by the shadow of an army, but with the reputation of irresistible success."

Such was the bold and successful exploit of Diebitsch, and the result of it was the Treaty of Adrianople, in quick succession to that of Akkerman, which was itself to be as quickly succeeded by that of London. By the treaty, however, of Adrianople, Russia obtained the Sulina mouth of the Danube, the conquests in Asia on the Armenian frontier, and the definite cession of Imeretia, Mingrelia, and Guriel; and further stipulations in favour of the Danubian principalities. An annual tribute was to be paid to the Porte, but for the first two years it was not to be exacted. Servia was equally benefited; all the clauses in the Treaty of Akkerman that bore upon Servia were to be carried into immediate effect, and ratified by the Sultans. The Dardanelles were to be open to Russian merchant ships. An indemnity for damage done to Russian commerce, and payment for the costs of the war, amounting to nearly five million were added. Such were the direct results of the Treaty of Adrianople. But, besides this, there was the engagement to agree to the stipulations of the Treaty of London; while the Treaty of London meant neither more nor less than the independence of Greece.

The Treaty of Adrianople, Aug. 28, 1829.

In 1830 the French began the conquest of Algiers, nominally a dependency of the Porte, but practically independent.

In 1832 Mehemet Ali, under the generalship of his son Ibrahim, reduced Syria, and, with equal ease, Asia Minor; so that he threatened Constantinople from Scutari. The other great powers found it inconvenient to interfere, and, by so doing, left the mediation between the Sultan and his rebellious vassal to Russia. It is not surprising, then, that fresh concessions were made by the Porte, and that, by the Treaty of Unkiar Skelessi, the Sultan consented, when required by the Czar, to close the Dardanelles against the armed vessels of any other power.

The Treaty of Unkiar Skelessi, 8th July, 1833.

In 1839 war again broke out between the Sultan and Mehemet

Ali. Now, however, there was an alliance between the Porte, England, Russia, Austria, and Prussia; but not with France. Mehemet Ali had retreated, under the pressure of Russia, from Scutari; but he returned to his vice-royalty with the intention of converting it into an hereditary monarchy. He has discontinued the payment of tribute, and substituted for the ordinary Turkish troops that guarded the prophet's tomb at Mecca, Arab troops of his own. Constructively, the change implies a denial of the sovereignty of the Sultan as Caliph; and it was a claim that the high-spirited and energetic Mahmoud lost no time in resisting, and that by both an army and a fleet. The army was defeated by Mehemet's son Ibrahim, at Nezib, in Assyria; and the fleet was delivered up to Mehemet Ali himself, in the harbour of Alexandria, by Achmet Pacha, its admiral. The loss of the battle is attributed to the venality and treachery of the commander Hafiz Pasha. This, though a probable, is scarcely a necessary, explanation for the loss of a battle. The treachery of the admiral's is less doubtful.

Before the news of the battle of Nezib reached Constantinople, Mahmoud II. was succeeded by Abdul Medjid, and the question of the following three years was the settlement of the affairs in Egypt. The error into which the other European powers had fallen in 1839, that of leaving the arrangements between the Sultan and his vassal so exclusively to Russia, was avoided; for a lesson was read to them upon this point in the Treaty of Unkiar Skelessi. There was, then, a treaty of July 15, 1840, by which the terms between Mehemet Ali and the new Sultan Abdul Medjid were defined and sanctioned by England, Russia, Austria, Prussia, and the Porte. But to this France was *not* a signitory, and it is certain that in this Mehemet Ali thought himself justified in demurring to its terms. He reckoned that some umbrage might be taken by France; that she had an interest in Egypt; and that she favoured her independence. At any rate, he refused to accede to the requisition of the Porte and its four powers; and as it was in Syria that his resistance was chiefly carried on, and as the fortified places in Syria were, as a rule, accessible by sea, the chief share in coercing him lay with the English; and the English fleet, under Admirals Stopford and Napier, by the bombardment of Beyrout and the capture, is considered to have done its work effectively. At any rate, the Pasha was brought to terms. The Turkish fleet was restored, the troops of the Pasha were withdrawn from Candia, and, in the final settlement of Feb. 13, 1841, the French, along with the other four powers, were signatories. By this the Pashalik of Egypt was confirmed to Mehemet Ali and his descendants in the male line, with a charge to the Sultan of one-fourth of its revenue, and a certain amount of naval and military support when required. In the same year a convention as to the rights of Turkey to control the navigation of the Dardanelles was signed by England, Austria, Prussia, Russia, and France. It was signed in London, July 13, 1841. In this is specified—

"ART. I.—His Highness the Sultan, on the one part, declares that he is firmly resolved to maintain for the future the principle invariably established as the ancient rule of his Empire, and in virtue of which it has at all times been prohibited for the ships of war of foreign powers to enter the Straits of the Dardanelles and of the Bosphorus; and, so long as the Porte is at peace, His Highness will admit no foreign ships of war into the said Straits.

"ART. II.—And their Majesties, the Queen of the United Kingdom of Great Britain and Ireland, the Emperor of Austria, King of Hungary and Bohemia, the King of the French, the King of Prussia, and the Emperor of All the Russias, on the other part, engage to respect the determination of the Sultan, and to conform themselves to the principles thus declared."

"The formal recognition," writes Sir Edward Creasy, "of the Dardanelles and the Bosphorus as being mere Turkish streams, and not highways for the fleets of all nations (as seas in general are), was of great value for Turkey. But still the convention of 1841 did not free the Porte from the chain by which the Treaty of Hunkiar Iskelessi had bound it to Russia. That liberation was not to be effected without the aid of the armed force as well as of the diplomacy of the Western powers. It was fortunate for the Ottoman Empire that a pacific period of twelve years intervened before the struggle for that liberation commenced; and that time was given for the development of measures of internal reform."

After this comes a period of peace for twelve years, and then the Crimean war, with the details of which the present work is not here connected.

CHAPTER III.

Religious Creeds and Sects of the Ottoman Empire.—General View.—
Sunnite and Shiite Mahometanism.—The Wahabis.—Judaism, Judean
and Samaritan.—Three forms of Syrian Christianity: Nestorian, Eutychian, Romanist.

THE consideration of the Christianity of the Greek, Albanian,
and Slavonic parts of the Empire makes no part of the present
chapter. In respect to this the general statement that, with
a few exceptions, it is the Christianity of the Eastern rather
than the Western, or the Greek rather than the Latin, Church
is sufficient. In Asia, however, the case is different. Of
Christianity in Asia there is not very much, but what there is
is of a peculiar and mixed character. Neither is there, within
the pale of Mahometanism, any important amount of sec-
tarianism. The Turks, as thoroughly as the Arabs themselves,
are orthodox Sunnites; but the Persians—of course, from the
Turkish point of view,—are heretics and Shiites; and of the Shiite
creed, *eo nomine*, there are certainly some dissenting subjects of
the Porte. They are not either Georgians or Armenians, and
but few of them are either Turks or Arabs; while, of Persia
proper, a very small part belongs to the Porte. But there is
all over Turkey the influence of the Persian literature; and, on
the frontier of Turkey, there is the debateable ground, march,
or boundary of the Kurd districts. They appear in the maps
as "Kurdistan," part of which is assigned to Persia and part to
Turkey. But, beyond Kurdistan, there are Kurds, sometimes
in continuity, sometimes sporadic; and wherever we get Kurds
we get the Persian language and the Shiite creed. We get,
too, a good deal more in the way of miscellaneous sorts of barbarism and savagery; for there is not much good to be said about

the Kurds. The extent, however, to which they trespass with impunity is a measure of the weakness of the Governments that tolerate them ; and, in this respect, there is but little difference between Turkey and Persia.

In Arabia itself, the land of the Prophet, the most important of all the schisms in Mahometanism broke out towards the end of the last century, and still exists, though no longer to a dangerous extent. This is that of the Wahabis, or followers of Abdul Wahab, an Arab of the Beni Tenim tribe. Burckhardt, who, with a more than ordinary familiarity with the vernacular Arabic, and with a personal familiarity with the Arabs which no traveller with the exception of Wallin has approached, who was, also, in the country during the war of Mehemet Ali, commits himself most decidedly to Wahab's orthodoxy. He was a reformer, not a heretic. His followers (writes Burckhardt) were the Puritans of Mahometanism ; strict adherents to the orthodox teaching of Abu Hanifeh, one of the four great masters of the law, and pronounced by a syndic at Cairo to be orthodox ; no doctrinal heresy being imputed to them. Still, they must have gone far in a heterodox direction. They anathematized all carnal indulgences. They anathematized tobacco. They denounced poetry. They impugned the over-valuation of even Mahomet himself. They despised pilgrimages and plundered pilgrims.

The religious doctrine, however, is one thing, the political power another. The latter was developed by Ibn Saud, born at the beginning of the present century. He sacked Mecca. He threatened Syria and Egypt. It was he whom Mehemet Ali conquered. The following is one of his proclamations :—

Ibu Saoud to the Inhabitants of Mekka, the highly honoured.

Praise be to God, the only God ! who has no co-partner—to whom belongs dominion, and who is omnipotent.

In the name of the all-merciful God ! It is necessary that every chosen servant of God should have a true knowledge of the Almighty, for in the word of God (the Korán) we read, Know that there is no God but one God! Bokháry,* may God have mercy upon him! said, First, learn, then speak and act. If it be asked, What are the three foundations of knowledge ? answer, The servant's knowledge of his Lord, of his religion, and of his Prophet.

* The compiler of Mohammed's traditions.

And first, as to the Knowledge of God; if they ask of thee, Who is thy Lord? answer, My Lord is God, through whose favour and grace I have been bred up; him I adore, and adore none but him. In proof of which we read (in the Korán), Praise be to the Lord of all creatures! Whatever exists besides God belongs to the class of creatures, and I myself am one of this created world. If they ask further of thee, How didst thou know thy Lord? answer, By the signs of his omnipotence and creation. In proof of which we read, And of his signs are the night and the day, the sun and the moon; and of his creation, heaven and earth, and whatever is upon them and whatever they contain. And we likewise read, The Lord is God, who created heaven and earth. If it be asked, For what purpose did God create thee? answer, To adore him. In proof of this we read, I created spirits and men to be adored by them. If it be asked, What does God command? answer, The Unity; which means, to adore him exclusively and solely; and what he above all prohibits is the association with him, or the adoring of any other god besides himself. In proof of which we read, Adore God and do not associate with him any other thing or being. The adoration by which thou art to worship him, thou evincest by the Islám; by faith and alms, by prayers, vows, sacrifices, by resignation, fear, hope, love, respect, humility, timidity, and by imploring his aid and protection.

In proof of the necessity of prayers we read, Pray, and I shall grant your wishes. Prayers, therefore, are true adoration. In proof of the necessity of making vows we read, Fulfil your vows and dread the day of which the evils have been foretold. To prove the necessity of slaughtering victims, we read, Pray to God, and kill victims. And the Prophet, may God's mercy be upon him! said, Cursed be he who sacrifices to any other but God.

The foundation of knowledge is the religion of Islám, which is submission to the Almighty. In proof of which we read, " The religion before God is Islám. And to this refers the saying of the Prophet, on whom be the peace of God! The chief of all business is Islám. If they ask, How many are the principal duties of our religion? answer, Islám, faith, and good works. Each of these is divided into different parts:—Jelím has five, viz.—the profession that there is no God but God, and that Mohammed is his prophet—the performance of the prescribed prayers—the distribution of alms—the observance of the fast of Ramadhán, and the pilgrimage to the holy house of God. In proof of the truth of the profession of faith, we read, God declares that there is no God but himself; and the meaning of the expression, There is no God but God, confirms that there is but one God, and that nothing in this world is to be adored but God. And in proof of the profession, that Mohammed is the prophet of God, we read, And Mohammed is nothing but a prophet. Our duty is to obey his commands, to believe what he related, to renounce what he forbade; and it is by following his precepts that we evince our devotion to God. The reason for joining these two professions, viz. in saying, There is no god but God, and Mohammed is his prophet; is to show our piety and perfect obedience. In proof of prayers and alms, we read, Nothing was commanded but that they should adore God, with the true religion alone, that they should perform prayers, and distribute alms. In proof of fasts, we read, O ye true believers, we have ordained for you the fasts! And in proof of the pilgrimage, we read, And God exacts the pilgrimage from those who are able to undertake the journey.

As a further proof of these five fundamental parts of the Islám, may be quoted the tradition of Ibn Omar, who says, The Prophet, may God's mercy be with him, declared that the Islám rests upon five requisites; the prayers, the alms, the fast, the pilgrimage, and the profession that there is no god but God. The second of the principal duties of religion is the faith. It comprises seventy-nine ramifications. The highest of them is the declaration, There is no God but God; and the lowest, the removal of all deception from the road of the faithful. Shame is one of those ramifications. The faith divides into six parts. These are: to believe in God and his angels, and the revealed books, and his prophets, and the last day, and the omnipotence of God, from whom all good and evil proceed. In proof of which we read, This is not righteousness, to turn your faces towards the east or the west; but he is righteous who believes in God, and the last day, and the angels, and the sacred book, and the prophets. And in proof of the omnipotence, it is said, We created everything through our power. The third of the principal duties of religion consists in good works. These are comprised within one single precept, which is Adore God, as if thou didst see him; and if thou canst not see him, know that he sees thee. In proof of which we read, He who turns his face towards the Almighty and confides in him, he is the well-doer, he holds fast by the firmest handle.

The third foundation of knowledge is the knowledge of our prophet Mohammed, may God's mercy and peace be with him! Mohammed the son of Abdullah the son of Abd el Motalleb, the son of Hashem, the son of Menaf, whose parentage ascends to Adam, who was himself a descendant of Ismayl, the son of Ibrahím, with whom and with our prophet may God's mercy dwell! Mohammed, may God's mercy be with him! is a delegate whom we dare not adore, and a prophet whom we dare not belie; but we must obey and follow him, for it has been ordained to spirits and to mortals to be his followers. He was born and appointed prophet at Mekka; his flight and his death were at Medinah. From him, to whom may God show his mercy! we have the saying, I am the prophet, this is no false assertion, I am the son of Abd el Motalleb! If it be asked, Is he a mortal? answer, Yes; he is a mortal. In proof of which we read, Say, I am but a mortal like yourselves to whom it is revealed that your God is but one God. If it be asked, Is he sent to any particular class of mankind? answer, No; he is sent to the whole race. In proof of which we read, O men, I am God's prophet sent to you all! If it be asked, Can any other religion, but his, be acceptable? answer, No other can be accepted; for we read, Whoever shall follow any other religion than Islám, will be rejected. And if it be asked, Does any prophet come after him? answer, No prophet comes after him; for after him comes the last day. In proof of which we read, He was father to none of your men, but the prophet of God, and the seal (that is the last) of all the prophets.

This was issued by Saud a little before his final and unsuccessful struggle with Mehemet Ali. The break-up, however, of

the Wahabi schism, like the break-up of the power of the Dereh
Beys, though, for many of the purposes of the politician, it is
an important reality, is in many other cases more nominal than
real, because (as has so often been either stated or suggested) the
political power of an institution is far less vital than the social.
That no such a chief as Ibn Saud is now minitant in Arabia is
true ; but that the Wahabi doctrines are obliterated is far from
being the case.   Among the genuine Beduins they are common,
especially among those of the great Shammar tribe.   Of these,
the occupants of the Dzhebel Shammar, the original district of
the division, give the nearest approach to the old Wahabi creed
in its primitive strictness, which elsewhere has abated some of
its harshness.   Whether pure, however, or modified, it has lost
much of its political importance, and, whether pure or modified,
it belongs to Arabia Proper rather than the Arab part of Turkey;
indeed, of the two Mahometan sects, the Metawileh, though
much less is known about them, are probably the more
important.

Of the *Jews*, the most numerous are those whose origin is
comparatively recent; the most interesting the descendants of
the original Judeans.   These are found in Gallilee rather than
in Judea Proper; the neighbourhood of Tiberias and two or
three less important districts being their chief localities.   In
Jerusalem itself the population is chiefly of recent origin, consisting of immigrants from Spain, descendants of the refugees
from the persecution under Ferdinand and Isabella.

A third class is that of the *Karaits;* but these are at present
the most numerous in Russia.

The fourth division is that of the mixed Jews, the Ashkenazim,
as they are called, from the numerous occupancies of Asia,
Africa, and Western Europe.

The fragments of a fragment, however, are the *Samaritans*.

Too small to command attention as an element in our
politics, the remnant which is still to be found in the neighbourhood of its old metropolis has only within the present year
been visited and described in any detail.   All that is known
respecting its present condition may be found in the interesting
account of Mr. Grove's personal visit to Mount Gerizim.   The

Pentateuch, the only part of the Old Testament which the Samaritans recognise, differs from that of the Jews in some important readings and in its alphabet. The language, however, is the same for both. In their Chronicle, whilst the language is Arabic, the alphabet is Samaritan. Mr. Grove doubts whether the present Samaritans of Syria, all of whom are assembled in a single village near Nablúz, amount to more than a hundred individuals. A few more are to be found in Cairo. Milman, in his "History of the Jews," states that even at the present time there are to be found in the Ottoman Empire *Sabbathaists*, and that *Sabbathaism* still exists as a sect of Judaism. Such sects are rare. Such Sabbathaism, however, as can be found at present dates from about 1666, when an impostor known as Sabbathai Levi gave himself out as the Messiah. Another impostor of the same period, who called himself the Prophet Mehdi, excited the fanaticism of the Kurds. Both were treated with impartial contempt by the Mahometans. The Jewish Antichrist became a door-keeper, and the Prophet of Kurdistan was made a page of the treasure chamber. "The Ottomans," writes Sir Edward Creasy,* observed the progress of Levi "with religious anxiety; not from any belief in his alleged character, but, on the contrary, from the fear that he was the Dedjal, or Antichrist, who, according to the Mahometan creed, is to appear among mankind in the last days of the world."

So much for the peculiarities in the way of creed for the three great denominations in which there is little difference between the language and the race. The Wahabis are as undoubted Arabs as they are undeniable Mahometans. The Shiites are Persian; and no one supposes that the Jew is other than what he is always considered, *i.e.*, a descendant of the great families of the Old Testament, the Book of Maccabees, and the history of Josephus. In none of these is there, to any appreciable extent, communities, or nations of which the blood is other than Persian, Arabic, or Hebrew; in none are they whole populations whose language is Hebrew, Arabic, or

* History of the Ottoman Turks, p. 298.

Persian, but whose blood is Greek, or Georgian, or Armenian, or Slavonic, or what not. The broad and patent differences between Turk and Arab, Arab and Persian, are not the points towards which our attention is henceforth more especially directed. They are strong, patent, clear, and numerous. Hence, they speak for themselves. But with the Arab and the Syrian this is not the case. There are several points on which they differ, and it is not very difficult to enumerate them. The difficult point is to know whether, when we have traced a cha- racteristic to the locality, and connected it with some special population, we ever actually know what that population is. It may have its habitat in Syria; but that will scarcely make it Syrian. Its language may be the Arabic; but that will not make it Arabian. The most that either of these characteristics can do, is to establish a presumption—a strong one in some cases, and a weak one in others.

The influence of the Arabs upon the world's history is known. So, in a general way, is that of the Turks. So is the contrast between the Turk and the Arabic languages. So, also, the real or supposed differences of their anatomical conformations. In the language of the lax ethnologist, the Turk is Mongol; the Arab Caucasian. The Turk affinities are with the Fins, Mon- golians, and Tatars; the Arab with the Jews and Phenicians. Never mind the exact value of these distinctions. They express something; though the main fact is this, that all the south part of the Ottoman Empire is Arab, or Arabiform.

The Arab is not the only member of the family to which he belongs; the family known as the Semitic. He is, undoubtedly, the one which, at present, is the most prominent; but he has only been this since the days of Mahomet. The Jews belong to the same family, and it is certain that before the spread of Mahometanism they were, at least, as important as any branch of the Arabian stock; indeed, immeasurably more important than all Arabia put together. We need not be of the seed of Abraham to understand this. It is enough if we are Christians, and have read our Bible. Above all, it is not the true Arab who is the Turkish subject. Arabia Proper is all but inde- pendent. The Arab—as opposed to the Turkish—portions of the Ottoman Empire are Syria and Egypt; and these are, at best, but Arabic and Syrian, Arabic and Hebrew, Arabic and Phenician, Arabic and Coptic, Arabic and Berber; in other words they are, one and all, Arabic in language but other than Arabic in blood.

There is a notable antipathy between the two divisions, an antipathy which it is difficult to either generalize or analyze. It is manifestly not an antipathy of creed. It is scarcely one of race, whatever that term may imply. It is not one based on historical remembrances like those that sustain the nationality of Poland and Italy. The history of the Arab subjects of the Porte is neither one and undivisible, nor definite. Egypt has one history, Syria another; both, as far as their more glorious epochs are concerned, forgotten, for all sentimental purposes, by the existing Syrians and Egyptians. The dislike, however, exists; and it seems to be the result of innumerable individual antipathies. The Turk is lordly, overbearing, and arrogant; the Greek hates and fears him. The Arab, who, as a Mahometan bearing arms, is more on an equality, fears him less, hates him less; but still is far from loving him.

This complex of individual and concrete enmities makes up a general distrust and repugnance, which is wholly different from many of the ordinary forms of national antipathy. Of these several are compatible with friendship and respect for individuals; indeed, the dislike of the nation in general, for some obscure or lax reason, is, in many European countries, perfectly compatible with a high esteem for nine-tenths of the individuals which compose it. This applies to the Turkish Empire in general. Syria, however, and Mesopotamia are in a different predicament. They are not in the semi-independent condition of Egypt. They are in a geographical continuity with the true Turk parts of Turkey. They are of great practical political importance. They, doubtless, gravitate towards Egypt; indeed, it is only through European interference that they are not already Egyptian. Beyond, however, the general facts of their Arab character; of their geographical position, the import of which is patent from a simple inspection of the map; and of the misgovernment common to them and the rest of the Ottoman

Empire, there would be little concerning them to add to what has already been written if it were not for the extraordinary complexities of their religious sects and heresies which, along with Kurdistan and the southern part of Armenia, they exhibit.

There are at least the following :—

1. The Wahabi (Arabian) } already noticed.
2. Jews and Samaritans }
3. Christians.
    a. Nestorians, Nsara Messihaye, Chaldani.
    b. Jacobites.
    c. Maronites.
    d. Converts to Romanism.
4. Haranites and Mendeans, or the so-called Christians of St. John.
5. Yezids.
6. Druzes.
7. Ismaeli, Assassins.
8. Nosrani, Nasariyeh, or Ansari.
9. Mutuali or Metawili.

In Asia Minor there are three forms of Christianity, and geographically they are in contact with one another ; but as creeds they stand widely apart. Only one of them belongs to a recognised church, the other two having arisen out of heresies ; the earliest out of the heresy condemned, by the Council of Ephesus, and the latter out of the heresy condemned at the Council of Chalcedon. Hence, both are more than fourteen centuries old, and both are departures from the Greek Church. On the other hand, the third form of Christianity, or that which is other than heretic, is that of the Church of Rome, and it is probable that in no part of his domain is the Pope better served than he is in these *partibus infidelium.*

Of the two heretical divisions, the one condemned at Ephesus is the most numerous, and it is that which is known as Nestorianism.

The Council of Ephesus sat on the opinions of Nestorius. Theologically, Nestorius was a Syrian ; his Christianity being that of the Syrian discipline, which was based on the Syriac translation of the Scriptures then existing, and, perhaps, two hundred years old. At any rate, Syria had a lettered language, and its Church had its great doctrinal authorities and controversialists; some writing in Greek, some in the vernacular. We may call them Fathers. It was, however, in Germanicia that Nestorius was born, and Germanicia I believe to have been Turk. His refinements upon the current doctrine as to Christ's place in the Trinity may, simply as a matter of history, have had a Manichean origin. At the same time they may merely have arisen out of the half-intellectual, half-emotional feeling of which Manicheism was an independent, though an earlier, manifestation. Nestorius had subscribed to the Nicæan creed, and had been called to the Bishopric of Constantinople. But the Manhood of Christ, in the mind of Nestorius, could only be, at one and the same time, blended with the Godhead, and purified from the contamination of matter by the separation of Christ the Virgin-born from God the Pre-existent. This was done by making the Virgin mother Χριστότοκος and denying her to be Θεότοκος. She was the mother of the incarnate Christ, but not the mother of the eternal God. A quasi-separation of the Saviour from the second hypostasis in the Trinity was the inference from this; but it was intolerable at Rome, intolerable at Constantinople, most especially intolerable at Alexandria, of which the notorious Cyrill was then bishop.

The doctrine was condemned, Nestorius deposed, and banished. But many Syrian and Anatolian bishops continued to maintain either his cause or his principles; some firmly, some indifferently. Some supported his doctrines, some merely opposed his great enemy Cyrill. In Syria, in Cilicia, in Bithynia, and in Cappadocia, some bishop or other did this. The true Nestorianism, however, was rarer. It took ground in the districts where it is now found; and, as will be shown elsewhere, it has not been without its effects in the history of the world at large.

It is to the Council of *Ephesus* that we trace the first of our two divisions. From the Council of *Chalcedon* we must deduce the second. Before the middle of the seventh century another heresy has been condemned, and the Council that condemns it is that of Chalcedon. The doctrine of the Double or Single nature has been refined on; and, instead of *nature*, the polemics of the time of Heraclius wrote *will*. Monothelitism was then the term for which blood was spilt and Christianity divided. As the name of Nestorius is associated with the Council of Ephesus, so is that of Eutychian with that of Chalcedon.

Ephesian, Chalcedonian, Roman Catholic—these are the three terms which have hitherto been used. And they have been used because they supply definite and tangible points of history by which the three denominations may be distinguished from each other. They are not, however, recognised names. The current names are *Jacobite, Nestorian,* and *Chaldani* or *Chaldæan*. But these are European rather than Asiatic; scholastic or theological rather than vernacular. It is one thing for learned men in England or France to call the adherents to the creed condemned at Ephesus *Nestorians* : it is another thing for the adherents themselves to recognise the name thus bestowed upon them *ab extra*. The term by which the Jacobites and Nestorians most willingly designate themselves is *Nsara Meshihaye=Messianic Nazarenes,* or Christians. They also call themselves *Suraye* or Syrians.

(1.) The doctrines condemned by the Council of Ephesus have the greatest number of supporters; perhaps, as many as seventy thousand.

(2.) The doctrines condemned by the Council of Chalcedon have the fewest ; and, what is more, the list of their adherents decreases annually. The number of their *villages* is as follows:—

In the Jebel Túr (to the south of Diarbekir,

		their stronghold)	. 150
,,	parts about Orfah .	. . .	. 50
,,	,, Kharput	. .	. 15
,,	,, Diarbekir	. . .	. 6
,,	,, Mosul .	. . .	. 5
,,	,, Damascus	.	. 4

230

The explanation of the decrease is found in the history of the—

(3.) Roman Catholic converts from the two preceding denominations. The approximate number of these is—

		Families.
In the Diocese of Mosul	. . . .	160
„ Amida	. . .	466
„ Sert	. . .	300
„ Kerkush	. . .	218
„ Jezirah	. . .	179
„ Diarbekir	. .	150
„ Khosraw	. . .	150
„ Bagdad	. . .	60
„ Mardin	. . .	60
	Total	1743

Adding to these the Roman Catholic Syrians beyond the dioceses here enumerated, Mr. Badger, the chief authority for the present condition of these three denominations, considers that they may amount altogether to twenty thousand—more numerous than the Chalcedonian, less numerous than the Ephesian, heretics, at whose expense they increase.

The intervention of Rome dates from the middle of the sixteenth century, when Syrian Christianity broke into the fragments of a fragment. The bishoprics of Mosul, Amida (Diarbekir), like the Slavonic bishopric of Montenegro and the Electoral bishoprics of the German Empire, had become hereditary; and that in the families of Elias, Joseph, and Simeon, respectively. Feuds arose. The decision of Rome was appealed to. By 1681 either the whole province, or the chief see, had been named *Chaldæa*, just as a Byzantine theme, in nearly the same parts, had been so named. It was a Roman see *in partibus infidelium;* so that *Chaldæa*, as applied to it, is an old indigenous name just as *Belgium* is one as applied to the kingdom of King Leopold, *i.e.*, not at all.

Except the Roman Catholics, we cannot invest these Christian populations with much political importance. They are all forbidden to bear arms, but it is only for the orthodox that the influence from the Vatican is exercised. The numbers, too, of the two sects put together is far less than that of the Romanists taken singly. And, moreover, it is a number that decreases. The Romanists exert themselves in making proselytes, and their

5

exertions are successful, especially in the Nestorian division and in the southern provinces; indeed, in Syria Proper, the Christianity of the sects is in a fair way of becoming extinct.

Yet the exceptions are numerous. Among the Chaldani proselytism still goes on. The Chaldani, however, may be held to represent the Papal intervention of the sixteenth century. The number of the converts made recently and sporadically is uncertain. The only figures I have met with are the following for the town of Aleppo :—

	Families.
Greeks of the Greek Church . .	100
„ Latin „ . .	1,000
Armenians of the Greek Church .	180
„ Latin „ . .	600
Syrians of the Greek Church . .	?
„ Latin „ . .	350

That these numbers are only approximate is plain. They give, however, a great preponderance of Latins. Indeed, it is so decided, that it is only by taking in the members of the Eastern Church from other districts that the majority in favour of it can be made good.

It is the Chalcedonian creed upon which these proselytizing Westerns more especially encroach, and it is from their conversions in Damascus, Mosul, and Diarbekir that the numbers of the heterodox villages run so low. The four villages of Damascus are all that is left in that Pashalik; whilst in those of Aleppo and Bagdad the obliteration of the older creed is even more complete. Perhaps it is wholly so. In Jebel Túr, on the other hand, the encroachment is at its *minimum*.

Like the Chaldani, the Maronites are Roman Catholics; but, unlike the Chaldani, they are Romanists of long standing. They were Romanist as opposed to Greek as early as the sixth and seventh centuries, and they were also orthodox as opposed to the Monophyists and the Monothelites. Being this, they represent the last members of the Roman Church in the East, and also the Roman Church before the Mahometan conquest.

In such lands of Monophysitism as Syria and Mesopotamia we naturally expect that Monothelitism will prevail. It seems

to have done so. Still there were decided supporters of the
Double Will even in Syria, and none more decided than Sophronius, Bishop of Jerusalem. It was the sad fate of Sophronius
to be bishop when his metropolis was taken by the Mahometans,
and still sadder was his function of taking the conqueror over
the city and pointing out to him the Holy Places. He had more
especially to show the very site of the Temple, in order that the
Khalif might be able to build a mosque on it. "Now indeed is
the abomination of desolation on the Holy of Holies!"
was his miserable exclamation. But he had prepared
A.D. 636.
the way for his own, his creed's, and his country's degradation.
He had been the life and soul of the Antimonothelites. The
town was in the hands of Mahometans when he took Stephen,
Bishop of Dora, to the site of Golgotha, and said, "To that
God who on this very place was crucified for thee, at his second
coming to judge the quick and the dead, thou shalt render thy
account, if thou delayest or art remiss in the defence of his
imperilled faith. Go thou forth in my place. As thou knowest,
on account of this Saracen invasion, now fallen upon us for
our sins, I cannot bodily strive for the truth, and before the
world proclaim to the end of the earth, to the apostolic throne
of Rome, the tenets of orthodoxy."

The last words of this speech deserve special attention. They
show the extent to which he looked towards Rome. Syria was
largely Monothelite. The Emperor was Monothelite. Rome
alone was, at one and the same time, authoritative and
orthodox.

During the Monothelite and the Iconoclast period, we find
an unusual number of Syrian Popes—more, indeed, than at any
other period of the papal history—John V., Sergius I., Sisinnius, and Constantine—all between A.D. 685 and A.D. 716.
Again, Gregory III., who succeeded Gregory II. A.D. 731,
was a Syrian.

Again, this was the time of the greatest of all the orthodox
Syrian fathers, John of Damascus, who taught his theology
in the capital of the Kalifs, the town he takes his name from.

Of the difference between the spirit of the Third Council of
Constantinople which condemned, and of the Second of Nicæa

which restored, images, the following extracts give a suggestive sketch :—

" Anathema against the double-minded Germanus, the worshipper of wood! Anathema against George, the falsifier of the traditions of the fathers! Anathema against Mansar, the Saracen in heart, the traitor to the Empire; Mansar the teacher of impiety, the false interpreter of Holy Scripture !"

Again—

" We all believe, we all assent, we all subscribe. This is the faith of the apostles, this is the faith of the Church, this is the faith of the orthodox, this is the faith of the world. We, who adore the Trinity, worship images. Whoever does not the like, anathema upon him! Anathema on all who call images idols! Anathema on all who communicate with them who do not worship images! Anathema upon Theodorus, falsely called Bishop of Ephesus; against Sisinnius of Perga, against Basilius with the ill-omened name! Anathema against the new Arius, Nestorius and Dioscorus, Anastasius; against Constantine and Nicetas! Everlasting glory to the orthodox Germanus, to John of Damascus! To Gregory of Rome, everlasting glory! Everlasting glory to the preachers of truth !"

This, then, is the phase of Christianity which the Maronite creed represents; and if, at the present moment, it is Roman with some considerable differences, the time and conditions of its origin and the events which have taken place since it parted from the Eastern Church explain them. The contact with Mahometanism has abated their image worship. The possession of an old translation of the Scriptures gives them a vernacular Bible. Thirdly, priests marry. With all this the Maronites are reasonably considered to be more Roman in their orthodoxy than the Romans themselves.

Of the word *Maronite,* a full explanation is given by Asemanni; himself, *the* learned Maronite, κατ᾽ ἐξόχην. If we look to his text only, all is clear; and the notice of *Maro,* or *Maron,* the eponymus of the sect, is a definite piece of authentic biography. It is also the notice on which the common doctrines concerning him run. But the case becomes altered when we turn our eyes from the report to the evidence, and ask the names, dates, and value of Asemanni's authorities. What he quotes is an ancient Arabic manuscript according to the abstract or translation made by a Bishop Gabriel Barclaius in 1495, *i.e.* some 700 years after Maro himself. Nor is the objection thus suggested improved by a reference to the earlier notices. Cedrenus makes

the Maronites, or Mardaits, the men of a *Maurus Mons*. However, they were bold soldiers, and spread their arms and creed
as far as Jerusalem; even into Armenia. As for Maro himself,
he was an abbot of about A.D. 700, pre-eminent for his successful opposition to the Monophysites and Monethelites; in
other words, to the Melkhites. *Meleko=king,* and *Melkhite* is
said to be the term applied to the Monethelites and Monophysites, who espoused the cause of the Emperor; in other
words, to the *Imperialists.* It is a word which has a fair
amount of prominence in ecclesiastical history. Perhaps it is
as good a *collective* name as any other for the Jacobites, the
Nestorians, and their heterodox congeners.

Jacobite came from *Jacob* Baradæus, or Barhadades, also
called Zanzalus, who was Bishop of Edessa. He *lay heavily*
(incubuit) on the diocese, says Asemanni, from
Died A.D. 889. A.D. 844 to A.D. 852. He was the pre-eminent
supporter of Sergius the Monophysite Patriarch against Ephraim
the Catholic Patriarch of Antioch. He is also called the
Mafrian of his church, an Armenian title.

Thus far the creeds under notice have been, one and all,
referable of one of the three great religions of Europe and of
Western Asia; in other words, they have been Jewish, Christian,
or Mahometan. With those that are now about to present
themselves the case will be different. They are not easily
classified in respect to their relations with one another, nor
are they easily assignable to any definite or classificational
denomination.

CHAPTER IV.

Religious Creeds and Sects of the Ottoman Empire.—Haranites and Mendeans.—Druzes.—Ismaeli.—Nasarieh, Nosrani, or Ansari.—Mutuali.

THE creed of the Haranites, or Haraniya, is, according to
its votaries, one of the oldest in the world; older than that of
the Jews, inasmuch as it dates from the ancestors of both Lot
and Abraham, from the times anterior to the arrival of Abraham
in Judea, to the times, indeed, of Nimrod, "the mighty hunter
before the Lord." This is a date of no slight antiquity, and
with this we may reasonably be satisfied. But the Sabean
traditions go farther, for they carry us to the times before the
Flood, and tell us of the books of Enoch, of Seth, and even of
Adam himself; inasmuch as Sabi, from whom is said to have
come the name of Sabean, was a son of Seth. About the books,
however, of Enoch, Seth, and Adam we may reasonably have
our doubts; but the book of Isaac is mentioned by the Jewish
writers of the middle ages, and so is the Book of Psalms, and
so is another work on morality in general. The Jews also
state that when they made the pilgrimage to Haran, the Sabians
paid respect to a black cock and a black bull, and that when
they prayed they turned their faces towards the north star.

It is in the parts about the site of Nineveh and Bagdad that
we get upon ground with which the Prophets and the Books of
Kings have long made us familiar—to districts in which Moses
and Jacob sought their wives, and then to the "Ur of the
Chaldees," which was the birthplace of Abraham and Lot.
There is little Christianity here, for we are not on the soil of
Syria, but in Mesopotamia and Assyria. But the best guide

for us in our geography is the town of Harran in the modern, of Haran in the scriptural, and of Charrhæ in the classical maps. This is the country of the Haraniya, or Haranites. They are often called the Christians of St. John the Baptist; often, too, called the Sabeans; but the most convenient name is Haranite.

It is the district which, in the Book of Genesis, is especially assigned to Nimrod, and in which stood the Tower of Babel; and its great cities are Haran and Calneh and Akkad. Nineveh is not named in this, the earliest notice of them. This is the land of Haraniya, and we know the general history of the country for nearly three thousand years. Harran, Haran, or Charræ stands on the boundaries of Syria, Assyria, and Armenia; and of the oldest religion in each of these three countries, whether it was the worship of Baal, the religion of the Magi, or a special and peculiar form of Paganism, fragments of it are preserved in the strange heterogeneous creed of the present Haraniya. After the fall of Nineveh and of Babylon the country became Persian, and after the conquest of Persia by Alexander the Great it became Greek, and after the fall of the Macedonian Empire, Roman. Then it continued to be debateable ground between the Romans and the Parthians, until, finally, it became Mahometan, and from the religion of every one of its masters the creed of the present Haraniya has taken up something. We learn from the old coinage that the Greek was the chief influence; and so late as the tenth century we find that one family at least deduced their descent from the Heraclidæ, and called themselves Beni Heraclish, *i.e.*, Sons of Hercules. But whether, upon the whole, the Greek or the Syrian influence prevailed is disputed. The few facts we know are instructive. The chief objects of worship were the heavenly bodies. Hatria, or Hatris, was the city in the moon; Charrhæ, that in which the sun was buried. The moon was androgynous —man and woman at once; while those who worshipped it as a male were lords over their wives; those who worshipped her as a female were ruled by them. This is not much; but the little that there is is curious and characteristic.

Immediately above and below the junction of the Tigris and Euphrates, in the parts about the cities Washit and Bassora,

lies the country of the Mendeans, but not in immediate geographical contact with the Haranites. They lie to the south of
them, and they lie in a different kind of country. The Haranites belong to the elevated platform of the parts between the
Euphrates and the Tigris. The Mendaites lie, in happy neglect
and obscurity, in the marshes or fens of the parts about the
junction of the two rivers, and almost to the outfall of the two
united streams. The Haranites lie to the north of Bagdad,
the Mendaites to the south.

It is the sun-worship, then, of the times before Judaism to
which the Mendaites and the Haranites probably adhere. And
under this head they may be classed. From the pale of Mahometanism they must be wholly excluded, so that, as a class,
they have a very definite place among the several sects and
denominations of Asiatic Turkey. With Christianity their
connection is still slighter. It has been suggested that they
got the name Sabean from the frequency and ceremonious
character of their ablutions, and that this name led to that of
John the Baptist; but the question is a dark one. What is
more certain is the fact that, at the time of Mahomet, they had
their scriptures. This we know, because Mahomet classed their
creed with Christianity and Judaism as a scriptural, or canonical,
one, *i.e.*, as the " Religion of a Book." As such, it was indulged
with something like toleration, though there was not much of
it. However, it was on this account that the Haranites assumed it for themselves. It gave them privileges. They
probably deserved them. The worship of the heavenly bodies
is by no means the most ignoble creed of the pagan world;
and, whatever may have been the case at one time, the adoration
of the Sabeans was of a spiritual character. It was not to the
sun, moon, and stars, as mere luminous bodies, that they addressed their prayers. It was rather to the spirits that directed
their movements. Nor were these spirits omnipotent, still less
were they self-existing. The unity of a God, and his paramount
rule over the universe, was certainly a part of the Sabean creed.
It may have been overlaid by baser matter, but that it was
acknowledged is stated by Jewish writers and not denied by
Mahometan.

Such is the sketch of two creeds in two different districts, both of which are considered *Sabean*. There is a difference, however, in the propriety of the application of the term, and, according to Chwollson, it is to the Mendeans that it originally was applied. The Haranites assumed it; but it does not follow from this that the two religions were identical, though it is probable that they were closely connected. At any rate, the two geographical names *Mendean* and *Haranite* are both safe and convenient. Between them there is a much closer connection than there is between either and the one that now follows.

Whatever may be the details as to the origin and extraction of the Yezids, it is almost certain that they give us the nearest representation of the old creed of this part of Asia as it stood before the diffusion of either Christianity or Mahometanism. It is, apparently, older than both; and by each it has been encroached upon and displaced. Hence the present Yezid localities are discontinuous or sporadic, indicating the fragments of a once continuous religion. From this point of view they cover a large field; probably a larger one than has been explored. Like most other fragments of either languages or creeds, it is in the mountain districts rather than in the level country that they are to be found. Hence it is to the north of the desert of Sinjar, along the eastern affluents of the Euphrates, along the main stream of the Tigris itself, and on the drainages of the Zab and Khabúr that they appear; to the west of the Sinjar mountains, to the east of Julamerik, and to the north of Diarbekir—Diarbekir, Julamerik, Mosul, and Amadieh being the towns which, in the ordinary maps, best indicate their neighbourhood. Some lie as far north as Georgia. But these are immigrants.

Politically, they approach the boundaries of Persia and Russia. Ethnologically, they come in contact with the Arabs, the Turks, the Armenians, and the Laz; and, above all, the Kurds. Indeed, in language and features they are themselves Kurd. Their hymns are in Arabic. A little Arabic is understood by the Sheikhs. But the language of the people is Kurd. I believe wholly so. They make no converts: nor if they did, are either Arabs or Turks, and still less the Armenians, easily converted. If, then, there be any foreign blood among them, it has long lost its original characteristics. The Yezid is a Kurd, with a Kurd physiognomy—spare frame, dark skin, prominent nose, projecting brow, retreating forehead, black hair. Except that some of them are shorter and more squarely-built than others, and some square, rather oval in face, this is the concurrent testimony of independent observers respecting the Yezids.

The Sinjar mountains are their chief occupancy. Here is the residence of the chief Sheikh; here, their chief burial-place; here, above all, their chief sanctuary and place of pilgrimage, Sheikh Adi. For these parts the ten tribes are those of—

1. Heska.	6. Beit Khaled.
2. Mendka.	7. Amera.
3. Hubaba.	8. Al Dakhi.
4. Merkhan.	9. Semoki.
5. Bukra.	10. Kerani.

The Yezid dioceses, for this is a term which their general organization suggests, are four:—

1. Sinjar.	2. Northern Armenia.
2. Diarbekir.	3. Northern Syria.

In each of these the Kawals hold an annual visitation; the Kawals being one of the four orders of priests.

1. The Pirs are the first. A Pir is an *emeritus* Sheikh, one who, from his superior sanctity, is invested with a halo of sanctity during even his lifetime. He is a prophet rather than a Sheikh.

2. The Sheikhs are the mullahs, doctors, or superior teachers;

3. The Kawals, the working, or inferior clergy;

4. The Fakirs, the humbler officials, who light lamps, keep the shrines in order, and the like.

The Yezid Holy of Holies is the tomb of the Sheikh Adi. Around is the semblance of a village, consisting of temporary lodges, each appropriated to a particular tribe; whilst each part of the valley is known by the name of the tribe that lodges in it during the festival.

A fluted cone on a square base—this is the Yezid tomb, and it is sufficiently general and characteristic to denote a Yezid village.

Until lately the current notion of the Yezid was that he was a Devil-worshipper. He is, and he is not. He fears offending the

Evil Spirit. He propitiates him as he best can. He never curses him. Bless him he cannot. So he never mentions him at all. It pains him to hear his name from others. An imprecation of Mr. Layard's, unconsciously and incompletely uttered, manifestly and seriously gave pain to his guest. Mr. Layard would have called a lad about him a young *Satan*, but when he got as far as *Shait*— checked himself. It was too late. The bolt had been shot, and uneasiness, unwillingly, created. This horror of the name runs even into the eschewal of the semblance of it; so that, in some instances, the Yezid language, like those of Polynesia, *taboos* certain words. Any word beginning with *shat*, no matter what it mean, is avoided, and some approximate synonym used in its stead. Even *kaitan*, though very good Kurd for a *fringe*, is not allowed. In like manner *naal*=horse-shoe, is considered to be too near in sound to *laan*=*curse*, to be a proper Yezid expression. That all this may be referable to the old Persian doctrine of the Two Principles is likely; indeed, it is nearly certain as a matter of history, that such is the case. Without, however, any such antecedent, it is explicable on general principles. Numerous rude tribes hold that the Good Deity requires no positive propitiations, and that it is only the Evil one who takes offence at being neglected. Even Satan, then, is not so purely malevolent as to be beyond propitiation. Nor is he incapable of gratitude.

"Dost thou believe that God is righteous and all-merciful," said one of the Yezids of Russian Armenia to Haxthausen.

"I do."

"Was not Satan the best beloved of all the archangels, and will not God take pity on him who has been exiled so many thousand years, and restore to him his dominion over the world he created? Will not Satan then reward the poor Yezids who alone have never spoken ill of him, and have suffered so much for him?"

Next to Satan are the seven archangels, Gabriel, Michael, Raphael, Azrael, Dedrael, Azraphael, and Shemkeel; the name of this last being a compound of *Shems*, the Arabic for *Sun*.

The element, however, in the Yezid creed which has given rise to the most speculation, and which, after all the criticism that has been expended upon it, is still obscure, is the respect paid to the image of a bird. There are several copies of it, one, at least, for each of the four districts; but the original has never been seen by anyone but a Yezid, and this is kept at Sheikh Adi. Never has one fallen in the hands of a Turk or Arab. Kawal Yussuf, on one of his missions as he was crossing the desert on his way to Sinjar, nearly lost one. He saw a body of Arabs coming down upon him. But he buried the sacred emblem and disentombed it when the danger had gone by. Mr. Layard saw one of the fac-similes. At Redwan, on the Upper Tigris, his host conducted him into a darkened room. A red coverlet was removed with every sign of respect by the Kawals, who bowed and kissed the corners as they removed it. On a stand of metal stood the rude image of a bird. On certain occasions the original is exhibited to the faithful. The name of this image is Melik Taus; Melik being an Arabic word for King (also meaning Angel) and Taus being the Persian for Peacock; but also capable of meaning Cock. It is an old Persian word, being found as such in the Acharnenses.

The image; its sanctity; its name—these are the positive acts known about the Melik Taus; all beyond being speculation. And what they give, if we limit ourselves to plain literal and grammatical sense, is King Peacock. The reader who knows this knows as much as anyone who is neither a Sheikh nor a Kawal; perhaps, as much as the Kawals and the Sheikhs themselves.

The following is the explanation of this bird-worship as given by a Yezid to an American missionary:—

"When Christ was on the cross, in the absence of his friends, the Devil, in the fashion of a dervish, took him down, and carried him to heaven. The Marys soon came, and seeing that their Lord was not there, inquired of the dervish where he was. They could not believe his answer; but they promised to do so, if he would take the pieces of a cooked chicken from which he was eating, and bring the animal to life. He assented to the proposal; and, bringing back bone to his bone, the *cock* crew! The dervish then announced his real character, and they expressed their astonishment by a burst of adoration. Having informed them that he would thenceforth always appear to his beloved in the shape of a beautiful bird, he departed."

Individually, I believe that originally Malek *Taus* was, word for word, Malek *Daúd*, or *Daúdh*, i. e. King *David*.

The Yezids have been cruelly afflicted: and that, both by the Pashas of Bagdad and Mosul, who are supposed to be under the authority of the Sultan, and those Kurd chieftains which are, for all the purposes of oppression and robbery, independent. And this is but the result of their position. Their creed is not only other than Mahometan, but it is, in the eyes of a Mahometan, a creed without a Scripture ; a creed that is open to persecution beyond that of the Jews and Christians, or the men whose religion shows a Book. It is a creed, too, which has no powerful congeners ; in other words, there is nothing like it in high places elsewhere. The Fire-worshippers, even if they acknowledged the relationship, could do nothing in the way of maintenance or protection.

As far, then, as they have any religious sympathies, they have them with the Christians of the parts around them ; towards whom common suffering engenders a something like kindliness. We must remember that, like the Albanian Christians, the Yezids bear arms ; that their country is impracticable ; that they know every rock and defile in it ; that they are Kurds in language, and, in the opinion of the present writers, in blood also Hence, they practise savage and bloody reprisals on the Mahometans. But with the Christians they have friendly communion. In this they resemble another class of sectional religionists, in a very different part of Asia ; viz. the Siaposh of Kafiristan : whose religion, like that of the Yezids, has no definite congeners. Indeed, it is, to some extent, the Yezidism of the East. It partakes of the nature of Fire-worship, though with a large, but unrecognized, amount of Indian elements either as a basis or an incorporation. Like the Yezid, the Siaposh spares the Christian—the Frank as he calls him—but kills all Mahometans, whom accident or razzias may deliver into his hands. Yezidism, too, and the infidelity of the Siaposh Kafir, are the only creeds south of Siberia, and north of Assam, which are so far pagan, as to be neither Mahometan nor Christian, neither Buddhist nor Brahmin. The Brahminism of the latter, like its Fire-worship, of which it has elements common with Yezidism, is only approximate— rudimentary or fragmentary as the case may be.

The absence of any canonic Scriptures for the Yezid creed has already been noticed : and so has the disadvantage of its non-existence. It excuses injustice and oppression on the part of the Mahometans. A recognized Scripture, however, is one thing ; a body of religious compositions of non-canonic authority another. The latter may exist, even when the former is wanting. And that such is the case with the Yezids is to be hoped ; perhaps, it is to be expected. A report as to the existence of *some*

Yezid book is afloat ; though no one, not even Mr. Layard who has been so favoured in his opportunities and has made such good use of them, has been able to inspect, or even see, it. Still, it may exist. With a persecuted creed, with a sporadic body of believers, the doctrine *de non apparentibus et non existentibus eadem habenda est ratio* fails to hold good. On the other hand, where the want of a book is a disadvantage and a reproach, the concoction of one, for the occasion, becomes probable.

As it is, however, the following is the only known Yezid composition. It is given as it stands in Mr. Badger's Nestorian Rituals, a work to which something in the present, but more in the next, chapter is due.

The Eulogy of Sheikh Adi.

" My wisdom knoweth the truth of things,
And my truth hath mingled with me.
My real descent is from myself :
I have not known evil to be with me.
All creation is under my control ;
Through me are the habitable parts and the deserts,
And every created thing is subservient to me.
And I am he that decreeth and causeth existence.
I am he that spake the true word,
And I am he that dispenseth power, and I am the ruler of the earth.
And I am he that guideth mankind to worship my majesty.
And they came unto me, and kissed my feet.
And I am he that pervadeth the highest heavens ;
And I am he that cried in the wilderness ;
And I am the Sheikh, the one, the only one ;
And I am he that by myself revealeth things ;
And I am he to whom the book of glad tidings came down
From my Lord, who cleaveth the mountains ;
And I am he to whom all men came,
Obedient to me they kissed my feet.
I am the mouth, the moisture of whose spittle
Is as my honey, wherewith I constitute my confidents.
And by his light he hath lighted the lamp of the morning.
I guide him that seeketh my direction.
And I am he that placed Adam in my paradise ;
And I am he that made Nimrod a hot burning fire ;
And I am he that guideth Ahmet, mine elect,
I gifted him with my way and guidance.
Mine are all existences together.
They are my gifts and under my direction.
And I am he that possesseth all majesty,
And beneficence and charity are from my grace.
And I am he that entereth the heart in my zeal,
And I shine through the power of my awfulness and majesty.
And I am he, to whom the lion of the desert came,

I rebuked him, and he became like stone;
And I am he to whom the serpent came,
And by my will I made him like dust.
And I am he who shook the rock and made it tremble,
And sweet water flowed therefrom on every side.
And I am he that brought down an authentic herity,
A book whereby I will guide the prudent ones.
And I am he that enacted a powerful law,
And its promulgation was my gift.
And I am he that brought from the fountain water
Limpid and sweeter than all waters :
And I am he that disclosed it in my mercy,
And in my might I called it the white (fountain).
And I am he to whom the Lord of heaven said :
Thou art the ruler and governor of the universe.
And I am he who manifested some of my wonders,
And some of my virtues are seen in the things that exist.
And I am he to whom the flinty mountains bow,
They are under me, and ask to do my pleasure.
And I am he before whose majesty the wild beasts wept,
They came and worshipped and kissed my feet.
I am Adi of the mark, a wanderer,—
The All-Merciful has distinguished me with names,
And my seat and throne are the wide-spread earth.
In the depth of my knowledge there is no God but me.
These things are subservient to my power,
How, then, can he deny me, O ! mine enemies?
Do not deny me, O men, but yield,
That in the day of the resurrection you may be happy in **meeting me.**
He who dies enraptured with me, I will cast him
In the midst of Paradise, after my pleasure, and by my will.
But he who dies neglectful of me,
Shall be punished with my contempt and rod.
And I declare that I am the essential one ;
I create and provide for those who do my will,
And the world is lighted with some of my gifts.
I am the great and majestic king ;
It is I who provide for the wants of men.
I have made known to you, O congregation, some of my ways.
Who desireth me must forsake the world.
I am he that spake a true word ;
The highest heavens are for those who obey me.
I sought out truth, and became the establisher of truth ;
And with a similar truth shall they attain to the highest like me." *

The legends, traditions, and floating opinions concerning both
the ethnological and the religious relations are so numerous, and
so heterogeneous, as to point in several directions at once.

* From the paper of Mr. Ainsworth's, in the Transactions of the Ethnological
Society, from which nearly the whole of this chapter is taken, I learn that there
is a second translation of this poem by Mr. Rassam.

There is an opinion that they come from the south, *i. e.* from the *lower* Euphrates, and there are high authorities who on this opinion lay considerable stress.

Again, the family of their chief affects a descent from the Ommiads of the Kalifat; and this is only one out of many facts which points towards Arabia. Nor is it the most important one. The Arab elements of the Yezid ritual and the Arab titles of the Yezid authorities, if they stood alone, would go far towards the doctrine that it was either Arabia or Syria, before those countries became Mahometan, which Yezidism more especially represented.

Then comes the statement of Hadzhi Khalfah which connects them with Mahometanism, but not with Arabia : making them Persian and Sufi, rather than aught else.

The Yezids reckon themselves disciples of Sheikh Adi. or Hadi, who was one of the Merwanian Khalifs. The Yezids were originally Sufites, who have fallen into error and darkness. Those whom they call their Sheikhs wear black turbans, whence they are called Kara Bash (black heads). They never hide their women. They buy places in Paradise from their Sheiks, and on no account curse the Devil or Yezid. The Sheikh Hadi has made our fast and prayer a part of their abominable faith, and they say that, at the day of judgment he will cause numbers to enter into Paradise. They have a great enmity to the doctors of law.

Then come the two following legends.* They are essentially the same. Yet the first, *eo nomine* Yezid, is from the north of Media, whilst the second is a tradition of the Fire-worshippers of Seistan in the south of Persia.

(1.)

Monseignore Tommaso, Bishop of Marquise, relates that when this Elias, after having been chosen bishop of Mogham—a city on the frontiers of Persia, and near the Caspian Sea—proceeded to enter on the duties of his diocese, he found it occupied by a barbarous people, immersed in superstition and idolatry.

The bishop, however, commenced his instructions: and his flock confessed that they received them with pleasure, were convinced of their truth, and were inclined to return to the true God, but that they were terrified at the thought of abandoning Yezid, the object of religious veneration of their ancestors. This idol, they said, conscious of approaching rejection and contempt, would not fail to revenge itself by their total destruction. Elias desired to be led to this object of their adoration. They conducted him to the summit of a neighbouring hill, from whence a dark wood extended into the valley below. From the bosom of this rose a plane-tree of enormous height, majestic in the spread of its boughs and deep obscurity of its shade; but, transported with holy zeal, he demanded a hatchet, and rushing to the valley, sought the idol, whom he found lowering with a dark and menacing aspect. Nothing daunted, however, he raised the axe, smote down the image of the prince of darkness, and continued his work till not only was the mighty tree laid prostrate, but every one of the numerous younger shoots, termed by the barbarians the children of Yezid, was likewise demolished.

(2.)

In former times there existed, they say, a prophet named Hanlalah, whose life was prolonged to the measure of a thousand years. He was their ruler and benefactor; and, as by his agency, their flocks gave birth to young miraculously once a-week; though ignorant of the use of money, they enjoyed all the comforts of life with much gratitude to him. At length, however, he died, and was suc-ceeded by his son, whom Satan, presuming on his inexperience, tempted to sin, by entering into a large mulberry tree, from whence he addressed the successor of Hanlalah, and called on him to worship the prince of darkness. Astonished, yet unshaken, the youth resisted the temptation. But the miracle proved too much for the constancy of his flock, who began to turn to the worship of the devil. The young prophet, enraged at this, seized an axe and a saw, and prepared to cut down the tree, when he was arrested by the appearance of a human form, who exclaimed, "Rash boy, desist! turn to me, and let us wrestle for victory: if you conquer, then fell the tree."

The prophet consented, and vanquished his opponent, who, however, bought his own safety and that of the tree by the promise of a weekly treasure. After seven days the holy victor again visited the tree, to claim the gold or fell it to the ground; but Satan persuaded him to hazard another struggle, on promise that if conquered again the amount should be doubled. The second rencounter proved fatal to the youth, who was put to death by his spiritual antagonist; and the results confirmed the tribes over whom he had ruled in the worship of the tree and its tutelary demon.

This legend of the tree, however, is merely one detail out of many. The most general affinity of Yezidism with Fire-worship lies in the definitude of the Yezid recognition of the Evil Prin-ciple; certainly the most prominent, and perhaps the most charac-teristic element of the creed.

With Christianity the recognition of the Scriptures connects it. But, in this recognition, the Old Testament commands more respect than the New; so that it is with either Judaizing Christianity or Christianizing Judaism, rather than with Chris-tianity in its more purified forms, that the connection chiefly lies. Of this, however, the full import is pre-eminently obscure. There was much in both Judaism and Christianity that was less Judaic and Christian, in the limited sense of the terms, than it was something anterior to (at least) the later elements of each. How difficult is it to say where the St. John of the Mendeans is separated from the St. John of the New Testament: where the Elias of the numerous floating superstitions of Caucasus, Media, and even early Germany, is other than the Elias for whom our Saviour was taken; other than the Elijah of the Old Testament. Yet the triple connection, though obscure, is real; whilst the prophet Elijah is older than either the Christianity of St. John or the Talmud, older than the Fire-worship of the Sassanidæ. Again, how far is the oriental belief a pure and proper tradition, or how far a mere educt from the text of the Old Testament misstated, misinterpreted, metamorphosed? But besides the name of Iliyas, that of Esa, or Jesus, is Yezid.

Add to this the points of resemblance which inquirers minutely versed in the False Gospels, in the Talmud, and in the details of the Arabian superstitions before the time of Mahomet, could, doubtless, suggest, and the difficulties of our analysis become painfully visible. Much, however, as it may leave unexplained, there is still one principle which it inculcates, viz., the composite character of creeds like Yezidism and the difficulty of pronouncing what they are off-hand. They have too much of something else to be substantive religions; and, as they admit foreign elements from more quarters than one, the question of the relation which any one of them bears to the others may still remain, even when the extraneous elements themselves have been enumerated, insoluble—all the more so for the connected religions being themselves complex. There is always room for refinement and analysis. The Fire-worship of the Sassanidæ is one thing; the Fire-worship which was incorporated with Christianity and became Manicheism is another. If Yezidism have grown out of the former it represents a separate substantive religion; if out of the latter, it represents a Christian heresy.

The Haranite and Yezid creeds belong to Mesopotamia rather than to Syria. The creeds of the Druzes, the Ismaeli, and Nozrani or Ansari, belong to Syria rather than to Mesopotamia. Without doubt there is in these both a Christian and a Mahometan element; but the Christianity is that of the heretics of the fifth and sixth centuries, and the Mahometanism that of the Shiites. Hence it is mainly in their geography that the two groups differ.

The Druzes occupy the Lebanon east of the Maronites and south of the Ansariyeh. Some of their superstitions present themselves in the history of the Knights Templars; for the towns of Antioch and Edessa were among the first conquests

of the Crusaders; so that the contact with the Orders was considerable. As far as the three following pairs of names go, the first
of which points to Judaism, the second to Christianity, the third
to Mahometanism, it would seem as if the Druzes had gone on
the principle of finding two contemporaries and reversing the
order of their importance. Thus, between Adam and Abel, Jesus
and St. Peter, Mahomet and Ali, there is a double relation;
that of Incarnate Deity, and human Prophet; but whilst Adam,
Jesus, and Mahomet represent Humanity, it is Abel, St. Peter,
and Ali, who give the Incarnate Deity. I take this as I find it,
as the most notable fact in their strange creed; indeed, as the
only one of much importance known to me.

The Druze Avatar, to borrow an expression from the Indian
mythology, is stranger still. It is important, however, as showing the historical origin of, at least, a portion of the creed.
After the dynasty of the first Kalifs had come to an end, after the
seat of the Kalifat had been removed from Damascus to Bagdad,
and when Ægypt, separated from the Empire of the Abbassides,
was under the rule of the Fatemites, arose an apostle named
Hamza. He assisted in the violent persecutions, directed against
both the Jews and the Christians, of the sixth Fatemite king,
Hakem, who was born at Cairo, A.D. 1004, who ascended the
throne when he was eleven years old, and who, in his thirtieth
year became the Druze epoch: this meaning that the Druzes date
from A.D. 1034. More than this, the bad mad Fatemite Hakem
is the Druze Avatar; the last Incarnation of the Deity.

The reign of Hakem is a matter of history. So are his
persecutions. So also the strangeness of his temper and character. But Hamza, Addi, and Darazi, have no personal verisimilitude. Hamza is sometimes called Addi; Addi, Hamza—
Addi, be it noted, being the name of the great Yezid Sheikh, as
well as that of the legendary founder of the Syrian Church.
Darazi, meanwhile, composes the Druze Scriptures; heads the
exodus from Ægypt into Syria; and, as is shown on the face of its
history, gives his name to the settlers. Full of Scriptural terms,
especially those that figure in the apocryphal writings, the Druze
theology is also full of abstractions savouring strongly of a
corrupted and misunderstood Christianity—the Soul, the Word,
the Following, the Preceding, and the like. The following

6 *

extracts show this. They are selected from Mr. Chameaud's translation of a Druze book, made about ten years ago. Each has been chosen for the illustration of a different principle of the creed. They form about a fifth of the whole work. The first gives the origin of evil, in its thoroughly pseudo-spiritual aspect.

The Ocean of Time.

CHAPTER I.

THE Creator, the supreme, created all things. The first thing He created was the minister Universal Mind, the praises of God be upon him! and the Creator gave to Mind the power to create, classify, and arrange all things.

The Spirit has the following attributes:—The Virgin of Power, The Receiver of Revelation, The Knower of the Wishes, The Explainer of Commands, The Spring of Light, The Will of Production, The Chosen of the Creator, and so forth.

It was this Spirit, or Mind, known by the above attributes, that arrayed the world.

The Mind is the Pen which writes upon stone, and the stone which it writes upon is The Soul.

The Mind is a perfect being, which being is at liberty to act, and is possessed of a free will; all he ordains or creates is in accordance with the will of the Creator.

When the Creator created Mind, He made him possessed of a free will, and with power to separate, or to remain and dwell with the Creator.

Ultimately Mind rebelled and abandoned the Creator, and thus became the spirit of sin, which sin was predestined to create the devil.

And the existence or creation of the devil occasioned the creation of another spirit called Universal Soul, and this spirit was the cause of the creation of all things existing.

The devil is perfect sin, and the creation of this spirit was permitted by the Creator, to show the unlimited power of the Creator in creating an opposite spirit to God.

Now when Mind rebelled against the Creator, the Creator threw him out of heaven; but Mind knew that this was done by the Creator to test his faith, and to punish him for his sin; so he repented and asked for forgiveness, and implored help against the devil.

And the Creator pitied Mind, and created him a helpmate called Universal Soul; this spirit God created from the spirits of the knowledge of good and evil.

Then Mind told Soul to yield obedience to the Creator, and Soul yielded, and became a helpmate of Mind; and these two spirits tried to force into submission to the Creator the evil spirit or devil.

They came to the evil one, Mind from behind, and Soul from before, in this fashion to marshal the devil into the presence of the Creator; but the devil evaded them, being unguarded on either side, which enabled him to escape from them to the right and left.

The Mind and Soul, finding this to be the case, required each of them a helpmate: Mind required a helpmate to keep the evil one from the right side, Soul one to guard him on the left, so as to hem in the devil between them, and prevent his escape on any side.

So they moved and immediately two spirits were created; the one called **Word**, and the other the Preceding.

The devil now found himself hemmed in on all four sides, and felt the want of a spirit to help him; and as to all things there must be an opposite, the Creator knowing the thoughts of the devil, inspired Mind, and thus created him a supporter; and when this supporter was created it was against the wishes of Soul.

The Mind and Soul commanded this supporter to yield to the Creator, and he yielded and worshipped the Creator.

And the Creator commanded the supporter to yield to Mind and Soul, but being instigated by the devil and tempted to disobedience, this supporter refused submission to Mind and Soul; whereupon, being cast out of heaven, he clung to the devil.

Then the Creator inspired Mind, and Mind inspired Soul, and created the Word (as already said).

And the Word could do good and evil.

And the Mind and Soul told Word to yield to the Creator, and the Word yielded; and the four spirits Mind, Devil, Soul, and the supporter, having inspired Word, created Preceding, who had good and evil in him, but more of the former than the latter; so that Preceding yielded ready obedience to the Creator, and was also subservient to Mind and Soul.

Now all these spirits above enumerated inspired Preceding, and thus created Ultimum, the last spirit created, and he yielded to the Creator.

And the Creator commanded Ultimum to be subservient to Mind, Soul, Word, and Preceding; and Ultimum was subservient.

Now all these spirits were true spirits before they entered the modern world, and their generation is as follows: the Creator created Mind, and Mind created Soul, and Soul created Word, and Word created Preceding, and Preceding created Ultimum, and Ultimum created the heavens and the earth and all therein.

And it came to pass that the aforesaid five spirits came to the devil, Mind from behind, Soul from before, Word from the left, and Preceding and Ultimum from the right, in order to force him to yield submission to the Creator; but the devil refused submission, and finding himself confined on all sides, with no means of issue, except upwards and downwards, and as, moreover, he feared fleeing upwards, where he must needs encounter the Creator, the devil fled downwards, and this was the origin of hell.

CHAPTER VIII.

Enoch, Sharkh, and Shutneel.

Hareth was serving in the priesthood with all the other angels, and he was among them when the Creator commanded them to be subjected to Shutneel.

And the Angels worshipped Shutneel, but Hareth refused and abandoned Paradise, and, quitting its borders, all the disciples of Falsehood fell with him, and Paradise was rid of their presence.

The Paradise of the Creator extended all over the earth, and the disciples of truth entered therein, and received the commands of Shutneel, the doctor.

And they kept apart from those who deny the Unity of God, and turned out the disciples of Falsehood from among them.

Then were established the order of Truth, and the words of verity (God's peace be upon them).

And the priesthood [belonged to Shutneel, who is Adam the happy; and Hareth and his followers were jealous and plotted contrivances to deprive him of his paradise, and to establish an enmity between him and his race.

Now these deceivers never desisted from their object ; they came and said, " We have a piece of advice to give to you, O our lord, Enoch ; and to your partner, Sharkh, which is good for you both."

This they kept repeating until they were admitted into the presence of Enoch and his partner, Sharkh.

When they came before them they worshipped them ; and Enoch, who is the second Adam, said, " Perhaps you have repented and seek forgiveness for your blasphemy and disobedience to the priesthood in having assisted Ibliss and his associates."

But the deceiver replied, " No, I swear by your head and by the Creator, I have come to give you advice by reason of the interest I take in your welfare, and to warn you against the injustice of Shutneel in having compelled you to be subjected to him.

" I have heard our Lord the Creator (praises be to Him !) say that the priesthood belonged only to Enoch and Sharkh, caitiffs in Paradise."

Hereupon Enoch made him swear, and he swore to him.

And as it was the custom that whosoever swore by God falsely should be punished, no one dared to swear by him falsely.

And when the deceiver swore to Enoch and Sharkh that he was sincere in what he said, true in his deeds, and most pure in his words, they believed him, and fell into sin in many ways.

First, by neglecting the commandments of Shutneel.

Secondly, by changing the priesthood from the person to whom it belonged.

Thirdly, by changing the will of the Creator (praises be to Him !) and opposing what he commanded them ; for the Creator had said, " Do not approach this tree, that ye be not of the unjust."

Fourthly, by believing in the words of one they knew to be deceitful.

And fifthly, by accepting advice from the father of deceit.

Now after they had committed these sins, and had so far forgotten themselves, Enoch and Sharkh awoke to a sense of what they had done and perceived their baseness.

Knowing that Shutneel was aware of their thoughts, and that they had no other way left them but that of repentance and of suing for forgiveness, they went to Shutneel.

They went to him crying, repenting of, and confessing their sins, and spoke to the following effect :—

" Thou art the forgiver, and we are the transgressors, thou art the pardoner of sins, thou art the merciful, thou art the Creator, thou art the element, oh! our God, forgive us."

With such like words they sued for mercy.

And when Shutneel knew that Enoch and Sharkh were truly repentant he begged the Creator to forgive them and to restore them to the position they formerly occupied.

The creatures who committed this sin were five in number, Enoch, Sharkh, Aneel, Tabookh, and Hibal.

And Enoch is The Soul, Sharkh is my lord the Word, Aneel is the Plaintiff, and Tabookh, their speaker.

And the deceiver is the supporter of the devil, not Ibliss, and he blasphemed against Shutneel.

Moses, Jesus, Mahomet, Hakem.

CHAPTER XI.

And from the seed of Abraham prophets appeared, like unto Isaac, Jacob, Joseph, and others.

Then appeared Moses the son of Imram, and the people of truth followed his law, and the interpretation of his supporter, who was Joshua, the son of Nun.

Then there appeared other prophets, and their power in the knowledge of the unity was as the amount of saliva in the throat of man.

And these were Isaiah, Hezekiah, Nathaniel, Daniel, Doodoosalem, and the like from among the prophets.

From among the respectable doctors Pythagoras, Plato, and Aristotle; the peace of God be upon them!

CHAPTER XII.

Now when Jesus, the son of Joseph, appeared with the New Testament, and established himself as the Lord, the Messiah who is Jesus (the peace of God be upon him!) he was accompanied by his four apostles, John, Matthew, Mark, and Luke (the peace of God be upon them!) and the people of Truth profited by his revelations, although they pretended to the truth, in the law, and copied the law of Moses in explaining the law of Jesus.

Then appeared Simon the happy, and the people of Truth were on his side until the time of the seven priests had passed away.

And the strength of the belief of the seven priests in the unity, was as the amount of saliva in the throat of man.

After this, Mohamed, the son of Abdalla, appeared with his law, which is the law of Islam.

And Mohamed established Ebn Abi Taleb as his supporter, and all the disciples of Truth followed the law of Islam, as they had done every other law that had preceded it.

Now Mahomed was in the time of Suleiman, the Persian.

When Ali Ebn Ali Taleb came forward with his explanations of the law of Islam, the people of Truth believed in them, and continued therein, until seven priests had passed away after him.

These seven priests were of the seed of Mohamed, and are Hassan, Hussein, Ali Ebn Abi il Hussein, Ebn Mohamed Ali, Jaffr Ebn Mohamed, Ismael Ebn Jaffar, and the name of the seventh is not known.

The time of Mohamed Ebn Abdalla was more evident and more demonstrative of power than all the epochs that preceded him; consequently, they pretended for singleness in Ebn Ali Taleb; moreover because the prophets Noah, Abraham, Moses, and Jesus foretold the appearance of a man, the highest of the high, whose rank is great, whose name be glorified.

This was Ali Ebn Abi Taleb.

When the term of the priesthood of Mohamed Ebn Abdalla was completed, Mohamed Ebn Ismael, the prophet, appeared, whose law is the final of all laws inciting to the right path; and he is from the seed of Eli Ebn Taleb.

And to Mohamed Ebn Ismael there is a supporter secretly established in Paradise, and no one knows his name, because he does not appear in the manifestation of the law which we have.

But it is certain that Mohamed is a prophet, and that God has sent him an evident book, and he has an open law and a secret law, and his works are the works of the eloquent that have passed before him.

Not that Mohamed is not like unto one of them, but that he is their partner against injustice.

And he has brought forward the law, the invitation to annihilation, the establishment of a delegate, and the promulgation of licentiousness.

CHAPTER XV.

At the completion of this era of the world, there commenced a second era and the wisdom of God thought proper to produce Kaem, the Almighty, with Sayeed il Muhdi.

And those who recognized the unity of God were steadfast in the secrets of Truth, and in the faith of Ali Ebn Ali Taleb, his progeny.

And the secrets of Truth succeeded from one to another until Sayeed il Muhdi, and from Sayeed il Muhdi the secrets of Truth reached the Lord of Truth (may his name be reverenced !), and the people recognized Kaem as a powerful God, because they had witnessed his miracles, and because he made manifest to them wonderful miracles whilst he was an infant under the guardianship of Sayeed il Muhdi.

When Il Kaem grew up, he took to the priesthood, and when he appeared in public, mounted on horseback, with the soldiers in his service, Sayeed il Muhdi used to walk before him, calling aloud, " I am the servant and slave of our Lord Il Kaem, and the priesthood was a thing in my consignment, and he has taken it from me."

After this Sayeed died, and his soul passed to Makhled Ebn Kebdad, one of the kings of the west.

Now, before Sayeed died, he had been an enemy of Keis Dad, the father of Makhded.

And when Makhded grew up, and his age was six, he was informed that Sayeed had been the enemy of his father, so he prepared to fight, and assembled his soldiers to go against Il Kaem (may his name be reverenced !).

And when Makhled was eleven years old, the number of his soldiers reached four hundred thousand.

The reason of his assembling all these was, because the Almighty had said, " Behold the people of the cursed and abominable Makhled Ebn Kebdad, surnamed Abi Yazeed, there are no people who are more sinful, more disorderly, and greater drunkards."

Now, Abi Yazeed desired to have a contention with Il Kaem (may his glory be sanctified !), and among his soldiers there was cheapness, and health, and peace, whilst to Il Kaem's soldiers there was only his presence and the presence of the forty-six.

And the soldiers of Il Kaem were few ; but he granted them his assistance and majesty, and went forth in person with them to fight Abn Yazeed.

And he defeated them, and killed them, and destroyed them, and revenged himself ; and when this great miracle became known, the faith of Il Kaem, the most glorious, reached the country of the West, and was promulgated all over the earth.

CHAPTER XVI.

At the close of the time of the Almighty Kaem, the Creator most praised manifested himself bodily and in the priesthood in Mansoor, and it was apparently visible that he was the son of Il Kaem, and that Il Kaem had transferred upon him the priesthood, and had clothed him with the Caliphat, and assigned his power to him.

And the faith of Mansoor was promulgated all over the earth, and made known to all assemblies, and Mansoor performed miracles, and changed some of the articles of the law, as the Almighty Kaem had also done before him, and his priesthood took place in the country of the West.

After Mansoor came the chief Maaz in the priesthood, and the faith was assigned to him, and he acted as did Mansoor, and his time began in the country of the West.

And Maaz sent Abdalla, whose name was Gouhair, with soldiers to Egypt, and he defeated the sons of Abbas, and conquered Cairo.

After this, the Almighty Maaz went to Cairo, and concluded his faith in that city.

After Maaz appeared the chief Azeez the Almighty, and his appearance took place in Cairo, and to him Maaz consigned the priesthood.

And the Almighty Azeez manifested signs which explained and made evident the unity, and he performed miracles which could not be performed by any one unless inspired by God.

And he proclaimed his faith, and his miracles were known throughout the world, and there remained not a single man who did receive the faith. Praises be to him whose grace has been so promulgated by reason of his mercy !

Then the Creator most praised appeared in Hakem ; may his power be glorified in Cairo !

And the five chiefs, Il Kaem, Mansoor, Maaz, Azeez, and Hakem appeared as though they were sons of each other ; and this secret priesthood passed together with the heavenly posts, from the post of Zacharias to the post of Hakem (may his power be glorified !), until it reached its real proprietor, Hamza, who, in truth, is the Kaem ; the celebrated Hamza Ebn Ali ; the blessings of God be upon him !

To the ordinary orthodox Sunnite Mahometanism all this is as decidedly opposed as it is to any creed in the world. To the Shiite Mahometanism of Persia, as modified by Sufism, it is somewhat less antagonistic. The practical view that the Druze takes of Mahomet is given in the following catechism :—

Q. What shall we say of Mohammed ?
A. He was a devil and the son of fornication.

Q. And why do we read in his books, and confess him to be a prophet, and weep at funerals like Moslems ?
A. By compulsion, for his religion was propagated by the sword ; therefore we read with the tongue, but not with the heart. This is not forbidden by our Lord Hakem.

Q. Why do we pray to Mohammed before men ?
A. We pray to Mohammed Mokdad, who is Solomon the Persian, the true Messiah ; but Mohammed the Koreishite, is a devil, the accursed son of fornication.

Q. Why do we publicly testify on the Koran, but deny its truth among our-selves ?
A. We deny it because it praises Mohammed the Koreishite. The words repeated are true, but taken from the Gospel which was dictated to four ministers by Solomon the Persian.

Q. What are our views and language with reference to the deluge which the Christians and the rest of the people say drowned the world?

A. The deluge is Mohammed the Koreishite and his sect who flooded the world.

I have suggested the doctrine that contact with the crusading Franks of the military orders may have had something to do with some of the ceremonies and secrets of the Nasariyeh. With the Druzes the evidence of this improves. The notice of them in D'Herbelot, written before the elaborate and valuable monograph of De Sacy, makes them little more than Syrian Franks. It is short. Indeed, all that it tells us is, that they considered themselves Frank in origin and that they were specially connected with the family of Lorraine.

One of the charges, truly or falsely, made against the Druzes, is that they worship the image of a calf; and this was one of the charges made against the Knights Templars during the process so infamously instituted against the Order by Philip the Fair.

It is only a fragment of their creed that is known; and it may be added that even the historical account of their origin is clouded with doubts. The statement, for instance, that *Darazi* was a man's name, that a man so called wrote a book, and that it was from the book and the man that the sect took its name, is traversed by the probability of the term *Dur*, *Dru*, or *Dr*, being a term as old as the Macedonian period. The suggestion that the older form *Durz* gives us the *-tur-* in *I-tur-æa* (? whence *Keturah* as an *eponymus*) is none of my own; but one that has been current since the time of Herbelot. The exact details by which the letter-changes are justified I have not seen. I only know that, so far as the geography is concerned, the etymology is eminently satisfactory. The ancient Ituræa, or Trachonitis, lying between the Hauran, Damascus, and the southern spurs of the Anti-libanus is just the region from which the Druzes of the Lebanon may reasonably be deduced; whilst, of the south-eastern Druzes, it is the exact locality. Hence, whatever may be the origin of the name, the descent of, at least, a large portion of the Druzes is, almost certainly, Iturean.

This, of course, is not the origin assigned to them by those who deduce them from Ægypt. Nor is it the one suggested by M. Chameneaud, the translator of the strange book from which so much has just been taken, and, as such, an authority of no slight influence. It is on the following extract that M. Chameneaud founds his doctrine that they were the Hivites :—

Judges, Chapter III.

1. Now these are the nations which the Lord left, to prove Israel by them, even as many of Israel as had not known all the wars of Canaan;

2. Only that the generations of the children of Israel might know, to teach them war, at the least such as before knew nothing thereof;

3. Namely, five lords of the Philistines, and all the Canaanites, and the Sidonians, and the *Hivites* that dwelt in mount Lebanon, from mount Baal-hermon unto the entering in of Hamath.

4. And they were to prove Israel by them, to know whether they would hearken unto the commandments of the Lord, which he commanded their fathers by the hand of Moses.

5. And the children of Israel dwelt among the Canaanites, Hittites, and Amorites, and Perizzites, and *Hivites*, and Jebusites :

6. And they took their daughters to be their wives, and gave their daughters to their sons, and served their gods.

7. And the children of Israel did evil in the sight of the Lord, and forgat the Lord their God, and served Baalim and the groves.

The descent from the Hivites implies that it is the Druzes of the Lebanon who most especially represent the denomination; which may or may not be the case. The two doctrines, however, are by no means incompatible; inasmuch as, if we scrutinize the details of the Hivites, we find that they are specially mentioned as extending to Mount Hermon; in other words, that Mount Hermon was a part of Lebanon, a fact which brings them into contact with Ituræa. By a further extension, it gives Bashan and half Gilead to either the same people or their confederates. In short, it gives the eastern Druzes the half-share of Manasseh and all Gad, with parts of Asher and Napthali, and a district in Central Phenicia, between Berytus and Tyre.

In any other country but Syria, the question would be comparatively unimportant. In Syria, however, from the complexity of its creeds and genealogies, as well as from their high interest, the minutest details deserve notice.

With those who look upon the Druze and its allied creeds as mere offsets of Mahometanism, the heresy which commands the most attention is that of the Karmathians, indeed it is upon the the Karmathians that the *Ismaeliyeh* are more especially affiliated; and, as Baalbek is one of the cities which the Karmathians took, the affiliation is probable enough; though it must not be con-

strued so as to exclude the Nasariyeh and the Druzes from
the same, direct or indirect, partial or complete, connection. The
same applies to the Assassins. The Ismaeliyeh need not have
been Assassins; though the Assassins may have been a special
branch of the Ismaeliyeh. As stated before, the localities differ.
The Ismaeliyeh district is the Kelat-el-Masaad to the west of
Hamah, and on the head-waters of the Orontes. It is almost a
south-eastern prolongation of the Nasariyeh area, as well as
a north-western one of the Druzes of Damascus and the
Hauran.

For the Karmathian heresy itself, the year A.D. 900 is a convenient date. The creed was then in full vigour. It had arisen
a few years before, in the two hundred and seventy-seventh year
of the Hejirah. Karmath, an Arabian of Kufa (I follow
Gibbon), undertook to purify and spiritualize Mahometanism.
He was the Guide, the Director, the Demonstrator of the Word, the
Holy Spirit, the Camel, the Herald of the Messiah, the Favoured
of Mahomet, the Son of Ali, St. John, and the Angel Gabriel.
He was either a new prophet or a new incarnation. He attacked
the ceremonial part of the Koran. He treated the pilgrims
to Mecca, and the Holy City itself, with scant respect; indeed,
he massacred some thousands of the first, and sacked and defiled
the second. He polluted the holy well of Zemzem. He tore-up
the veil of the Temple. He removed the Kaaba—he or his
followers, Abu Saud, the father, and Abu Taher, his son.
Baalbek in Syria, and Bassora on the frontier of Persia, he
sacked. He crossed the Tigris. The Kalif sent a deputy to
him, who enlarged on the vast power and multitudinous armies of
his master and recommended prudence and submission.

Abu Taher to one of his men.—Plunge a dagger into thy
heart.

To another.—Throw thyself into the Tigris.

To a third.—Cast thyself from that precipice.

And when each, without hesitation or delay, had done as the
chief had commanded him, the imam turned round to the deputy,
and said:—

"Tell thy master what thou hast seen. He had not three such
men in all his armies. To-morrow he shall be before the dogs."

The essentials of this threat were made good; and a great,

though not a permanent, Karmathian conquest followed. That it spread in the direction of Phenicia we learn from the express statement that Baalbek was one of the cities it involved.

Though I have taken an exception to the doctrine that the Ismaeliyeh are either the descendants or the representatives of the Assassins of the Crusades, more especially of those whose occupancy was the mountain district near Acre, I by no means object to the converse of the proposition, or the doctrine that the Assassins of the Crusades were Ismaeliyehs. As far as assassination was concerned, the Ismaeliyeh form of fanaticism may have been found far beyond the proper boundaries of Ismaeliyehism : indeed, the ordinary Assassins may have been Nasariyeh with a certain recognition of the Ismaeliyeh discipline—*i. e.* the duty of assassination when ordered by a superior to whom implicit obedience was due. They may also have been true Ismaeliyeh extended westwards. What follows, however, is the history of the Ismaeliyeh, *eo nomine* and *iis locis.*

It begins, if we take the name as an epoch, in the seventh generation from Mahomet's son-in-law, Ali.

With Ali, began the great schism between the Sunnites and the Shiites.

Of the Sunnites nothing need here be said.

The Shiites fell into four primary divisions.

Of these one was that of the *Imami,* or the men whose doctrine was determined by their notion as to the character of the Imam.

The Imami were one of a dichotomy.

Whilst the Kaissaniyeh and the Seidiyeh made the true successor to Mahomet simply a human being, (differing only as to who he was,) the Imami and the Gulhat spiritualized him into an Avatar ; in other words, they agreed with one another in recognizing the doctrine of an Incarnation.

The Imami fell into two divisions.

The *Twelve*-imam sectaries made the series of revealed Imams end with Mohammed Ben Hassan Askeri, the twelfth from Ali.

The *Seven*-imam doctrine stopped at Ismael, the son of Dzhafir Sadik ; Ismael being the seventh from Ali ; the order being :—

1. Ali.
2. Hassan.
3. Hussein.
4. Ali Sein-al-alabidin.
5. Mohammed Bekir.
6. Dzhaffer Sadik.
7. Ismael, who died before his father.

The Fatemites of Ægypt were of this line; and so good did their title seem to be, that the great Kalif Almansor, Abbassid as he was, is said to have named Ali Risa the Eighth of the Twelve-men Imams, as his successor. He did so, however, to the great offence of the other Abbassids; and, under the pressure that their claims developed, a committee of doctors sat upon the question of the succession. This committee decided in favour of the powers that were; and, as it is from Sunnite accounts that Western Europe takes its chief notions of Mahometanism, the validity of the Fatemite, the Ismaeli, and the Twelve-men Imami claims has generally been summarily dismissed. However, they were not so treated by a great subsequent authority, the Kadi Abubekir Bakilani, who held the opposite opinion; an opinion with which the modern historian (Von Hammer) from whom is taken all concerning the Ismaeliyeh which is here laid before the reader, apparently agrees.

Mahommed	was the son of	Ismael;
Dzhafir Mosadik	„	Mohammed;
Mohammed Hab	„	Dzafir Mosadik;
Obeid Allah	„	Mohammed.

Obeid Allah was the fourth in descent from the seventh Imam, and the founder of Ismaeliyehism. He, it was, who asserted his rights to the Kalifat; his father, grandfather, and great-grandfather, having been unrevealed, or latent Imams.

Let us still remember that the Ismaeliyeh doctrine is Shiite rather than Sunnite, that the Shiites are pre-eminently Persian, and that Persia, as the land of Fire-worship, Zoroastrianism, Magianism, Manichism, the Two Principles, and much of the same sort, is the quarter in which we must seek the chief influences which in the way of spirituality and transcendentalism modify Mahometanism. During the first two centuries of the Hejira the ordinary phenomena present themselves. There is the struggle of the pure typical and orthodox Sassanian Fire-worship, whatever that was, with ordinary Mahometanism. But besides this, there were Mahometan and fire-worshipping sectarians. There were, amongst others, the followers of Mazdak, whose influence on the politics of the Persian Empire, under the reign of Khosroes Nushirvan, has commanded the attention (and what escaped the notice?) of Gibbon. There were, amongst others, the followers of Hakem Ben Hashem; of whom, under that name, few English readers have heard; but who to the reader of Lalla Rookh is the real Veiled Prophet of Khorasan. There is also Babek, of less notoriety but greater power, who was a Per-sianized Mahometan; and Karmath, of whom notice has already been taken. The evidence that he also was all but a Fire-worshipper is satisfactory. He was the disciple of Hussein, who was the disciple of Ahmed, who was the son of Abdallah, the son of Maimun Kaddah, the son of Daissas the Dualist. He it was that used for his own purposes the malcontent spirit of the Ismaeliyeh; he, who more especially organized the secret-society element in their political organization.

It developed itself still further in Cairo, under the Fatemites, whose dynasty, in Von Hammer, seems to have been mainly supported by secret societies. As an historical fact this is highly improbable. However, the following is a sketch of what we may call the Ismaeliyeh Lodge of Ægypt in the tenth century. Its name was the Society of Wisdom. The candidates were dressed in white. Every day the chief visited the Kalif, and either read to him an essay, or took a written receipt for one having been heard by his Holiness. The pupils, on the master's return, touched the signature with their foreheads. The institution was subsidized to the amount of two hundred and fifty-seven thousand ducats. The noviciate was put on his trial and promised implicit obedience. When sufficiently puzzled by points of casuistry, he was told that the only explanation of them lay in the authority of the Imam. When more advanced, he learned how everything went by sevens; how God had made seven planets, seven heavens, seven earths, seven seas, seven colours, seven musical sounds, seven metals, seven Imams, seven lawgivers, each of which altered the doctrine of his predecessors. There were the speaking apostles. But, besides them, there were seven mutes. The seven speaking prophets were Adam, Noah, Abraham, Moses, Jesus, Mahomet, Ismael; their seven assistants, Seth, Shem, Ishmael (the son of Abraham), Aaron, Simeon, Ali, and Mahomet the son of Ismael.

The highest doctrines were transcendental inculcations of in- differentism, embellished by the names of Plato, Aristotle, and Pythagoras; the practical upshot of them being that nothing was true and everything allowed, that naught was to be believed and anything to be dared.

When, taking leave of the institution, we address ourselves to the individual men who invested it with life and influence, the first name that presents itself is that of Hassan Sabah. His father Ali was a Persian of Rei, a Shiite, of doubtful orthodoxy; of which he was so definitely accused that, in order to place himself above suspicion, he sent his son to sit at the feet of the famous Mowafek of Nishabur; unrivalled as a teacher, unquestioned as a Sunnite. All Mowafek's pupils got on well in after-life; and among them three were conspicuous. The first was Omar Kiam, whose habits were those of an intellectual Epicurean, who loved astronomy better than anything but poetry, and poetry better than anything but his ease. The next was Nizam-ul-Mulk, who became the vizier of Malek Shah. The third was the founder of the Assassins, Hassan Ben Sabah himself.

"As all the disciples of Mowakef," said he, one day, to the other two, "become successful in the world, let us promise that whoever succeeds first shall share his good fortune with the other two."

"Agreed."

When Nizam-ul-Mulk became vizier, Omar Kiam was the first who found him out; but high office at court, of which his old friend thought him worthy, had no charms for him. He was satisfied with being made Astronomer Royal. He has left behind him, however, more verses than observations.

Then came, some ten years afterwards, Hassan Saba, who was also promoted—only, however, to endanger the place of his bene- factor by vile but eminently skilful intrigues. However, he failed and was banished. Keeping himself concealed in the house of a friend at Ispahan, he wound up a tirade against Malek Shah and his vizier, by saying, "that with two devoted friends to do his bidding he would soon have overturned both the Turk and the peasant," *i. e.* the Sultan and his vizier. His host thought him mad ; and when dinner came set before him a pot of aromatics and saffron, a diet-drink which was esteemed useful in cerebral affections. After this Hassan left Ispahan, and threw himself into that vortex of intrigue and mystery with which Fatemite Ægypt was overflowing. The following is his own account of himself :—

From my childhood, from my seventh year, my sole effort has been to extend the bounds of my knowledge, and to increase my capacities. Like my fathers I was educated in the tenets of the twelve imans (Imanie) and I formed acquaintance with an Ismaeliyeh Refik (Fellow) called Emise Dharab, with whom I cemented bonds of friendship. My opinion was, that the doctrine of Ismaeliyehs was like that of the philosophers, and that the ruler of Egypt was one of the initiated ; whenever, therefore, Emise spoke in favour of their principles, I disputed with him, and there was a great deal of discussion between us concerning points of faith. I did not in the least admit the justice of the reproaches which Emise lavished on my sect ; nevertheless, they left a deep impression on my mind. In the meanwhile he left me, and I was attacked by a severe fit of illness, during which I blamed my obstinacy in not having embraced the doctrine of the Ismailiyehs, which was the true one ; and I dreaded lest, should death await me, from which God preserved me, I might die without obtaining a knowledge of the truth. At length I recovered, and met with another Ismailiyeh, Abu-Nedshm-Saraj, whom I questioned concerning the truth of this doctrine ; Abunedshm explained it to me in the most circumstantial manner that I came fully to understand it. Lastly, I found a Dai (missionary) called Mumin, to whom the Sheikh Abdolmelek-ben-Attash, the president of the missions of Isak, had granted permission to exercise that office. I entreated him to accept my homage in the name of the Fatimite Khalif ; this he at first refused, because I was of higher rank than himself ; but as I urged it most pressingly he at length acquiesced. Now when the Sheikh Abdolmelek arrived at Rei, and had become acquainted with my opinions in conversation, my demeanour pleased him so, that he immediately invested me with the office of Dai (religious and political missionary). He said to me 'Thou must go to Egypt to enjoy the happiness of serving the Imam Mostanssur (the reigning Fatimite Khalif)." On the Sheikh Abdolmelek's departure from Rei, on his route to Ispahan, I journeyed into Egypt."

Where he was received with honour. But the Kalif named either the more unpopular, or the more unfit, of his sons as his successor ; and it was to the losing party that Hassan attached himself. Reluctantly his imperial patron ordered him into prison. But a tower, the strongest in Damietta, fell to the ground without any visible cause, and the fall was converted into a miracle in favour of Hassan. So he was shipped off. Then a storm drove him on the coast of Syria :

and there he preached the doctrine of the Seven Imams and of the Fatemite claims to the Kalifat. He then seems to have traversed all Persia, from Bagdad and Kerman on the south to the frontier of Turkistan on the north. The district, however, of the Rudbar, to the south of the Caspian, on the boundaries of Dilem and Irak, was his final resting-place. There he gained the castle of Alamut, the citadel of the eastern and earlier branch of his abominable sect. There he resisted more than one attack of the captains of Malek Shah. Thence he spread his arms and influence around, nominally for the Fatemite Kalif, really for himself. He was not a sultan, not an emir. He was no prince. He was the Grand Master of a brotherhood rather than an ordinary sovereign; and it is remarkable that, in the way of date, his settlement in Dilem was exactly contemporary with that of the first crusaders in Palestine. Still more remarkable is the parallelism between his order and those of the Crusaders. He himself was the Sheikh. Immediately under him were the Dailkebirs, lieutenants, bishops, overseers, or administrators of the three provinces of Dzhebal, Kohistan, and Syria. Then came the Dai or initiated missionaries, then the Refiks or associates, then the Fedavi or devotee murderers, then the Lassik or novices, and lastly the uninitiated mass.

This was the working, political, or active organization: superadded to which was a concurrent one of a more spiritual, and a very unintelligible, kind. I give, however, the details of it, in order to show how thoroughly the number seven runs through it:—

1. The Imam, divinely appointed.

2. The Hudzhet, or the Proof, who take orders from the Imam.

3. The Sumassa, who take order from the Hudzhet.

4. The Dai.

5. The Messuni, or Freed.

6. The Mukellebi, or Hounds who beat about for either proselytes or victims.

7. The Mumini or believers in general.

Their discipline consisted in the unscrupulous application of a knowledge of the weak parts of human nature and a system of casuistry. The introductory rule comprised such maxims as:—

Sow not on a barren soil.

Speak not in a house where there is a lamp.

Waste not words on the incapable.

Speak not in the presence of a lawyer.

The second set of rules was for gaining confidence by flattering passions and humouring weaknesses. The third was for raising religious doubts and leaving them for the authority of a superior to settle. The fourth rule was that of implicit and unquestioning obedience, with oaths to sanction it. The fifth course, one of instruction, was somewhat historical. It taught the opinions of the wise and good men of all ages, so far at least as they could be wrested to a conformation of the peculiar doctrines of Ismaeliyehism. The sixth delivered a recapitulation of all hitherto learnt. The seventh was essentially esoteric and delivered in full, and delivered the allegorical or non-natural sense in which all the positive and literal injunctions of the Koran were to be taken. As all was doubtful nothing was prohibited.

Such was the school, college, garrison, or court, at Alamut, in which, as a spider in his web, sat the wicked old Hassan.

The chief disciples, and most intimate confidants of the first Sheikh were Reis Mosaffer, Hussein of Kaini, Abulfettah, and Kia Busurgomid; all, apparently, Persians from the northern provinces. Under these were their conquests effected and their assassinations achieved. For the possession of rich towns and fertile valleys they cared but little. What they most especially coveted was fortresses on inaccessible rocks. Hence, the line of their acquisitions has a physical or a geological outline: and Assassin castles appear sporadically and at distances from one another wherever there is the necessary condition of a mountain-range. Of the eastern Assassins the districts to the south of the Caspian at the foot of Dermavend, and the Persian Kohistan were the chief habitats. Their foremost, perhaps their earliest victim, was Nizam-ul-Mulk himself, the old school-fellow, friend, and patron of Hassan. Hated as benefactors are hated by the ungrateful and envious, and feared as the powerful vizier of Malek Shah, it was not long after that Sultan's attempt to reduce Hussein Kaini that Nizam-ul-Mulk was stabbed. The sultan died soon afterwards; supposed to have been poisoned. His death was followed by anarchy; and during the dispute between the brothers Barkyarok and Mohammed for the possession of Irak and Khorasan, some important acquisitions to the power of Hassan Saba were effected. They consisted of the castles of the Shah Durye, of Derkul, and

7 *

Khalendzhan near Ispahan; of Wastamkuh, of Tambur and Khalovkhan; of Damaghan, Firuskuh, and Kirdkuh; of Tabs, Kain, and Toon; of Esdahan and Lamsir, all in Persia.

Such are their chief actions in the field. Of the individuals whom they murdered, the list, though incomplete, is full enough to show the character of their warfare. They struck at the men in power. Three kinsmen of the reigning sultans and three viziers I find mentioned by name as their victims. The Sultan Sandzhar himself was only warned. One morning when he awoke, he found a dagger stuck in the ground close to his head. A few days afterwards he received the following note : "Had we not been well-disposed towards the Sultan, we might have plunged the dagger into his heart instead of the ground."

Sandzhar, either because such warnings moved him, or because (as some of his acts incline us to believe) he was not unfavourable to the institution, would willingly have made peace with them on the three following conditions :—

1. That they should build no more castles.
2. That they should purchase no more arms.
3. That they should make no more proselytes.

But the doctors of the law and Koran forbade a compromise. Their opposition, however, only delayed the settlement. A few years later, peace was concluded between Hassan and Sandzhar; greatly to the favour of the former. The Ismaeliyeh of the district of Kirdkuh were freed from all impost, and an annual subsidy was assigned to them, charged upon the revenues of the district of Kumis.

Hassan was now old. He had survived his old schoolfellows, the Vizier whose murder he had procured, and the astronomer. Reis Mosaffer, too, director, or grand master in Damghan, after receiving a visit of honour from Sultan Sandzhak, had gone down to the grave as an honoured and aged patriarch. Abulfettah had been tortured to death in Syria; having failed to defend the city of Apamea against the crusader Tancred, who gave him over to the vengeance of the sons of Khalaf the ejected governor. Hussein Kaini, though one of the triumvirate of the first assassins, had been himself assassinated; the suspected murderer being Ostad, one of the two sons of Hassan himself. For this he was ordered to death by his father; and, along with him, his brother.

So, now, Hassan, not only old but childless, feels his end approaching, and sends for the two best-deserving of the Dais—for Abu Ali, from Kaswin, and for Kia Busurgomid, from Lamsir; between whom he divides his power. To Abu Ali is allotted the external command and the civil administration: to Busurgomid the supreme spiritual power.

After this, Hassan died as quietly as if, instead of being a murderer and the father of murderers, he had passed a long life in the temperate and chastened exercise of both mind and body. Yet he had never, for thirty-five years, left the castle of Alamut; and only twice had he moved from his chamber to his terrace. He had merely received reports and issued orders. The murders and battles followed as a matter of course. In like manner had lived his successor whilst at Lamsir. To Lamsir Busurgomid had confined himself as strictly as Hassan had confined himself to Alamut.

All this has been the history of the eastern rather than the western branch of the Ismaeliyeh; of the Assassins of Persia rather than of the Assassins of Syria. This is because Persia is the country in which the institution originally developed itself, the Persian castle of Alamut being the metropolis of the creed. On the other hand, however, we must remember that it was in Ægypt that it appears to have begun; and, connecting it, in its origin, with Ægypt, we must bear in mind Ægypt's vicinity to Syria.

The exact details of the introduction of the Ismaeliyeh creed into Syria are uncertain. We have seen that, in his escape from Ægypt, Hassan Sabah landed in the north of that country, where he promulgated his doctrines. Still, they may have crossed the frontier from Ægypt before the time of Hassan. However, it is pretty certain that there were Assassins in Syria as early as there were crusaders; and, deadly enemies as they were to the Franks afterwards, it is on the side of the Christians, rather than the Mahometans, that they first appear. The Count de St. Gilles is besieging the fortress of Hosnal-a-Kurd, when the Prince of Emesa, as he is moving to its relief, is assassinated. It was, however, as the enemy of Risvan, Prince of Aleppo, rather than as the Mahometan warrior, that he fell; Risvan of Aleppo, with whom lies the disgrace of having been the employer of the first Assassins of Syria. The agent who commanded his support was a physician, astrologer, and poisoner. The next was Abutaher

Essaigh, a Persian goldsmith, the commandant of Sarmin, a strong fort to the south of Aleppo. Abutaher had received Abulfettah, Hassan Saba's nephew, as a resident emissary within the walls; this being much the same as making over the fort to the Assassins. A few years afterwards the inhabitants of Apamea rebelled against their governor, and invoked the aid of Abutaher. It was granted. Khalaf, the governor, was assassinated, and the town was held as a garrison of Risvan's. Only, however, to be taken by the Crusaders under Tancred; whose conquest of it brought about the death of Abulfettah, already noticed.

Abutaher, however, was ransomed, and for some years he is the most prominent member of the Syrian branch of his vile order. An attack upon a caravan, which miscarried and was repudiated; an attack on the fortress of Shisher, which also miscarried; the murder of Newdud, Prince of Mosul, stabbed at noon-day, in the great square of Damascus,—these are the chief events which are assigned to the Assassins of the parts about Aleppo, under the direction of Abutaher and during the reign of Risvan.

However much it might suit a wicked prince to avail himself of the daggers of the Assassins for the purpose of accomplishing some particular object, it is plain that the permanent reliance on them is a political impossibility. They might, at any time, turn against their patron. Either feeling this, or actuated by some higher motive, the son of Risvan, a youth of sixteen, began his reign by an attempted extermination of the sect. Nor was it an insignificant one. Three hundred put to death and two hundred imprisoned are the numbers for that part of the Ismaeliyeh (or as it is also called the Bathenian* persecution) which has come down to us in the most definite form. Wide as these examples must have spread, they were utterly insufficient. All that followed the attempts of Akhras and his eunuch minister was revenge, and again revenge—assassination in the light of day; assassination under the shade of night; open razzias of armed men; solitary stabbings.

The Kalif of Bagdad had to receive the Atabeg of Damascus the Governor of Khorasan being present. Mistaken for the

---

* Though this word is differently derived, I suggest that it is merely the geographical term *Batancan*.

Atabeg, the Governor was stabbed by the third of three Fedavi; two of whom had failed, and all of whom were slaughtered on the spot.

The Governor of Aleppo, with two of his sons, was on the way to the court of the Emir Ilghazi. The three were murdered on the road.

The following year, this same Emir Ilghazi received a message from Abu Mohammed, the head of the Ismaeliyeh, at Aleppo demanding the fortress of Sherif. Such demands were frequent. They were also effective. Rarely was a bold denial hazarded; as rarely was a straightforward transfer made at once. Prevarication was the rule. Consent was given; but orders for the fortress to be either demolished or spoilt were superadded. Thus it was with Sherif. Ilghazi gave it up; but, before his orders reached Aleppo, the people had pulled down the walls and filled up the ditches. So famous a prince as Nureddin prevaricated in like manner with Bertlaha.

The thread of the Ismaeliyeh history is that of a labyrinth. This is because the scenes of action are numerous, and irregularly distributed; whilst the capital, in which the Sheikh sat resident and immovable, was generally distant from the most notable of them. The work is done in Syria: the order is given, and the reports received in Persia. Not that Persia is by any means without a history of its own; at times, as bad and bloody as that of Syria itself. It has also an Ismaelite literature; for more than one of the Sheikhs were either lovers of literature or pretenders to a literary taste. We shall hear of them as vain and ambitious preachers; as innovators upon their own innovations upon Mahometanism; as reformers of their imperfect system, i. e. as men who, by making the bad worse and the wicked wickeder, treated themselves as purifiers of doctrine and menders of discipline. Syria, however, is all that we need, here, look to—making an exception only in favour of the names by which the succession was kept up. These are always borne by occupants of the original metropolis, the fort of Alamut.

1. Hassan I. (Saba)	was succeeded by	Kia Busurgomid.
2. Kia Busurgomid	,,	Mohammed I.
3. Mohammed I.	,,	Hassan II.
4. Hassan II.	,,	Mohammed II.

5. Mohammed II. was succeeded by Hassan III.

6. Hassan III. (Jelaleddin) ,, Mohammed III.

7. Mohammed III. ,, Rokneddin Khorshah,
the last Sheik of the Order.

Such the order of succession in the mountain metropolis. In Syria, the history falls into six periods :—

1. The first ends with the occupancy of Sarnin by Abulfettah ;

2. The second, with that of Banias ;

3. The third, with the removal from Banias to Masaad, the present locality of the fragments of the sect ;

4. The fourth, with the accession of Rashededdin Sinan ;

5. The fifth, with the Mameluk Conquest ;

6. The sixth, with our own times.

Under Kia Busurgomid, Damascus, to a great extent, takes the place of Aleppo ; and it is the Vizier of Damascus who most especially intrigues with, and employs, the Assassins. We know what will come of the connection. There will be a short friendship ; a discovery of either treachery, or danger ; a reaction ; a bloody and vindictive massacre. The whole history is a cycle of such enormities. The main details, however, gather round the names of Behram, Ismail, and Abulwefa. It is Behram who works his way to the confidence of the Vizier of Damascus, from whom he obtains the town of Banias. Dreaded, however, as the Ismaeliyeh were by the Sunnite Turks, it was not by the Sunnites that their power was broken. In the valley of Taim, an outlying portion of the Baalbek district, an Ismaeliyeh army was cut to pieces by a combined force of Nasariyeh, Druzes, and *Magians* —so the name stands—by which is, probably, meant the Mutuali. Ismail, like Behram (whom he succeeded in the administration of Banias) a Persian, on the news of the defeat, entrusts his plans to the triply treacherous Abulwefa ; who, whilst pretending to act with the Emir of Damascus, enters into a secret treaty with the Christian King of Jerusalem and the Knights Templars to deliver Damascus into the hands of the Crusaders and to take Tyre in exchange. The plot miscarries and the Ismaeliyeh in Damascus are massacred. Meanwhile, the Crusaders take Banias and hold it for three years.

That more individuals were assassinated in the reign of Kia

Busurgomid than in any other, can scarcely be stated with safety. What, however, we may state, without hesitation, is, that during the times under notice, more crowned heads and more high officials were stricken down than at any other period. The Prince of Mosul, the Vizier of the Sultan Sandzak, the Emir of Damascus (his son), the Mufti of Kaswin, the Reis of Ispahan, the Reis of Tabriz, one Kalif of Ægypt, two of Bagdad—of these we know the names, titles, and dates: the rank having ensured a record of their fate. Of those who died unregistered, who can even guess the number? We can hope that the murders of the poor and weak bore no proportion to those of the great and powerful; and, considering the general character of the Assassin policy, that, like lightning, it struck chiefly at the highest, this is, by no means, an unreasonable hope.

Kia Busurgomid nominated his son as his successor; thus determining that the headship of the Order should be hereditary. In Mohammed's reign, which was, in all its essentials, a mere continuation of Busurgomid's, the Fatemite dynasty came to its end, and Ægypt was conquered by Nureddin, and his lieutenant the famous Saladin. The throne under which Ismaelitism first developed itself had now fallen.

Between 1330 and 1340 the castles of Kadmos, Kahaf, and Massiat came into the possession of the Ismaeliyeh; the first two by purchase, the second by conquest. Henceforth the sect is to be studied in its present locality.

Hassan II. was the preacher and reformer we have already alluded to. He proclaimed himself a Fatemite Imam; substituted the allegorical or non-natural interpretation for the literal and grammatical sense of the Koran; effectually separated Ismaelitism from Mahometanism; and authorized by both example and precept the doctrine that everything was doubtful and nothing forbidden. The effect was uncontrolled licence and licentiousness.

His son ruled much after the same fashion.

Such was Ismaelitism in the metropolis.

In Syria Saladin was Sultan: whilst, in Ægypt, the Fatemites were no more.

Saladin was every Assassin's enemy. Thrice was his life attempted. Thrice the attempt failed. The details here have not only a general, but an English, interest. The son of

Nureddin was a minor; his minister a eunuch, Gumushtegin. The movements and countermovements on the parts of Saladin and Gumushtegin belong to the general history of Syria. Suffice it to say that Gumushtegin suborned the Assassins. They failed and fell absolutely into the hands of Saladin; who, on the point of taking their stronghold Massaat, was dissuaded from it by his uncle the Emir of Hamah, who was over-persuaded by Rashi-deddin Sinan, the head of the Ismaeliyeh, of whom more will soon be said. On the condition that he should, to the end of his natural life, be safe from assassination, he granted them peace. And the agreement was kept. Von Hammer, speculating on the motives that thus kept the daggers of the Assassins in their sheaths, and made the person of the great Sultan sacred, suggests more than one reason for their faithful abstinence from his blood. The previous failures may have frightened them. The balance of power may have commanded their attention. The sanctity of a treaty may possibly have withheld them from treachery. The old saw of Honour among Thieves, probably, conveys the true expla-nation. Safe, however, as far as the Assassins were concerned, Saladin remained till the day of his death.

Now comes the notice of their famous embassy to Amaury, King of Jerusalem, connected, by the events with which it closed, with the terrible name of Richard I. of England. The ambas-sadors offered the baptism and conversion of their sect on condition of peace, friendship, and the remission of their tribute of two thousand ducats. As they were on the way homewards with the news of the acceptance of their terms, Walter de Dumesnil, under the orders of the Grand Master of the Templars, Odo de St. Amand, set-upon them from an ambuscade and killed the envoy. The scandal spread, and Amaury demanded at the hands of Odo the punishment of Dumesnil. It was nominal: whereupon Amaury bided his time, and, at a meeting at Sidon, dragged from their hospital and imprisoned several of the Templars—himself dying soon afterwards. The Grand Master himself was taken prisoner by Saladin at the battle of Sidon. All hope of converting the Ismaeliyeh was now gone; and they were free to be used as Assassins.

Nothing has hitherto been said of the Christians whom they murdered. It may now be noted that Raymond, the Count of

Tripoli, had been murdered by them about forty years before the time under notice, and that, now, they murdered Conrad the great Marquis of Montserrat, a kinsman of Leopold of Austria, and an enemy of Richard of England.

The charge of having suborned them to this unhappy act was laid against the Lion-hearted King by his contemporaries, and has been echoed by our own. It is a likely one. Bad as the deed was, it would be far from the worst for which that cruel king has to answer. At the same time, it is not on the arguments of Von Hammer that he can be convicted. A letter from the Old Man of the Mountain of the time—probably Rashideddin Sinan—exculpates him. It runs as follows:—

To Leopold, Duke of Austria, the Old Man of the Mountain sends, greeting.

"Seeing that many kings and princes, beyond the sea, accuse the Lord Richard, King of England, of the death of the Marquiss, I swear, by the God who reigns for ever, and by the laws which we observe, that he had no share in his death; the cause of the Marquiss's death was as follows:—

"One of our brethren journeying in a ship, from Salteleya to our parts, was driven by a tempest, near to Tyre, and the Marquiss had him seized and put to death, and laid hands on his money. Now, we sent our messengers to the Marquiss, requiring him to restore our brother's money, and give us satisfaction for our brother's death, of which he accused Reginald, Lord of Sidon, but we ascertained the truth, by means of our friends, that it was the Marquiss himself who caused him to be slain, and his money to be seized.

"And again we sent another messenger to him, by name Eurisus, whom he would have thrown into the sea, had not our friends caused him to depart hastily from Tyre. He came quickly to us, and told us these things. We, therefore, from that hour have desired to slay the Marquiss. So, then, we sent two brethren to Tyre, who killed him openly, and almost before the whole people of Tyre.

"This, therefore, was the cause of the Marquiss's death; and we tell you of a truth, that the Lord Richard, King of England, hath had no share in this death of the Marquiss; and they who, on that account, ill-treat the King of England, do it unjustly, and without cause.

"Know ye for certain, that we slay no man in this world for any gain or reward, unless he have first injured us.

"And know, that we have drawn up these present letters in our palace, in our castle of Massiat, in the middle of September, in the fifteen hundred and fifteenth year after Alexander."

This Von Hammer treats as a forgery. The date condemns it. The Hejira, or the accession of Hassan II., was the true Ismaeliyeh era. Again, in a second letter, mentioned by William of Newbury, the Sheikh calls himself *simplicitas nostra*, an unlikely phrase. Be it so. Von Hammer's error, and it is a notable one, consists in entirely ignoring the fact that both letters, which are in Latin only, are translations: indeed, he leaves it doubtful whether he does not actually believe that Latin was the diplomatic language between the Assassins and the Crusaders. How far the charge is made good on other grounds is another matter. All that the present writer does is to condemn as a maresnest the Austrian doctrine of the letter being a forgery; and, he does so, because he has a vague notion that if Leopold and Von Hammer had not been Austrians it would not have been put forward.

At this time the number of Assassins, high and low, is placed at about sixty thousand. Their forts were ten: the three that have already been named, and Akkar, Hosn-al-ekiad, Safita, Alika, Hosn-al-ekiad, Sihinn, and Sarmin. Rashideddin Sinan was their Sheikh, and under him the connection with the Persian metropolis of Alamut appears to cease. Naturally. Rashideddin held himself higher than either Sheikh or Imam. He gave out that it was an incarnation of the deity. Except in a coarse dress of hair he never showed himself. No one saw him eat, drink, sleep, or spit. He preached from a rock, and the sun rose and set upon his discourses. However, once, when he mixed with his followers on the level ground, he was observed to limp. The accident that had crippled him nearly cost him his life. It was only by his eloquence that he escaped being murdered as an impostor. He escaped to become, practically, the founder of the new Syrian discipline. The little that the existing Ismaeliyeh know about their early history attaches itself to the name of Rashideddin Sinan, and the few books they have are supposed to be of Rashideddin's writing. Like those of the Druzes they are a mixture of the Koran and the Bible.

Of Hassan III.—Dzhelaleddin Hassan—the character is wholly exceptional. He undid, as far as he could, the work of his latitudinarian father and grandfather; restored Mahometanism; and was recognized as a Mahometan prince by his contemporary sovereigns. Von Hammer, after expressly stating that not so much as one murder can be laid to his charge, takes exceptions to his motives and his sincerity.

> " Brand him who will with base report,
> He shall be free of mine."

A degenerate Assassin, he seems to have been a respectable ruler. His son, however, was much like his other ancestors.

With Rokneddin Kharshah, the Persian sheikship ended; destroyed by the Mongols.

The same Mongols broke, rather than destroyed, the power of the Assassins of Syria; the final overthrow of whom was reserved for the Ægyptian sultan, Bibars—no Fatemite, but one of the ablest and most powerful of the new dynasty of Mamlúks. Under his reign the Crusaders still took tribute from the Ismaeliyeh; and it was this sign of subjection which the tributaries were willing to transfer. Bibars, in a treaty, made A.D. 1265, with the Knights of St. John, had made the abolition of the Ismaeliyeh payments one of its conditions. The following year he received an embassy, with a sum of money, and with the petition "that what had hitherto been paid to the Franks, should, in future, be paid to the Sultan, and serve for the pay of the defenders of the true faith." Three years afterwards, when Bibars was marching against the Franks, the commanders of the different towns did him homage. Nedzhmeddin, however, the head of the Order, only requested a diminution of the tribute. This cost him his place; Sarameddin, the commandant of Alika, being put over his head. In the name of the sultan of Ægypt Sarameddin governed all the castles of the Assassins.

A reconciliation, partaking of the nature of a compromise, with Nedzhmeddin followed. The late sheikh, now more than seventy years old, threw himself, with his son, on the clemency of Bibars; who, taking from him an annual tribute of twenty thousand drachmas, and from Sarameddin one of two thousand gold pieces, allowed the two to divide the authority between them as they best could. But, when Sarameddin fell into disgrace, *all* the power returned to Nedzhmeddin, whose son Shemseddin was retained at Cairo as a hostage. Eventually the father joined him. Having learned that suspicions were rising against him, he presented himself at the Sultan's court in person, offering to give up all the castles in Syria and to pass the remnant of his life in Ægypt. Shemseddin, when this was agreed to, left Ægypt for Syria in order to induce the Assassins to complete the surrender. This was no easy matter; Menifa, Kadmus, Massiat, Sihun, and more especially Kehef, resisted; the last-named citadel with extraordinary obstinacy. That commissions of murder were issued is what we expect. Still they scarcely seem to have been the main weapon. There was much brave fighting, much personal adventure, much heroic endurance. Of the Hamsa Nameh, or narrative of the actions of Hamsa, we only know that it was composed. Of the Ismaeliyeh heroes, however, in this their last great struggle, Hamsa was the greatest.

The Syrian Ismaeliyeh of the present time, occupants of eighteen villages in the parts about Massiat, are under the rule of a sheikh, or emir, nominated by the Governor of Hamah. They fall into two divisions, the Suveidani and the Khisrevi; the former taking their name from one of the former sheikhs, and the latter from Khisr Ilias.

In 1809 there was a war between the Ismaeliyeh and the Nasariyeh, when the latter sacked Massiat; from which, however, they were themselves expelled by the Governor of Hamah.

The *Nasariyeh.*—Of this denomination the Pashaliks of Aleppo and Tripoli give us the chief localities. Antioch on the north, and the Nahr-el-Kelb on the south, are their boundaries, their habitats being the villages of the hill-country. In these, to which they are strongly attached, they till the soil with a fair amount of industry and skill; and have the credit of being somewhat less warlike than the other mountain tribes. The names of four divisions of them are known: Kamariyeh, Shamseyeh, Kleleseyeh, and Shimaleyeh. Are these denominations religious, tribal, or both?

The Nasariyeh hate Mahometans; but are willing, when they visit the towns, to comport themselves as true believers. They keep as holidays Christmas Day, Epiphany, New Year's Day, the Fourth of April, and the Seventeenth of April. They have secret signs, mysterious words, initiative ceremonies.

Of the *Mutuali* I know little; nor can I say whether they are anything, either worse or better, than simple Shiites of Persian or Kurd origin. They are active soldiers, and their valour is respected, though as a body they are neither numerous nor widely diffused. The parts about Baalbek, the ancient Heliopolis, are their occupancy.

CHAPTER V.

Albania.—Despotat of Epirus.—Scanderbeg.—Ali Pasha.—Albanians in Greece.

FEW countries have clearer and more definite natural boundaries than Albania. In few countries, too, is the intermixture of extraneous elements less. The patches of foreign settlers with the outward and visible characteristics of language, name, and nationality, are few; and the amount of foreign blood, disguised by Albanian characteristics, is small. Still, there are certain settlements of Valachians, Slavonians, and Greeks, which, though they are few as compared with similar heterogeneities elsewhere, are still too notable to be ignored. Upon the whole, however, the Albanian stock, within the limits of Albania, is, comparatively speaking, pure.

But the Albanians are, by no means, limited to Albania. In Italy, and Sicily, they are numerous. There are some in Russia, some in Austria, an inordinate number in Greece. Indeed, much of Greece is more Albanian than Greek.

That the population is as uniform in its character as the land on which it lives is, by no means, the case. On the contrary, it is signalized by differences of dialect which in their extreme forms almost amount to differences of language; by differences of religion; by differences of nationality. On the other hand, the general character of the men and women is the same throughout. We may call them Albanians. We may call them Arnauts. We may call them Skipetar. The first name is the ordinary European one; the second is the one applied by the Turks; the third the one applied by the Albanians themselves.

Though shepherds, robbers, and soldiers, the Albanians must not be looked upon as exclusively landsmen. Those of the islands exhibit great naval aptitude. As sailors they are both bold and skilful.

They marry young; and become betrothed still younger. When this is the case the principals have but a small voice in the marriage preliminaries. The parents effect these long before the sons and daughters are adolescent.

The best traits in the Skipetar character are their love of liberty, their love of their country, their courage, and their confidence in each other. Hence their chief representatives in history have been warriors; first and foremost of whom stands George Castriotes, Little Alexander, or Scanderbeg. That there was Skipetar blood in more than one of the heroes of antiquity is nearly certain. There was Skipetar blood in the veins of more than one of the kings of the Hellenic world. Pyrrhus, for instance, and the Temenids of Macedonia were, probably, more or less Skipetar.

In the details of their division the primary sections are those of the Gheghs and the Tosks: the Gheghs on the north, the Tosks on the south. The chief character is the language; the valley of Skumbi or Stirnatza, between Berat and Elbassan being, there or thereabouts, the boundary between the two forms of it. That the two dialects are mutually unintelligible has been over-boldly and over-hastily asserted. It is doubtful whether, even, the most northern sub-dialect of the one and the most southern of the other, verify this statement. That there is anything like an approximation to mutual unintelligibility on the frontier is out of the question. Still, the division is natural. It is with the Slavonians that the Gheghs, with the Greeks that the Tosks, come the most in contact. Again, when a Skipetar is a Christian his Christianity is that of his frontier, so that the Christianity of the Tosks is that of the Greek, the Christianity of the Gheghs that of the Latin Church. Of the Latin Christians the Mirdits are the chief tribe. Among the Lyapid and Tshamid divisions of the Tosks, the Greek Church has its chief adherents. The mass, however, professes Mahometanism; though not often with bigotry and not always with sincerity.

The singularly mild form of their Mahometanism is referable

to several causes. In the first place, their Christianity was always of an imperfect character, being underlaid from the beginning to the end by the original paganism which, at the present time, crops out on every occasion where a superstition can find a chance of showing itself. It was more Greek than Latin, though not without Latin elements. Neither was the Greek part of it typically Greek. No vernacular translation of the Scriptures helped to fix the language, as vernacular translations fixed the Slavonic of Bulgaria, Servia, and Dalmatia. No notable saints, no polemic bishops, figure in their annals. Monasteries were never numerous in their rude and suspicious mountains. All this favoured the natural vitality of the old mythology.

Secondly. Many of the conversions were made from political motives : to save an estate, to keep an office, to take a place in a privileged class. In many families the Mahometanism is scarcely three generations old.

Thirdly. Amongst the Christians themselves the two rival denominations were prevented from quarrelling with one another by their geographical position. The Romanist Mirdits lay on the north, the orthodox Tshamids and Lyapids on the south. Between them lay the great block of the Mahometanism of the middle district as a breakwater to their natural intolerance.

Fourthly. There was never much religious persecution : which was wanting not because the Ottomans were tolerant, but because (from a variety of reasons differing with the difference of circumstances) the Christians of Albania managed to keep the right of bearing arms, and knew well how to wield them. For this they had to thank their own bold tempers and the impracticable nature of their occupancies.

In all this we get the explanation of a fact upon which the historian of the Greek Revolution has founded a safe generalization and remarked that whilst, with the Greeks, the ecclesiastic spirit was stronger than the national, the national, with the Albanians, was stronger than the ecclesiastic. The fact itself, whatever may be its explanation, is beyond doubt ; a fact which makes itself apparent in every page of the later history of Greece—wherein we find Albanians and Greeks fighting side by side, for the political freedom of the soil of Greece—the adopted country of an inordinate number of Albanian colonists—the country in which, notwithstanding the difference of blood and language, the Albanians comported themselves as Greeks.

Nor have these characteristics been exhibited without reason. If ever the time come when the Greek Kingdom shall strengthen itself at the expense of the Turkish, whatever may be the doubts as to the amalgamation of the Bulgarians and Rumanyos in a Great Byzantine Empire, the practicability of a fusion between the Greeks and Albanians, even if everything else be denied, must be recognized. Greece, at the present time, is, to a great extent, Albanian; and, if it had not been for its Albanian element, would, in all probability, never have been independent Greece. With Albania released from Turkey, a similar series of migrations in the opposite direction is likely: in which case Albania would be partially Hellenized — the Albanians holding the hills, the Greeks the towns. On the other hand, however, the Albanians are, by no means, either malcontents or bad subjects of the Porte.

It were well for many Christian countries if they were so—well for Christendom in general; for it is through the unscrupulous instrumentality of the Albanian garrisons that the worst acts in the Ottoman history have been perpetrated. Faithful to his pay the Albanian is as careless of human suffering as he is bold, as rapacious as he is trusty. Faithful he is and brave he is, but brave and faithful after the fashion of a brave and faithful mercenary.

From the compactness of its area the Albanian nationality is isolated; by which I mean that the Albanian has no near kinsmen elsewhere by whom his political sympathies are extended beyond the frontiers of his own country. Such relations as exist between Servia and Bulgaria, between Alsatia and Germany, between Lower Canada and France, whatever may be their value, have no existence in the Skipetar world. Except in the case of its colonies it is self-contained. Albania, if united with any second nation, must be united with one which differs in many important ethnological characteristics from itself.

From the tenor of its previous history, itself determined by the physical conditions of the country, the Albanian nationality is local, sectional, and provincial, rather than general: in other words, it consists of a series of small nationalities rather than of one great one. The country has never played a prominent and acknowledged part in the world's history. An Albanian empire, *eo nomine*, has never existed. An Albanian kingdom has only been approximated. There is no such thing as a royal Albanian dynasty. The nearest approaches to anything of this kind have been made by certain Bulgarian and Wallachian principalities founded in Albania. But even these, except in Byzantine history, have never been of importance. What there is instead of this, is a series of tribual captains, of guerilla chieftains, of (at the best) popular heroes whose fame has been co-extensive with the small domain of Albanian language; the greatest of whom, the only one whose exploits have arrested the attention of the general historian, was Scanderbeg.

In ethnology, so wanting has it been in method and principle, the exertion of a *minimum* of common-sense or the recognition of the most patent presumption takes the guise of a discovery. Hence, the doctrine broached by Thunman, that the modern Albanians are neither more nor less than the descendants of the ancient Illyrians, has been looked upon by some as a valuable suggestion, by others as a bold hypothesis. Yet it is simply the *primâ facie* view. What should they be else? It is not, however, on the mere presumptions that the doctrine rests. Local names and glosses confirm it; and there are few critics, at the present time, who doubt it. The exact details of the boundaries are another matter. So is the original extent of the area. How far Albania ran northwards before it touched the Slavonic frontier, how far it ran east and south before it touched the Hellenic, are questions of more or less. Questions, too, of more or less are those touching the blood of Pyrrhus, Philip, and Alexander, Epirots and Macedonians who were certainly in blood more or less what a Greek would call Barbarian. That the Gheghs represent the Illyrians in the limited sense of the term rather than the Epirots, and the Tosks the Epirots rather than the Illyrians, is likely.

But, except in the ethnology of the Celts and Germans, there is nothing in the classical writings more indefinite than the boundaries of Illyria, on every side but that of the sea. The division between Epirus and Greece could never have been very decided; though between the more barbaric and more Hellenizing tribes there may have been a political frontier. Then there was the boundary on the east between Illyria and Macedon, and then, on the north-east, between Illyria and Thrace; and here there were ethnological distinction as well. The difference between the Illyrians, the Thracians, and (we may add) the Celts, was a prominent element in ancient ethnology. As a *race*, the Illyrians were put on the high level of the ubiquitous Celts, and Noricum was called by Strabo *Illyrian*. Again, the northern boundary of the race was carried far in the direction of the Danube; so that much of Pannonia passes for having been Illyrian.

Finally, it was mainly on the sea-coast and on the Hellenizing part of Epirus that there was any accurate geography. The inland districts were but little known.

In respect to Albanian history, if we begin at the very beginning, we must make it so early as (speaking catachrestically) to make it *pre*-historic. This means that we must go back to the time of the Odyssey. After this comes the Athenian period, or the days of the Peloponnesian war. Here we get adequate notices of the southern districts under the name "*Epirus*," and of the northern under that of "*Illyria*." Then comes the time when the great Macedonian Empire is cut up into Roman provinces; and then the division of the Roman Empire itself. Until the time of the Ottoman conquest it was, theoretically, a question as to which of the two rival empires Albania belonged; if, indeed, it belonged to either. After the death of George Castriotes, or Scanderbeg, it certainly was not Roman at all. The special campaign, however, by which it was conquered has yet to be discovered; neither do we know anything of the details of its reduction. All we know is that it followed the fate of the countries of its three frontiers—Bosnia on the north, Macedonia on the east, and Greece on the south. Neither have we any history of it as a compact and independent state. There was a Bulgarian kingdom pure and simple; a Bulgaro-Wallachian kingdom, and a Servian kingdom; in all of which some portion of Albania, either really or nominally, made a part. But of a consolidated state, whether regal or republican, coextensive with the very natural boundary of the country as a nation we know nothing. So it was when Mahomet II. fought against Scanderbeg, and so it was when Pyrrhus invaded

Italy. In the time of Pyrrhus there was a Greek kingdom on the Greco-Macedonian frontier, and in the time of Scanderbeg there was a principality on the north; but there is not a consolidated Albania.

No parallels run exactly on all fours; but, in the way of approximate illustrations, we may find something like Albania in the Highlands of Scotland, in Switzerland, and, in what comes most appropriate to the present subject, the Ottoman and Persian part of the Kurd country—Kurdistan. That the national, or ethnological, characteristics of the Albanians in general is of a very definite and decided character has already been indicated.

When we lose sight of Albania as a part of the Roman Empire, we must look to the early histories of Hungary and of Venice; and from these we get but little information. Albania seems to have been independent of both; so far, at least, as the terra firma of the continent is concerned. The islands seem to have been Venetian before the thirteenth century; and at an equally early date certain ports seem to have been occupied by the Normans.

With the Fourth Crusade we get something like a consecutive history, though not a continuous one.

At the beginning of the thirteenth century the history of Albania, which means Epirus and part of Illyria, takes a separate form; though its connections with Servia, Bulgaria, Greece, and Venice, must be borne in mind.

When Constantinople, A.D. 1204, was taken by the Franks, Michael I. of Epirus, a cousin of the two Emperors, Isaac II. and Alexius III., was illegitimate. Theodore, his brother, was legitimate. Manuel and Constantine, legitimate or illegitimate, were the brothers or half-brothers of Theodore. The Emperor in Nicæa is also named Theodore.

Michael fled to Epirus; married an Epirot lady; contracted power; founded a principality; took, under the Nicæan Emperor, the title of Despot; ruled in Epirus till assassinated.

Theodore, his brother, who had sworn allegiance to his Imperial namesake at Nicæa, succeeded; conquered the Constantinopolitan Emperor; threw off his allegiance; reduced

Thessalonica and called himself Emperor; threatened Constantinople; was defeated by Asan, the King of Bulgaria, and blinded. His brother, Manuel, succeeded. Meanwhile, Asan had married Theodore's daughter, whose father returned to Bulgaria; but, as a blind man, was constrained to place the government in the hands of his son John, with the title of Despot.

Constantine, during these events, holds authority in Thessaly. Manuel escapes to Nicæa. He attacks John and Theodore; but the latter, in the capacity of ambassador and plenipotentiary from his son, persuades them to make a family compact against both the Greeks and the Franks. This leaves John Emperor of Thessalonica, though unable to hold the empire. Reduced by the Emperor of Nicæa, he is satisfied with the recognition of his Despotats in Epirus and Thessalonica, though fated to lose both. Thessalonica goes back to the empire; Epirus to Michael II., a natural son of Michael I. Epirus, however, has extended its frontiers; whilst the old blind Theodore retains the district of Vodhena in Thessalia. But this lasts only for a time. John III. confirms Michael in the title of Despot of Epirus, and Michael acknowledges John III. as Emperor. But Theodore intrigues. Michael and John quarrel. The former gives up Theodore and relinquishes a part of his Despotat. The battle of Pelagonia weakens him still more. He partially recovers his strength; and is succeeded by his son Nicephorus, who reduces parts of Etolia and Acarnania. Attacked by the Greeks and the Genoese, he is assisted by the Count of Cephalonia, with whom he contracts alliances; dies, and is succeeded by his son Thomas. The Count of Cephalonia murders his nephew Thomas, who is murdered by his brother John, who is murdered by his wife Anne; and thus the Cephalonian Counts of the family of Tocco become the Despots of Epirus. By 1350, however, the northern part of Albania is conquered by the King of Servia, Stephen Dushan.

Early in the thirteenth century we find Albanians in Greece. The Emperor Manuel Palæologus in the Morea was constrained to defend the Morea against the Turkish corsairs, who were now formidable. He taxed his subjects in order to raise a fleet, and a rebellion was the result; a rebellion which he succeeded, with the assistance of a body of *Albanian* mercenaries, in putting down.

I now follow Finlay, whose general carefulness makes him a trustworthy guide even when he ventures on the dangerous risk of a negative assertion, in drawing attention to this Albanian company as the *first* upon record which mixed itself up with the affairs of Greece. The intruders who had preceded them were Slavonians; but from this time forwards the Slavonian name loses importance, whilst the Albanian gains it. We shall, henceforth, hear but little of the Slavonians of Taygetus and Skortos; but much concerning the Albanians.

About the same date with the earliest notice of an Albanian element in the Morea is that of the earliest notice of the *Ottoman Turks*. Cantacuzene, we may remember, was a usurper; so that the title of his son to the Despotat was a bad one. John V. deputed Asan to supersede him. The son, however, of the usurper kept his place during his lifetime. Theodore Palæologus, the son of the Emperor, succeeded him, and finding that his despotism was threatened by the resistance of his subjects, called in, in support of his authority, a body of auxiliaries under Evrenos, one of the ablest of Amurath's generals. There had been piracy on the coast of the Morea long before this; but of Ottoman soldiers on the soil of the peninsula this (I again quote Finlay) is the *first* notice.

And now, though the Imperial power is but small, that of the Franks is less. Indeed, it is waning. So is the language and nationality of the Slavonians; whilst colonization from Albania increases. Hardier and ruder than the children of the soil, the Skipetar, year after year, increase in number. Some come as squatters, some as farmers; so that rents were increased to the colonists. Their spirit, then at its highest, for the fame of their countryman, Scanderbeg, had reached them, and an actual conquest of the Morea seemed scarcely an illegitimate aspiration. And many malcontent Greeks encouraged and joined them, one of whom was a noble, who thought that by adapting himself to their nationality, he might make them instrumental to his ambition. Instead of his Greek name Manuel he called himself by the Albanian name

Ghin, whilst his wife, who was a Maria, affected that of Cuchia. The insurgents were, on the whole, successful. On each side, however, Ottoman intervention was invoked. It was exerted so as to protect the Greeks without crushing the Albanians. Indeed, they kept the cattle they had stolen and retained their lands at a fixed rent.

Then comes the time of the famous George Castriotes, or Scanderbeg. His father was the lord of a small district in Epirus, and George himself one of four brothers. All the four were sent to Adrianople as hostages; and, of these, three died, perhaps, by poison. All had been circumcised; all trained as soldiers in the Ottoman army; and in this George had so conspicuously distinguished himself, that the Turks gave him the name of Iskender Beg, Scanderbeg, or the Lord Alexander. He escaped, however, to his native land; and, having been admitted within the walls of Croya, proclaimed himself the avenger of his family and country. This position he maintained for about a quarter of a century. Under extreme pressure, he applied to the Pope, Pius II., for a refuge in Italy, where he died at Lissus, in the Venetian territory. The town of Croya, with which his name is most especially associated, was not part of his paternal domain, but a Turkish fortress which he recovered. That he made over his rights in Epirus to Venice is probable. It is doubtful, however, what they were.

Be this as it may, it was not long after his death that Croya was retaken. It is now a mere village. The siege of Scutari soon followed that of Croya, and Scutari was taken also. In both cases a large body of the inhabitants sought and found shelter in Venetia.

It is not easy to give in a single chapter anything like a consecutive history of Albania for the next three centuries—there or thereabouts; nor even for the whole of the reign of Mahomet II. is the history continuous. It is in the earlier part of it, and between the conquest of Trebizond and the repulse at Belgrade, that we first find him on or within the frontier of Albania and in contact with Scanderbeg. The result of this campaign seems to have been the complete conquest of Bosnia and the Duchy of St. Saba (Herzegovina), and something like an agreement with Scanderbeg, whom he acknowledges as Lord of Albania and Epirus; after which there seems to have been peace in the country till towards the end of the reign. The events that then take place succeed the conquests of Mahomet in Greece, the Negropont, and other of the less important islands. This implies that the war is more especially against Venice; not without an alliance between the Turk and the Duke of Milan. That Venice, at this time, was threatened by an Ottoman fleet, and that, subsequently, the Sultan took possession of the country and town of Otranto, has already been stated. He retired from Italy as we know; but it seems to be in connection with this campaign, in the last year of the reign of Mahomet II., that Albania became a part of the Ottoman Empire.

It was not, however, conquered as a whole; nor is it easy to see how the central districts lost their independence at all. We can readily understand how Epirus might be treated as little more than a part of Greece; and that, after the death of Scanderbeg, Croya and Scutari were reduced as possessions of Venice we know to a certainty. Indentations, too, on the northern and eastern frontiers might be conceded as parts of Macedonia, or of the Bulgaro-Wallachian kingdom, or of the indefinite and ephemeral character of Stephan Dushan might be ceded in such a manner as to imply the transfer of the whole country; but of either a campaign in detail or a single great battle that decided the fate of Albania in mass I find no evidence.

During the war with Austria, in the year before the battle of Salankemen, 1689, one of the captains of Northern Albania, named Karpos, assumes, under the suzerainty of the Emperor, the title of Kral, and makes Egri-palanka the seat of his kraldom. He joins the Austrians in a battle which was fought in the neighbourhood of Usküp, in Northern Macedonia, where the whole army is defeated, and Karpos is publicly executed. The victorious army was led by the third of the Kiuprili Viziers, and was of an unusually heterogeneous constitution; Turks, of course, but, more especially, Hungarians, under Teleki, the Hungarian rebel, and, from a greater distance, Tatars of the Crimea, under their Khan, Ghirai.

I know of no name of any leader of Albanians on Albanian soil and with an Albanian army between the time of Karpos and Ali Pasha, though there is never a time when the Albanian element in the Turkish armies elsewhere is not conspicuous. But they appear as Albanian captains in some foreign fortress, doing their duty honestly, effectively, and remorselessly— always without fear, and thoroughly faithful as long as they are regularly paid. *Point d'argent point de Suisse*; and it is with the Swiss guards in this respect, as admirable soldiers on foreign service, that the Albanians are most readily compared. It was Khalil Patrona, an Albanian, who, in 1730, superseded Achmet III. by Mahmoud I.; and it was Bairactar who, at the head of his Albanian regiments, preserved and enthroned Mahmoud IV. This was in 1804; so that Bairactar was a contemporary of Ali Pasha of Janina.

We can scarcely call this notorious Ali Pasha one of the " *worthies* " of Albania; of which only two seem to be generally recognised—Pyrrhus and Scanderbeg. Of the great family of the Kiuprilis, the most that can be said is that they were of Albanian origin. Ali Pasha, however, call him what we will, and whatever else he may have been, was wholly Albanian. He was of the Ghegh or southern, rather than of the Tosk or northern, division; and the town of Tepeleen was his birthplace. His father died whilst Ali was under age, and that as a member of a reduced family; for the name was one of some note, but which had lost much of its hereditary prerogative. The mother, of an ambitious and vindictive temper, did all she could to inspire her son with the ambition of getting back the position of his ancestry, and of avenging himself on its enemies. He became an associate and then the captain in a band of Klepths. From a Klepth he bacame a soldier, and, by the year 1788, had done such good service for the Sultan that he obtained the Pashalik of Tricala in Thessaly. Thence he rose to that of Jannina, in his native country, and in the southern part of it. This was the time when to be a Pasha was to be a rebel; and from this time till his assassination, Ali Pasha was one of the most conspicuous. But he was a scourge to his subjects.

The tyranny of Ali Pasha led to their revolt, and the movements in Albania, of which the Suliot revolt was one, were among the chief preliminaries to the emancipation of Greece.

With the unsettled times of the Venetian war, the history of Suli begins. As Christians of the Greek Church the Suliots loved the Venetians no better than the Turks; and the Turks, aware of this, relaxed their restrictions and allowed them to bear arms. The habits thus engendered took root, and Suli became a military community in a natural fortress; with a gorge in front and impracticable mountains on each side. But, like a fortress, it was stinted in its supply of food and land, and a chronic system of either robbery or black-mail, was the result. In 1780 the number of Suliot families which bore arms was about a hundred. When Ali began his attacks, nineteen pharas gave four hundred and fifty, and about fifteen hundred fighting-men, distributed over four villages, with the historical names of Djavella, and Botzaris among their chief. Speaking roughly, we may give each family a traitor and each a patriot. If one Botzaris or Djavella gave his services to Ali, some other of the name died in a death-struggle against him. Still, the names of Botzaris and Djavella are best known from their bad deeds.

The attacks of Ali against Suli lasted about fifteen years. At one time he was suspected of being only half in A.D. 1788-1803. earnest against them and of prolonging the war for purposes of his own. His stimulated energy, however, left no room for doubt as to his ultimate intentions. Nor was repression, if repression only had been intended, unneeded. The tillers of the soil suffered from either inroads or exactions, in excuse of which the poverty and circumscription of the soil of the Suli were pleaded before indulgent judges; for both Russia and France sympathized, or intrigued, with these brave and efficient marauders. Much of what is now going on in Montenegro went on during the last years of the last century in the four villages; Kako Suli (well-named), Avariko, Samoneva, and Kiapha, a miniature Lacedæmon.

With George Botzaris Suli lost seventy families, or about one hundred soldiers. Djavella took off others. Kako Suli was betrayed by Pyho Gousi. Avariko followed. To Kiapha alone attaches the interest which the name of Suliot inspires. The man whom no bribes seduced, no dangers terrified, and no promises deceived, was an Albanian, of mysterious origin, who had dropped upon Suli as it were from the skies. He is said to have been a native of Andros. His name was Samuel; but he called himself The Last Judgment, a term which suggests the secret of his authority. The ecclesistical dynasts had joined with Ali against the Suliots. The Bishop of Arta had forbidden the Christians of his diocese to assist them. The Bishop of Paramythia had allowed Ali to dictate a letter to the same effect. The spiritual censure of the Metropolitan of Joannina had been directed against them. But the Church, in the eyes of Samuel, was selling itself to Mahomet; and, full of his mission, he made light of both its censures and its exhortations. It was, probably, no difficult matter to infuse his own spirit of insubordination into the hearts of the Suliots. They made him their military chief.

He had charge of the hill of Kughni, and the village of Kiapha. All around was conquered or coerced. The men guarded the paths; while the women carried them water and provisions under the fire of the besiegers, who treated them as combatants. The number of the families was three hundred; but their resistance was sufficiently

Dec. 12, 1803. prolonged to induce Ali to offer terms; and a capitulation was signed, by which Kughni and Kiapha were delivered up to Veli Pasha and Photo Djavella.

The Suliots who had concluded separate treaties with Ali had betaken themselves to Zalongo. The terms of the capitulation of Kughni and Kiapha were never meant to be kept; for, after permission had been given to Zervas and Drako to retire with their pharas to Parga, Ali placed an ambuscade on their road. They escaped it; but the treachery was the same. In like manner, Ali surprised Zalongo. Some of its defenders were made slaves of; some were killed fighting; some threw themselves from the rock rather than fall into the hand of Ali; and of these the greater part were women. Some dashed their infants down first. Such is the general picture, which is, perhaps, vague and indistinct. Let us remember that the whole garrison was but a fraction of a fraction of the reduced Suliot population, and then see whether we can find a numerical return. Sixty men, twenty-two women, and four children—these are the imperfect statistics for the occupants of Zalongo who died dashed to pieces. Samuel, in Kughni, when he saw that all was lost, retired to the powder-magazine and lit a match. We know what comes when resolute men do this.

Though the Suliots are the most notable warriors of their class (the class of the semi-independent, privileged, and Christian Albanians), the Chimariots and Parginots are in the same category. By the Treaty of Campo Formio, the Venetian dependencies off and in Albania became French, and Ali Pasha was the Friend of the French, to whom he represented the Chimariots as rebels to his lord the Sultan, and reduced them by a bloody massacre for himself.

In 1798, however, he ejects the French themselves from all the fortresses on the continent which they held under their title from Venice, Parga alone remaining independent.

In 1800, everything which had ever been Venetian is made over to Turkey. This gave Parga to the Sultan as its nominal, but to Ali as its real, master. Even the Sultan assented to its remaining as it was; so that for nineteen years its cession was in abeyance. In 1819, however, England was called upon to make good the convention of 1800, and Parga was unwillingly ceded. Rather than submit to Ali, the Parginots emigrated in a body. England gave them up unwillingly, but under the legitimate compulsion of a treaty, and received them in the Ionian Islands.

*　　*　　*　　*　　*　　*

In the way of blood, race, or descent, the Albanians are comparatively pure. Still, there is considerable intermixture in the north and in the south, the middle districts being the purest. At some uncertain period, but in connection with the extension of the Bulgarian and Vallachian kingdom, a considerable Vlach element was introduced into Albania, which, apparently from Albania, extended itself into Thessaly. But within the limits of Albania itself there were, at least, four settlements; and they exist at the present time.

1. In the parts about Moscopolis and Kastoria, to the east of Berat. The exact boundaries of this region are uncertain. Maltebrun, however, states that to the north of Kastoria five languages are spoken, viz., the Greek, the Albanian, the Servian,

the Turk, and the Vallachian. Unless by " *Servian* " he means
" *Bulgarian*," he might have added a *fourth*.

2. On the head-waters of the River Arta.

3. On the head-waters of the Aspropotamos. Both these
districts are Albanian. The population, however, extends across
the mountains into Greece.

4. The parts about Karpenis. All these Vlachs are *Kutzo*
Vallachians.

Again, there was rarely a time when some part of Albania
was not under the dominion of either Bulgaria or Servia; and
when this was the case, the city of Ochrida was a favoured
town, with something like a metropolitan prerogative. It was
this in the time of the Bulgaro-Wallachian dynasty, and this in
the time of the great Servian Kral Dushan Khan.

There are probably other Servian localities. I find it stated
by Finlay, on the high authority of Colonel Leake, that the
Bulgarian language was spoken within the present generation
(as it, perhaps, is spoken at the present moment) in some
villages to the south of Akrida.

Meanwhile, the Greek language deeply indents the southern
frontier, whilst along the sea-coast there is much Venetian blood.

With all this, *central* Albania is one of the most pure-blooded
countries in Europe; though, out of Albania itself, there is
much Albanian blood elsewhere, especially in Greece and Italy.

In Greece.

*Attica, Megara and Salamis . . .	30,000
Bœotia (*nearly all*)	25,000
Phocis	(?) 5,000
Valley of the Spercheios . . .	10,000
†South Andros	25,000
North Eubœa	6,000
Argolis and Poros	25,000
Korinth and Akhaia	15,000
South Arkadia	10,000
Hydra (*all*)	12,000
Spezzia (*all*)	10,000
	173,000

* All, except the towns of Athens, Megara, and the Piræus.

† All, except the town of Carysto.

In *Italy* the true colonists are—

1. *Skipitar*, or *Albanians*, of which there is a vast population in Calabria and Sicily. In numbers—

Calabria Ulteriore	4,407
„ Citeriore	30,812
Basilicata	10,090
Capitanata	13,463
Terra d'Otranto	6,844
Abruzzo Ulteriore	220
Sicily	19,743
	85,579

In *Russia* there is an Albanian colony in the Government of Ekaterinoslav.

* * * * *

There is no portion of the Ottoman Empire that can better be left to itself than Albania. There are a few villages on the frontier in which the majority of the occupants may be Montenegriners, and, if these added to that principality, the only difficulty should be that of determining the boundaries. Albania is the natural limit of Slavonia on the Adriatic. If Epirus wishes to be Greek, well and good; but if it is merely Greece that wants Epirus, the question takes a very different form. Nor should Italy's desire for a footing on the mainland (the islands are already Greek) be encouraged. As Albania stands at the present time, it is a compact and well-defined district. Nor are the Albanians the worse instruments in Turkish warfare. In guerilla warfare they show most to disadvantage when they mix themselves up with the non-official campaigns of the Greeks. In the Turkish service they are chiefly employed in distant garrisons, much as the Swiss were when they took service under the Pope. So employed, they obey orders of any kind without fear and without compulsion; but they are not as the Janissaries, and not as the Circassians and Bazi-Basúks, unmanageable and ungovernable. They are not tender-hearted, and, like the Swiss, expect to be paid for their services. With the Slavonians, except those of the Montenegro frontier, they live on comparatively amicable terms; and, when the Mahometan holidays and the Christian fall on different days, the herdsmen of the frontier take upon themselves the charge of the pastures of their neighbours. On the boundaries of Montenegro, however, the feeling is somewhat different, and the two countries are much in the condition of the men of the Scottish border in the time of our ancestors. But in these districts there are the barbarous traditions of the *vendetta,* and the blood of kinsmen on either side must be retaliated.

CHAPTER V.

Bulgaria and the Bulgarians.—Their Ethnological Elements.—Their early History.—Latin and Paulician Elements in the Bulgarian Creed.—Rumelia. —Bosnia.—Croatia.—Herzegovina.

THE Bulgarians at the present time are, to all appearance, Slavonians. Their language is a well-marked dialect of the Slavonic, yet not without one very important characteristic and some minor ones. Their creed is that of the Greek Church. This they have held from the time of their first conversion; and many high authorities hold that the language of the old Slavonic translation of the Scriptures is Bulgarian.

If it were not for certain complicating points of detail it would be unnecessary to refine on this view. Two facts, how-ever, have engendered the doctrine that the blood is not entirely Slavonic; in other words, that the Bulgarians are either Turks or Fins who have adopted the Slavonic language. The reasons for this are sufficiently valid to justify the view to a certain extent; though there are serious obstacles to accepting it without reserve.

Such is the question of blood or race. It is not one upon which opinion is undivided; neither is there any absolute uni-formity in respect to the ecclesiastical position of the Bulgarians. The earliest Christianity of them was certainly that of the Greek Church; and, at the present time, it is the Christianity of the Eastern Empire which is notoriously predominant. But what if it be that only *some* Bulgarians took their faith from Con-stantinople? What if others took it from Rome? What, too, if the Roman converts may have been the earlier? There are manifestly the elements of a controversy upon this point, and that an important one.

In connection with these two questions, one ethnological and one political, I shall begin with the break-up of the Roman Empire, without, at present, considering the complex and obscure details of the early history of the Roman province of Lower Mœsia.

How far the Romans introduced the Latin language is uncertain. The Mœsias were certainly not provinces which were thoroughly Romanized. I imagine that the original language was never wholly displaced by the Latin; perhaps only to a very slight degree. Still, some Roman elements were introduced. Upon these their most notable graft was one effected in the third century by the Goths and Vandals.

The Emperor Severus is succeeded by his son Caracalla, and in the reign of Caracalla the name *Goth* first appears ; the population to which it applies being then occupants of the country of the ancient *Getæ ;* and from this time forwards until the time of a Gothic king in Rome there is a continuous system of Gothic wars, sometimes on one, sometimes on the other, side of the Danube—in Mœsia most especially. There is a Gothic war under Maximus and Balbinus; a Gothic war under the Gordians; a Gothic war, disastrous to the Romans, under Decius, A.D. 251. in which that vigorous and brave Emperor met his death on the field of battle. His successor, Gallus, bought a peace.

At the beginning of their migration, the Goths were in alliance with the Vandals, and, as they moved down the Danube, they seemed to have succeeded in forming an offensive alliance with almost all the nations of their ever-changing frontier. They reach the mouth of the river, and effect naval victories as well as military ones. They plunder Trebizond in the east, Byzantium in the south. Cyzicus, Ephesus, Athens, Crete, the cities of the Illyrian sea-board are all plundered by them. A great victory by Claudius Gothicus checked them, and Aurelian drove them across the Danube; but he ceded Dacia to the barbarians, who, with the new comers, held it until it was reduced and consolidated into a kingdom under Attila. But between the Goths and Huns hostilities set in, and the former re-crossed the Danube to fight their way to Italy, France, and Spain. All this would be foreign to the ethnology of Mœsia, if it were not for the fact that, during the migration, a colony had settled therein; one which, after *Mœsia* had become *Bulgaria*, still remained. The foot of the mountains in the parts about Nicopolis was the country of what Jornandes, who supplies the notice, calls the Gothi Minores. They were poor, simple, and peaceful; shepherds and herdsmen; living largely on milk. They were Christians. Ulphilas, their bishop, had translated the Scriptures into their language; indeed, they were the men whose language, under the exceptionable name Mœso-Gothic, has come down to us as the earliest specimen of the German. The blood, then, of the peasants about Nicopolis is, in some small degree, that of the peasants of Thuringia; not unmixed with a Slavonic element from the Vandals.

Up to this time our history is that of a Roman province, *i.e.* Mœsia (Inferior); and this it will continue to be for the next two centuries. "*Mœsia*" is the name it bears in the time of Alani, and of Attila; but in that of Theodoric we meet with a new name. It is in a panegyric by Ennodius, addressed to Theodoric, that the name *Bulgaria* first appears; and with this appear the difficulties which traverse the inferences from the present Slavonism of its people. It connects them, by implication, with a Turk tribe, the *Huns.*

" I see before me," says the bombastic panegyrist, who, however, from the simple fact of his being a contemporary, is a valuable witness for such facts as are incapable of exaggeration, "Libertem, the chief of the Bulgarians, prostrate, yet alive: alive, lest he should be missing in your monuments; broken, lest he should be an encouragement to the arrogant. This is the nation which, before your time, took all it wanted; in which he who would earn titles must shed the blood of an enemy; the nation to which the field of battle was the blazon of blood; the redder the sword the greater the honour;—a nation that was never to be starved, for horse's milk with horse's flesh is a delicacy to the Bulgarian. Who can withstand the enemy who is both fed and carried by his steed ? All the world was once accessible to them. Now they abstain from that part of it only which you protect." Zeuss, who opens his identification of the Bulgarians with the Huns with this passage, remarks, with reason, that, to a new nation, language like this, even in the mouth of a professed encomiast, can scarcely apply; though it may easily apply to an old and famous nation with a new name. He adds that Procopius, though he has much to say concerning the Bulgarians, really uses the word Hun. Lastly, he shows that one name, at least, that of the Onoguri, is mentioned both as Hun and as Bulgarian.

But a simple Turk basis will not explain the name. Word for word, *Bulga*-ria is *Volga*. Place for place, there is, on the Volga, not only a Bulgarian country but a Great Bulgaria. From these parts came, without doubt, the Magyars of Hungary. Why not, then, the Bulgarians? Besides this, the minute details of the invasion of the Magyars are obscure, and excellent reasons may be given for believing that they were not the first members of the stock who set foot in Europe as conquerors.

If so, a Turk overlaid a Ugrian or Fin element. Yet within two hundred years from the notice of Ennodius, and within a hundred from the time of Procopius, the history of the Bulgarians becomes clear, definite, and authentic; clear, definite, and, at the same time, undeniably and purely Slavonic; and so it continues till now. With this before us we must be curiously careful to limit our interpretation of the opposing facts to the bare necessities they impose on us. Ignore them we cannot.

The hypothesis I suggest is the following :—

1. That the name Bulgaria was limited, in the first instance, to what its name denotes, the valley of a river, and that it applied only to the country immediately along the course of the Danube.

2. That either there were Asiatic Bulgarians in the Hun armies, or that the Huns had, before they left Asia, taken up the word in question from the Ugrians, with whom they were in contact, or upon whose land they had encroached. That it was a word common to the two languages from the beginning I think unlikely; though upon this point I should be glad to be corrected by some special Turk scholar.

Let Bulgaria, then, mean the banks of the Danube, and there is no objection to its having been Hun; but, on the contrary, good reason for making it so. Until the time of Valens the frontier was kept tolerably clear. In the reign of Valens it was invaded; not, however, by the Huns, but by the Goths, whom the Huns drove out of what is now Moldavia, and who recrossed the Danube. Attila at the height of his power held a band of fifty miles in breadth on the south of the Danube; fifty miles, and no more. After his death the Slavonians were more formidable than the Huns.

3. That the second element in the word is the *-uarii* and *-wære* in the German names *Cantuarii* and *Cantwære*=Men of Kent; the name being Gothic in its origin and geographical in its import. The word *Volgy*, on the other hand, is a recognized Fin, or Ugrian, term for the valley of a river, like *Wady* in Arabic; but it is also applied to the river itself—notably in the Spanish names *Guad*iana and *Gud*alquiver. But it may be objected that *Bulgaria* is a hybrid word. Granted; but so is the *Cant-* in *Cant*ware and *Cant*erbury. The Germans who gave it were the Goths of Theodoric. The Fins who supplied the "*Volgy*" were either actual Fins or Turks from the drainage of the *Volga*.

The *Avars* appear for the first time in the reign of Justinian. They never conquered Bulgaria; and even if they had done so, their invasion would not account for the use of the term in a speech to Theodoric. All that is absolutely required for the panegyric of Ennodius is a population of Huns on the Danube. They need not even have been on both sides of it.

How early the Bulgarians became Slavonized we cannot tell. Nor yet can we give the details of the Bulgarian kingdom on its origin. We only know that during the prevalence of the Hun name that of the Bulgarian was unknown; and that soon after the break-up of the kingdom of Attila the word Bulgarian presents itself. As a rule, they are the enemies of the empire; and, as a rule, they are allied with the Slavonians.

They are pagans and warriors; warriors, too, who join their allies in distant as well as near enterprizes. There was a Bulgarian element in the Langobard invasion of Italy; and, afterwards, a permanent Bulgarian settlement in the parts about Sæpinum, Bovianum, and Osernia.

About the middle of the eighth century, Constantine V. put a check upon their ordinary practice of ravaging the frontier, and, by the abduction of the population as slaves, made it an approximate solitude. He repaired the fortifications of the marches and mountain passes, and built others. He rejected the demands of the King, who, on the plea that some of the forts had been planted on Bulgarian ground, had applied for the payment of an annual tribute. He repelled the invading army, which had approached the very walls of Constantinople. He made peace on favourable terms; and, when it was broken, carried the war into the country of the enemy. An occasional repulse never dismayed him. The wreck of his fleet of more than two thousand vessels, upon which he had embarked his infantry, only suspended his activity. He acted again on the offensive; again made peace; which was again broken.

In 775 he died, bequeathing to his successors the coercion of the Bulgarians as a condition of the security of the northern provinces of his empire. Their power, however, though more than once broken, was never annihilated, until the time of the Ottomans.

Soon after the Avar invasion the Bulgarian kingdom of Krum, Bogoris and their pagan predecessors began. By this time the whole land, whatever it may have been before, is Slavonic. But it is now about to become Christian. Theodora is the Empress in Constantinople, and her contemporary in Rome is Pope Nicholas I.

" There is a strange uniformity," writes the historian of Latin Christianity, " in the instruments employed in the conversion of barbarous princes, and, through the princes, of their barbarous subjects. A female of rank and influence, a zealous monk, some national calamity; no sooner do these three agencies coincide than the land opens itself to Christianity."* And in accordance with, or rather as exposition of, this remark, the history of the conversion of Bulgarians runs thus:—Bogoris was their king. His sister had lived, as a captive, for upwards

* Milman, book v. chap. 8.

of thirty-eight years at Constantinople, during a part of which time Theodosius Cupharas had lived as a slave in Bulgaria. An exchange took place; when a pestilence broke out, and raged until Bogoris prayed to the God of his restored and Christian sister, when it abated. The impression of this on the king was strong, on his subjects somewhat weak. In vain were they addressed in their own language by the two brothers, Cyril and Methodius; in vain did a painting, by Methodius, of the horrors of the Last Judgment appeal through their sight to their fears.

This was at the time when the Greek Church was divided between the upholders and the abominators of the worship of images; the Empress Theodora being one of the upholders. She replied to the request of Bogoris that the hands of the two monks might be strengthened in their mission, by sending a bishop, who should baptize the King. But this could only be done secretly; and when the secret came to light the people broke out in defence of the old gods. With only forty-eight attendants, and the cross on his breast, Bogoris affronted the revolt. The insurgents fled. Such of the nobles, however, as Bogoris could lay hand on he put to death.

Thus far the work is Greek. It is in Constantinople that the royal princess has found her new creed. It is a Greek monk by whom her brother is half persuaded to be a Christian. It is two Greek monks by whom the Gospel is preached to the people; and it is a Greek bishop who baptizes Bogoris; henceforward to be known as Micael. Above all, it is on the Greek that the Cyrillian alphabet, the alphabet in which the first translation of the Scriptures into the language of the Eastern Slavonians was made, is founded.

The authority, however, of the Pope was not unknown to the Bulgarian convert; and better known than the authority of the Pope were the scandalous factions to which the Photian and Ignatian quarrel had given rise. It was when this was at its height that a visit, either accidental or well timed, of some Latin missionaries suggested to King Bogoris, who was in doubts as to some fourscore points of discipline, a reference to Rome. To the one hundred and six questions thus referred the answers of Nicolas I. were prompt, prudent, parental.

" Would the king be forgiven the murder of his nobles?"

" Upon doing penance, Yes. But such severity was not to be repeated. Apostates only were to be punished. Where there was no conversion God alone was to judge the obstinate."

" Were prayers for their fathers who had died in darkness and unbelief to be offered?" " By no means."

" Were holy places to serve as asylums?" " Yes. Even murderers, if they could reach a church, were to be protected by the bishop."

" May we fight?"

" Wars will, doubtless, continue; but let the banner be the cross, not the horse-tail as of old."

" May we fight on holy days?" " Not on days which are merely looked upon as lucky, and not on the strength of old saws or auguries. When you go to the war, go to the Church first."

" Be less severe and less ready with some of your punishments." A Greek had baptized some Bulgarians. By the inspiration of God, Bogoris, having found out that he was not a priest, cut off his nose and ears, scourged, and expelled him. For this inhumanity he is blamed by Nicolas, who admits the validity of the baptism.

The custom of the king was to eat his meals alone. Let him be more sociable in this matter.

The oaths were taken on the sword. Take them on the Gospels instead.

Polygamy and marriage within the degrees are strictly forbidden.

So, in a general way, is the adoption of the errors of the Greeks and Armenians.

The bearer of these answers was Formosus, afterwards Pope. That the Latin writers credit him with the primary conversion of the Bulgarians is not to be wondered at. The tendency of the Western writers is all in this direction. That Formosus was the Apostle of Bulgarians, that Bulgaria had been Roman from the time of Pope Damasus, that Bulgaria was part and parcel of the province of Illyricum, are the definite elements in the Roman claim. It was urgently pressed by all the early

successors of Nicolas; and it has never been formally withdrawn. It was resisted from the beginning, by even the
Romanizing Ignatius, who, when the Greek bishops were
ordered to withdraw from the Roman soil of Bulgaria, was not
only Patriarch of Constantinople, but Patriarch through the
influence and decision of Rome. Yet he resisted the cession
of Bulgaria.

In the thirteenth century Bulgaria was the centre of what
is called Western Manicheism. The germs of this reached
Bulgaria from Asia. With a special reverence, implied by the
denomination they bore, for the writings of St. Paul, combined
with certain doctrines excerpted from the still surviving Manicheism of Syria and Asia Minor, the *Paulicians*, from their
theological metropolis of Samosata, spread from the Tigris to
the Dardanelles; and thence into Bulgaria. Persecuted during
the ninth century by the Byzantine Emperors and Empresses,
they rose in revolt. Tephrice, to the south of Trebizond,
became their stronghold. They leagued with the Mahometans.
They ravaged Asia Minor. Constantine Copronymus waged a
war against them, and, with their own consent, transplanted a
vast colony into Rumelia; a fact to be remembered in our
analysis of the very heterogeneous blood of that province.
John Zimiskes founded a second colony in Mount Hæmus. It
probably consisted of Armenians and Lazes, as well as Greeks
and Turks. From Bulgaria it spread westward, especially in
France, where the horrible Albigensian Crusade arrested and,
perhaps, extirpated it. Even here, however, it was known as
the Bulgarian heresy; as it was in Italy, Hungary, Germany,
and Poland. What remains of this in Bulgaria, and how far
it underlies the ordinary orthodox creed, is a question which is
suggested rather than raised.

In 1204 Constantinople, as is well known, was sacked, and
for a time became a Frank Empire, by the Venetians and the
allied powers of the west, of the Fourth Crusade; and during
the reign of the first Emperor, Theodore, breaks out a war with
Bulgaria; Innocent III. being Pope. The relations between
the great Pontiff, the Frank Emperor at Constantinople, and
the King of Bulgaria are remarkable. The Pope had con-

demned the attack upon Constantinople, the Venetians he laid
under an interdict; the Franks he had threatened with one.
The success, however, of the offenders was gradually reconciling
him to the offence. The Venetian nominee to the Patriarchate,
though not the details of his nomination, had been approved.
The establishment of a Latin church in the East had begun.
The Emperor had asked for a supply of breviaries and missals,
of rituals, ministers, and monks; and Innocent had appealed
to the prelates of France in support of the request. "Samaria,"
he wrote, "had returned to Jerusalem. God had transferred
the empire of the Greeks from the proud to the lowly, from
the superstitious to the religious, from the schismatics to the
catholics, from the disobedient to the devoted servants of God."

Meanwhile the King of Bulgaria had received the royal
unction from one of his legates, submitted the Bulgarian to
Rome; and, in the eye of the Pope, at least, he was a spiritual
subject from whom he might expect support and obedience.
The object of the Bulgarian was a share in the spoils of the
Eastern empire. He was now a Latin sovereign, and, as a Latin
sovereign and a frontager, had an interest in the distribution
of the territory. So, having taken offence at the rejection of
his offers of alliance, his activity on the other side moved the
Emperor, the old Doge Dandolo, and the Count of Blois, with
all the troops they could command, against him. The Count
was left dead on the field of battle. The Emperor was taken
prisoner. His brother, who took upon himself the administration of the empire, lost no time in applying for the intercession
of the Pope; and the Pope, in a mild letter, reminded the Bulgarian king that the consecrated banner which he had received
was given him that he should rule in peace. There "is an
army collecting in France and Germany, and it is your interest
to make peace with the occupants of Constantinople by re-
storing to them their Emperor. This is a suggestion, not a
command." On his own part he would lay his injunction on
the Emperor Henry to abstain from all invasion of the borders
of Bulgaria. That kingdom, so devoutly dedicated to St. Peter
and the Church of Rome, was to remain in its inviolable
security! The Bulgarian replied that "he had offered terms

of peace to the Latins, which they had rejected with contempt; they had demanded the surrender of all the territories which they accused him of having usurped from the Empire of Constantinople, themselves being the real usurpers. These lands he occupied by a better right than that by which they held Constantinople. He had received his crown from the Supreme Pontiff; they had violently seized and invested themselves with that of the Eastern Empire; the Empire which belonged to him rather than to them. He was fighting under the banner consecrated by St. Peter: they with the cross on their shoulders, which they had falsely assumed. He had been defied, had fought in self-defence, had won a glorious victory, which he ascribed to the intercession of the Prince of the Apostles. As to the Emperor, his release was impossible. He had gone the way of all flesh."

Johannes, for this was the name of the Bulgarian king, stood better in the eyes of the Pope than in those of the Crusaders; for we have seen that he fought against them, took their king prisoner, and made away with him. Amongst his troops was a body of *Cumanians*. Of these more will be said in the sequel. At present it is enough to remark that they were Turks—Turks other than Ottoman and *Præ*-Ottoman.

Both the Western and the Eastern Church may claim a share in the introduction of Christianity into Albania, and we may reasonably believe that up to the time of Mahomet II., and the completion of the Ottoman conquest, the whole country was Christian. At any rate, it was divided into bishoprics; the Greek creed predominating in the south, the Latin in the north; just as we expect from the difference of the two frontiers. But the residuum of the original paganism was great, and is so at the present time. That a heresy had been imported from Bulgaria to Western Europe we have seen. It was quashed by the Albigensian crusade. This, also, was under the Pontificate of Innocent III.

Though belonging to the Greek Church, the Bulgarians are not fond of hearing themselves called Greek Christians; or, rather, the term *Greek Church* is exceptionable. The name in which its adherents delight is that of the Orthodox Church;

indeed, out of Greece, the other term is, more or less, offensive. Neither is the Greek language loved; still less the Greek individual. It is probable, indeed, that a Greek, provided that he be neither a soldier nor an official, is more disliked by the Bulgarian than a Turk. And the Turks of the Bulgarian villages are, as a rule, neither; but, on the contrary, plain cultivators like themselves.

There is, as we naturally expect, some Mahometanism in Bulgaria. But it is, only to a very slight extent, of the same character as that of Bosnia and Herzegovina; though in respect to the mixture of the Latin and Greek forms of Christianity, the three provinces agrees. In Bosnia and Herzegovina the Mahometanism is of long standing, and dates from the Ottoman conquest. The land-holders apostatized in order to keep their estates, so that, even at the present time, the difference of creed coincides with a difference of class. In Bulgaria the converts to Mahometanism are of later date, and there is less uniformity in the motives that made them converts. They have the credit of being more hostile to their Christian fellow-subjects than the ordinary Mahometans. This is likely enough as a fact; but, whether a fact or not, it is the ordinary charge made against converts, and, whether rightly or wrongly, is sure to be made.

The class-name of these converts is *Pomak*; but more will be said about them in the sequel.

*   *   *   *   *

Of *Rumelia* it may be said that, considering the fact of such a city as Constantinople being its capital, it is one of the most unexplored districts in Europe. If the present writer were the first who made this remark it might not go for much. It might only show that he had overlooked some competent and sufficient authority. But it is a common one. Few who write about the Ottomans at all go much beyond the precincts of Constantinople. Those, however, who, instead of the capital, have to speak about the country, generally find it due to themselves to excuse the imperfection of their details by a notice of the want of materials. The statistician, the archæologist, the chorographer, the military historian, all do this; and the political ethnologist must do the same.

In a general way, all that he can state of Rumelia is, that whilst the urban population is Greek, or Turk, the population of the villages and hamlets is Bulgarian; that the proportion of the Greeks of the towns is greater on the coast than inland; that more than half the population of the whole province is centred in Constantinople; and that in Constantinople itself, independent of the Greek and other foreign Quarters, there is a mixture of blood at once extensive and heterogeneous. Constantinople, however, is the capital of the Ottoman Empire. The capital of Rumelia, the oldest occupancy of the Ottomans in Europe, was Adrianople. Its census, like those of all eastern towns, is scarcely a census at all. A hundred and thirty thousand inhabitants, in its most flourishing times, it may possibly have held. At any rate, this is one of the numbers that have been given for its population. Eighty-five thousand, of which thirty thousand are Mahometans, is another. Both, however, are merely the estimates of travellers; and, in such estimates, the formula is nearly the same throughout. The first remark, when the population of an Eastern town is under notice, is that some previous traveller put it at such a number; the next is that the number is too high by about half; the third is that the population has decreased since such or such an event (the war of such a year, the migration of such a one, and the like); the fourth is, that, at the present time, it contains so many hearths, houses, or families, of which so many are Mahometan, so many Christian. As far as it goes this method is good; but it applies only to the localities visited by the observer.

By far the fullest list of towns and villages thus dealt with, which has come under my notice, is, that of Lieutenant-general Jochmus, of the Russian service, who, in 1847, made a careful exploration of the Eastern half of the Balkan, or range of Mount Hæmus. Starting from Constantinople he made Tirnova his furthest point. Along and on each side of his somewhat devious route lay the villages of the following list, for which he has supplied us with data of the kind in question. No excuse is made for giving it *in extenso*. In all questions concerning the future fate of the Ottoman Empire, the real proportion of its Turk to the non-Turk elements is of primary importance; yet just in those parts where the analysis is most complicated our *data* are the fewest.

Abbreviations.

T. Turkish	G. Greek	M. Mahometan
B. Bulgarian	J. Jewish	C. Christian.
	A. Armenian	

Villages.

Village.	Houses.	Village.	Houses.	Village.	Houses.
Natash	. 120 T.B.	Dobral	. . 40 T.	Yakovzi	. . 50 B.
Chatalcha	. 120 T.	Marata .	. . 30 T.	Kovanlik .	. 70 B.
————	. 180 C.	Yenikoi	. . 30 G.B.	Ravaditza	. 400 B.
Avren .	. . 50 T.B.	Hojakoi	. . 20 T.	Osman Bazaar	700 T.
Yenikoi	. . 40 B.	Aivatshik	. 20 T.	————	—— 100 B.
Serai	. . . 250 T.C.	Karamancha	. 20 T.	Ishehol	. . 30 T.
Bunarhissar	. 120 T.	Kaldumay	. 25 T.	Chatuk	. . 150 M.
————	. 120 G.	Shimanli .	. 50 T.	Sadova	. . 45 T.
————	. 130 B.	Karatepe	. 25 T.	Keder-Fekli .	60 T.
Yene .	. . 20 T.	Abkli .	. . 25 T.	Peklatch .	. 25 T.
—— .	. . 150 G.	Nabat .	. . 600 M.	Malenich .	. 40 T.
—— .	. . 50 B.	Korkeshah	. 25 T.	Rubja .	. . 50 T.
*Kirk-kelesia	600 T.	Yenijekoi	. 25 T.	Murad-dere .	40 T.
————	1000 B.G.J.	Balabariche	. 30 T.	Chalik Kavak	80 M.
Erekli .	. . 50 T.	Isinplu	. . 25 T.	Bairam-dere.	60 T.
Dolet-agach	. 40 B.†	Papaskoi .	. 100 B.	Bekie .	. . 55 T.
Karabunar	. 30 B.	—— .	. . 50 T.	Lubnitza .	. 60 T.
Rusukastro	. 5 T.	Kazan .	. . 912 B.	Mereke .	. 60 T.
————	. 35 B.	Selimne .	. 1000 T.	Buyuk Chenka	80 T.
Aidos .	. . 200 T.	————	950 B.J.A.	Kara Ahmed	
—— .	. . 100 B.	Kapinlu .	. 100 M.	Mahalesi	. 40 T.
Topjiler .	. 40 T.	Mindi .	. . 100 B.	Butresk .	. 45 T.
Kaibilar .	. 50 T.	Slatar .	. . 150 B.	Köpri-koi	. 40 T.B.
Faki .	. . 50 B.	Yenikoi	. 120 B.T.	Kadikoi	. . 100 T.B.
Kutshuk Ali.	50 M.	Chülün	. . 120 B.	Fellakoi	. . 30 T.B.?
Bana .	. . 6 G.‡	Kesrova .	. ? B.	Aiasma	. . 80 T.B.?
Chavderlik	. 30 T.	Chehdecke	. 100 T.B.	Markovcha	. 120 T.B.?
Nadir .	. . 10 T.	Laila .	. . 100 T.	Kutefcha .	. 30 T.B.?
§Uflakni	. 30 T.	Karasiler .	. 50 T.	Madara .	. 40 M.?
Boghazdere .	40 T.	Hassan Faki	. 40 T.B.	Kasbein .	. 45 M.?
Karanla .	. 35 T.	Zurtkoi	. . 50 T.	Velshin .	. 30 M.?
Rudcha .	. 30 T.	Ereskli	. . 200 M.	Paravate .	. 220 ?
Kamtshik Maha-		LowerBebrova	300 M.	Testajikoi	. 40 M.
lesi .	. . 80 T.	Illiena	. . 600 B.	Avren	. . 60 B.‖

It is only to the villages of a single road in Rumelia and only to the south-eastern part of Bulgaria that this list applies. At Tirnova on the west, and at Shumla on the north, our authority

---

* Reduced by ¼.   † Recent colonists.
‡ The Greeks of Bana dress like Bulgarians.
§ The name suggests a Valachian element.
‖ Transactions of the Royal Geographical Society. Vol. 24. Read Nov. 28, 1853. The date of the observations is 1847.

leaves us; so that, even if he had exhausted all the villages of his circuit, the details of more than three-fourths of the remainder of Bulgaria would want elucidating. And this they *do* want. That the further we go from the Turkish frontier the smaller will be the number of the Turks is likely; though in the great fortresses along the Danube we must expect to find them numerous. That there are Servians in the west and Vallachians in the north-east, is probable; indeed, it is known that such is the case. The numbers, however, and the proportions are unknown. It is submitted that anything that throws light on such a question as this is of value.

Of the towns Kasan seems to be most Bulgarian; and as it was the district about Kasan that has supplied the fewest elements to the Bulgarian emigrations we may fairly look upon it as the centre of the nationality.

In Rumelia I believe that the mountain-range of Rhodope is Bulgarian.

It is not, however, upon the history of Rumelia that we need go into detail. Except in respect to its future, and the extent to which it may, possibly, be divided between Bulgaria and the suburbs of Constantinople, nothing need be said at present. Its history is that of the capital, which is much the same as the history of the Empire in general. To some extent this is the case with Bulgaria. There is little to be said about it until it becomes to be a battle-field; and it is only since the full development of the Russian policy that it has become this. It is not till the year 1773, in the reign of Abdul Hamid, and just before the Treaty of Kainairdji, that we first find the Russians in Bulgaria. I cannot altogether venture on the negative statement that no hostile army since the time of Mahomet II. had been thus near the capital. Austria, however, rarely got further east than Widdin, and the Danube does not seem to have been crossed from Wallachia.

During the Fanariote period in the Danubian Principalities, the influence of Russia increased, and her subsequent conquests in the Crimea and Bessarabia greatly strengthened. In the campaign, then, of 1771–1774, the Danube is passed, and the barrier of Balkan is threatened. This is a new phase in Turkish

history; and there are more points than one in the history of
the invasion that claim notice. The prominent one is the
terrible disorganization of the administration. There was
some show of vigour in Constantinople, and some activity in
the way of extemporising an army. There were soldiers good
in quality and sufficient in number that were despatched to
the Danube, and who reached the place of their destination.
But there were no commanders, real or nominal, to lead them.
Hence, different companies put themselves under anyone who
set himself up for an officer; and gave themselves up either to
the pillage of the peaceful population around them, or to faction
fights among themselves; and all this in the sight of the enemy
on the other side of the river.

The next campaign arises out of the compact between
Napoleon and the Czar at Tilsit, 1808. This was when England and Russia were allied with one another against Turkey.
Russia's portion in the contemplated partition of Europe was,
inter alia, Vallachia, Moldavia, and Rumelia.

France did as little as possible for her ally. Nevertheless,
her generals took some fortresses, one of which was Silistria.

Before Shumla they failed. Bosniak Aga was the brave and
active captain who raised the siege; but he neglected to follow
up his advantages, or, rather, he took special pains *not* to make
the most of them. And that reasonably. He was himself a
rebel against the Sultan, and did what he did for his country
in the capacity of patriot rather than a subject. Nor did he
stand alone in this respect. All over the Empire the subordinate officers were malcontents, and the Pashas open and
undisguised rebels. So it was in Albania, so it was in Servia,
so it was in Bulgaria, and so it was—and was to be—in
Egypt.

The third campaign on Bulgarian ground was that of Diebitsch, which has already been noticed. The last but one was
that of the Crimean war; and the last, the one which is still
unfinished.

CHAPTER VI.

THE chief text for the notices of the present chapter is a well known passage from Constantine Porphyrogenita to the fact that—" *all Greece was Slavonized.*" That this means that the ancient Hellas became Slavonic in the way that the Russian Governments of Vladimer, or Moscow, became Russian no one imagines. The passage, however, though it has never been wrested to such an import as this, has been made to carry more than it can fairly bear, though it bears much.

It is not necessary to begin with the Greece of the Athenian and the Macedonian time, nor yet with those of Rome anterior to its decline.

There were *Goths* in Greece as early as the reign of Gallienus; and where there were Goths at that time there were also *Vandals*. But these are not very important.

After the Goths and Vandals come the *Huns*, of whom the earliest notice is that of Procopius, who carries a large army of them through the pass of Thermopylæ as early as A.D. 540. That these were Bulgarians under another name is probable; but even if we suppose them to have been the true Huns of the Turk stock there is good reason for believing, indeed there is the express evidence of the historian, that they were accompanied by Slavonians. Turk, however, or Slave, there was a foreign element of some sort.

In 581-2, another great invasion is mentioned, and within ten years later a third; the invaders in this last being the *Avars*. "These Avars," writes the Patriarch Nicholaos to the Emperor

10

Alexis, "had held possession of the Peloponessus for two hundred and eighteen years, and had so completely separated it from the Byzantine empire that no Byzantine official dared to put his foot in the country." This is from a notice of the foundation of the Bishopric of Patras, by Nicephorus I. in 807, the date from which the two hundred and eighteen years must be calculated.

The Avars were members of the Turk stock. I think they were this, because, unlike *Hun*, Avar is a name used with tolerable accuracy and precision. Still, there are good reasons for attaching a great host of Slavonians to their armies. As Patras was besieged by them they must have penetrated beyond the Isthmus.

The authority for this statement is manifestly anything but a cotemporary; and such is the case with, I believe, the rest of our witnesses. But this is merely partially an objection. Our evidence is insufficient only for a part of the question, viz., the exact details of the invasion or invasions. To the fact of the country being *Slavonized* at the time of the writers it is decisive. But the Patriarch Nicholaos is, by no means, our only authority. The year 581-2, or the third year of the Emperor Tiberius, is specially mentioned by more than one writer; and the circumstances connected with it are exactly of the kind which we expect *à priori*. The strong reign of Justinian I. is over, and the Avars are the dominant nation. Tiberius contrives to come to something like terms with them; but only for a while. His successor Maurice is their most formidable enemy; indeed, the only formidable one they had. His reign is throughout a series of wars ably conducted against their great Khan Baian. The terrible enemy is kept at bay; but, under the worthless Phocas, the Avar power endangers the very existence of the Empire. Heraclius succeeds him; and, until we come to the time of the Paleologi and the Ottoman Sultans, no emperor is more beset than Heraclius by misfortunes of all kinds. There are Avars on the west; and we know what these are. There is the powerful King of Persia, Khosroes Nushirvan, and the full flood of Mahometan conquest in the east; and, against these, Heraclius has to uphold the integrity of the Empire. Over and over again the confusion and troubles of the reign of this Emperor are alluded to in Byzantine history; indeed, it is an epoch from which the so-called *Slavonization* of Hellas is dated. Even in the present work they will have to be alluded to elsewhere.

But, be this as it may, the fourth year of the reign of Tiberius is our leading epoch. We shall see how continuous and well authenticated is the history that follows it, and how thoroughly it suits with the whole history of the next four centuries.

"*Avar*" is the name in the notice of Nicholaos; but the fact that there were Slavonians as well is undoubted. Menander, for the fourth year of Tiberius, states—

1. That 100,000 Slavonians were collected in Thrace.

2. That Tiberius invited the Khan of the Avars, Baian, then on a friendly footing with the Empire, to assist in coercing them. But, under his successor Maurice, the Avars and the Emperor had a war—not wholly without success on the part of Maurice, but with gross disgrace on the part of Phocas. Then, writes Theophanes, Heraclius found "the affairs of the Empire out of joint; for the barbarians made Europe a desert, and the Persians overturned all Asia." And the epitomizer of Strabo writes—"and now Scythian Slavonians occupy all Epirus, and almost all Greece, Peloponnesus, and Macedonia." In the ninth century we find them occupying not only the level countries, but the mountains; and that under the name of *Klephths*—this being, I believe, the first time the word occurs in this sense.

Constantine II., A.D. 657, fights against them. And here we may remember that it is in a statement of Constantine Porphyrogenitas, we get, for the first time a *King of Bulgaria*. Justinian (Rhinotmetus), too, of the Heraclian dynasty, fights against them in 687. So, in 758, does Constantine Copronymus. In 782 the Empress Irene sends against them the Patrician Stauracius, who conquers them not only in Macedonia but in Peloponnesus; and in all these later wars we hear nothing more about the Avars. "*Slavonian*" is the usual name. If any second occurs it is "*Bulgarian*" or

10 *

" Scythian." " And now," writes the epitomator of Strabo, "the names *Pisatæ,* and *Kaukones,* and *Pylii* are nowhere. It is *Scythians* who occupy their places."

Thus far, then, the history of these *Slavonizers of Hellas* has begun with that of the Avars, continued with that of the Bulgarians, and ended with the amalgamation of the invaders with the older occupiers of the land. We never hear a word about their ejection. But the inroads seem to have ended before the tenth century. They will be renewed; but by A.D. 950 the Bulgarians will have been reduced by the victories of John Zimisces and Basil II. (Bulgaroctonus), and the Slavonization in blood, with an amalgamation in language, will have become more or less complete. This, I submit, is the history of Macedon and Greece from the reign of Justinian and the rise of the Avars to that of Basil II. and the overthrow of the Bulgarians.

Assuredly we may say that the statement *" all Greece was Slavonized"* is one of considerable import. But the Slavonic element, though the one that is the most conspicuous in the evidence, and the most permanent in its effects, is, by no means, the only one. It was Avar in the first instance; and the Avars were Turks. Nor was the Slavonism of all one kind. The Bulgarian division of the great stock was, probably, the first and foremost. But some of the Slavonizers were Servian, and some—not a few—Russian, and that from distant parts of Russia. In the Vallachian elements the majority spoke a language of Latin origin; and, if the proposed doctrine as to the origin of the word *Kutzo* be true, there were among the Vallachians themselves descendants of one of the numerous sections and sub-sections of the Hun nation; not to mention the Albanians of the frontier and of the second kingdom of Bulgaria.

In the Morea there is another ethnological element, and a double process in connection with it. Bajazet I., who, in person, overran the whole of Greece, not only introduced into the Morea a large body of Turks—Tatars and Turkomans from Asia,—but transported from their own country thirty thousand Greeks.

Add to these the *Albanian* element, which has been already noticed; and the Frank settlements of the thirteenth and fourteenth centuries—French, Norman, Italian, and Spanish (Catalonian).

The valley of the Apidanus looks like another of these Non-Hellenic localities. Just where it joins the Peneus stands the village of *Kutzochevo*. Follow the stream to its bifurcation, and you come to a *Vlakho* Iani. Cross the water-shed, and near the mouth of the Sperchius stands Zeitoun, in the country of the Maleans, on the Sinus Maliacus, not far to the north of Thermopylæ. Roughly speaking, and for the sake of bringing in two old familiar names, let us say that the evidence of *Valachian* occupancy extends from Larissa to Thermopylæ, taking in parts of Pelasgiotis, Thessaliotis, Phthiotis, and the Maliensis, with Pharsalia and Thaumakia on the west, and Pheræ on the east; being part, also, of the Pelasgian Argos with the range of Pelion and the battle-ground of the Centaurs and Lapithæ between it and the sea. I conclude with remarking that the modern name of Pelion is Zagora, a Slavonic word meaning *over the mountain*. It applies to a town on the eastern slope; and, consequently, places the Slavonians who applied it on the west. This gives the south-eastern quarter of Thessaly, more or less, to two intrusive populations. Zeitouni is brought in because it is mentioned by Benjamin of Tudela as the southern limit of what he calls Great Vallachia. "Here are the confines of Vallachia, a country the inhabitants of which are called Vlachi. They are as nimble as deer, and descend from the mountains into the plains of Greece, committing robberies and making booty. Nobody ventures to make war upon them, nor can any king bring them to submission; and they do not profess the Christian faith. Their names are of Jewish origin, and some even say they have been Jews; which nation they call brethren. Whenever they meet an Israelite they rob, but never kill, him as they do the Greeks. They profess no religious creed."

That the names of Samuel, Simeon, Gabriel, Daniel, and Moses appear in almost every page of Vallachian history, is a remark of Finlay's, from whom the preceding extract is taken.

When did these Vallachians enter this part of Thessaly, and whence came they? Anna Comnena mentions them as being the masters of several Thessalian towns. Kinnamos observes the affinity between their language and the Latin. Finlay suggests the year 1040 as a probable approximate date for their introduction, under Basil II., who, he thinks, may have introduced them in order to re-people the country which the Bulgarians had depopulated.

In dealing, however, with this question, we must by no means overlook the term *Kutzo*. In more than one of the ordinary works on the Rumanyo language, the Vallachians of Greece—not these (for they are scarcely to be found speaking their original language in the valley of Apidanus), but some others, which will be mentioned in the sequel—are called Kutzo-Vallachians, a compound which is explained to mean Lame, *i.e.* False Vallachians, or something equally disparaging. The writers, however, who lay this before us overlook the following notice, while Zeuss, to whom it is due, though he suggests the connection between the Kutzi and the Vallachians, seems unaware of the existence of the compound which adds so much in favour of his hypothesis.

1. Codinus mentions the Bishopric of the Kutziagri as one of the sees of Thessaly.

2. In the heading of a chapter in the Life of the Archbishop of Thessalonica are the words "Civil war between the city and Maurus and Kuver the *Bulgarian.*"

3. In a life of John, Archbishop of Salonica, who lived in the latter half of the seventh century, is the statement that the Khan of the Avars brought back from Pannonia and the parts about Sirmium a number of men out of captivity, whom he claimed as his own subjects, and who, when they reached his dominions, mixed themselves with the Avars and Bulgarians; that he placed over them a captain named Kuver (Κουβερ); that Kuver affected independence; that he carried the Captivity with him, and, finally, that the whole mass moved towards Thessalonica—whence arose the war alluded to in the second notice.

The connection of the Kutziaguri with what we may call the

Kutz element in the *Kutzo*-Vallachians was suggested (as afore-said) by Zeuss, apparently without knowing that they were called anything but simple Vallachians. The next suggestion is the present author's. The Kutziaguri were the nation to which the captain Kuver belonged; and they were Turks of either the Hun or Avar name. But the men over whom he was placed, and whom the Avar king claimed, were Ru-manyos — probably ordinary Rumanyos of Dacia, but not impossibly of Pannonia.

Here we find in an account of, perhaps, the ninth century, that in the time of Archbishop John, the *Dragovitæ*, the Sagu-datæ, the Velegezetæ, the Vaiunetæ, and the Berzetæ, invaded the Chachidic Peninsula. Most of these names occur else-where. The Bishop of Philippopolis styles himself the Exarch of all Europe and Dragovintia. The Sagudates and the Dra-govites are specially mentioned as paying tribute to the Scythian empire on that frontier. The names Sougdaia and *Souodalia* are again the names of bishoprics; and that they are the names of a Sagudat see is likely. The King of Bulgaria threatens Verzetia. The Velegezetæ are placed in Thessaly. Finally, there is a Thessalian Bishop of the Εζερος, *Ezero*, or *Lake;* one of the Smoleni; and one of the Galazi; words which may be compared with Smolensk and Galacz—whilst *Susdal* is the name of a district east of Moscow. But, though this is enough to establish a Slavonic migration, it scarcely makes it Russian. The invasion, however, was made by sea. More than this, it was made in boats made out of single trees—monoxyla—a fact which suggests the likelihood of the origin of the migrations having been high up some of the rivers of Russia. More than this. In Nestor we get the name Dragovitæ in its true natural form *Dragoviczi*, accompanied with the statement that the men who bore the name dwelt between the Dwina and the Pripecz.

Lastly, we have, more than once in Constantine Porphyro-genita, the words 'Ρῶς and Ρωσία, applied to not only the Krivitzi, the Lentzinini, the Ultini, and the Dervinini, but to the *Druguvitæ*, who are, undoubtedly, the *Dragovitæ* already mentioned. (See Zeuss, &c., p. 623.)

The *Norman* name now comes under notice.

Four times did the Normans, who had fixed themselves as rulers, attempt the conquest of Constantinople, or, at least, a dismemberment of the great Byzantine empire. There was a narrow stream of salt water between Italy and Greece; and what was that to men whose original home had been on the Eyder and the firths of Norway? men whose arms, except by the Arabs of Spain, had never been foiled; who saw in the wealth of Constantinople even a greater prize than the crown of England, so lately won by one of their countrymen.

About twenty years, then, after the battle of Hastings, A.D. 1081, Robert Guiscard sailed from Brindisi with an armament of thirty thousand men and a hundred and fifty ships, but succeeded only in reducing Corfu and in landing in Epirus.

The Eastern is the most Hellenic side of Thessaly as to blood; Zagora being so in the way of politics. This means that the part taken in the Revolution is the test. The occupants of Zagora are left to govern themselves, through magistrates of their own election. In ordinary times the district thrives; but in 1820 there had been a failure in the product of both the silk and oil, and distress weighed heavy on the dense and industrious population. Forty-five thousand inhabitants to twenty-four village communities is the population ascribed by Finlay to Zagora at this time; Turkish occupancy being the exception. Nevertheless, in Lekhoria, they were numerous enough for six hundred of them to be massacred by the insurgents, who, after some intestine quarrels, established a Thessalo-Magnesian Senate. The reduction of Volo was the chief object of the movement in these parts, but Volo was relieved. Trichen held out the longest, inasmuch as it was not reduced until 1823, when, on the surrender of its vessels, and the admission of a Turkish garrison, an amnesty was granted.

The Vallachians of the district of the water-shed between the Peneus and the Aspropotamo were among the first to revolt; for, like the Christian Albanians of Hellas, the Vallachians acted as Greeks. They were coerced, however, by Kurshid Pasha.

In noting that the Revolution was suppressed with comparative ease in Thessaly, we must remember that Larissa is the most Turkish town south of Saloniki; and that in Macedonia, as in Thessaly, there is a settlement of Anatolian Turks.

The following is a list of the feudatories of Achaia from Count Beugnot's *Assizes de Jerusalem,* as given by Finlay.

It shows the extent, if not of Greek and French intermixture, of, at least, the surface over which the two elements came in contact.

Secular.

District.	Holder.	No. of Fiefs.
1. Kalamata . .	Geoffrey de Villehardouin .	. (?)
2. Akova . . .	Walter de Rosières . .	. 22
3. Karitena (Skorta)	Hugh de Brières . .	. 24
4. Patras . .	William de Alaman .	. (?)
5. Vostitza . .	Hugh de Charpigny .	. 8
6. Chalandritza .	Robert de Tremouille .	. 4
7. Kalavryta . .	Otho de Tournay . .	. 12
8. Nikli . . .	William (?) . .	. 6
9. Veligosti . .	Mathew de Mons . .	. 4
10. Gritzena . .	Luke (?) . .	. 4
11. Geraka . .	Guy de Nivelet . .	. 6
12. Passava . .	John de Neuilly . .	. 4

Ecclesiastic.

1. Archbishop of Patras	8
2. Bishp of Olerios	4
3. ———— Modon	4
4. ———— Coron	4
5. ———— Veligosti	4
6. ———— Nikli, Moukhli (Amyclæ) . . .	4
7. ———— Lacedæmon	4

Military Orders.

1. Knights of St. John . .	. 4
2. ———— The Temple .	. 4
3. The Teutonic Order . .	. 4

In an account of St. Willibald's pilgrimage to Jerusalem, A.D. 723, the saint is said, after leaving Sicily, to have touched at Manafasia, *i.e.* Monemvasia, in the *Slavonian* land.

Between 842 and 852 the Melingi and Ezeritæ were conquered by Theoktistos under the regency of Theodora during the minority of her son Michael III.; but only for a time.

Between 920 and 944 they are again in arms; are threatened with extermination; are constrained to pay tribute; are supported by an allied population of Slavesians; and, finally, are allowed to elect their own chiefs. The partial independence that this privilege procured them lasted more than two hundred years; for Slavonians were found in the Morea by the Franks about 1205, in Laconia, in Arcadia, and in Elis. The latest notice of their language carries it into the fourteenth century.

Of the three kingdoms that, beyond the boundaries of Rumelia, were the first to be conquered by the Ottomans, Bulgaria was the earliest, then Servia, and, as the third, Bosnia.

When Bosnia ceased to be a Roman province, its history, until it became Turkish, was chiefly connected with that of Venice and Hungary, both Christian countries; so that of the original Paganism of Bosnia we know nothing. The *name* first appears in Constantine Porphyrogeneta.

It is in the time of the Frank conquest of Constantinople (1204), that we find, to a certain extent, the histories of Bosnia and Bulgaria running parallel; though of Bulgaria, previous to this date, we know much more than we do of Bosnia. Pope Innocent III., who, as we have seen, was recognised as spiritual lord by Johannes of Bulgaria, is, more decidedly and undoubtedly, exercising like power in Bosnia, which is, then, no kingdom, but a Banate under the suzerainty of Hungary.

In 1197 Kulin is the Ban. It is the obnoxious heresy of Paulician which has been alluded to as an introduction into Europe from Bulgaria, which he favours. He is summoned to Rome, and returns, having given plausible explanations and fair promises both to his suzerain, the King of Hungary, and the Pope. Still the heresy increased; and in 1222 it took the shape of an insurrection, and after that, until the Ottoman conquest, there was either a religious war or a decided ascendency on the side of the schismatic. It was the same creed that had been adopted by the Albigenses.

During this period the Banat became a kingdom; and, in the early part of the fifteenth century, under Tuartko I., the sect is decidedly dominant.

What is now known as Herzegovina was, at this time, the Duchy of St. Saba; and of this Stephen Cosaccia was the Duke, while John Paulovitch was Voivode of Montenegro. Bajazet I. and Amurath II. are the Sultans in Constantinople. But Servia and Bulgaria are no longer kingdoms.

The Turks, too, pending these religious disturbances and a disputed succession between a second Tuartko and Ostoya Christich, bring in the Hungarians on the one side and the Turks on the other. Stephen (Cristich), the Turk nominee, becomes a vassal and tributary to Amurath II.; is murdered by his illegitimate son Stephen Tomasovitsh, crowned, and, having failed to pay tribute to the Sultan, put to death by Mahomet II. And by the campaign of 1463 Bosnia became a Turkish province.

The Duke of St. Saba was constrained to send his son, Stephen, to Constantinople as a hostage. There he became a Mahometan, and under the name of Ahmet, a son-in-law of Bajazet II., and a Vizier.

CHAPTER VII.

Turks other than Ottoman.—The Sultan and the Czar.—General Character.

THE Turks of the Ottoman, and the Slavonians of the Russian, Empire are pre-eminently representative populations. Each represents a creed, and each represents a race or family. The Czar's is the great power of the Slavonic, the Sultan's that of the Turk, world. And both the Turks and the Slavonians are among the most important families of mankind. The Turk class, however, is the smaller, and it is, perhaps, the simpler one also. In some senses it is certainly so. The great majority of the Turks is, in language at least, less unlike an Osmanli than a Bohemian is unlike a Russian; though when we go farther and take into consideration the whole complex of the characteristics of the different sections of the two groups, it is doubtful whether the observation applies. The civilization of the Slavonians is of a much more uniform character than that of the Turks; and no Slavonian differs in this respect from another so much as a Yakut from the shores of the Arctic Sea, or a Karakalpak from the frontier of Mongolia differs from a Turk of Constantinople. Yet it is nearly certain that these differences are chiefly due to circumstances of comparatively recent occurrence; so that what applies to the Turks of the present day would not have applied five hundred years ago. Before the diffusion of the Mahometan religion, the difference between one Turk and another must have been but slight; for it must be remembered that there are, at present, not only Mahometan, but Christian, Pagan, and, probably, Buddhist

Turks; these differences of creed giving rise to distinctions which, when all Central Asia was simply pagan, must have amounted to very little.

But, though the Ottoman Empire is to the Turk much as Russia is to the Slavonic world, there are Turks who know but little and care less about the Sultan. Many of them are Christians; a few Pagans; none enthusiastic or even decided, Mahometans. Still less do they place the Sultan above the Czar; for, whatever may be the case with the Mahometans of Kazan or Orenburg, the Pagan and Christian Turks of Siberia are as good Russian subjects as they would be if there were no such an individual as the Sultan. But Russia has the parallels, and more than the parallels, of these in the comparative indifference of the Bohemian Tsheks and the positive hostility of Poland. Still, Panslavonism has its analogue in Turkey; and with form and organization it might act upon the Usbeks * of Khiva and Bokhara much as Russian influence tells upon Servia, Bulgaria, and Montenegro. And, in all probability, there has been at different times more of it than appears on the face of history. That the religious feeling has been appealed to over and over again there is ample evidence. The appeals to that of nationality or race have been fewer and less patent; probably because the chief enemies with which Turkey has had to contend have been Christians, against whom the appeal to religion was sufficient.

In creed the Sultan is, at least, the equal of the Czar as the representative of a great section of a great creed. If Christianity fall into the Latin, the Greek, and the Protestant Churches, and if, of the Greek Church, the Czar, layman as he is, is the ever visible symbol, Mahometanism, with its divisions into the Shiites, and the Sunnites, has a similar symbol for Sunnitism in the Sultan. It was a little before the extinction of the Kalifat that this title arose; Mahmud of Ghuzni being, as far as we may make a negative statement, the first who assumed it. The highest before his time was, probably, Khan or Khaghan. In the Sultan every Sunnite sees the successor and equivalent of the Kalif, and, with a few exceptions, every

---

* This was written before the late conquests by Russia in Turkestan.

Turk who is a Mahometan at all is a Sunnite. The Shah of Persia is scarcely this in the eyes of the Shiite, though the Persian language and the Shiite creed coincide as closely as do the Turkish and the Sunnite. The difference, however, is accidental rather than real. The Sultan is more of a symbol in Mahometanism than the Shah, inasmuch as, being on the frontier of the Mahometan world, it is he who most looks like the bulwark of the faith.

Again. Of the Mahometan populations which are neither Turk nor Persian there are more which are Sunnite than Shiite; in other words, there is more of the Turkish doctrine beyond Turkestan than there is of the Persian beyond Persia. The great Arab division of the Mahometan world is chiefly Sunnite; and of the two Mahometan kingdoms which (though at long intervals) the nearest approach Turkey and Persia, the former is wholly Sunnite, the latter partially so. Morocco, with its population of Arabs and Berbers, is Turk in creed; Bokhara is the same in respect to its dynasty and the dominant population.

Arabia itself is more Turk both in creed and political feeling than Persian; indeed, a portion of it is nominally Turk. That it is a land which has never been thoroughly and permanently reduced is true; but it is also true that the loose and current statements as to its absolute independence are exaggerated. It has been held in partial subjection by Rome, and it is held to some extent at the present time in an imperfect state of vassalage by the Porte. Hence, the relations between Russia and Greece repeat themselves in those between Turkey and Arabia. The mother countries of the two creeds, and the sources of the civilization which these creeds carried with them, were Greece and Arabia. The political power, however, is in other hands. The eldest son, so to say, of the Greek Church is Russia; the eldest son of Islam is Turkey—*eldest son* meaning the Representative Power.

We see a Shiite influence in the history of the great Caucasian war under Shamil; but see it very rarely in the relations of the Mahometans who come in contact with Europe. On the Indian frontier, indeed, Persia has an influence of the kind in question; but it is in no wise to be compared with that of the Sultan in Europe.

Neither must we forget that the Mahometans of the Crusades were Turks; and that this means the only real Mahometans who have even been prominent in the history of France, England, and the Empire. In Spain it was different. The infidels with whom the Spaniards have the credit of having waged a chronic, national, and separate crusade of their own were the true original Mahometans of Arabia. But it was only in Spain and Africa that these were formidable. The Kalifat broke up before the Crusades began, and the infidels who interrupted the pilgrimages to Jerusalem, the infidels against whom Peter the Hermit preached, the infidels against whom Richard I. drew his sword, the infidels who held Jerusalem, were Turks; Turks under the Sultan of Iconium.

The great Tatar conqueror Tamerlane, or Timor, was also a Turk; a fact which leads us to ask how far the Turk language and Turk history coincide with the Turk blood. They do so but partially. In the recognition of a strong Turk element in the Mongol armies, I only follow current opinion; going no further than the facts suggested by the names Timur and The Great Mogul. The Great Mogul was so named because he was a descendant of Baber, who was a descendant of Timur, who passed for a descendant of Tshingiz. Whether he were so in reality is doubtful. It is only certain, on one side, that, dynastically, he was considered as such; and that, on the other, he was a Turk, who knew the Mongols of his frontier only as strangers and enemies, who, in all probability, could speak no word of Mongol, and who had, at most, in his army, only a few companies who could do so. Whatever the Mongols were elsewhere, the Moguls of India were Tshagatai Turks. They affected a Mongol lineage; just as Timur professed a descent from Tshingis, whilst the Tshagatai tribe to which he belonged took its name from Tshingis's huntsman, Zagatai. This is a matter of history. *Mutatis mutandis*, I believe that Tshingis himself connected his line with the Mantshus. At any rate his Mongol son bore the name of a Mantshu predecessor. But this is general rather than special ethnology.

They are a foreign population. But this, as a characteristic, is of no great importance. Most populations are foreign ; most were, at some time or other, intruders on the soil which they afterwards treated as their own.

They are strangers of recent introduction. Four hundred years junior in the date of their original conquest to the Norman conquerors of England ; seven hundred years junior to the Mahometan occupants of Spain, they are, in respect to the antiquity of their tenure, the *novi homines* of Europe ; and on the strength of their being this a good deal of declamation has been wasted. That the Ottoman Empire is a mere encampment, that the Ottoman Turks are mere squatters, that the Ottomans hold Constantinople by sufferance, that they should be driven back to the deserts and steppes of their original Asia, are flowers of rhetoric which may be found in writings of influential authors; just as, in the works of their antagonists, exaggerations of the validity of the Ottoman title and panegyrics upon the efficiency of the Ottoman reforms take suspicious prominence. As far as the question of time is concerned, the title of the Ottomans of Constantinople is what that of the English was to London in the reign of Edgar, and that of the Magyars to Hungary in the year 1300.

They are Asiatics. As a simple matter of geography this is as true as the truest of the preceding propositions. Othman was born in Asia Minor, and the germ of his kingdom lay in Bithynia. On this there is thorough unanimity of opinion, though on the value, or want of value, of the orientalism of Asia as contrasted with the occidentalism of Europe there is, in the way of weighty opinion, any amount of diversity. What the mere fact of an origin in Asia carries with it, be it for good or be it for bad, is so thoroughly connected with the particular conditions of time and place as to be utterly unsusceptible of any useful generalization.

They are Mahometans. Being this, they are certainly in a strong contrast to the Christians of Europe. And it may be added that they are Mahometans who have outlived the time when there was even an approximation to equality of power on the part of the two creeds. They are Mahometans on Christian ground, and on ground that will scarcely become Mahometan. They are exceptional Mahometans in a Christian system. The difficulties created by their position are great; but for four hundred years they have not been great enough to prevent the Christians doing political business with them. Still, their Mahometanism is a great distinctive feature; one, indeed, which takes more political prominence than all the rest put together. As Mahometans they are, to a great extent, impracticable members of the European system; and they would be this if they were ever so civilized, ever so European. On the contrary, if Christian, they might be parvenus, Asiatics, and barbarians without much culpability. Besides this, they are not only Mahometans, but they are likely to remain so.

They are, according to many writers on ethnology, Mongolians, the term *Mongolian* being used in a technical, if not a scientific, sense, and the phrase meaning that they belong to a division of mankind different from, and, perhaps, inferior to, the great Caucasian race. In France this notion of race has a greater prevalence than in England, and, in America, for obvious reasons, more prevalence than in France. The Ottomans certainly belong to a division which is in some respects natural, in some artificial, which includes the Mongolians Proper, the Mantshus, the Chinese, the Fins, and others; but what Mongolism carries with it is a point of which the recognized elucidator is unborn. Under any view, however, the Turks, whether from the original osculancy of the classes, or from intermixture, are the most Caucasian (so-called) of the (so-called) Mongols.

They are barbarians. A good deal of the connotation of this term is that of the term Asiatic also. In the eyes of a Greek, they would, doubtless, have been barbarous. In the eyes of a Parisian or a Londoner they are, more or less, barbarous now. But it is not against the ancient Greek, with his merits appraised by himself, or with the Englishman or Frenchman of the nineteenth century, also taken at his own valuation, that either the old Ottoman or the modern Turk is to be matched. His true measure is to be found in Servia, Bosnia, Wallachia, and Albania; and, with these regions as a standard, it is not

11

too much to say that the rudest Ottoman of any century is not below the rudest Skipetar of the same date, the most civilized Vallachian not above the most enlightened Ottoman.

What the Ottomans *do* belong to is this. They belong to a class of which many members, at the present moment, may fairly be called barbarians; of these cognizance will be taken when the Turks of Siberia come under notice. They also belong to a class of which the most civilized members were rude and illiterate, when Greece and Italy were classical. Thirdly, they belong to a class of which they themselves are the most civilized members, but who are not civilized after the fashion of the nations of Western Europe. I am not prepared to say that, in some cases, this difference is not a difference of kind rather than degree.

Asia Minor is Turk as South Britain is English. It may not have been so originally; neither was England originally English. It is so, however, at the present time; and that decidedly, decidedly but not exclusively: just as South Britain is not exclusively and originally English.

With Asia Minor, however, of which the Euphrates seems both now and of old to have been the boundary on the east, it is convenient to associate Armenia and Kurdistan; indeed, that part of Mesopotamia in which the population is Kurd rather than Arab.

The general view of the district thus defined is as follows:—

The mass of the population is Turkish.

The Ægean islands are Greek. So are Proconesus, the peninsula of Cyzicus, and, perhaps, the majority of the Trapezuntines.

The north-eastern extremity is Laz; the Laz form of the Georgian language being spoken as far south and east as the parts about Baiburt and Trebizond.

The eastern frontier, so far as it is other than Turk, is Armenian and Kurd.

On the south and south-east the population becomes Arab.

Turks, Greeks, Lazes, Armenians, Kurds, Arabs—these are our factors for the political ethnology of the parts under notice.

The difference between the ordinary Anatolian Turk of Asia

Minor and the Turk of that special section which bears the name of *Ottoman* or *Osmanli* has already been indicated.

And now Macedonia comes under notice; for, in Macedonia, over and above the ordinary Ottoman of Constantinople, certain fragmentary representatives in Europe of the original Seljukians of Iconium present themselves, even in these latter days. We may call them, in opposition to the Ottomans, Anatolians, or Karamanians, or, what they call themselves, Koniarids.

Even in Europe there are Turks that are other than Ottoman. This is the case with the Tatars of Bessarabia—the *Budjack Tatars*.

Then there are the *Yuruks*.

Then the *Koniarids*.

In Macedonia and Thessaly, and in the parts about Serres and Saloniki the names *Yuruk* and *Koniarid* first occur. Both names apply to the Turks of Asia Minor rather than to the Ottomans. The former is the term applied to the numerous migratory nomads of the Turkoman type in Anatolia; the latter a derivative from *Konieh* or *Iconium*. The time of the Norman invasions, and the time of the earliest Ottoman conquests, are dates assigned to these settlements; and as there is no necessity for referring all the ancestors of all the Koniarids and Yuruks to any single immigration, both may be correct. That some of them are older occupants of European soil than the oldest Ottomans is certain; certain, too, that they represent the old Seljuk Turks of Iconium and Karamania; certain, too, that, compared with the Turks of Constantinople, they are pre-eminently pure in blood. They cultivate the soil. As a body they are industrious, self-relying, and attached to their villages. They bear arms, and constitute in the military organization of the Porte a class by themselves. Left to manage themselves, they are, in some sense, a privileged class; and, even at the present time, some of the powers of the old Dereh Beys are still exercised by their headmen. No class of Turks supplies fewer officials, or men who seek employment in the capital; indeed, the Yuruk and Koniarid capital is Saloniki rather than Constantinople. Kavalla, one of the Koniarid villages, was the birthplace of Mehemet Ali, whose uncle was

11 *

headman of the district. And this is why it was stated, at the very beginning of this book, that, though the Sultan of Constantinople was a true Ottoman, the Khedive of Egypt was not. The Koniarids, as Karamanians, interrupted the victories of the first Sultans. The great Koniarid of the last generation is likely, in Egypt, at least, to plant his dynasty. Either offended or oppressed, he left Macedonia for Egypt with a few followers. The chief Yuruk villages are Gumertzina, Drama, Nevrykopo, Strumitza, Radhovitzi, Tifkis, Karadagh.

There is another Koniarid district in the north of Thessaly.

Thus much for the Ottoman Turks, and, to a certain extent, for the Turks of Iconium ; under whatever name, Iconian, Koniarid, Anatolian, or Karamanian, we choose to designate the representatives of the stock with which the Ottomans are most closely connected, and from which they may, not improbably, be directly deduced. Solyman Shah may or may not have been a Turk of another division ; but it is certain that Othman was a liegeman to the Sultan of Iconium. Be this, however, as it may, after the thorough reduction of Asia Minor the history of the Koniarids is almost identified with the history of the Ottomans up to the present time. What it may be hereafter is another question.

This distinction is important ; and we shall do well to get a clear conception of the original character of the dynasties which, after the reign of Bajazet II., the father of Selim I., the conqueror of Syria and Egypt, constituted the Mahometan part of the Ottoman Empire as it stood in the reign of Solyman I.

The dynasty of Syria was that of the Atabegs.

That of Egypt the dynasty of the Mamelukes.

That of the Barbary States is divided, and its history obscure. But it represented not so much any secondary conquest, like that of the Seljukian Turks, over the successors of the first Caliphs, as the original conquest, as old as the eighth century, of the immediate followers of Mahomet himself. It represented the conquest of the northern coast of Africa, out of which grew that of Spain. It was no part of the Seljukian domain.

And here I hope I may enter a protest against one, at least, of the partially recognised elements in the genealogy of the patriarchal Othman. He is, almost certainly, the son of Ertogrul; not so certainly the grandson of Solyman. Most certainly no descendant of anyone named Seljuk. The real Seljuk seems to me to be the historical Seleucus, neither more nor less; so that when Syria was reduced by the founders of a new dynasty, the name of its most noted ruler was adopted by the conquerors.

CHAPTER VIII.

The Turks other than Ottoman.—Their Area.—The Alani.—The Huns.—The Avars.—The Khazars.—The Petshinegs.—The Uz.—The Cumanians.—The Tshuvash.

Of the Turks represented by the Ottoman Empire not one single occupant of the soil of Asia Minor, of Europe, or of Africa, was on ground originally Turk; nor was there a single acre of their vast dominion that had not been foreign soil to their ancestors, and those ancestors not very remote. The date of the first Turk inroads south of the Caucasus and west of Persia and Armenia, so far as it is traceable from the time of Othman and upwards, is certainly subsequent to the Hejira, and, probably, no earlier than the break-up of the Califat.

This, however, has already been enlarged on; and, by reading what has just been set down backwards, we are prepared for the reverse statement of the Turks now coming under notice. These are the Turks of the original Turkish area; and of this it may be said that not one of them is in contact with their congeners of the south and west. There is the whole of Persia, the Caspian, and the Caucasus between them.

It is not necessary, even in the early history of the Turks of Western and North-Western Asia, to go back to the earliest notices of their possible or probable history, i.e., to the Scythians of Herodotus, or, indeed, to any names anterior to the time of the Gothic and Vandal inroads. When we come to these, however, it is necessary to know who were the nations on the east; in other words, how far the history of the Eastern Empire from the time of Valens, A.D. 375, when the Goths crossed the

Danube, there were Turks, Slavonians, and, probably, the ancestors of the future Russians in the background.

(1.) In the continuous history of these the first name is that of the *Alani*. In respect to this I may remark that the second syllable seems to be long—"*Alāni*," rather than "*Alăni*." In Dionysius Periegetes, they are noticed as the occupants of the valley of the Danube. He writes—

Τοῦ μὲν πρὸς βορέην τετανυσμένα φῦλα νέμονται
Πολλὰ μάλ᾽ ἑξείης Μαιώτιδος ἐς στόμα λίμνης·
Γερμανοί, Σαμάται τε Γέται θ᾽ ἅμα Βαστάρναι τε,
Δακῶν τ᾽ ἄσπετος αἶα καὶ ἀλκήεντες Ἀλανοὶ (v. 302).

It is not certain, however, that the Alani were Turks, though they are specially called *Caucasigenæ* by Sidonius Apollinaris. It is also certain that they occupied some part of the Caucasian range in its north-western half. I believe, however, that they are generally considered to be Circassian rather than Turk, though the question is not beyond a doubt. That the geography points to Circassia is certain; for the country of the Alani lay between Trebizond and the Volga, and it was the route of more than one ambassador between Turkestan and Constantinople, both going and returning. Still, this, even in the reign of Justinian, may have been in the direction of the Caspian more or less Tatar.

(2.) The Alani are certainly earlier than the *Huns*, and their history is more varied. At the same time, the Huns are the nation of which we hear the most. Only, however, for a short period. They are formidable to the Romans during the last quarter of the fourth century, and, for about ten years in the middle of the fifth, they have a terrible representative in Attila. But before his time, and after it, the name is of only secondary importance. The evidence of the bearers of it having been Turks, is better than that in favour of the Alani being such; indeed, except by those who consider them Mongol (in the strict sense of the term), their Turk affinities are pretty generally recognised. It is not to be supposed that before the time of Ruas, the grandfather of Attila, there was no such name as "*Hun*" in Europe. At any rate Ptolemy names the "Χοῦνοι," and that in European Scythia.

(3.) After the Huns, the *Avars* of whom the first notice is between 461 and 465. With these the evidence of their being Turks improves. They seem to have been nearly congeners of the Huns. Their occupancy was the north-western part of Hungary, especially the Interamnium of the Thiess and Danube. But they extended their arms westward, and, for more than two centuries, the whole district of what is now Upper and Lower Austria was held by the Avars. The so-called Hungarian campaigns of Charlemagne were mainly against these intrusive and over-well established Avars; but their power, their language, and their very name had been obliterated, and this obliteration of them became a bye-word.

(4.) The *Khazars* are mentioned by Theophanes as Turks from the east, who assisted the Emperor Heraclius against Chosroes, King of Persia. They conquered the Goths of the Crimea, and took tribute from the Viatitsh, the Severski, and the Polyani. The Viatitsh were, probably, Ugrians or Finns. The Severski and Polyani may have been either Russians or Lithuanians, or one Russian and the other Lithuanian. The Khazars, however, were Turks—Τοῦρκοι ἀπο τῆς ἑώας.

(5.) The *Petshinegs*—Πατζινάκιται, Peczinegi, Postinagi, Pincenates, Petinei, Pezini, Besseni, Bessi, from which we get "*Bessarabia;*" whilst from some others comes the name "*Budjak,*" as applied to the Tatars of that district.

(6.) The *U'z* or *U'zes.*—These are the least conspicuous of the denominations here enumerated; and—

(7.) The *Cumanians* are the last of them.

Such is the general view of the seven chief denominations connected with the history of Rome between the time of the Goths and Vandals in the fourth century, and the great Mongolian inroad of the thirteenth. There are seven denominations; and others of less importance are connected with them. Moreover, each of the seven has not only a special history of its own, but one in which there is always some uncertainty. There is, indeed, of some sort or other, a question connected with every one of them. Hence each will now be considered *in extenso*, and that in the order they stand; for the sequence is chronological. The Alani connect our history with that of the decline of the Western Empire; the Cumani bring it down to the time of Othman, and more than one of his successors.

The *Alani.*—These stand by themselves. It is not only doubtful whether they were Turks, but it is certain that they began their career of conquest before the year 375, the date of the exodus of the Goths from Dacia. Moreover, their whole history is peculiar, and but slightly connected with that of the Huns and Avars. We know, however, the most about them; inasmuch as they are mentioned by the writers of both the Eastern and Western Empire. Indeed, they are noticed by the Jewish historian Josephus. Pliny, however, seems to be the first writer who mentions them. Others speak to their personal appearance. It seems, on this point, to be generally agreed that they were better-looking men than the Huns; and this passes as a reason for making them Circassians. Lucian tells us that they wore less hair than the Scythians; for one of his characters, Makentes, who understood both the Alanian and the Scythian language, had to pass off for a Scythian. So he cut off some of his hair, "for the Alani wear less hair than the Scythians."

The Alans enter into the service of Rome, and, as usual, serve at first in Pannonia. But they soon divide; and a part, under Candax, settles in Mœsia. Another company joins the Burgundians, and we hear of them, under Respendial, at Mentz, in an army out of which will grow the independent kingdom of Burgundy. Others, under Goar, serve under Ætius in Gaul; and Sangiban, their king, has to fight against Attila at Chalons. But it is thought prudent to keep the contingent of the Frank king in his rear, so as to prevent him from changing sides.

A more important union than this with the Burgundians was that of the Alans, the Vandals, and the Suevi. The result of this was the invasion and partition of Spain, where the special Vandali *Silingi* (Vandals of Silesia) took the province of Bætica; the other Vandals, along with the Suevi, Galicia; and the Alani, Lusitania and the Carthaginiensis. Nor was this all. From the Carthaginiensis they proceeded to Carthage itself; a *Vandal* conquest. I know of no other Eastern barbarians except the Heruli who committed themselves to the sea, and no other that went so far from home, as these Alans. However, before they joined Genseric they had been nearly cut to pieces by their old associates.

The King of the Vandals of Lusitania was Atax. In Carthage the title of Gelimer was "*Rex Wandalorum et Alanorum.*"

The Alani, of whom the name lasts the longest, are those of Gaul. Their last king but one is Eochar, their last Beorgor. They are, within a few years, the contemporaries of the last Emperor of Rome, Romulus Augustulus.

Ending with him and beginning before the defection of the Burgundians, the history of the Alans nearly coincides with that of the dissolution of the Western Empire.

The *Huns.*—The current history of the Hun invasion is both indefinite and complicated; and, what is more important, it lies open to a very serious objection. It assumes that there was an invasion at all; or, at least, that there was a specified time when the Huns were strangers to Europe. There was such a time undoubtedly; for there are few districts that, ever since they have had any occupants at all, have always had them of the same race, blood, family, or whatever we choose to call the aborigines. There was, therefore, a time when the ancestors of the Huns dwelt elsewhere; a time when the occupants of what was afterwards the Hun area in Europe were other than Huns. But this time, in the case of the Huns under notice, was not the fourth century of the Christian era, and, possibly, not in the fourth B.C. It probably was earlier than this; early enough to be pre-historic. This, however, is not the ordinary view of the question.

The statement of Procopius as to the origin of the Huns is simply mythical, and that manifestly. It is to the effect that two brothers, Utugur and Kutugur, followed a stag across the Cimmerian Bosphorus, and, so doing, showed their countrymen the way into Europe. There is no date to this. The statement, however, has its value. Both "*Cutugur*" and "*Utugur*" are real national names, and that of populations generally believed to have been either Hun or allied to the Huns. This view the notice of Procopius confirms.

Then there is the date A.D. 375. This is the year when the Goths effect their exodus from Dacia to the opposite province of Mœsia, *i.e.* the year in which the Goths crossed the Danube. In many respects the epoch is a notable one; for it is within a few years from the conversion of the first Germans to Christianity; and these Germans—Goths, Ostrogoths, Visigoths, and Mœsogoths—are all held to have crossed the Danube under the pressure of the Huns, who are now *novi homines*, and unwelcome intruders in Dacia.

Now it is to the interval between this year and the year 458 that the history of the Huns is confined; and, if it were not for the ten years of the reign of Attila, it would not be a history of any remarkable importance. As it is, it is a very obscure one. Attila is the only individual of whom we have any adequate account; and, for some cause or other, or rather from a mixture of several causes, it has never been the practice to speak of Attila without exaggeration. A great deal, if we look either to the character of the king or the nation in respect to their prowess, their ferocity, and their conquering power, which is so commonly assigned to the Huns, is conventional rather than real. We are too much in the habit of making them exceptionally barbarous, numerous, and terrible.

As it is with the king and the people, so it is with the land; for the Hun geography, like the Hun ethnology, must be limited. To the proper domain of Attila may be safely assigned the Interamnium of the Theiss and Danube. That he held this, and made it the district of his capital, we know from the unimpeachable evidence of Priscus. Nor need we doubt that he held the rest of what is now called Hungary, both in the direction of Styria and the direction of Vallachia. The Aluta, however, was probably his limit eastwards: his possession of Transylvania being doubtful. Of actual territory I cannot find an acre more than this, except in the dicta of the historians. What Attila really commanded, and that only towards the end of his life, was a very large army made up of a great variety of elements, and one of which some of the constituents may have come from a great distance, and borne strange names. The Huns were, as a nation, simply what the

Ottomans were, viz., members of a vast and widespread family, of which, like the Ottomans when they crossed the Bosphorus, they were first represented as threatening the majesty of Rome.

In respect to the original country of the Huns of Attila, our best landmark is the locality of the Utugurs ; and this, for the time of Justinian, we get from Procopius, who states that they bordered on the Gothi Tetraxitæ. Now these, we know, were on the neck of the Crimea, and also, from other notices, that a part of their frontier touched the Don. To the Don, then, we trace the Utugurs, the most undoubted members of the Hun denomination.

Of the personal names prior to Attila, Ruas or Rugilas, and Ultis are the most important. Litttle, however, is known about them, for, with the exception of the account of Priscus' embassy to Attila himself, the chief notices of the Huns are from authors of later date than the events.

The tribes conquered by Ruas were the *Amilzuri*, the *Itimari*, the *Tonosures*, and the *Boisci ;* and of these all we know is that Rugilas, or Ruas, conquered them. Such was one of the earliest Hun conquests, probably made in the reign of Valens, certainly before that of Honorius.

Ultis seems to have fought his battles in the next reign, that of Theodosius ; and the notice of him is, with the exception of those of Attila and his sons, the most important we have. The movement of the Huns in general seems always to have been in the direction of Pannonia ; and it is on the Pannonian side of the Danube that we, thus early, read of Ultis. For the troops under him we get the names *Sciri* and *Carpodaci*, the former of whom I hold to have been Turks, and the latter what their name denotes—*Daci* from the *Carpathians ;* probably the same as the Carpi, who, in the Gothic campaigns, claim a higher place as warriors than even the Goths themselves. These last were, almost certainly, other than Turk. However, they are defeated, and that by Theodosius himself, who constrained them to re-pass the Danube.

This we get from Zosimus ; and it is probable that the following account, by Sozomenus, is an expansion of the same event.

It is interesting, however, from what the writer tells us of the Sciri. Ultis had crossed the river, and then re-crossed it, so that his defeat was a complete one, and his escape difficult. The Sciri of his army were well nigh exterminated. These, continues the author, were barbarians, but, before they met with this defeat, numerous. Here, however, they were over-taken in their flight; some slain, others taken alive, others sent in chains to Constantinople. Then it was considered necessary to break them up as a body. Hence many were given away as slaves, and all sold cheap. Some, however, were sent into Asia as colonists. Of these the writer states that he had himself seen several, in Bithynia, in the parts about Mount Olympus.

There were Sciri, however, who, both earlier and later than the time of Sozomenus, might be found elsewhere; nearer to the scene of their defeat, and in a district that still preserves their name, and, possibly, much of their blood. It is these *Sciri* from whom we get the present name *Stiria*, or *Steiermark*. Not, however, because it was their mother country, but because it was the district in which they settled, and that at the time under notice. The Sciri in the army of Ultis were not like the Carpodacæ. The Carpodacæ belonged to the frontier of the invaded country, and had been Dacians and Carpi from time immemorial. The Sciri had not even had to join Ultis in his march. They had been part and parcel of the original army. For we know their locality, and we know that not long before the time of Ultis they were the occupants of the parts about Olbia. More, however, will be said upon this point when the Avars come under notice; for the relation between the Avars, the Sciri, and the Huns, and the Turks in general, is the point which is most especially under consideration—much more so than the mere glimpses we have of the marches and conflicts of the early Huns and the exaggerated conquests of the later.

How their dominion has come down to us in such an ex-aggerated form as that in which it now presents itself is a question; whatever it may be in respect to the reality of its basis, it is certainly a great fact in the history of opinion. It began early. A cotemporary with Attila himself, Sidonius Apollinaris, writes :—

" Barbaries totas in se confuderat Arctos
    Gallia, pugnacem Rugum, comitante *Gelono*,
    Gepida trux sequitur, Scirum Burgundio cogit.
    Chunus, Bellonotus, Neurus, Basterna, Toringus,
    Bructerus, umbrosâ vel quem Nicer alluit unda
    Prorumpit Francus; cecidit cito secta bipenni
    Hercynia in lintres, et Rhenum texuit alno ;
    Et jam terrificis diffuderat Attila turmis
    In campos se, Belga, tuos."

Ad Avitum.

Again, with additional names :—

    " Quidquid languidus axis
    Cardine Sithonio sub Parrhase parturit ursa,
    Hoc totum tua signa pavet. Bastarna, Suevus,
    Pannonius, Neurus, Chunus, Geta, Dacus, Alanus,
    Bellonotus, Rugus, Burgundio, *Vesus, Alites,*
    Bisalta, Ostrogothus, *Procrustes*, Sarmata, *Moschus*,
    Post aquilas venere tuas ; tibi militat omnis
    Caucasus, et Scythicæ potor Tanaiticus undæ."

Ad Majorianum.

The "*Gelonus*" may be invested with something like personality, for in the following lines he is characterized by a special aptitude :—

    " Vincitur illuc
    Cursu Herulus, Chunus jaculis, Francusque natatu,
    Sauromata clypeo, Salius pede, falce *Gelonus*."

Nevertheless, for the circumstance with which this faction may invest its bearer, it is doubtful whether "*Gelonus*" was a real name at the time of any definite population so called, or any known locality. It seems to represent little more than a reminiscence of the older classics ; though it should be added that, along with other names equally poetical, it appears in the *prose* narrative of Ammianus Marcellinus. The population meant was, doubtless, the *Alani*, who appear to have been the *Geloni* of Herodotus, and whose language, which he said was

Hellenic solecistically spoken, has always been one of the several peculiarities so conspicuously prominent in the equivocal history of the Alani, Alauni, Geloni, Budini, Hellenes Solœcizontes, and what not.

But upon their equivocal position in the way of *ethnology* enough has been written already. *Geographically*, they are not far from the frontier here indicated. What the present writer more especially inculcates is, that where we find old names like those in Sidonius in verse, and in Ammianus before him in prose, the extent to which they mixed up the ethnology of one period with that of another is considerable; that of the older period being indefinite and equivocal.

As for the "*Alites*" and "*Procrustes*," I have failed to find anything like them, either near or distant, early or late.

In the "*Neurus*" there is nothing improbable, for it is a name which is found in Herodotus (iv. 100). The *Neuri* here constitute one division out of four; the other three being the *Agathyrsi*, the *Melanchlœni*, and the *Androphagi*. These last are specially stated to speak a language other than Scythian. Respecting the others, nothing is said about their language; the customs of the Neuri and the Melanchlæni being Scythian, and those of the *Agathyrsi* Thracian. These appear for the last time in the times now under notice; and the explanation of the name is a point on which there is a division of opinion. Zeuss* suggests that they may have been "*Khazars*"—word for word. His suggestions upon this point (pp. 709, 714, 715) are well worth close consideration. They are to the effect that the *Akatziri, Akatiri Hunni*, of Priscus, of the time of the sons of Attila, were not only the *Agathyrsi* of the writers before, but the *Khazars* of the writers after him. It is a point, however, upon which, individually, I have for years had to suspend my judgment.

Upon the geography of the "*Neuri*" I speak with more confidence, and place them in the parts about Pinsk; these being within a moderate distance from the camp of Attila, between 52° and 58° North Lat. This is on the Lithuanic or Western frontier of the present Russia.

* Zeuss, D.N., p. 278.

The " *Ves* " may have occupied a corresponding area on the
Eastern side, and have been Fins whose language was known
under that name; inasmuch as a language, so called, is spoken
at the present time, though somewhat farther north, *i.e.* in the
Governments of St. Petersburg and Novogorod. In the eleventh
century Nestor mentions the " *Ves* " as a population. Earlier
still, Jormandes names them as subjects of Hermanric. They
were probably an element in the mixed population of Dacia.
The " *Bisaltæ* " and " *Bastarnæ* " were simply Thracians and
Getæ; and " *Moschi* " belongs to the geography of Caucasus.

The names we know more about are not of the sort that is
indicative of any inordinate extent of dominion. The " *Toringus* "
was the " *Thuringian;* " and this is the first time that we meet
the word *totidem literis*; for, hitherto, we have heard of
nothing but " *Hermunduri.* " Thuringia was simply a country
that Attila passed through; but, except for the special occasion,
it can scarcely be called even a Hun dependency, for we know
that at this very time it had a king of its own, *Basinus*, with
Basina for a queen, and also a daughter, who was the mother
of the great Clovis. That the *Bructeri* from the Lippe and the
Franks from the *Neckar* were anything more than temporary
associates is out of the question.

The " *Gepidæ*," whatever they were in the time of the Catalaunian campaign, and whatever they were in reality, when we
find them in the sixth century, undoubtedly look like a nation
from a considerable distance; for, according to Jornandes, they
came from the mouth of the Vistula. Hence, if we admit this
as evidence for the time of Sidonius, either the actual dominion
of Attila, or of the extent of his alliances, may have reached not
only the Rhine and the Don, but even the Baltic. Nor am I
prepared to say that they did not. I am only showing that
Attila's dominion covered a great deal of space, either in the
maps or in the imaginations of the writers not far from his
time.

And now we see not only its constitution but the limits of
the countries which made it up. Its nucleus was the Hungary
of the present time. It included, at the beginning of the Hun
career, soldiers from its frontier on the east and north-east;

such as the *Basternæ* and the *Bisaltæ* from Thrace and the country of the Getæ, and the *Vesi* from the southern part of the Fin area and the contiguous kingdom of Hermanric. And it added, as it approached Gaul, the *Thuringi*, the *Bructeri*, and the *Franks* of the Neckar. It was a *colluvies gentium* even before it reached the Catalaunian plains. It was specially wondered at as such; and its heterogeneousness, along with the geographical and ethnological differences between the extreme components of it, did much to make it the fear and the wonder for which it has passed from the beginning to the present time.

Then there was the success and the peremptory character of Attila himself. Also the striking circumstances of his death and funeral. Neither were his people of the cast of countenance with which the Gauls and the Romans of the East were familiar, though in Pannonia and Dacia it must have been well known. Ammianus describes it, and the exaggeration of its hideousness culminates in the virulent writing of Jornandes.

If there is exaggeration here, there is more of it when we approach our own times. I cannot carry the ethnography of the old writers farther than the Baltic on the north, the Rhine on the west, and the Volga on the east; nor, if we consider this area simply as a region from which soldiers might be collected, is it too much. The real question is the proportion it bore to the realm, dominion, kingdom, khanate, or empire of the great barbarian. I believe this proportion to have been very small indeed.

But the exaggeration continued and increased; and when what the ancients call *Scythia* came to be known to their descendants as *Tatary* and *Mongolia*, it was not difficult to make the dominion of Attila co-extensive with the race, stock, or family to which he and his subjects undoubtedly belonged. And so it was that when the literature of China began to be recognised, and when the closely allied histories of Mongolia and Turkestan were studied by the Oriental scholars of the century, it was an easy matter, by the time of Gibbon, to bring the great Hun area up to the Wall of China—and so far east was it brought—in one sense rightly, in another wrongly.

For, if we change the special kingdom of the Huns of Attila for the whole of that part of the world which was occupied by the Turkish Tatars and the Mongolian Calmucks, there is at the bottom of it not only a certain amount of verisimilitude but an actual verity. There *is*, in its way, a unity which connects not only the different divisions and sub-divisions of the two denominations, but the two denominations—Turk and Mongol—themselves. More than this, there is sometimes an actual and recognized suzerain, such as was Tshingizkhan in the thirteenth century; but there is not a shadow of reason to believe that Attila was anything of this kind; though the Disabulus of the time of Justinian—of whom more will be said in the sequel—may have considered himself as such.

The chronology of the Huns is as insufficient as the geography; and nine-tenths of the historical evidence that has come down to us applies only to the reign of Attila. Of special value on this point is that of Priscus. For the beginning of the Hun period our best authority, Ammianus Marcellinus, leaves us within the first three years; and what he tells us applies to the Goths rather than the Huns.

For the interval the all-important statement is a single date—an important one, because it implies another. It is to the effect that in the Consulate of Hierius and Ardabur the Pannoniæ were recovered by the Romans from the Huns. This was A.D. 427, and before the reign of Attila. Moreover, we get the additional statement that the provinces thus recovered had been held by the Huns *fifty years*.

This takes us back to A.D. 377—only two years after the crossing of the Danube by the Goths, which is unanimously assigned to A.D. 375.

It is in the filling-up and the continuation of the history of the Huns during this half century that we are most especially at fault. Ammianus is a trustworthy authority for the first few years; and for the time of Attila, Priscus, and the writers of the Western Empire, and Cassiodorus in the time of Theodoric, are our best lights. But the little we know about the intervening period is mainly due to incidental notices; the most important of them being from two writers of Church

History, Socrates and Solzomenus, and relating more to their theology than their wars. Then, in the sixth century, comes Jornandes—a good authority for the parts immediately of his own time, but when he comes to topography, and meddles with the ethnology and origin of the Goths, of no more account than our own Geoffrey of Monmouth.

But this is the character of all the writers of the Eastern Empire. They always introduce their hypotheses; and, unfortunately, these have, up to the present time, passed for history. It is no part of the present work to analyze either this special one of Jornandes, or those of others of the same class. It is enough to inform his readers that Jornandes identifies the Goths with the Getæ, the Getæ with the Scythians, and adopts as the antecedents of the countrymen of Theodoric everything that can be found from Homer downwards about anything, Getic or Scythian, that he can find in the course of his reading; for he is a firm believer of anything whatever that is to be found in a book. The result is that, *inter alios et alias*, Alexander the Great and Thamyris, and the old kings of Egypt, were Goths : indeed, he finds the Goths everywhere, and deduces them indirectly from every country but Germany, of which he shows a most remarkable ignorance, and leaves it out of his account altogether. Neither does he seem to have known the language of his Goths.

Of the fifty years' occupancy, then, of the Pannonias we know next to nothing. The most important notice is the following:—

A.D. 481, the panegyrist Pacatus, on enlarging upon a victory by Theodosius over Maximus, the usurper in *Gaul*, makes a special reference to the loss of the Pannonias—*perdidi infortunata Pannonias, lugeo funus Illyrici*. On the other hand, however, he enlarges upon the extent to which "those *Goths, Huns,* and *Alani*" (*Gothus ille, et Hunnus, et Alani*), "formerly the enemies of the Empire, were now obedient soldiers in the Roman service, who have learnt the Roman watchwords and the Roman words of command, and who now follow the standard they opposed."

Here we have, in the fourth year of the Hun rule, one allusion to the loss of the provinces, and another of something like amity between the Huns and the Romans; and in the same reign we have already had the great victory of Theodosius over the Huns and Sciri. There is a gap in the evidence here.

As for the details of the crossing of the Danube, our evidence is even worse; especially in respect as to the doctrine that the movement of the Goths was, in the way of cause and effect, connected with pressure on the part of the Huns, before whom the Goths are said to have fled. Of anything like this there is not a particle of evidence; nor can we see our way to it as a probability.

The state of what we may call either *"Hungary"* or *"Dacia"* in the reign of Valens was, in the way of geography, as follows. The Goths had one portion of the area, the Huns another; and in the direction of Pannonia, the Huns lay between the Gothic and the Roman frontiers. The *Thervings* (for *Visigoth* is a later name) held all Transylvania up to the Dniester. By the Dniester they were separated from the *Grutungs* (*Ostrogoths*), whose domain was called *Vallis Grutungorum;* while the Transylvanian part of the Therving territory was called *Caucoland=* (*Highland*), a German compound. There is no evidence of any Huns in either district, nor yet behind it; the reasons for the belief that the Huns pushed them either southward or westward consisting only in the *ex post facto* hypothesis that they came from beyond the Don. They did this undoubtedly; but not in the time of Valens, in whose time the Hun part of Dacia was as distinct from the Gothic as Brittany is from Normandy. On the west side of Transylvania Athanaric had built a wall against them.

On the other hand, the Huns occupied the valley of the Maros and the Interamnium of the Theiss and the Danube; the level plains; and, so doing, abutted on Pannonia. So far as they were continuous with their congeners of the parts between the Don and the Volga, the communication seems to have been to the north, and not the east, of the great Goth area; *i.e. viâ* Buchovinia, Podolia, and Ekaterinoslav. But there is no evidence that the communication was kept up, or that a single Hun, before the time of Attila, came from any part of Asia, or pressed upon any part of Gothland. When we hear of them in connection with the Goths it is along the frontier of the Danube, and on the side of the Romans; so that if there is any *vis a tergo* at all it must have been the Goths rather than the Huns who exerted it. Wallachia and Moldavia seem to have the occupancy of a different nation—the " *Thaifalæ.*"

So much for the geography. The political view coincides with it. The so-called Gothic crossing of the Danube was only one out of many; some being Goths, others Huns. The one of 375 was certainly not the last, nor does it seem to be the first. But, whether for the last or the first, or for any intermediate one, of pressure on the part of the Huns there is no definite sign; though it is not denied that there are expressions from writers which suggest it. There *is* a war which is connected with some passage or other in or about 375. There is a campaign against the Goths in the reign of Valens. But the assailants, here, are not the Huns but the Romans.

What I submit to the consideration of the reader is as follows :—

1. That the Goths and the Huns held definite and distinct parts of the *non*-Wallachian parts of " *Dacia* " or " *Hungary* "— Wallachia and parts of Moldavia being held by the *Thaifalæ*; so that the Thaifalæ held the middle district on the northern side of the Danube.

2. That the Gothic area faced the Roman on the *eastern* extremity, or on the lower part of the Danube; Moldavia and Bessarabia.

3. That the Huns held the parts on the *west*, or the parts on the bend of the river, *i.e.* the valleys of the Maros and Theiss; and that there is no evidence of any hostile contact between the two causing either a Hun or a Goth to cross the river.

4. That, nevertheless, *both* crossed it, more than once. But this was *proprio motu; i.e.* with no pressure of the one upon the other either way.

5. That there was no sudden advent of the Huns from Asia, so as to create a *vis a tergo*, propelling the Goths southwards; but rather that the Huns, who lay *between* the Goths and the

Danube, may have been there *in situ* from any length of time previously.

6. That the relations to one another and to the Romans were nearly as follows:—

  a. There was fighting between the Thervings, or Visigoths, of Transylvania (*Caucoland*) and the Huns, *within the limits of Dacia;* the war, for which we have special evidence, being one in which Athanaric, the Judge of the Thervings (Visigoths), so far from crossing the Danube, subdued the Slavonians of Caucoland, and built a wall on the Hun frontier as a defence against the men of the valley of the Maros; from which wall to the Dniester (the frontier of the Ostrogoths) his domain extended.

  b. That, besides their wars with the Huns, the Thervings (Visigoths) had a religious feud between themselves; *i.e.* one between the Arian and the orthodox Christians.

  c. That both had their wars against the Romans.

  d. That, in these wars, both made peace for a time; and that, when this was done, a certain portion of the combatants generally entered the Roman service as soldiers.

  e. That this readiness to be taken into the pay of the Empire had much more to do with the crossings of the Danube, on the parts of both the Goth and the Hun, than any pressure exerted by the one upon the other.

Nevertheless, in suggesting all this, I do not deny that the great passage of the Lower Danube in 375 was something very like a national migration; nor yet that there is something like evidence as to a dislike on the part of the Goths to their contact with the Huns.

There is a passage in which tells that "when the report of Athanaric's troubles spread among the other Goths, the greater part of his followers, being pinched as to the necessities of life, sought a domicile remote from the knowledge of the barbarians."

There is another, and a stronger one, to the effect that "in the beginning of the reign of Theodosius, the nation of the

Scythians, *driven out* (ἐξελαυνόμενοι) by the Huns, crossed the Danube. The leaders were those highest in race and dignity."

The first of these is from Ammianus, a cotemporary to the events he describes; the other from Eunapius, subsequent to them. What do they tell us? Simply that there was a war between the Huns and the Thervings on the line of Athanaric's wall, on the western frontier of Transylvania; that there were concurrent wars with the Romans; that the Emperor Valens cut his way from the Danube, through the Hun country, to the Therving frontier; that he weakened the power of the Therving judge, Athanaric; that attacks on the part of the Huns followed; that Athanaric was annoyed and, perhaps, distressed by them; that his distress became known; that the "greater part of his people sought a district remote from all knowledge of the barbarians." This place of refuge, I hold, was not on the north of the Danube, but in the parts near its mouth—the parts where the Therving (*Visigoth*) frontier on the east approached that of the Grutungs (*Ostrogoths*) on the south-east; in other words, it was from one part of the Gothic area to another—both lying at this time south of the Danube.

Such is the sketch, not so much of the actual history of the Hun district, of *Hungary* or *Dacia*, as of the evidence concerning it upon which the current opinion as to its general character rests. For the beginning of it, we have seen that there is confusion as to the relations of the Goths and the Huns. For the end, we have seen that there is exaggeration as to the character of Attila as a potentate and conqueror. For the interval, especially for the fifty years during which the *Pannoniæ* were Hun occupancies, we have seen little more, in the way of detail, than a blank. The one great fact, however, which is undoubtedly real, is that of the conquest (almost certainly by Attila) of the Gothic part of his domain. At the beginning all the country between the western frontier of Transilvania and the Don was Gothic—Visigoth or Ostrogoth, as the case may be. But this we get from inference. Eastern and North-Eastern Dacia was Goth in 375; in 450 it was Hun. It was the realm of either Athanaric or the successors of Hermanric in the time of Valens; and it was Hun before the

death of Honorius.   But I have not found the details of its
conquest.   All we know is that it must have taken place.

After the break up of the dominion of Attila, the only conquerors of much historical importance are either called *Avars*,
or *" Avars or Huns "* (*Avares qui et Chuni*).   The least that
we infer from this double appellation is, that the history of the
Huns is superseded by that of the Avars.   How far the Avars
were absolute Huns under another name, or *vice versâ*, I cannot
say.   There was some difference between them.   But I think
that it is a very slight one.

Again, when the Huns lost their dominion in *Dacia* (*Hungary*), they were superseded by the *Gepidæ*; and *Dacia*, by
A.D. 500, had become *Gepidia*.   But as, before 600, it was
recovered by the Avars, it will be under the notice of that denomination that the short, but important, history of the Gepidæ
will be considered.

The *Avars.*—Whatever may be the dimensions of the power
and influence of the Huns, that of the Avars has been greater;
indeed, though less conspicuous as a nation, the Avars have
had both a longer and a more varied history than their predecessors.   They have not, perhaps, had a ruler who ever had
the terrible notoriety, or who has borne such bad names, as
the exaggerated Attila; but they have had a really great king
in Baian, and, in him, the founder of a kingdom of longer
duration than Attila's.   Baian's foundation lasted from the
time of Justinian to that of Charlemagne, and ran farther
westward into Europe than either that of the Huns who preceded, or that of the Ottomans who came after it; and it was
mainly against the Franks that it was held.

Now comes a perplexing question—How far were the two
denominations different?   Were the Avars Huns, or the Huns
Avars?   How far were either or both Turks?

As early as A.D. 465, or earlier, we get a single notice of
them.   It stands alone for the time.   It is a strange one.   But
it comes from a cotemporary writer—Priscus.

It runs thus:—" At that time the *Saraguri, Urugi,* and
Onoguri sent ambassadors to the Eastern Romans; these being
nations dispossessed of their own country by the attacks of the

Saviri, whom the Avars had expelled; the Avars themselves being emigrants from a land of their own on the coast of the Ocean, on account of the appearance of a host of griffins (γρῶπες), concerning which it was the saying that they would not go away before they had devoured the whole human race." This, then, it was that drove the Avars from their own country upon the Saviri, and the Saviri—to whom the tale seems most especially to belong—upon the Urugi and their neighbours.

At the first view this statement seems to condemn itself, and, with its story of the insatiable griffins, looks simply supernatural and mythic. We cannot but at once ignore such an origin. On the other hand, however, we must remember that one of the most notable characteristics of the Byzantine historians is their accuracy in the geography and ethnology of their own times, in contrast to the remarkable erroneousness of their speculations as to anything connected with the question of origin and original affinity. They are as pre-eminently safe in the former as worthless in the latter department. Again, we must remember that the present authority, Priscus, is not only writing of an event which took place during his lifetime, but upon one in Hun history; and as a writer upon this he is admittedly *instar omnium*. He was the ambassador to the court, such as it was, of Attila himself, and every statement that comes from him is of more than ordinary value. We must believe, then, what he says, not only about the Avars, but what he adds in respect to the Saraguri, Urugi, Onoguri, and Saviri.

So much for the statement of Priscus—eminently trustworthy, except where its erroneousness betrays itself, and remarkable for its isolation. It will not be till A.D. 558 that we hear anything more about the Avars. Then, however, they are emigrants.

Sarosius is the king of the Alans; and him the Avars ask to introduce them (ὡς δι' αὐτου γνώριμοι γένοιντο) to the Romans. This he does, through Justin, who was then the commander in Lazistan (ἡ Λαζικη). Then comes the arrogant and extravagant speech of their legate Kandich, to the effect that " we, the Avars, are of all men the greatest and most powerful, invincible, and irresistible; but we are willing to come to an agreement with the Emperor Justinian, and become associates of the Empire, defend it well, and receive for our services honourable presents, yearly stipends, and the possession of a fertile district "

This is one account, in which the name of these sturdy beggars is " *Avar*," purely and simply. But in another it is the " *Var* " and the " *Chuni* " (Ουαρ καὶ Χοῦννι), who only call themselves *Avars*. This is from Theophylact, *not* a cotemporary authority. " *Chunni*," word for word, is " *Hun*," and Χοῦνοι, as the name is found in Ptolemy. These were a small part of a larger tribe. They were runaways. They were living in Europe. They called themselves *Avars*. The title of their ruler was *Khagan*. They pressed upon the Hunuguri, the Savirs, and Sarselt—a new name, but one as shall hereafter be known as a fortress on the Don, on the frontier between the Khazars and the Petshineks, and other Hun tribes. They frighten them, and get bought off. The intruders then went and gave themselves out as *Avars*; for the Avars were the most active tribe of the Scythians.

Is there any doubt as to " *Var* " being, word for word, *Avar*, and " *Chunni* " word for word *Hun* ? If there be, the following sentence from the same writer dispels it :—" Even to our own times the Ψευδάβαροι, for so it is more appropriate to call them, are distributed according to their genealogies and their old names ; and some call themselves (ὀνομάζονται) *Var*, and some are called (πρὸς αγορεύονται) *Chunni*.

In the next passage from Menander we have the two names turned into one, and " *Var et Chunni* " becomes " *Varchonitæ*."

The matter, however, of this is more curious than the form. The date is A.D. 575 ; and about this time there was more than one legation between the capital of the Khakhan of the Turks and Constantinople. And we can easily imagine that, *inter alia*, something may be said about the *Var*, *Chuni*, *Varchonites*, or *Avars*, which will dispel the ambiguity. Something *was* said about them, and that somewhat offensively. "These *Varchonites*," said Turxanth, the son of Disabulus, " are our slaves and runaways whom you have taken into alliance. They are our subjects ; and when I choose they shall come to me. I will send in my cavalry as a scourge after them, and when they see it they shall fly to the uttermost parts of the earth. I know not only the course of the Ister, but the Hebrus; and I know how they crossed them—those slaves of ours, the Varchonites." This is the language of a man who is not thinking of how the Varchonites got from Asia into Europe; but rather of how, when in Europe, they got into the Roman Empire.

Again, in 568, Maniach, who, like Turxanth, is delivering an answer to an embassy from Justinian, says: "Tell us, what the number of these Avars is, and if there be any *still* with you (εἰ πνες ἔτι παρ' ὑμῖν); there are some who *still* (ἔτι) love us. Those who some time back ran away (δηπούθεν) are, I suppose, *about* (ἀμφὶ) twenty thousand." This is not the language of one asking for information concerning any recent exodus of his subjects, but rather that of one who wishes to know about the remains of an old one. Some of them, he thinks, may *still* retain some friendship for us.

The immediate effect of the embassy was that the Emperor Justinian found it convenient to get rid of his Avars, true or false, as the case might be. So he took them into his pay; and, accordingly, the first of their services was to turn upon the Utigurs and Savirs, and (a new denomination) the *Zali*, either Turks, like themselves, or Caucasians. Also against the *Antæ*, who were Slavonians. But this was not what the Emperor wanted. His special wish was to keep them away from Constantinople; their ambition being to be taken into the personal service of the Empire. But, be this as it may, Lower Mœsia (Bulgaria) was the quarters that Justinian meant for them.

The next Emperor, Justin, was more peremptory. The applicants to his predecessor seem to have remained in the parts about the Don, and to have applied for more desirable quarters through an embassy to Constantinople. "And here," writes Menander, "they did not care to remain in the capital to no purpose, nor yet to leave it without some result. Eventually, however, they decided upon going back to their tribesmen (ὁμοφόλοι), and, with them, to unite in some inroad on the Franks, wondering at the apology (ἀπολογία) of the Emperor."

From this time begins the continuous history of the Avars, *eo nomine*. Avars in the definite sense of the word ; Avars who were neither *Var* and *Chunni*, nor *Varchonites*, nor yet *Pseudavari*, but Avars, so far as the name goes, pure, simple, and unmistakeable.

It is not, however, in Lower Mœsia that we shall find them; though that was the province assigned to, or intended for, them by Justinian. Just where we found the Huns under Ultis, in the reign of Theodosius I., there we find the Avars under Baian in the reign of Justin II. ; and, on their frontier, the Lombards in the direction of Italy, and the Gepidæ in the old domain of Attila. We know how the Avars and Langobards made a compact against these Gepidæ, and the result of it. The Langobards invaded Italy, and the Avars recovered Dacia. The Emperor, it may be added, favoured the Lombards, and, so far, may be said to have favoured the Avars. But this is all. As a general rule, the relations between these last and the Empire were hostile.

In the reigns of Justin II. and Tiberius the hostilities are at first on the frontier, chiefly for the possession of Sirmium, which more than once changes its masters. Then the Avars have a fleet as well as an army, and by sea they beleaguer Constantinople. But Tiberius consents to pay tribute, and gets them to help him in coercing the Slavonians. Sirmium, however, again becomes Avar. But the great struggle against their great king Baian takes place in the reign of Maurice, and this is spread over the whole valley of the Danube, and beyond the Balkan. Twice under Maurice did the Avars invest Constantinople, and twice did he, partly by arms and partly by tribute, keep them at bay. And then the worthless Phocas succeeded him. And then came the Emperor of many enemies, Heraclius; twice, in the west, besieged in his capital by the Avars, and, in the east, throughout his reign engaged in a hopeless war against the Persians, now inflamed by the fearless and aggressive spirit of Mahometanism. It was for the Bulgarians, rather than for the Avars, that the empire under Heraclius was thus distracted.

Of the Avar inroads in Macedonia and Greece, it was the

Slavonians rather than the Avars that became the dominant population. Dalmatia, like Macedonia, was overrun; nor was Albania wholly unmolested. Vast, however, as this area was, it gave no permanent territory to the Avars. The farther the invader's hordes moved from Thrace, the smaller became the Avar element, and the longer the occupancy lasted the more Slavonic it became. Thus, Macedonia may have been, in the first instance, as much Avar as Slav. In the Peloponnesus, however, there seems to have been no appreciable Avar element.

"Has the man," is the indignant and poetic repudiation of anything like dependence by the Slavonian Dauritas—"has such a man been born, and warmed by the beams of the sun, who hath the power thus to subject us? It is our wont to take what belongs to others; not that others should take what is ours. Upon this we stand firm, so long as there shall be battles and swords." I give this as it stands in Zeuss, and am willing to believe that such were the *ipsissima verba* of Dauritas. At the same time I cannot but think that I have heard something like it before, and that in metre. I subjoin* the original as it stands in Zeuss.

The Frank cotemporaries of Baian are Chlotaire I. and Sigisbert I. At the death of Chlotaire the Avars invade Thuringia. Where the campaign began we know not; but we know that two battles were fought on the same battle-field. Gregory of Tours, a Frank and a cotemporary, is the primary authority; and, rather as a good patriot than a bad geographer, he writes that the battles were fought in the Gauls (Gallias), and that the Franks, under Sigisbert, conquered, and made peace. By implication we must understand that the *Huns* (*Chuni*), for this is what he calls them, went either back or backward: for he writes in the sequel, " *Chuni vero iterum in Gallias venire conabantur adversus quos Sigisbertus cum exercitu dirigit.*" He then gives the details, to the effect that " when they ought to begin the conflict, the Huns, those amongst them

---

* Zeuss, D. N., p. 731.—Καὶ τὶς ἄρα, ἔφασαν, οὗτος πέφυκεν ἀνθρώπων, καί ταῖς τοῦ ἡλίου θέρεται ακτῖσιν, ὃς τὴν καθ' ἡμᾶς ὑπήκουον ποιήσεται δύναμιν; κρατεῖν γεγὰρ ἡμεῖς τῆς ἀλλοτρίας ἐιώθαμεν, καὶ οὐκ ἕτεροι τῆς ἡμεδαπῆς καὶ ταῦτα ἡμῖν ἐν βεβαίῳ, μέχρι πόλεμοι τε ὦσι καὶ ξίφη.

who were skilled in magic, presented different fantasies (*diversas eis fantasias ostendunt*), and conquered the Franks easily. Then the army takes flight, and the king is left surrounded by the enemy. But Sigisbert was accomplished and artful, and those whom he could not conquer by valour he subdued by the art of making gifts. So he made them accordingly; and it was agreed that so long as he lived there should be peace between them." On the other side, the king, who was called a Khakhan (*Gaganus*), made gifts in return.

Paulus Diaconus gives the same account with an improvement in the geography and ethnology. He tells us that the battle was fought in Thuringia, near the Elbe; and calls the Avars by their right name, so far correcting the text of Gregory. But he adds, what we fail to find in Gregory, that the second battle was fought on the same field as the first.

I think it likely, from the two accounts and the subseqnent history of the Franks, that this was a defensive war on the part of the Avars. It was fought near the frontiers of Thuringia and Bavaria; and that it was a hostile movement in the direction of that province, which was the next addition to the now powerful empire of the Franks. A third account, by Menander, states that the Avars were starving, but that they were relieved by Sigisbert, on the promise that they should leave the country within three days. And this they did.

Paulus Diaconus, as we have seen, calls the *Chuni* of Gregory "*Avares*"; but he adds the name as a synonym—*Chuni qui et Avares*.

So he does in another place; for there was another war under Childebert and the famous Brunechild. And here again the battle-field is in Thuringia; and here, again, the names are "*Huni, qui et Avares*."

The conflicts after this between the Avars and the Franks are defensive, and the Avars are the allies of the Slavonians of Bavaria and Stiria, which are now either partially or wholly Frank.

In the direction of Italy but few attempts at conquest were made. The old alliance between the Avars and the Langobards had something to do with this; nor was the fighting power of the conquerors of Italy wholly uninfluential. At any rate no one knew it better than the Avars. Still there were differences; and one, at least, was serious—the siege by the Avars of Friuli. On the whole, however, the relations of the two concurrent, and to some extent allied, kingdoms were peaceful.

Except these two, I find, in my great and indispensable authority, Zeuss, no other wars on Frank soil between the Franks and the Avars; and, except certain minor cases of indirect assistance given by the Avars to the Slavonians of Stiria and Carinthia against the Frank conquerors, any other instance of intercourse. Nor will there be any before the fortieth year of the reign of Chlotaire II., A.D. 625.

Thus long has Avaria existed without any signs of decay, though it is evident that this may be due to the little we know about it. It will last, like the twin dynasty of the Langobards, many years longer. Yet it never comes to any brilliant climax; and Baian, under whom it took birth, is the first and last of its heroes. But under Chlotaire II. and Dagobert we get *"the beginning of the end."* This is the time when its frontier is first contracted, though to what extent we know not. There is no foreign enemy and no pitched battle. There is the germ of a great war, and the beginning of a vast national struggle which is still going on; a contest of twelve centuries already, and likely to last—the conflict between Western Germany and North-Eastern Slavonia. This is what grew out of the *Domain of Samo.*

The Domain of Samo was a result of a partial dismemberment of the kingdom of Avaria, a part cut off from the western extremity. This is all that the Avars have to do with. The rest was fought out between the Slaves and the Franks. But it was by the domain of Samo that the Avars lost territory.

Samo, writes Fredegar, the continuation of Gregory of Tours, was a Frank merchant from Sens. The boundary of Avaria was the Ens, and the mass of the population Slaves. The Avars were, probably, a dominant minority; and we know what this is. Their subjects are oppressed. They rebel, and they make Samo their champion. Fredegar writes that they made him their king. How far the rebellion spread, and what it took away from

Avaria, is unknown. Probably it extended to the Hungarian frontier. But beyond being the *causa mali,* the Avars seem to have taken no part in it. There is fighting between the Slaves and the Franks; and Dervan, a Serb of the parts between the Saale and Elbe, though he had long been friendly to the Franks, betakes himself *ad regnum Samonis.* In this there were probably few or no true Avars. In other words, it was as in Macedonia. The Avars had become Slavonized. This is the state of Avaria during the whole of the reign of Dagobert. That the dynasty of Samo ended with Samo himself is what we expect. There is no sign of the Avars of Hungary doing anything to dethrone him; and it is certain that neither the Franks nor the Bavarians allowed Avaria to become a principality.

The successor of Dagobert was Clovis II., the first of *Rois Faineants.* The mayor was Pepin of Landen. But there was much that employed the mayors nearer home; and nothing beyond a few casual notices of the Avars before the time of Charlemagne. Bavaria, with the exception of the parts between the Ens and the Wienerwald, is the only part of Bavaria that is not Frank; and from this we can scarcely expect anything like offensive warfare. It is well for these Avars of this out-lying district that they are not coerced by the Franks. But the seventh century is not a time when the Frank power is formidable. The little opportunity that the Avars had of invading their neighbours was on the side of Italy and Croatia. But there is no evidence either of gain or loss in the way of territory on this side. But whether there is much or little to be known about the Avars of the sixth and seventh centuries, it must be remembered all our knowledge applies to a mere fraction of their history; that of the Avars of Pannonia as opposed to Dacia, and of Austria as opposed to Hungary; and this means the Avaria of the German and Slavonic frontiers. Of that vast tract of country north of the Danube, and extending from Moravia to Moldavia, and from the Danube to the Carpathians, we know nothing; nor shall we till the time of Charlemagne.

In A.D. 782 the Avars send an embassy to him *pacis causa;* but in 788 they make a double onset on the Franks, one in the parts about Friuli, and one in Bavaria. In the latter they are beaten in two battles, probably by the Bavarians, unassisted. In 790 there is a contest as to the boundaries. This brought down Charlemagne himself upon the Avars in their own territory, and that with an army on each side of the Danube. In this campaign he drove them into the Wienerwald. Here, the Franks marched as far west as the mouth of the Raab. Then we have sure evidence of internal disunion; the murder of the Khaghan; and the result is the campaign which sealed the fate of Avaria. It is under the direction of Erich, Duke of Friuli, Charles's illegitimate son Pepin, and a Slavonian auxiliary named Vonomyr. Then it is that Pepin invades the " *Campus,*" and breaks into the " *Hringi.*"

These *Hringi, Ringi,* or *Rinni,* were *Rings;* for the word is not Avar, but German. The Avar word was *hegi.* In 979 we read of a place near the confluence of the Erlaf with the Danube called *Erdyasthegi,* a compound, wherein the first part of the word is Slavonic. What these *Rings* were we learn from a curious conversation between a monk of St. Gallen and a soldier named Adalbert. It is substantially a report of a dialogue. I have, with a very slight change, put it in the form of one; somewhat abbreviated.

Adalbert: The land of the Avars is bound by five *rings* (*circulos*).

The Monk (who thinks he means wattled hurdles—*circulos vimineos*) : And what is there wonderful in that, *Domine?*

Adalbert: Nine *hegin.*

The Monk (more curiously, thinking that he was speaking of hurdles round corn fields) : Rings!

Adalbert: One ring is so large that it would take-in all the country between Zurich and Constance—stumps of oak, beech, and fir; twenty feet from side to side; twenty feet high; the part between, all stone, or hard lime; at the top of this, big turves; between these, pollard trees, like those we see here, with shoots and leaves from the stumps of them; between these, villages and granges (*vici et villæ*) within call of each other; then buildings (*edificea*), with walls so thick, and doors so narrow, that you could not, if you tried to rob them, get into

13

them, much less get out (*portæ non satis late erant constitutæ per quas latrocinandi gratia non solum exteriores sed etiam interiores exire solebant*).

"The second village is like the first in its building—ten German miles, which make forty Italian; extends in like manner to the third; and so on to the ninth; some circles larger than others.

"From circle to circle, holdings and dwelling-houses (*possessiones et habitacula*) on every side, so that you might signal by sounding a trumpet. To these fastnesses, for more than two hundred years, all the wealth of all kinds of the people of the West were brought together, at the time when the Goths and Vandals were making the Eastern world a wilderness."

There is another word, which looks like a German one, but which may be Avar, or even Slavonic—"*Befulci.*" It occurs in Fredegar, our authority for the *regnum Samonis*. The system of the *Befulci* was one of the grievances of the Slavonians.

"The *Befulci*," writes Fredegar, "who were Vends (*Winidi Befulci Præfulci*), from the earliest time belonged to the Chuni; and when the Huns (*Chuni*) went with an army against any nation whatever, they—the Huns—stood with their army in muster before the camp; but the Vends fought. If the Befulci got the better, the Huns, then, moved forwards to take the spoil; but if the Vends were conquered, they resumed the fight with the help of the Huns. Therefore, they were called *Befulci* (*Befulei, Præfulci*) by the Huns, because in the double conflict of the combat (*duplici congressione certaminis*) in pitched battles (*vesita prælia*), they went before the Huns."

Now this, better than any derivation or any definition, tells us what the *Befulci* were, and what they had to do; and this is the main point. It may, or may not be, an Avar word. It is difficult, however, to give an exact rendering of it.

There are, however, at the present time, two words in Turkish, either of which may have been the original one. These are *Azab*, and *Akindji*, both common in the accounts of the Ottoman campaigns; and either of them, with an allowance for the difference of date, gives us a fair notion of the function of these miserable *Befulci*. The following is from a writer[*] of the beginning of the seventeenth century :—

" Besides these Janizars he hath the Azapi (properly belonging to the Gallies), a base Besonio, fitter for the spade than the sword, entertained rather with numbers to tire, than by prowess to defeat armies, opposing them to all dangerous services ; yea, to fill trenches with their slain carcasses, and then to make bridges with their slaughtered bodies, for the Janizars to pass over to the breaches. And as the Romans had their legions and auxiliaries, the one the flower of their chivalry, the other as an aid or augmentation, even so the Turk accounteth his stipendiary horsemen or Timariots the sinews of his arms ; the Alcanzi (such as he presseth out of towns and villages) scarecrows, and for ostentation; the Janizars as the Prætorian legions, and the Azapi as a rabble of peasants ; being, indeed, mere hinds, and tied to serve on horseback for certain privileges which they hold, in number about thirty or forty thousand, without allowance of any pay, save what they get by spoil and rapine.

" Besides these he hath at command the Tatars as auxiliaries, whereof there are likely threescore thousand, who live by spoil, and serve also without pay. In their marches they scour the country two days' journey before. Next them follow the Achangi, then the Timariots, then those few Azamoglani that be ; and, lastly, the Janizars. The Chauses ride on horseback (and carry bows and arrows, besides their maces and simiters), after whom followeth the Sultan, with the officers of the Court, and archers of his guard ; the Spahies, as aforesaid, encircling the flanks of this brave battle. The pages, eunuchs, and carriages, followed by another fort of auxiliaries, called voluntaries, make the rear ; and these follow only upon hope to be entertained in their rooms of the slain Spahies and Janizars ; their commanders being nothing curious (in these times) to receive those that be not the sons of Christians into orders. Thus have we lively described his forces at land.

A.D. 630, there was a debated succession in Pannonia, the Avars electing one king, and the *Bulgarians* another. The

---

* Relations of the most famous Kingdoms, &c. thorowout the World, &c., pp. 515, 516. London, 1630.

former prevail; and nine thousand Bulgarians, with their wives and children, are constrained to seek a refuge among the Franks. Thereupon, Dagobert commands them to remain during the winter in Bavaria, in order that time may be allowed for considering what next was to be done. So they are quartered upon the different householders of the country; and when they have thus been dispersed, Dagobert orders a general massacre of them. Then, in one and the same night, every Bavarian puts to death the Bulgarians that he is sheltering under his roof. The few that escaped, to the amount of seven hundred in all (*vivis, uxoribus et liberis*), under Alticeus as their captain, settle in the Slavonian March (*Marca Winidorum*), of which Wallucus was the Marquis. There they lived many years. This is the notice of Fredegar, the Frank historian. The Langobard authority, Paulus Diaconus, seems to supply a continuation of it. He does not profess to know why; but, in the reign of Grimoald, a leader of the Bulgarians, named *Alzeco*, offered his services to that king, who received them, and settled then in certain districts to the north of Naples, of which Sepianum, Bovianum, and Isernia, are mentioned by name. Alzeco, himself, became the Duke of Gastaldium, and in the time of the historian the Bulgarian language was still spoken in the above-named districts.

The history of the Huns, such as it is, is mainly the history of the beginning and the end of a name; and, such as it is, the history of the Avars has been much of the same kind.

When the history of the Huns ended, that of the Gepidæ began, while that of the Avars was closely connected with the downfall of the Gepidæ.

Fragmentary as are details for the Hun and Avar kingdoms, those for the intermediate kingdom of the Gepidæ are still more so.

For these the most valuable, and the most worthless, are due to the same author—Jornandes. What the Gepid dominion was in the first half of the sixth century no one knew better than he; and he calls it "*Gepidia*," from the *Gepidæ*, who succeeded the Huns; and that over the whole of Dacia (*totius Daciæ*)." Nothing is more trustworthy or more to the purpose

t han this; for this is what Jornandes, as a well-informed cotemporary, could scarcely fail to know.

But when he comes to tell us how it was that the Gepidæ
became the kinsmen (*parentes*) of the Goths, the case is
altered; for this connexion he refers to a pre-historic period.

Hence, at some unknown time, but as Zeuss believes within
the range of trustworthy tradition, it was in the islands at the
mouth of the Vistula that the Goths and Gepidæ were neighbours; and, when both left their homes on the Baltic and
migrated to *Gothiscandia* in three ships, the vessel of the
Gepidæ was the slowest of them, and from this the sluggish
navigators took their name—"nam lingua eorum pigra
'*gepanta*' decitur." This, according to Jornandes, was no
nappropriate designation; inasmuch as the Gepidæ were really
both slow in temperament, and heavy of frame. "*Gepidojos*"
was the name of the island on which they stayed behind; and
the occupiers of it in the time of Jornandes were of the "*gens
Vividaria*" (*i.e.* "*Vitivaria*"). The legend here is Lithuanic,
and, as such, applicable, in geography, to the country of the
Gothones, or *Guttones*; and we know what comes of this when
the *Goths* get, at one and the same time, to be treated as
Gothones, as *Getæ*, and as *Germani*. The Germans of Dacia are
deduced from the Lower Vistula, and with them their neighbours the Gepidæ; and much more in the same way besides.

Than all this nothing is less trustworthy, less to the purpose,
and more misleading; for this is what Jornandes writes, as a
speculative logographer, for a region of which he knew litttle,
and for a time of which he knew nothing. Upon the whole,
however, it is to be feared that he passes for a safe authority
on both points, and nearly all that he tells us is believed.

Be this, however, as it may, we get upon safe ground about
the middle of the third century, though with less certainty for
the earlier dates than the later. Thus, if Zeuss be right in
identifying the "*Si-cobotes*" of Capitolinus with the *Gepidæ*,
we meet them as early as the reign of Marcus Antonius. If,
wrong in this, he be right in identifying them with the "*Piti*"
of the *Tabula Pentingenana*, we have them as early as the re-
reputed date of that document; *i.e.* in the reign of Alexander

Severus. If the same writer be correct in identifying them with the *Si*-gipedes of Trebellius Pollio, we have them in the reign of Claudius. But whether any or all of these suggestions be right or wrong, we have them unequivocally in the reign of Probus; for which Vopiscus writes that that Emperor translated from other nations, as settlers in the Roman dominion, along with *Grautungs* (afterwards " *Ostrogoths* ") and *Vandals*, certain *Gepidæ*.[*] In the reign of Diocletian, we learn from the panegyrist Mamertinus that the Thervings (afterwards *Visigoths*) fought against the Vandals and *Gipedes*; and that in Dacia. Whether this was on their own or on foreign soil we are not informed.

They were, probably, in contact and alliance with the Grutungs. However, whether this were the case or not, the connexion between the *Gepidæ* and the *Grutungs* is the first known fact in their history. And this connexion continues till the disappearance of their name. Nor is it ephemeral; though there is dissension and warfare during the interval, which spreads over more than two centuries.

Mamertinus wrote not only before the time of Attila, but before the division of the Empire. With the exception, however, of a notice by St. Jerome of the Gepidæ as plunderers on Roman ground, we hear no more of them until the great battle on the Catalaunian Plain. Here the fierce Gepid (*Gepida trux*) forms a part of the multitudinous and heterogeneous army of the terirble Hun—as we have already seen.

Then comes the break-up of Attila's empire, wherein the Gepidæ, under their great captain Ardarich, seem to be among the first of the rebels—here, again, in alliance with the Ostrogoths. It is then that they succeed the Huns as rulers over Dacia, which, under them, becomes, as far at least as the Aluta, " *Gepidia*."

In making this river the boundary of the Gepidæ, I follow Zeuss, the name in the text of his authorities being " *Ulca*" (as Zeuss suggests " *Ulta* "). In confirmation of this view the geographer of Ravenna makes two Dacias—a *Dacia Major* and a *Dacia Minor*; referring to Jordanus (*Jornandes*) for details.

---

[*] For all this, as for nearly the whole of the sequel, *see* Zeuss, p. 437.

But, without enlarging on this, we may turn to a notice of Ennodius, the panegyrist of Theodoric the Ostrogoth. He alludes to an Ostrogoth campaign on the same " *Ulta* " against the Gepidæ; the campaign being a successful though, probably, not a conclusive one. This indicates that the Gepid occupancy of Dacia took place before the time of Theodoric. The parts about Sirmium were probably on the boundary between the two nations. That the Gepidæ, however, remained in Dacia after the campaign of Theodoric is certain.

It is not till the reign of Justinian that the name of Avar appears—or rather *re*-appears; for we must bear in mind the isolated notice of Priscus. However, the Avars of the time of Justinian and his successors are the unequivocal Avars of the great Khakhan Baian; and their history, as we have seen, is continuous. When these appear, the Gepid dominion in Dacia is, probably, at its best. But the character of the frontier is altered. The power of the Goths is declining, and that of the Langobards increasing; while of the Gepidæ, the Langobards are the enemies that determine their doom. We have already seen that, by a compact with the Langobards, the Gepidæ were made over to the Avars.

In A.D. 600, the Roman general Priscus found only a remnant of them, viz., three villages beyond the Theiss. Paulus Diaconus writes that in his time they had no longer a king of their own; and that the few that remained were either subjects to the Langobards or groaning under the rule of the Huns. Lastly, a nameless writer from Salzburg states that the Huns (Avars) expelled the Romans, the Goths, and the Gepidæ; but that of the Gepidæ a few still remained.

In the reign of Charlemagne we have seen that the Avars were reduced by the Franks (A.D. 800 circ.); that in the reign of Arnulf (before A.D. 900) *their* name, like that of the Gepidæ whom they extinguished, was either dying out or dead; and that, as the Avars displaced the Gepidæ, the Magyars succeeded the Avars. Hence Dacia became Gepidia, and Gepidia became Avaria. Finally, Avaria itself became what it is now—Hungary.

This is much, perhaps too much, to have written about the

Avars ; and it is not improbable that, here and there, there may have been something like repetition. But the object of the writer has been two-fold. The history of the Avars is one thing, the history of the Avar districts another, especially with the view of ascertaining the extent to which its occupants were Turks. Even now, it has not been asked how far it was Turk before it was Hun,—in other words, when it was, more or less, *Scythian*. And, even now, it has not been asked, " *Who were the isolated Avars of Priscus ?* The first of these two questions is reserved for the sequel ; the latter comes conveniently in the notice that now follows :—

The *Turks*.—There is no such thing as a Turk invasion of Europe, *eo nomine*, before the time of the Ottomans ; though there is never a time when members of the Turk family, under some name or other, were not only making conquests on European ground, but, also, settling in them. Of these, how-ever, not one can be shown to have made its way by the Hellespont, or to have settled in Mœsia. This, however, is implied in the division already made between the Turk to the north of Persia, the Caucasus, and those to the south thereof. But this is no reason why the name " *Turk*" should not occur at any time anterior to that of the southern Turks. We may have known the name under notice long before they were known as invaders. That they *were* such was known, for embassies had passed between the Turks and the emperors of Constantinople at a comparatively earlier period. In short there was a By-zantine embassy at the court of the Turk so early as A.D. 568, and there was a return embassy from the Turkish ruler to the emperor, and a very instructive one it is, especially to the geographer.

These have already been noticed. They were concurrent, or nearly so, with the advent of the Avars during the reign of Justinian. But they were later by nearly a century than the Avars of Priscus, so that, in fact, the earliest notice of the Avars is older than the earliest notice of the Turks. The Avars, however, of Priscus stand alone, and their history is a fragment. As compared with their later namesakes, they are to the reader as the footstep in the sand was to Robinson

Crusoe—a mystery, but not one which long remains inexplicable.

It is not necessary to lay before the reader the fragmentary pieces of evidence that show the Turk affinities of both the Huns and Avars, along with other minor populations connected with them. These disjointed details in the way of evidence are supplied by the embassies alluded to. They have been carefully collected, well put together, and, what is more, I do not know that a single objection has been made to the legitimate and necessary inference deduced from them. Whatever and wherever these Turks of Asia were, they were of the same family with those of Europe. They were not very near the European frontier, neither were they as far from it eastwards as the most distant of the Turks of the present Turkestan, for these reach to the parts about Lop Nor, in Mongolia, and in the valley of the Yarkend abut upon the frontiers of Tibet and India. Nor do we expect them to be this, inasmuch as it is on the western boundary of the present Turkestan that we, in the first instance, look for them. There is some difficulty, however, in ascertaining their exact locality. They were in what is afterwards known as the *Uighur* country, or on its frontier, for the name 'Ογῶρ appears in Theophylact, our authority for the *Pseudabari*, or *False Avars*. Now these he connects with the *Til*, the Asiatic name for the *Volga*. But to this Zeuss reasonably objects, for the whole context shows that the country of both the Turks and the Ogor lay farther to the east. There was, as we learn from Theophylact himself, another name for the river (τῳ Μέλανι ποταμῳ), probably the translation of the common Turkish name *Karasu=Blackwater*. Moreover, the context tells us that the Ogor country was on the borders of Bactria and Sogdiana, on the parts about the extreme conquests of Alexander, and in, or near, the silk-producing countries; indeed it is probable that the introduction of the silkworm into Europe, which took place about this time, was one of the objects of the embassy* ; or, at least, had much more to do with them than either the True or the False Avars. The Ogor lay east of the Turks of Disabulus, so that we must assign

* Zeuss, D.N., p. 713, and note.

to them the western part of Turkestan. *Tashkend* is the country which is generally recognized as the one which best accords with these conditions, and here, or hereabouts, we may, provisionally, place the capital of Disabulus. It may have lain farther eastward, or farther southward, but it can scarcely have lain more westwardly. Between the Volga and the Amur, we require room for the Kirgiz, the Uz, the Cumanians, and other tribes of a ruder and more migratory character than that which we assign to the Turks; not to mention the distance between them and the Persian frontier, and also the present name "*Turkestan.*" Οὔγουροι, another form of *Ogor*, and *Uighur*, appear in Menander, and that in connection with the same embassy. These are placed east of the Volga. The Volga, however, seems to have been the limit of the area of which the Romans of Constantinople had any accurate knowledge. The *Kirghis* of what used to be called Independent Tartary are known to have borne their present name in the time of Disabulus, for a Kirghis female slave (χέρχις) is mentioned in one of the embassies. Yet no such name is found in any European writer.

*   *   *   *   *

This is as much as need be said at present about these Turks of Turkestan. We have not as yet found them on European soil, but as they seem to represent the original members of the Turk family in their original country, and, moreover, as they were known through embassies at Constantinople, it has been necessary to notice them. Besides all this, there is the relation between them and the Avars—True or False as the case may be.

And this I now venture to investigate.

The date assigned by Zeuss to the Avar embassy mentioned by Priscus is between A.D. 461 and A.D. 465. The first of these is exactly ten years after the battle of Chalons.

The second is A.D. 464, the year after the death of Ægidius; and this, as we shall see, is an event that has a remarkable bearing upon the history of those members of the Hun alliance and the Turk family which we may reasonably presume were affected by the death of Attila, and the dissolution of his empire. From this point of view, I assume for the present that the *Sciri* and *Alani* were, almost certainly, among these, and, probably, the *Heruli* also ; these last at this time being in Gaul, and associated with *Saxons* of the *Littus Saxonicum.*

The *Sciri* we have already noticed as united with the Huns in the reign of Theodosius.

The *Alani*, in the battle of Chalons, were on the side of the Romans. But their Hun proclivities were so notorious, and they were so suspected, that they were drawn up on the field of battle between the Goths and the Romans, so as to ensure against their going over to the Huns.

I think that these circumstances lead to something like joint action between the four denominations—Alani, Sciri, Heruli, and Saxones—during the life of the usurper Odoacer. These were first his allies, then his subjects ; and, it is now suggested that along with them under a temporary change of name were the Avars of Priscus.

This temporary, or intermediate, name I believe to have been *Turcilingi.*

It is immediately after the death of Ægidius that we meet with the name *Adovacrius,* and we must remember that this notice of him is by one of the earliest of the *Frank* writers, and one who, except for the action of Adovacrius in Gaul, had no other interest in the history of *Odoacer.*

However, after the death of Ægidius, we find *Adovacrius* at *Andegavi, i.e. Odoacer* at *Anjou,* and this A.D. 465, thirteen years after the battle of Chalons, and five before we read of Odoacer in Rhœtia.

Between 170–175 and 187, Odoacer is in Rhœtia; and after this he is king of Italy. Now it is during this latter period, and this only, that the name *Turcilingi* presents itself. And the following are the only notices of it that have come down to us. They all apply to the same king, khan, or captain —viz.: *Odoacer.* In Jornandes, Odoacer himself is a Rugian (*genere Rugus*), his supporters being crowds of *Turcilingi,* Sciri, Heruli, and auxiliaries from divers nations. In an anonymous author, the *Sciri* and *Heruli* are named as his supporters. Elsewhere, Odoacer, with a strong body of Heruli, and relying on the assistance of the *Turcilingi, or* Sciri, hastens to advance on Italy from the extreme boundaries of Pannonia.

In Paulus Draconus, Odoacer, having collected the nations under his dominion, *i.e.* the *Turcilingi* and Heruli, along with the Rugi, which had long been his own people, and, moreover, some populations of Italy, entered *Rugiland.*

Except so far as he is either King of Rugiland, or Emperor of Rome, his only subjects mentioned by name are the Heruli, the Sciri, and the *Turcilingi.*

Nor, except as subjects of Odoacer, are the *Turcilingi* mentioned anywhere, or by any one; nor is there, at the time of that ruler, any name like *Turcilingi*, or *Turk*, nearer than Tashkend. Yet within fifty years there will be embassies between Tashkend and Constantinople. There has already been one from the Avars of Priscus, and the others will be from the *Turks* in reference to the Avars.

I do not say that this *was*, or that it *must have been* the case, for proof on points like these is out of the question. We have no absolute certainty even that *Adovacrius* was *Odoacer.* It is all circumstantial evidence. But my inference is that it is in the history of the *Turcilingi* under Odoacer, that the history of the Avars of Priscus is continued; not absolutely up to that of the Avars of Baian, but in that direction.

It is not essential to this doctrine that *Odoacer* should be *Adovacrius,* or yet that the *Sciri* and *Heruli* should be Turks, though it makes the question simpler if these were so to a certainty. About Odoacer there seems to be no one who would say that he is *not* Adovacrius; but whether anyone would go farther and commit himself to an affirmation on the point is doubtful. With the Turk affinites of the Heruli and Sciri it is different. Zeuss, for one, positively claims the *Heruli* as Germans, and where Zeuss leads many follow. The *Sciri,* he admits, may possibly—perhaps, probably—be German also. With these he associates the *Turcilingi.* In the opinion of the present writer, Zeuss is in error throughout; but if in the matter of the Turcilingi he is right, the suggestion of the present writer is worthless.

Be this, however, as it may, I submit that, word for word,

" *Turcilingi*," is more like " *Turk* " than it is like *Ruticleii*
(Ῥουτίκλειοι). Yet this is the name by which it is identified. In
the Germany of Ptolemy (there is nothing of the sort in
Tacitus) we have, " after the Saxons, from the river Chalusus
to the river Suevus, the *Pharodini*, then the Sidini (Σιδεῖνοι) as
far as the Oder ('Ιαδούα), and under (ὑπ' ἀοτους) the Ruticleii as
far as the river Vistula." Zeuss accounts for this by the trans-
position of the " T " and " R," which gives *Turcleii*. This is,
no doubt, ingenious ; and if there were a single manuscript to
support it, the suggestion would be legitimate. But he gives
us nothing of the kind. Again, it would be legitimate if we
knew anything, *aliunde*, which identified, or even connected, the
history of the two. But, again, there is nothing of the kind.
In fact, both the *Ruticleii* and the *Turcilingi* appear only once
either in geography or in history. The name *Ruticleii* is found
but in one author, Ptolemy, and is absolutely an ἄπαξ λεγόμενον.
The name "*Turcilingi*" is found in more authors than one, but
it applies to the same population, at the same time, and that in
connexion with Odoacer only. From this point of view it is as
much an ἄπαξ λεγόμενον as *Ruticleii*.

But it may be said there must be other reasons for an
authority like Zeuss to write as he does. There are *other*
reasons ; but I leave it to the reader to judge whether there are
better ones. The *Ruticleii* of Ptolemy are on the frontier of
his *Sidini*. And the Sidini are Rugi, as the Rugi are Sidini.
What is the evidence of this ? Simply the converse of the
previous statement ; viz. : that the Turcilingi were the frontagers
of the Sidini. If this is not enough, there is more of the same
kind. The Heruli, which are associated with Odoacer along
with the Rugi (*Sidini*) and the Turcilingi (*Ruticleii*), are held
to be, *mutato nomine*, the Φαροδεῖνοι of Ptolemy, and also the
Suardones of Tacitus.

That Φαροδεῖνοι and *Suardones* may be the same word I do
not deny ; but how does this make either of them *Heruli* ?

" But there must be other and better reasons in the background," the reader may say. There are. Mention is made by
Tacitus of a population named Rugii ; but these are held to be,
at least, as far east as the Vistula, or, probably, the Niemen.

It is not easy to connect them with the *Sidini* and *Ruticleii*. Nor is it necessary to do so. We can get the word " *Rugi* " nearer home; and, what is more to the purpose, in probable contact with the *Ruticleii, Pharodini (Suardones)*, and *Sidini*.

We cannot, indeed, get a definite and continuous *Rugia*, or *Rugiland*, but we know where to find the " *Isle of Rugen* " on the west, and the " *Rugenwald* " on the east; and there is space enough between them for any amount of *Sidini* and *Ruticleii*. But this does not make it the *Rugiland* of the *Rugii* of Odoacer; nor yet the *Rugiland* of the *Herulian* and the *Turcilingian* frontier in the time of that ruler. There was another *Rugiland*; and the *Rugiland* of the time of Odoacer was simply the German name for *Rhœtia*. It was certainly the country of which he was the king; a usurper, no doubt, but still the country of which he was king, and the country from which he usurped the Empire. There is no doubt of this. He conquers Rhœtia before he conquers Italy; and Rhœtia before he conquers it was *Rugiland*. Odoacer was *genere Rugus*. And, even if this can be made to mean that he came from the Rugiland of the Baltic, the Felethei, Favas, Frederics, and the rest of the dynasty which he supplanted, did not. As for Odoacer himself, we never hear of him farther from Rhœtia than Anjou. All that we get besides is a Rugiland which is made to coincide with the frontiers of the Ruticleii and Suardones; these being what are supposed to be because they are on the frontiers of Rugiland. Meanwhile the Heruli are Suardones, or Pharodini, as the case may be ; and the Turcilingi are identified with the Ruticleii, for, as far as we can see at present, no reason beyond that of investing one of the most heterogeneous kingdoms in history with a uniformity.

In all these identifications there is a foregone conclusion— one to the effect that *all* the bearers of the name *Goth* were members of the German family, and that, unless there is special proof to the contrary, all the denominations connected with their history were the same. I am not prepared at present either to affirm or to deny this. All that I submit to the reader is the doctrine that the syllable " *Turc-* " in " *Turc-*ilingi" is the syllable " *Turk* " in " Τυρκ-αι " and " *Turk-ish*," and not

the syllables "*Rutic-*" in "*Rutic-*leii." The termination -*ling*
is, of course, German; perhaps of Gothic, perhaps of Suevran
origin—possibly of Langobard. The compound is a hybrid
one; but this is the rule rather than the exception in proper
names. *Po-lab-ing-i*, the term for the dwellers on the Lower
Elbe, is just such another compound, the first two syllables
being Slavonic.

I think we may now go farther in our inquiries, and ask how
it was that, if the evidence of Priscus be so good for the Avars
of his generation, it is so bad in the details of their origin?
Upon this point we can only say that he writes as learned
Byzantines wrote in general upon subjects like the present.
They almost always think it necessary to tell us not only what
a particular population or district is at the time it comes under
their notice, but what it was *ab origine*. It is manifest, then,
that though they may thoroughly understand one part of their
subject, they may easily be mistaken in another.

Sometimes we can get an inkling as to the nature of the
special *ignes fatui* that mislead them.

I think that, in the case of the Avars of Priscus, in
respect to the *mist* (τὸ ὀμιχλῶδες) we have the proverbial darkness of the *Cimmerian* region; and that the suggestion of a
flood is from Strabo's account of the Cimbri. Indeed, between
Strabo and Posidonius, we get the two elements—the land of
darkness and the land of floods—in the same series of speculations; *i.e.*, those on the origin of the Teutones and Cimbri.
The *gryphons* I take to be those of Herodotus, who troubled
the Arimaspians.

> "As when a gryphon, through the wilderness,
> Pursues the Arimaspian, who by stealth
> Had from his wakeful custody purloined
> The guarded gold; so eagerly the Fiend,
> O'er bog, or steep, through strait, rough, dense, or rare,
> With head, hands, wings, or feet, pursues his way,
> And swims, or sinks, or wades, or creeps, or flies."
>
> *Paradise Lost, Book II.*

But whatever may have been the original district of the

Huns of Priscus, it is certain that both the *Sciri* and the *Heruli*, who are the special associates of the Turcilingi in the army of Odoacer, came from the parts on the Mœotis. The Sciri are mentioned in the Olbiopolitan Inscription as having, in conjunction with the *Thisamatæ, Saudaratæ, Galatæ,* and *Scythæ,* harassed the Greek town of Olbia. The Heruli are specially stated to have come from the Mœotis, and that so early as the third century. In the fifth, as we have seen, they were in Gaul, still retaining what would now be called their " *Mongol* " physiognomy.

> " Hic glaucis *Herulus* genis vagatur
> Imos oceani colens recessus
> Algoso prope concolor profundo."
>
> *Sidonius Apollinaris.*

Such were the Avars of Priscus, and such their associates. What were they in the eyes of their suzerain in the time of Justinian, nearly a hundred years later than Priscus? It is beyond all doubt that it is upon the matter of the *Pseudavares,* or the Avars of the time being, that the main discussion between the ambassadors and Disabulus takes place. But it does not follow that the particular speeches which have come down to us belong to this part of the negotiations. I rather think that the Khan has changed the conversation from the newer Avars to the older ones; and that it is *their* history to which he alludes. Of the conquests of Attila he probably knew a great deal, and may have considered them as actual parts of the dominion of his ancestors; as in some degree, at some time they may really have been. But these have manifestly thrown off their allegiance, and the great Turk, their suzerain, speaks of them irreverently, not to say contemptuously.

Such seems the tenor of his conversation. Men in genera do not utter such sentences as " *I know where M. or N. have gone;*" and " *I know all about the rivers of their new country;*" and " *I think there are still some who are well-disposed to us*" (ἔτι στέργουσι τὰ ἡμέτερα), when they are speaking of mere runaways who have scarcely been three months away from them. Still less do they ask " *Are there any still among you?*" and then answer themselves by adding, "*I think there are about twenty thousand.*" I suggest, then, that it is not the Avars of the time of the speaker that the Khagan alludes to, but the Avars of Priscus—lost to sight, dear to memory.

* * * * *

The *Khazars*, with their name spelt in the ordinary way, first appear in the reign of Heraclius; and, when this is the case, the whole character of the history of the Roman world, as well as the evidence of its historiographers, undergoes a change. The date is nearly coincident with the spread of Mahometanism, and it belongs to the darker periods of the literature of Constantinople. The old series of events has changed its course, and the records of them have deteriorated. Nor is this change accidental. In the time of Heraclius there were two nearly concurrent epochs in the history of literature. In the reign of Justinian the old classical schools of Greece were closed, and we have no longer any of the later Pagan writers concurrent with the earlier Christian; no writers representing the eclectic mixture of religion and philosophy of the Emperor Julian; no writers who, after the manner of Eunapius, give us the history of their times from a pagan point of view. The reign of Heraclius, too, was the time of the last of the great fathers of the Eastern Church, John of Damascus; while, year by year, the knowledge of the political history of the East is becoming less and less in the West. On the other hand, Mahometan literature has begun, and it will be seen that, before we have done with the history of the Turks under notice, Arabian writers will be cited as authorities. There is, then, from the time of Heraclius until the time when the regular series of the later Byzantine historians begins, a break. And the effect of this, in the way of evidence, is what has already been indicated; viz., the rule that, whereas the later Byzantines are trustworthy authorities for the geography of their own times, they are anything but safe for their accounts of the origin and early migrations of the nations whose present geography they describe. This is strong language; but, when we consider, it is neither improbable or inexplicable? This difference between the unequal value of their statements concerning what

14

and where such and such populations are during the time of
the author, and what they were a certain number of generations
before his time, shows itself at an earlier period; for we have
seen it in Jornandes, in Theophylact, and in Priscus. But it
attains its *maximum* later, and more especially in the writings
of Constantine Porphyrogeneta.

When we find that any ethnological epoch is connected with
the reign of Heraclius we must suspend our judgment.

The Khazars seem to play the same part in the history of
Eastern Russia that the Avars played in that of Southern
Bavaria, or, if we prefer the later name, Austria; but with two
important differences. The Avars in Bavaria were intruders.
The Khazars in the parts about Khazan, for thus far north (and
farther) we can trace them, seem to have been older occupants
than the Russians. In these parts, however, the two frontiers
met; and I believe that it was through this northern portion
of the Khazar area that the Russians made *one* of their ways
to Novogorod. But more upon this point will be said in the
sequel. Again; the Avars cut their way into Bavaria by the
sword; representing, even more than the Huns, the fighting
power of the Turk family. The Khazars, on the other hand,
seem to have been, for Turks, comparatively a peaceful body of
settlers; indeed, merchants rather than men of war.

Like the Turks in general, and like more than one mercantile
country, they had their armies, and were lords over a definite
territory. We meet with the term *Chazaria* as the land of
the *Khazars*. There is also a *Bey* of Chazaria (Πέχ Χαξαρίας);
also a *King*. But upon the whole they seem to have been
the most quiet and the most civilized division of the Turk
name.

I must now refer the reader to what I have suggested in
respect to the import of the word Bulgaria,* and the doctrine
that, whatever it may be now, it began as a geographical term;
*Bulgarii=Bulgwære=*the occupants of a "*volgy,*" or the valley
of a river; and, in the word "*Volga,*" the river itself. There
are certainly two *Bulgarias*—a *Bulgaria* of the *Danube,* and a
Bulgaria of the *Volga.* That the initial letter "B" is to be

* See p. 133.

pronounced as " V " is a remark of Zeuss's.* The river Itil (Volga), writes an Arabian author, runs through Russia, then *Bulgaria*, then Burtasia, into the Khazar Sea (*i.e.* the Caspian). Nestor, too, a Russian authority, writes to the same effect. The Khazars he calls *Chwalisi*. *Great Bulgaria* was the name for this district.

It is not for nothing that this has been enlarged on. So long as we make *Bulgaria* a national name we get a series of difficulties, especially in respect to the language. Thus, let the speech of the Khazars be the same as that of the Turks, and also the same as that of the Bulgarians. The inference will be that the Turk is the same as the Bulgarian—which it is not. Again, let the language of the Bulgarians and the Hungarians be the same, and "*Hungarian*" means "*Magyar*." These statements are not imaginary, but real; and it is easy to see what sort of difficulties they raise—difficulties that disappear when we not only recognise more *Bulgarias* than one, but see the reason why there should be such.

If we carry the Khazar area as far north as Kazan, we can explain a difficulty. The word "*volgy*" has already been stated to have been a Ugrian, or Fin, gloss, and not a Turkish one. If so, it is difficult to account for its existence on the Danube before the time of the Magyars. But the Volga of the northern part of the Khazar district is well within the Fin boundary, and that at the present time. If so, the Khazars, though themselves pressed upon by the Russians, must, on their own part, have pressed upon the Fins. Be it so. There was no great displacement of the older population, for it is part of the view here submitted to the reader that the Khazars were merchants rather than conquerors; indeed, I believe that the name itself was not so much that of a tribe as that of a class.

The Khazars certainly seem to have come from a distance, and to have proceeded at least as far as Kazan, probably as far as Novogorod, possibly as far as Archangel; and, in all these cases, to have shown the Russians the way northward.

---

* Βούλγα, bei Byzantinern ist nicht *Boulga* aber *Voulga* zu lesen. Snorro Sturleson (for the country was known as a part of Gardariki or Novogorod), writes *Vulgara*, p. 722, and note.

In respect to their original locality, I think it was that of the Turks of Disabulus, the Turks of Turkestan, the Turks of the Persian frontier, and, as such, Turks more civilized than the Tatarlike Huns, Avars, Petshinegs, and Cumanians.

The Arab writers* divide the denomination into two sections, the *Black* Khazars and the *White* Khazars. Ouseley, from a Persian authority, gives the same division. Klaproth finds traces of the same distinction among the present Bashkirs; and, earlier still, Procopius, in writing about the Epthalites of the Persian frontier, states they alone of "the Huns" (for this is the family to which he assigns them) "are white of skin, and not ill-looking." Indeed, "*White Hun*" and "*Epthalite*" are occasionally used as synonyms.

This is as much as can well be said about the general history of the Khazars at present; but it may easily be imagined that, when they come to be considered as the forerunners of the Russians in their north-eastern movements towards the Baltic and the White Sea, towards Novogorod and Archangel, they will re-appear in another place. So they will when the account of Theophanes as to their origin has to be compared with one of Constantine Porphyrogeneta of the same kind. This is because the comparison between the two will be a good illustration of the worthlessness of the Byzantine accounts as to the origin of the populations they have to treat of.

The details of their history are few. Zeuss scarcely gives half a page to them; less than what he gives to them in his account of the Bulgarians. But this is not because he has more to say, but because he has to discuss their connection with Bulgaria.

It is in respect to their relations with other countries and other denominations that the external history of the Khazars is most connected, especially with that of Russia. But all this is just the question which the Byzantine historians are the least capable of illustrating. Of the little republic of Cherson, in the Crimea, they had some accurate knowledge; for this was a remnant of the old kingdom of Bosphorus. But beyond the Crimea there were no districts that the successors of Hera-

* Zeuss, pp. 723, 724, 725, and note.

clius knew in detail, as the statesmen and soldiers of Justinian's time knew the old province of Dacia; and no populations which they knew as the men of the previous centuries knew the Huns and Avars. At the same time there were always changes going on in the parts between the Volga and the Dnieper, or the Dnieper and the Danube; and these brought the Empire into contact with new enemies—sometimes directly, but oftener indirectly, and by changes which they effected in the character of the frontier.

The insufficiency of the Greek records to give us any adequate history of the parts beyond the Danube has already been indicated, and, to some extent, accounted for. During the ninth century we meet with a new series of authorities, the early Arabian writers. These we get for the East. For the West we have the historians of the Carlovingian Franks; those of the Merovingian period having already helped us in the details connected with the Avars. But with the Khazars we approach the history of the Hungary of the present time—the Hungary of the Magyars; and this is closely connected with that of the Turks. Then, before they come to the Mongol conquest, we have the earlier Russian records, and the notices of the Frank crusades beyond the Vistula; and then, before we have quite done with the Petshinecks and Cumanians, the earlier Scandinavian writers allude to the populations of Russia and the South.

In one sense these last are the most important of all, but only in the history of opinion. It is these who unsettle the whole question as to the foundation of the great Empire of the Czar. It is these who mainly, but not exclusively, teach us that when in the ninth century great things—such as the attacks on Constantinople, and the foundation of such towns as Kiev and Novogorod—are effected by the Ῥῶς, the bearers of that name are not to be considered what we now call *Russians*, but that they were *Swedes*. That nearly all Scandinavia and two-thirds of Russia hold this to be sound doctrine I cannot deny. Nor can I set aside this view. However, I write this to prepare the reader for a criticism of it; and that is why, when, perhaps, I ought to be writing of the Khazars and Ῥῶς, I have drawn attention, in the foregoing remarks, not only to the subject but to the evidence connected with it.

With the Avars and the Huns before them we had more to do with Rome than with Russia. With the Khazars and those that come after them we have more to do with Russia than with Rome.

For this reason I shall state the few facts that are given by Zeuss in his special notice of the Khazars, more for the sake of the geography and chronology, than for any other more immediate purpose; all collected from the Byzantine writers, and bearing on the history of the Empire. Those that he takes from his Arabian authorities tell us the most about the Khazars in their own country and about their relations to Russia; in fact, they make a very important part of their very incomplete history.

The notices of the first class are few, and can be laid before the reader with a *minimum* of commentary; all the more so because the first, second, and fourth will be noticed elsewhere.

They are as follows :—

1. That "the Turks from the east, whom they name Khazars," about A.D. 620 joined the Emperor Heraclius in his war against Chosroes, King of Persia; the Khazars being a powerful nation which held the whole coast as far as the Pontic Sea.

2. That they conquered the greater part of the Crimea. I put the statement thus because they seem to have been repulsed by the Gothi Tetraxitæ.

3. That the mother of the Emperor Leo was a Khazar.

4. That they took tribute from the Viatitsh, the Severians, and the Polyane; Russian, Lithuanian, or Fin tribes on the Dnieper.

5. That their territory extended from the Crimea to Sarkel; Sarkel being on the frontier of the Petshinegs. I think this *Sarkel* was the present capital of the Don Cossacks; *i.e.* Tsherkask; but it is a point upon which there are doubts.

Of the Arabic notices, one has already been alluded to*; but here it may be expanded. I think it gives us a measure of the

---

* See pp. 25 and 26.

extent to which the Khazars were a trading rather than a
fighting population. They seem, like the Europeans in the
early East Indian service, to have been civilians, with just
enough of forts and soldiers to be able to act on the defensive.
However, about A.D. 912, five hundred ships of the Pῶs appear
on the Don, in the parts where it bends eastwards in the
direction of the Volga, the parts where Selim the Second's
Vizier, Sokolli, contemplated a canal. They get leave from
the King of the Khazars to sail down his river, the Volga, into
the Caspian, and then and there to collect as much plunder
from the districts around it as they can; and, having done
this, to give the Khazars half of it, and return to their own
country. It was on the side of Georgia and Persia where the
most booty was to be got, and for the details of their inroad
we have a precise and minute account. Georgia and the district
of Aderbijan suffered most; for in the latter the Pῶs sacked
Ardebil, and this was, as the historian states, three days'
distance inland. Then, on the way back, they came to the
lands of Naptha (*Nefata*), or Babekeh (*Baku*), which belonged
to the King of Shirvan. Then, having put in at some small
islands off the coast, they were attacked by the king, Ali-ben-
Heisem. The Pῶs, however, were not easily ejected. Nevertheless, at the end of some months, they withdrew, sailed up
the Danube, and gave the King of the Khazars the share in the
booty that they had promised him.

The King of the Khazars had no ships; fortunately, writes
the Arabian historian, for the Mahometans. These are naturally incensed against both the Pῶs and the Khazars, so that
the Mahometans of the Caspian districts, and, along with them,
the Christians of the town of Itil, make war upon them—the
latter against the wish of the Khazar King or Khagan. It
seems that, having been paid according to agreement, they
acted as peace-makers. But in the end the Khazars and Pῶs are
defeated. After this, writes Masudi, they did not repeat their
attacks.

Not, at least, in Masudi's time, who was cotemporary with
the events he narrates. But in the time of Ibn-Haukal, another
cotemporary authority, there is another Pῶs invasion. By A.D.

968, "*Bulgar*," a small "town, once famous," has been plundered; the whole country, Khazar, Burtasian, and Bulgarian, has been overrun; and the invaders sail away to *Rum* and *Andalus*, *i.e.* to Constantinople and Spain.

Who the *Burtasii* were is not certain; their country lay between that of the Khazars and the Bulgarians—the parts about Khazan. Both these districts were equally Khazar and Bulgarian; yet the Burtasii, separated from both by name, lay between them and on the way from the one to the other. But the whole valley of the Volga was, geographically and by hypothesis, a *Bulg*-aria, and the population *Bulg*-uarii, or *Bulg*-arii.

I cannot account for these Burtasii. They seem to have intervened between Bulgaria and Chazaria, along the overland route, and in a straight line northwards, rather than along the line of the river Volga.

It is certainly under the name of Ῥῶς that the voyage from the Sea of Azof to the coast of Spain is effected. Yet it is not the Russians, but rather the Scandinavians, that, in the ninth century, were the great pirates of the West. There would be nothing remarkable in the return of these Ῥῶς if they had only sailed to Constantinople; for this they had already done more than once—in 858 as friends, and in 841 as formidable enemies. In both cases the country from whence they came immediately is that which we now know as *Russia*. Yet it is notorious that these Ῥῶς are generally and almost universally considered to have been not *Russians* but *Swedes*. I cannot refute this view; but that much can be said against adopting it to the extent to which it is usually adopted I hope to show in the sequel, and when the origin and development of the Russian Empire comes under consideration.

Of Khazar blood, either pure or mixed with that of the Avars, there is much in Hungary; and this is further mixed with that of the Petshinegs. This is on the frontier of Transylvania. The Kavars were one of the divisions of the Kazars, and they not only settled in Hungary, but taught the Hungarians "the language of the Khazars."

Before the Magyars became conspicuous in Hungary, the Avars of that country were called *Turks* by the writers of Constantinople; and so were the Magyars that displaced them. The Magyar language is Ugrian, or Fin, and this was known to Gibbon. But the connection with the Fins, which implies one with the Laplanders as well, has not been very willingly recognised in Hungary; so that it is not wonderful that during the late war some of them have persuaded themselves that their consanguinity is with the Turks. It is this to some extent; but not with the Ottomans.

There is another district in Hungary, where there is a Turk element. The Arabian historian, Jakut, in the thirteenth century, gives the following account of a Bashkir settlement in that country. He met in Aleppo many Mahometans, one of whom told him that he came from Hungary, where his co-religionists occupied thirty villages (pagi), which, though each of them had the dimensions of a small town, were not allowed to be surrounded by a wall, lest they should become unruly. They had long been converted. The Bulgaria here is the Bulgaria of the Danube, and the Bashkir converts probably Khazars.

Finally, the division which has already been noticed between the *White* and the *Black Khazars*, and the *White* and the *Black Huns*, repeats itself in Constantine Porphyrogeneta, in his account of the Hungarians (Magyars); and, according to the rule already laid down as to the value of Byzantine authorities concerning the *origin* of the nations they are writing about, is not only wrong, but manifestly wrong. The Hungarians, according to this writer, came from Asia; and one part of them went to Moldavia, and another to the east, on the frontier of the Khazars and of *Persia*. The original Turkish name was Savartoiasphali (Σαβαρτοιάσφαλοι). Now -*phal*- is the German "*pfahl*," and in any map of Hungary on a large scale there are several districts of which the name ends in this word. This, then, is German. And it is not the present writer, but Zeuss,[*] who suggests that " *Savart* " is, word for word, " *schwarz* "= " *black*." In like manner Nestor, writing as a Russian, makes two kinds of Hungarians, the *Black* and the *White*—the latter being the *Khazars*.

_____
[*] Zeuss, pp. 745 and 749, and notes.

The *Petshinegs—Pizenaci, Pecinatici, Pincenates, Pecinei, Petinei, Postinagi,* Πατζινακῖται, *Peczenjezi (Slavonic), Bisseui, Bessi (Hungarian).* The *Petshinegs,* writes Cedrenus, are Royal Scythians, divided into fourteen tribes, each with its own peculiar name. These were generally those of their chiefs. They dwelt in tents.

The fixed territory that can with the least uncertainty be assigned to the Petshinegs is Bessarabia; for there, at the present moment, their descendants, the *Budjak Tatars,* are still to be found. Beyond this, northwards, the Petshinegs lay along the coast as far as the Dnieper, and probably as far as the Donetz or the Don. They seem nowhere to have extended far inland.

The same is the case with their occupancies westward. They lie along the south bank of the Danube. They occasionally cross that river, invade Bulgaria, and even threaten the Empire. But, again, they are only a fringe or a border to the mainland. They are nowhere far inland, at least in Vallachia. In Transylvania and in Hungary they may have reached farther north; for in Transylvania, at least, they are mentioned in the early history of Hungary. But the general rule seems to be that they followed the coast, and ran along, or encircled, an inland district, without occupying it. Cedrenus writes that they had no houses; and Finlay notices the extent to which they neglected to establish themselves in the interior. The Uzes, of whom their king Tyrach was afraid, but who had no terrors for his general Keghenes, lay in the marshy districts, probably inland of the Petshinegs. We hear of them for the first time when they encroach upon the Khazars. Until we know the future fate of the present Budjak Tatars we have not heard the last of the Petshinegs.

Where they are supposed to have come from we have seen. Their original name seems to have been *Kangar;* which is also that of a Nogay tribe. If this be really the case it is probable that they took their European name from the island of *Peuce,* or its occupants, the *Peucini.* The nearest to the name, as a word, among the numerous forms of the word *Petshineg* (as it seems to have been pronounced), is " *Pecinei.*" This form

Zeuss assigns to the Western writers; and this means those who were the most familiar with the name "*Pencini*." On the other hand, the name most like "*Budjak*" is *Peczenjezi*.

In the tenth century the Petshinegs attack Kiev, and, somewhat later, we find them as far south as Salonica; this giving us the measure of their inroads. Another name for them was Kangar. They lived a long time in Europe before they exchanged the tent for the house. Formidable warriors and faithless allies, they appear in the greatest detail in the reign of Constantine Monomachus, between A.D. 1028 and A.D. 1054, when Tyrach is their king and Keghenes (? Khakan) his general. Like so many others of his class, Keghenes, whose actions as a soldier had excited the jealousy of his king, transferred his services to the Empire, followed by as many as twenty thousand men. Allowing himself to be converted to Christianity, he received the title of Patrician. From a fort on the Danube he made inroads on the country he fled from. Tyrach, whose remonstrances were neglected, crossed the Danube, with his army, on the ice; but disease thinned his ranks, and he surrendered. Keghenes recommended a wholesale slaughter, but his advice, either from policy or humanity, was neglected, and the prisoners were planted, as colonists, in the parts about Sardica and Naissus. Many of the nobles embraced Christianity. Of the remainder, fifteen thousand were sent to join the army in Armenia. On reaching Damatrys, one of their generals persuaded them to force their way back. They did so, and joined their countrymen the colonists. They then moved forward to the mouth of the River Osmos, and again to a place called the Hundred Hills. Keghenes was ordered to move against them, narrowly escaped assassination, was accused of complicity, and arrested. His followers joined their countrymen. The king, who had been taken captive, was released upon condition that he should bring back his countrymen to their allegiance; but he renounced his Christianity, and revenged himself by two successful battles. This restored Keghenes to favour. He defeated his countrymen, but was murdered after his victory. A truce of thirty years was the result.

We hear of another defeat of the Petshinegs in 1091, and

another in 1122, when they cross the Danube and threaten the passes of the Balkan. The Emperor, however, John II., Calojannes, who is with the army at Berrhœa, forces the passes, and completely defeats them. Here, again, we have a portion of the captives settled as colonists.

Of Petshineg blood, then, beyond the Petshineg area there is probably much; the most of it perhaps in Hungary. In the long account of Constantine Porphyrogenitus of the entrance of the Magyars into Hungary, the Petshineg admixture is conspicuous. This stands, in respect to its historical value, wholly apart from the speculations as to their origin, and tells us nothing improbable. The chief settlement of the Petshineg was on the Transylvanian frontier, where they formed a march boundary.

The *U'z* or *U'zes*.—Masudi mentions these early in the tenth century, but not as invaders of any part of Europe. It is in their own country, on the Eastern frontier of the Khazars, that we find them. Every winter, when the ice on the Volga will bear them, they cross it on horseback; but not with the leave of the Khan of the Khazars. On the Khazar side there is a special line of posts; and when these are insufficient, the Khan himself takes the command. We have seen that the Uzes of Europe were in contact with the Petshinegs, and this is nearly all we know about them.

The *Cumanians.*—Our authority for the Uzes, who knew both the Petshinegs and the Cumanians, considers that the Cumanians were the nobler of the two. His knowledge may have been imperfect, or his standard peculiar. The habits of the Cumanians may have been exaggerated, or they may have been looked upon with undue horror. As the account of them comes from Europeans, this is possible. The best, however, was bad. Nestor says they cared not what they ate; Otto of Frisingen that they devoured horseflesh; Henry the Lett that they drank not only mares' milk but mares' blood as well, and that their meat was eaten raw. However, the chroniclers had the satisfaction of adding that they were defeated. There is little doubt as to the area of the Cumanians. The Russians call them *Polowci* or *Poles,* a word meaning *Men of*

the plains. The German for this is *Waluwen,* the French *Valan.*
A Latin form is *Falones.* All this is simply the etymon of
the name of the Russian Government, *Volhynia.*

There were Cumanian settlements in Thrace, in Asia Minor,
and in Hungary.

The Cumanian history begins later than that of the Petshinegs; and, in the thirteenth century, Carpin and Rubriquis
found Cumanians between the Dnieper and the Volga.

The Cumanian, or Komanian, element in the blood of the
men who, as speaking the Magyar language, are legitimately
treated as Magyars, curious as it is, is something more than a
mere ethnological or philological curiosity. The Cumanians
were, with the exception of the Ottomans, the last of the Turks
who made, under a definite denomination, notable conquests in
Europe. In comparing them, indeed, with their congeners,
there is scarcely any need to take the Ottomans into the question.
The Ottomans were Turks of Asia Minor, comparatively civilized,
who crossed the Hellespont under a captain who was the recognized chief of either a well-known kingdom or of a part of
one. The Cumanian conquests represent a totally different
state of things. They represent the invasions from the parts
to the north and the east of Caucasus, the invasions of which
the original seat was Independent Tatary, and in which the
lines of migration were the Russian Governments of Saratov,
Caucasus, and Kherson. They represent invasions like those of
the old Scythians, the Petshinegs, and others. They represent
the barbarism and nomadism of Western Asia as encroaching
on the similar barbarism of Eastern Europe. Of the invaders
who come under this category the Cumanians were the last.
The Scythians played their fierce game some thousand years
before the Christian era. The Khazars did the same between
600 and 800. The Petshinegs came later; the Uzes later still.
The last of all were the Cumanians. As the Khazar name loses
importance, the Petshineg name emerges into prominence. The
less we hear of the Petshinegs the more we hear of the Cumanians. The twelfth, thirteenth, and fourteenth centuries
give the Cumanian era. That the same population may have
effected, either single-handed or in union with others, earlier

conquests is likely. It, apparently, did so; in Caucasus as well
as in Europe. But of the Cumanians, *eo nomine*, in Europe the
history is late. Nor is it favourable. After such or such
nation has been described in terms which imply the maximum
of ferocity, the wind-up is that there was one nation which was
worse : viz., that of the Cumanians.

Such their character. Such their date. The great Cumanian
locality was Volhynia. The *Volhynians* were the people of the
Volhynia, a *German* name for a *level country; i.e.* the very word
we have in the Dutch word *Valuwe* in Guelderland at the present moment. The Slavonians, however, called them *Polovczi*,
a word with the same meaning; *i.e. Poles,* or people of the
Polyane, Champagne, or *Levels.* Hence, a *Volhynian* and a
Polonian are the same. But the Volhynians and the Polovczi
were neither more nor less than so many Cumanian Turks who
had conquered Volhynia. What portion of it they held is
uncertain. It is only certain that, at the time of the Mongol
invasion, Volhynia (neither Polish nor Russian, and, at most, only
in part Lithuanic) was Cumanian. Of these Cumanians, under
their Slavonic name of Polovczi, the early Russian chronicles
have numerous notices. Some of them joined the Mongols.
Upon the whole, however, they seem to have fought a triangular
duel, being sometimes arrayed against the new invaders, sometimes against the Poles, Russians, Lithuanians, and Yatshvings,
on whose frontiers they had encroached.

Be this as it may, at the time of the inroads under notice thirty
thousand of them left Volhynia and the Volhynian frontier to
settle in Hungary. There they occupied a district in the Interamnium of the Danube and the Theiss, which, at the present
time, bears the names of the Great and the Little Cunsag, the
Little Cunsag being the larger of the two.

With the Cumanians ends the last of the long series of
special inroads from Asia made by mere divisions or sub-
divisions of the numerous denominations of the great Turk
family; beginning with that of the Alani, who may or may not
have been Turks, but who, in any case, were invaders from Asia;
and that of the same type as their successors. With the Huns
the evidence that such invaders were Turk improves. In respect

to the Avars there is no reasonable doubt. But until the Avar name has made itself known, there is no undoubted notice of the Turks *eo nomine*. And, even when we get it, it is not the name of an invader. Of the Turks, *eo nomine*, we only know that they sent an embassy to Constantinople, which was met by another from the Emperor to some distant part of Central Asia. Yet the Khazars crossed not only the Volga but the Don, and held a district in the present Government of the Don Cossacks, in the Crimea, in Bessarabia, and, probably in the parts beyond; a notable amount of territory, of which they were subsequently deprived by the Petshinegs. The Cumanian, however, was the last of these sectional invasions; and of Volhynia the Cumanians were the partial occupants in the twelfth and thirteenth centuries. In Hungary their language lasted much longer; indeed it was the last of the Turk dialects that kept its ground in that kingdom.

CHAPTER IX.

Non-Ottoman Turks.—The Mongol Conquest.—The Kiptshak.—The Four Khanates.—The present Population of them.—Tho Nogays, Bashkirs, Meshtsheriaks, Tyeptyars, Kirghis, Barabinski, Karagass, Koibals, Yakuts. Karakalpaks.—Doubtful Turks, tho Tshuvash.

In the thirteenth century more than half Asia and the great part of Europe trembled at the terrible name of the Mongols. But the prerogative of the Mongol denomination was of short duration. The great founder of his dynasty never reached the Volga, or even the Jaik. His conquests were in the east and south, in China, in Armenia, in Georgia, in Asia Minor, and in Persia and in Turkestan. The terrible conqueror in the direction of Europe was Batum; and the forces of Batum and his captains were constantly mixed, and probably more Turk than Mongol. A few tribes, *e.g.* the Kari and Kaslik, are specially named as Mongol; but the more important Uighurs and Tshagatai were Turks.

On the death of Uzbek Khan, the power of the Kiptshak declined; and it sank still lower in the time of Timur. In his reign two Khans disputed the succession, Toktamish and Urus Khan. Without laying undue stress on what is little more than a conjecture, I suggest the probability of *Urus* meaning *Russian*. It is, at any rate, a Mongol name for the Russians. If so, some of the native princes must have created an influence among the great vassals, or perhaps a partial and approximate equality.

Timur supported Toktamish; but, afterwards he not only abandoned, but raised up a third candidate, Timur-Kutluk, against him. But only to abandon him, in his turn, for the son of Urus Khan. From the anarchy that these movements suggest the Kiptshak never recovered. Out of its ruins arose the Khanats of Astrakan, Kazan, the Krimea, and Siberia; their origin being nearly contemporary, *i.e.* between 1375 and 1400. Their durations, however, were different. Kazan became Russian in 1552, Astrakan in 1554, the Crimea no earlier than 1783.

The two Northern Khanates, Kazan and Astrakan, were both the conquests of the same Czar, Ivan IV., Ivan Vasilievitsh, or Ivan the Terrible. The final annexation of the Crimea was not till 1783, in the reign of Catherine the Great. It was in the reign of Ivan IV. that the first recorded invasion of the parts beyond the Black Sea, of which an account has been given under the reign of Selim II., took place; and it seems to have been a defensive one; for, after the conquests of Kazan and Astrakan, we may easily believe that Ivan contemplated the reduction of the third Khanate, the one nearest Constantinople. Of the dates connected with the fourth, that of Siberia, it is not easy to speak definitely, either in respect to its history or its geography. Even as a part of the Kiptshak its boundaries were indefinite; inasmuch as the whole of the Khanate seems to have been, in the first instance, other than Turk, *i.e.*, Fin (Ugrian), Yeniscian (a term which will be explained in the sequel), Mongol, and even Tungusian (Mantshu). " *Siberia*," however, meaning *the North*, is a Russian word, *i.e.*, neither Turk nor Mongol; and, consequently, a term of comparatively recent origin.

Meanwhile it may be safely said, even about Siberia, that, like those of Kazan and Astrakan, its conquest *began* in the reign of Ivan IV.; and that in the pre-eminently daring inroad of Yermak the Kosak.

All the four, however, have been Russian for more than a century; and, at present, they are, of course, so many Russian Governments. Nevertheless, they still approximately coincide with so many Khanates.

The following are the recognised divisions of the Turk populations of Russia in Asia; and the classification for the present will be geographical and ethnological rather than historical.

The Tatars of *Kazan,* though commercial in their habits, are less numerous in the towns than the Russians. They are the most civilized of the family.

Between 1796 and 1800, they increased from 90,000 (there or thereabouts) to 120,000. In 1838, they amounted to 275,822.

Of the Turks of the khanat of *Astrakan*, some are to be found in the Government of Caucasus, and others in that of Astrakan itself. They are separated from one another by a Mongol district, of which more will be said in the sequel. The northern or eastern branch is in contact with the most western Kirghiz.

Some of these are Nogays. The whole may amount to 22,000.

In allotting all the Turks of the following Governments to the khanat of *Kazan*, I may err in some unimportant details, inasmuch as some of them may have had their origin beyond its frontiers. I give, however, the following table :—

In the Government of Kazan	.	.	.	308,574
———— Orenburg	.	.	.	230,080
———— Stauropol	.	.	.	96,037
———— Samar	.	.	.	83,927
———— Simbirsk	.	.	.	67,730
———— Viatka	.	.	.	57,944
———— Saratov	.	.	.	46,713
———— Penza	.	.	.	34,684
———— Nizhnigorod	.	.	.	22,788
———— Perm	.	.	.	17,271
———— Tambov	.	.	.	10,640
———— Riazan	.	.	.	4,725
———— Kostroma	.	.	.	262

In the city of Kazan itself with a population of more than 50,000 two-thirds are Russian, one-third Turk; the latter living apart and in the so-called Tartar town.

No longer the metropolis of a khanat it is still a town full of trade, industry, and intelligence; its University being the great seminary for missionaries and for agitators in behalf of religious and political designs of Russia in the direction of the east.

All travellers speak well of the Kazan Tartars. In the towns they have wholly sunk their original nomad character and are as truly industrial as so many Jews, Armenians, or Anglo-Saxons. In the country some of the old characteristics keep their ground. Yet, in the country, they are hard-working farmers—though shepherds and bee-masters also. In both, they are zealous and sincere, though not intolerant, Mahometans; less sensual, and less idle, than the Osmanli of Constantinople, and circumspect in business. In dress, they are accommodating themselves to that of the Russians.

The approximate measure of the old Bulgarian civilization is to be found in the ruins of Vrakhimov and Bolgari near Spask, on the left bank of the Volga, half-way between Kazan and Simbirsk. The coins found there are Cufic: the inscriptions Turkish, Arabic, and Armenian. Of the 47 Turkish legends 22 are referable to one year, the year of the Hegira, 623. As Vrakimov fell off Old Kazan rose; and as Old Kazan declined, the Kazan of the present time flourished.

Mutatis mutandis, the same phenomenon presents itself in Astrakan, where the ruins of Okak and Serai replace those of Vrakimov and Old Kazan.

Of the *Nogays* there are four divisions—one in the locality which they inhabited in the time of Peter the Great, two in settlements planted by that emperor, and a fourth in the Crimea, where it seems to have been settled under the khanat. Of these—

1. The Nogays of the original locality are the so-called Kundur Tartars of the Aktuba, one of the mouths of the Volga. They change their residence as well as their mode of life with the season, living during the summer in felt tents, and resorting when winter comes on to the town of Krasnoyarsk. Of these—

2. The Nogays of the Kuma and Kuban, along with—

3. The Nogays to the north of the Black Sea, are the offsets.

4. The Crimean Nogays are remarkable for the extent to which they have laid aside their migratory habits and become settled agriculturists. So far from their preferring the tent to the house, or the encampment to the village, they are amongst the most industrious of the Tartars of the Crimea.

Orenburg is the *Bashkir* country; for it is in Orenburg that the Bashkirs are the most numerous, and most wear the guise of an original population: the Tartars, as has been seen, being also numerous.

15*

In the Government of Orenburg . . .		332,358
———————— Perm	. . . .	40,746
———————— Samar	. . . .	15,351
———————— Viatka	. . . .	3,617
		398,072

Next, in order, come the Meshtsheriaks, and then, after a long interval, the Tshuvash, the Mordvins and the Tsherimis; followed by about 15,000 Germans, and a few Gipsies.

In language the Bashkirs are Tartars; in blood (I think) Ugrians. They are pastoral rather than agricultural, and quite as much military as pastoral: Mahometans in creed, and, to a great extent, nomads in habit. Before the conquest of Kazan, two other Khans, one in Siberia, and one in Independent Tartary, took tribute from a portion of the Bashkir country—the bulk of which belonged to Kazan. The Bashkirs, however, submitted to Russia, and after the foundation of Ufa were effectually protected by her. During the wars of the seventeenth century between the Kirghiz and the Siberians, the Bashkirs revolted—once in 1672, once in 1707, and once in 1740. They also moved with the Kosaks in Pugatsheff's rebellion. The first three of these revolts were headed by native chiefs. In 1735, a Kosak March, or boundary, had been established on the frontier; but since 1741 the Bashkirs themselves have, to a great extent, been converted into virtual Kosaks. Instead of paying tribute, they serve as soldiers, and submit to a military organization. The Starshins, judges, or elders, are appointed by Russia; who feebly represent the original nobility.

The *Meshtsheriaks* are mixed up with the Bashkirs, and, except that they remained faithful to Russia during the Bashkir rebellions, and that they are civilians rather than soldiers in habit, are little more than Bashkirs under another name—if, indeed, the names are not identical. They amount

In the Government of Orenburg to	. .	71,578
———————— Perm	. . . . .	5,783
———————— Saratov	. . . .	2,580
		79,941

The *Tyeptyar* are believed to be a mixture of Turks and

Ugrians, who crossed the Ural and submitted to Russia soon after the conquest of Kazan. They are imperfect Mahometans. Word for word, Tyeptyar seems to be *Kiptshak*.

The true occupancy of the *Kirghiz* is Independent Tartary. We shall, however, see how much it has forfeited its title to the name.

The Kirghiz fall into—

The Middle Hord	. . . . .	500,000
— Little ——	. . . . .	190,000
— Great ——	. . .	100,000
		790,000

The *Middle* Hord belongs almost as much to Siberia as to Tartary; its occupancy being the drainage of the Upper Ishim and the Upper Obi. In 1823 some of its sultans put themselves under the protection of Russia. At first they paid no tribute. Now they pay some. One of its tribes, the Naiman, has a Mongol name. Of two others, the Argin and the Turtul, more will be said anon; since they are names which re-appear on the Tshulim.

The *Little* Hord became, more or less, Russian about the middle of the last century; when the tribes under the chieftaincy of Abulkair, along with some others, invoked the protection of the Czar. Their allegiance, however, was doubtful. They made inroads across the frontier, and levied blackmail upon the caravans to and from Bokhara. To check this, their constitution was changed and the power of the khans was broken—with this, the integrity of the hord. Some went over to China, some to the Middle Hord, some to the khanat of Khiva. Finally, a division of 10,000 families settled in Astrakan. In 1812 the khanat was made hereditary in the family of Bakei. They lie a little to the right of the Volga, from which they are divided by the Kalmuks. On the south they are bounded by a small Turk district and the Caspian. A little to the north of them lie the Bashkir and German districts, the former in Orenburg, the latter in Saratov. They seem to be wholly cut off from the other Kirghiz: and amount to about 82,000. With the exception of *Katai*, which reminds us of the Mantshu *Kitan*, the names of the tribes of the Little Hord are purely Turk.

The *Great* Hord lies north and east, and reaches the drainage of the Upper Yenisei. The name of, at least, one of their tribes is Buriat; a name identical with that of the Buriat Mongols. How far this makes the Mongols Turkish, or the Kirghiz Mongol I have not inquired. In the Chinese geographers the name by which the most eastern of their tribes was known is Kilikisa, or Kirghiz.

In 1606, when the *Barabinski* submitted to Russia, a large portion of the Great Hord did the same; the Barabinski being the Turks of Barama, that dreary waste which lies between the Ishim and the Obi. In summer the Barabinski Tartars dwell in tents; in winter in huts; the huts being partially sunk in the ground. They are, for the most part, herdsmen, with a slight tendency to an imperfect agriculture. Shamanism is common; to the exclusion, I believe, of Mahometanism—but not to that of Christianity; which is making its way amongst them.

From the name of their country which is Bara*ma*, meaning the Bara country, and from *ma* being the ordinary Fin name for *land*, along with other facts which point to the same conclusion, I consider that the Barabinski are, more or less, Fin in blood. That they are old occupants of their present area I infer from their being Shamans rather than Mahometans. That some of them may have had the once terrible Avars amongst their ancestors I infer from the name.

They may amount to 3500 individuals paying *yasak* or tribute, Russia being the Power that holds them tributary. They call

The Russians	. . . .	*Urus*
„ Kirghiz	. . . . .	*Kasak*
„ Kalmuks.	. . . .	*Kalmuk*
„ Ostiaks	. . . . .	*Ishtak*

They fall into the following Aimâks: this Mongol term being the one I find in Klaproth.

In Turk.	In Russian.
1. Langga.	Tanuskaya Volost
2. Lubai.	Lubanskaya Volost.
3. Kulaba.	Turashkaya Volost.
4. Barama.	Barabinskaya Volost.
5. Tsoi.	Tshaiskaya Volost.
6. Terena.	Tereninskaya Volost.
7. Kargala.	Kargalinskaya Volost.

The *Tshulim* Tartars, occupants of a feeder of the Obi, so called, are said to approach the Mongols in their looks, and also to speak a dialect of the Turkish which has more than an ordinary amount of Mongol words. Pastoral rather than agricultural, and Christian rather than Mahometan, the Tshulim Turks, who amount to about 15,000, are also, to some extent, Shamanist. They move with seasons; live by fishing and hunting; and dwell, like the Barabinski, in huts sunk in the ground. That the climate is unhealthy is inferred from a notice of Bell's, who remarked the prevalence of a skin-disease amongst them, which left large white spots on their otherwise swarthy bodies. He attributes it to the exclusive use of fish and animal food. For a small population their tribes are numerous. Two are named Bura; which points to Barama. Besides these there is a Tutul tribe, and an Argen tribe; names which point to the Middle Hord of the Kirghiz.

Of the tribes of the Upper Tom, Verkho-Tomski, or Kuznetsk, the *Abintsi* are one; and with these ends the notice of the Tartars of the drainage of the Obi.

Of those of the Yenesey the most western are the *Katshtalar* or Katshinzi (the first form being Turk, the second Russian), so-called from the river which they occupy.

The *Boktalar*, or Boktintsi, lie below—

The *Kaidin* above—Abakansk.

The *Beltyr*, amounting to about 150 payers of tribute, lie on the right bank of the Abakan.

The *Biryus*, on the river so-called, originally belonged to the Verkho-Tomski Tartars. They are all poor, with a few horses, a few oxen, and a little rye. They have a chief (Bashlik) at the head of each of their four divisions.

The *Tubalar*, or Tubintsi, on the Tuba, though Turk in language, are believed to be Samoyed in blood. They are sometimes called Kirghiz: a fact which points to Independent Tartary. Indeed, I imagine, that it is from the Kirghiz that all these tribes of Siberia have been derived.

The preceding view of these minor divisions of the Siberian Turks is purely ethnological. The political classification, or the classification which is current with those Russian officials, who look chiefly to topographical boundaries and the most convenient way by which the tribute can be collected, is somewhat different. It gives four divisions.

1. *The Koibal* tribes of the Yenisey after it passes the Chinese frontier and becomes Russian and Siberian. —Some of the Koibals are subject to China: not that the Chinese call them so, but that the class, so far as it is natural rather than political, is Chinese as well as Russian. The Koibal area (politically speaking) is bounded by the Yenisey; the Tabat, a feeder of the Abakan; and the Sogda, a feeder of the Tuba. The tribes on the Tuba are mentioned elsewhere, and, *eo nomine*, as Tubalar or Tubinski. I imagine that they differ from the true Koibals, without being sure of it. This is because the Koibals (some or all) name themselves Tufa; a fact which suggests the probability of the Tubalar being a branch of them. If so, they are, in the present work, noticed twice over.

In 1830, the Koibals (the word being dealt with as a political term) amount to 635 males, and 493 females —total 1128.

In the way of *language*, the Koibals are Turks; the Koibal grammar of Castrèn being neither more nor less than a grammar of a Turk dialect spoken in Siberia, on the right bank of the Abakan.

In the way of *blood*, they are anything but Turk. Out of the eight divisions, which come under the denomination, five are Samoyed, three Yeniseian.

The *name*, however, is Samoyed. In Klaproth's Asia Polyglotta, there is a long Koibal vocabulary, collected during the last century, by Messerschmidt, which is simply Samoyed; and in 1847, a few grey-headed Koibals could still speak Samoyed.

2. *The Sagay.*—These lie between Askyz and the Upper Abakan; and amounted, in 1830, to 3897 males, and 4011 females; total 7908.

3. *The Katsha, Katshalar,* or *Katshinski.*—On the Lower Abakan, or between the Sagay and the Yenisey; also on the White Iyus. They amounted, in 1860, to 3460 males, and 3119 females; total, 6579. Castrèn, however, in 1847, puts them at 9436 in all. The Koibals and Sagay were Samoyeds and Yeniseians who had become Turk. The Katsha tribes have gone further. They are in the third stage and are Russian.

4. *The Kisilzi.*—This is the most northern of the four divisions; and, also, the most Russian. Perhaps, indeed, the Kisilzi

are wholly Russianized. They amounted, in 1830, to **2282** males, and 2080 females ; total, 5362.

The *Karagass*, conterminous with the Koibals and Soiot, occupy the valleys of the Oka, Uda, Biryus, and Kan, as nomads. In 1851, they amounted to 284 males, and 259 females ; total 543. They fall into five tribes.

1. The Kash.
2. The Kash Sareg.
3. The Tyogde.
4. The Kara Tyogde.
5. The Tyeptei.

The Kash are conterminous with the Soiot ; the Sareg Kash with the Kamash : the Tyeptei with the Buriats.

Castrèn visited the *Koibals.* He found them in extreme poverty ; but they were pleased when he asked about their language and their history. Yet the pleasure was dashed with mistrust. "Why do travellers visit us? Surely we must be of more value than other people." An old man who remembered the expedition of Pallas, told him, that since the foreigner visited them, all had gone bad. The cattle sickened when he went away. But "was that Pallas's fault?" The answer was, "that men don't come and pass weeks in the winter for nothing." The chief charge against him was, that he was an excavator of the *Tshuden-gräben,* and that he was a magician. Nor was this belief extinct. Castrèn, himself, who excavated as far as his opportunities would let him, was supposed to be looking after Tshúd skulls, out of which a decoction more effective than sarsaparilla was to be made. Still they let him dig and received him kindly ; though steeped in poverty to the very lips themselves. He found huts where the children ran naked, crying for food ; for which the dogs howled too. Yet they found a place for him by the fire. They found it, too, for a miserable beggar—vagabond and minstrel—who, on a two-stringed harp, sang the following song of Tyenar Kuss.

There was a Tartar whose name was Tyenar-Kuss ; he had a great many tents, more men, and still more cattle. He was very old. He took to himself a wife. He loved her much ; but he thought, in his own heart, that she never loved him. So he tried her love. He went out one morning, as if he went after some cattle that he said were missing. He went a little way ; but, before he had gone far, he threw himself down on the ground, and lay as if he were dead. The shepherds and herdsmen saw him ; and, as he never moved a limb, they thought he was dead. So they went back to his tribe, and said that he was lying dead. When his wife heard this, she took a horse, and rode to where he lay, and found him lying on the ground, just like a dead man ; never moving a limb. So she lay down by his side, and began to weep. But Tyenar-Kuss thought to himself that he must not put faith in his wife's tears ; so he lay as before. Then his wife took out a dagger, and said,—

"Thou seest, Tyenar-Kuss, that I will not abide any longer on the earth ; I will never roam about as a widow, and look for any other husband. I will never part from you, my husband—my wedded one ! "

But Tyenar-Kuss, though he heard all this, never moved a limb. He lay like a dead man. So the wife rose up, and took the dagger, and stabbed her breast with it, and fell dead by his side. And Tyenar-Kuss got up, and grieved that he had lost a good wife ; and, as long as he lived, never ceased to mourn for her.

They talked too about Irle-khan, and when they put on new logs or got warm, said, " Aye! Fire is a god." They said the same of water ; and the traveller was told that on certain occasions they threw the first-fruits into a river or lake. Some threw the first morsels of their meal towards the east. Those who did this did it to please Irle-khan. Displease Irle-khan and you will be punished as those are punished who give milk-and-water instead of milk.

Of the *Soiot* little is known. Most of them are Chinese.

There was a man, and his name was Toros. He was a Soiot ; but he lived within the boundaries of China. He paid tribute to the Chinese ; but he wished to escape this tribute. So he moved himself northwards—himself and his tribe. They were thirty-five in all ; and he wanted to settle in Siberia. This was two hundred years ago. His countrymen, who were Soiot, went after him, and followed hard on his track. He saw that they were near upon him, so he betook himself to the Toros Taskyl. It was a steep mountain, but he made a way. But his countrymen followed him : so he made a palisade. He cut down trees, and bound them together with bands ; and heaped up a wall of stones behind them. His countrymen still followed on his footsteps. They came to the wall : they came under the wall. Then Toros cut the bands, and the wall fell down, and the stones rolled ; and his countrymen were carried back. Not a man lived to tell the tale. But Toros dwelt with the Mator ; and the way is called Toros's Way till this day.

One of the Sayanian tribes is named *Sokha ;* the Sayanian tribes being held to be of Kirghiz origin. We have traced them as far north as the Upper Yenisey ; and we have yet to trace them further.

They lead to the division which gives its name to the Government of Yakutsk, of which they are, for a native population, the most civilized inhabitants. *Yakut*, however, is only the name which the Russians give them. The name they give themselves is Saikha, Sokha, or *Sokhalar*. It is believed to be the name of one of their early Khans; but this is unlikely; at any rate, he was the man who led them northwards, since the chief who separated them from the *Brath* (with which they made one nation) and led them from Lake Baikal to the Lower Lena, was not Sakha, but Deptsi Tarkhantegin. Word for word, *Brath* is *Buriat*. It points to the Buriat Mongols; and it also points to the Buriat Kirghiz of the Great Hord. It is with the latter that I more especially connect the Sakhalar or Yakut. At the same time, the names of the Baitung, the Yok Soyon, the Manga, and the Namin tribes are more Mongol and Turk. The two views, however, by no means exclude one another.

The most western of the Yakut are three small tribes on the Chatunga and in the parts about Dudinka, who lie in immediate contact with the Samoyeds, the Yeniseians, and the Tungús; with the latter of whom they have been confounded. Castrèn, indeed, says that all the world, the Samoyeds themselves included, have so confounded them. As far back, however, as 1856 Middendorf informed me of their true affinities.

In calling them Yakut, I merely mean that they speak the Yakut language; by no means holding that the blood and language coincide. Indeed, it is most likely that they do not.

There are three tribes. One of these is the *Dongót*, whose occupancy is about three days' journey from Dudinka, on the Noryl Lake. Word for word, Dongót seems to be Denka; and Denka is the name of a division of the Yeniseians, who, as far back as Messerschmidts' time, had nearly lost their language, and who were said to count only as far as five.

The next is the *Adgan*; the third, the *Dolgan*. They refer their origin to three brothers, Galkinga, Sakatin, and Büka, who left the Yakut country but recently—so recently, says Castrèn, that one of his existing descendants smoked out of the very pipe which Galkinga smoked. Whether this be a fact, a rhetorical way of saying that his tribe were new comers, or evidence as to the age of the pipe, I know not. The Samoyed call them *Aüa* =*Younger brothers*. The Russians apply the name Dolganen to all the three tribes. As a general rule, they are Pagans, a few only being converted to Christianity. They live on friendly terms, as their name denotes, with the Samoyeds.

This is a name which may surprise some of us; for the Samoyeds that we best know at present are full five degrees north of the implied frontier; indeed, they lie, for the greater part, well within the Arctic Circle. But even at the present time their language is spoken as far south as the district here indicated. Indeed, with a few possible exceptions, the Turks of the Khanate of Siberia were all intrusive, *i.e.* settlers on ground other than Turkish. Thus—

The *Barabinski* of *Bara-ma* (Fin for *Bara-land*) lie between the Ishim and the Obi. The original Fins were, probably, of the Ostiak division.

The *Tubalar, Koibals, Karagass, Katshalar*, and *Soiot* seem to be a mixture of Samoyeds and Yeniseians.

The *Tshulim* Turks and the *Tyeptar* are more or less Mongol.

Beyond all this there is some Tungusian blood, especially among the *Yakuts*; and, for the *Yakuts*, two other elements, viz. the Jukaghir and the Koriak, upon each of which something will be said when the minor populations of Siberia come under notice. One point, however, in the account of the great *Turk* family, with the use of the word in its widest sense, must be foreshadowed; viz., the fact that with the Ottoman Turks on one side, and the Siberian Turks on the other, each on ground untrodden by their earliest ancestors, we have the two extreme illustrations of change in the way of development and of change in the way of deterioration; the Turks in the parts beyond the Hellespont, and the Turks beyond the Lena.

Such are the divisions for the Turks of the parts *north* of Persia and the Caspian; or the Turks of the district in which the family originated as opposed to their congeners of the south, whether Ottoman or Seljukian; and it cannot be denied that there is a notable difference in their histories.

We may call the Turks that have just been enumerated the *Kiptshak*, or we may call them the " *Temudjinian* " Turks; for *Temudjin* was the original name of the great Tshingiz-Khan. But the real differences in the way of their origins and their histories, between the two great divisions, is of more importance than the name. Nor is the present classification absolutely complete for either of the two classes; since, although between the areas of the Seldzukian Turks and the Kiptshak there is the whole breadth of Persia, Armenia, and Caucasus, there are still certain divisions and sub-divisions in each group. There are members of the northern group who, without absolutely crossing over from Turkestan to Arabia, or even becoming more or less Persianized in the intermediate country, simply encroached upon the frontiers of Persia, Georgia, and Armenia, as the case may have been, while they were still in geographical continuity with their aboriginal districts. Something, then, has yet to be said about the present descendants of the Turks of Disabulus and his embassies, the Turks of the districts known as Great and Little Bokhara, as Chinese Tartary, as the Khanates of Tashkend, Khiva, Kokhan and the like; in short, as *Turkestan* in opposition to *Turkey*. To these we may add the *Turcomans*.

Then there is the question as to the antiquity of the Turk family in Europe, and the consanguinity of the Avars and Huns with the Scythians of Herodotus and their descendants. That these were not only members of the great Turk family, but that their history on the soil of Scythia Europea was continuous from the time of the Father of History to the fourth century is the strong conviction of the present writer. But it is not one upon which opinion is uniform. Nor is it easy to say in what direction it runs. There are those who hold that the Herodotean Scythians were Mongols. Others believe that before the Huns, who are the first in date of the Turks of the present investigations, the old Scythian population had disappeared; and that between the Scythians of the time of Philip of Macedon, and the Huns of that of Valens, there was no continuity. That the names which present themselves in Herodotus, unless we suppose that the *Kutuguri* of the Hun dominion to be his *Katiari*, are not to be found in the interval is true; but the disappearance of a name and the extinction of a nation to which it applied are widely different questions. Be this, however, as it may, the classification, so far as it has hitherto gone, is not exhaustive.

Thirdly, there is the somewhat unfamiliar denomination

" *Tshuvash.*" This leads us from the Turk family to that of the Fins, or Ugrians; and the fact which invests the name with interest is the doubtful and equivocal character of the Tshuvash ethnology. According to some authorities the bearers of this name, who speak a language which is held to be Ugrian, are also Ugrian in blood. According to others they are Ugrianized Turks, *i.e.*, Turks in blood, though Ugrian in language, and Christian in creed. Such are the two opinions in their simplest form. But, besides this, there is much in the way of subordinate detail. Is the language so undoubtedly Ugrian as it is stated to be? Is it not rather Turk in grammar, and Ugrian only in respect to its vocabulary? Is the creed so very Christian ? Is it not to some extent Mahometan ? Is it not to a great extent pagan?

Such are the points in question; points upon which the present writer has no decided opinion, but which he finds it necessary to indicate, inasmuch as the Turk family, and the Ugrian, or Fin (which will be next to come under notice), will graduate into one another through the section under notice.

The present *Tshuvash* population may amount to half a million, there or thereabouts; the statistical notice of them in Köppen being as follows :—

In the Government of Kazan		-	-	300,091
,,	,,	Simbirsk -	-	84,714
,,	,,	Samar -	-	29,926
,,	,,	Orenburg	-	8,352
,,	,,	Saratov -	-	6,852
,,	,,	Viatka -	-	17
				429,952

In the first of these Governments their number nearly equals that of Turks, who amount to about 308,574. The names by which they designate themselves are Vereyal, Khirdeyal, and Vyress. The Tsherimis call them *Kurkmari* or *Hill-men*, the Mordvins *Wiedke.* *Tshuvash*, itself, I take for a Tatar word.

That their Christianity is nominal, and that it is dashed not only with pagan but with Mahometan elements, is made evident by the following short sketch of their Pantheon.

Süldi Torà is the *God above ;* a kind God who lives in the sky, which he leaves only when he visits the earth on Fridays : when he descends to see whether any one breaks that day of rest by working. He has as many names as functions. One of them is *Syuda-tuvny Torà*, or the *God who makes Light :* another, *Tshon shoradan Torà*, or the *Soul-maker ;* another, *Sir-shu-askshe*, or the *Father of Land and Water ;* another, *Mun Torà*, or the *Great God ;* another, *Mun Yra Torà*, or the *Great Good God.* He has a mother, a wife, children, and several subordinates : such as *Toryn-uvynsthe-sürün*, or the *Forerunner ; Alyk ozhan*, the *Door-shutter*, *Pülüks*, the *Messenger :* the last being the term for an *Angel*

Asla-adi Tora, is the *Grandfather ; Kebe*, the *Judge; Pig-amber*, the *Hearth-God ; Pereget*, the *Giver of Wealth* or *Luck   Khvely Tora* is the *Sun God ; Oikh Tora*, the *Moon God ;* and *Sily Tora*, the *Wind God.*

Of the Terrestrial Deities, the chief are *Syol Tora*, the *Way God ; Kily Tóra*, the *House God ; Kardy Tóra*, the *Barn God ; Wurman Tóra*, the *Wood God*, and *Sirdi Patsha*, the *Lord of the Earth.*

In *Shoitan*, or *Satan*, and *Keremet Esrel*, the *Angel of Death*, we see Turk elements ; as (indeed) we see them in *Patsha*= *Pasha.* But *Shoitan* is, to a great extent, superseded by *Keremet ;* the Tshuvash analogue of the Jewish Satan in his character of Fallen Angel. Keremet was, originally, a being of equal power, knowledge, and beneficence, whose delight it was to traverse the world below, and to confer blessings on mankind. He would be doing this at the present time, had not Shoitan instigated some wicked men to murder him. This they did : and, having burnt his body, they gave the ashes to the winds. But the winds let them fall on the ground, and wherever they fell up sprung trees : and with these trees Keremet came to life again—but with a new and a bad disposition. He was, now, as malicious and mischie-vous, as he had once been kind and gentle. At first he haunted the woods ; but, when the woods decreased, he took the clearings and the villages ; so that, now, every village has its Keremet.

Yirikh is the god who causes the chief bodily ailments; and when these develope themselves it is the Tshuvash habit to have recourse to the conjuror rather than the physician. A private offering, in a comparatively quiet manner, suffices for their cure. The great festivals, however, at the beginning and at the end of harvest are more imposing. It is hard, however, for a stranger to observe them. The following is one of the few accounts we have of them.

It was near the village of Iseneva, on the side of a forest of oak-trees, that Lepechin, towards the end of the last century, when the superstitions of the Tshuvash were much more vigorous than at present, witnessed a Keremet sacrifice. It began as early as nine in the morning, and was unfinished at four in the afternoon, when his patience gave way, and he left the *Yonse*—for that is the name of the Seer, Wizard, Medicine-man, or Shaman in these parts—still muttering invocations and exorcisms. When he reached the appointed spot there was a kettle on the fire; four old men, who proved to be the chief officiators; and a great number of oxen, sheep, and cocks and hens. Whilst the bystanders hung their heads in respectful silence, the four old men, having prayed to Tora, and having waited until a row of buckets was filled with water, submitted the cattle and poultry to an ordeal by water. They dashed it on them suddenly, and noted such as ran away startled, and such as stood stupidly quiet. The latter they spared; inasmuch as it was held that animals of this temper were not received favourably by Tora. The others, which were huddled together in a heap, were then slaughtered; and their flesh boiled. But the bones, head, and bowels, were put by in rush baskets for burning. This took place after the feast on the flesh was over, when the ashes were given to the winds. As for the feathers of the birds—they are sown broadcast over the fields.

At the richer sacrifices, gold and silver coins are added to the offerings of the poultry and cattle. The modern Tshuvashes replace them by brass and copper ores. They also substitute little images for the sheep and oxen.

The Tshuvash Hades is a re-production of the world of our present state; and, when a man dies, his friends put tobacco pipes, and drams in his grave, celebrating (not without festivities) the anniversary of his death.

1.

A hundred and sixty beams I carried:
A room I built.
Twelve windows I made in it;
Out of two windows I looked myself.
At ten windows, sit ten young maidens.
The first time they looked out,
The second time they laughed.
I went from village to village,
Never found a grown-up maiden.
In one village I saw a maiden,
But I had no money:
" Come with me," I would have said
But I had not the heart to say it.

2.

I went from wood to wood,
But found no cherries:
I went from village to village,
But found no maidens.
I would eat the cherries;
They are a black morsel:
Good to eat with bread.
I would eat other berries,
They are a red morsel;
Good to eat with bread.
I would take the maiden,
The flaxen-haired maiden.
With her to live were sweet.

3.

I went and went along the way;
I came to a thick wood.
I sought out the nut-tree;
Milk came out of it.
Without meat I eat no bread.
I sought the elm;
A bee came out of it.
Out of the bee came honey;
Without honey I eat no bread.
I went and went along the way;
I came into the village.
The dogs of the village barked.
I cast my eye on a flaxen-haired maiden;
I wished to take her with me:
My father gave me no money:
The priest gave me no writing.

4.

The girls of our town—
The girls of our town—
Jump over the hedge like wolves
Over the hedge like wolves,

The girls of other towns—
The girls of other towns
Creep under the hedge like mice—
Under the hedge like mice.
The girls of our town—
The girls of our town,
They drive with two horses—
Drive with two horses.
The girls of other towns—
The girls of other towns,
They drive with two sows—
Drive with two sows.

5.

My father gave me a black horse:
Let me saddle him, thought I to myself.
The horse became an oak-tree.
My father gave me a white cow:
Let me milk it, thought I to myself.
The cow became a birch-tree.
My father gave me a red sheep:
Let me shear it, thought I to myself.
The sheep became a red stump.
My father gave me a silken girdle:
Let me bind it on, thought I to myself.
The girdle became a rush.
My father gave me a silken kerchief:
Let me put it in my girdle, thought I to myself.
The kerchief became a horn-beam leaf.

6.

On the road lies my field;
It bears no corn:
More's the pity.
I have a bay horse;
He won't stay on the road:
More's the pity.
I have a still stupid wife;
She has nothing to say:
More's the pity.

7.

I would walk along the road to the country,
But was afraid of the Russians.
I would walk along the road to the village,
But was afraid of the thieves.
I would walk along the road to the fields,
But was afraid of the wind.
I would walk through the wood,
But was afraid of bears and the wolves.
I would walk to the village,
But was afraid of the dogs.

I would walk to the corner of the village,
But was afraid of the young maids.

8.

Ah! my father! ah! my mother!
I wish I were a goose,
I would fly to my own village.
Were I the gate of the village,
And the villagers came ;
I would open and shut
Of my own free will.
Were I the gate of a palace,
And my father and mother came ;
I would open and shut
Of my own free will.
The moon shines over the land ;
The land is our march.
The stars rise over the way ;
The way is our road.
The snow-flakes fall ;
So falls our hair.
The rain runs down ;
So run our tears.
Lumps of ice float down the Volga ;
So float our bodies.
On the Anger stands an old oak ;
That's my father.
On the Anger stands an old birch ;
That's my mother.

9.

My father is woodman ;
My mother is breadmaker ;
My eldest brother is headborough ;
My next is post-boy ;
My youngest cooper ;
My eldest brother's wife is singer ;
My next brother's wife is dancer ;
My youngest brother's wife is harper
I, myself, am a spooner.

Another name still stands over for a short notice—that of the *Biserman* or *Bisermans*. All I know of them is, that they amount to about 4500 individuals in the Government of Viatka, that they are Ugrians in blood, and (I believe) language ; but that they are Mahometans in creed—*Biserman* being, word for word, *Mussulman*. They are, perhaps, neither more nor less than Votiak converts of some standing.

CHAPTER X.

The Fin or Ugrian Family.—Ugrians or Fins in Cúrland, Livonia, Estonia, the Governments of St. Petersburg, Novogorod.—Finlanders of the Duchy of Finland.—Tavastrian, Karelian, and Quain.—Their early Christianity. —Their present Popular Poetry.—The Kalevala.—The Laps.

THE Tshuvash of the last chapter, by being an equivocal population, or one of disputed affinities, leads us from the Turk family to the Fin, or Ugrian.

This, even now, occupies a very extensive territory; and originally it was one of still wider dimensions, one of a more varied population, and, thirdly, one of a continuous and unbroken area—which it is not at present.

The language of the Magyars of Hungary has long been recognized as Ugrian. In Hungary, then, we have the limit of the Fin area on the South. The Magyar area, however, is discontinuous.

On the North, we have in Lapland and the Samoyed country the Ugrians of the parts beyond the Arctic Circle.

Of the Fins on the Baltic, the most western locality is Courland; for thus far do Fins, or Ugrians, extend in the direction of Prussia. In Courland, however, the undoubted natives are Letts of the Lithuanian family; and the name that these Lithuanian Letts give to the Fins under notice is " *Lief.*" And this is the name by which they are generally known. They call themselves " *Sea-shore-men,*" and it is only when they speak Lettish, which they do no more than they can help, that they recognize the name. No definite account can be given of their origin; for, though " *Lief*" is a name which we may reasonably expect to find in *Livonia* or *Lief*land, it is not the one that we look for in Courland. Of *Liefs* in Livonia, as distinguished from the ordinary Fins of that Government, the number in A.D. 1840 was only twenty-two; and this, some few years after, was reduced to twelve, the occupancy of these being a small patch of country near the mouth of the river Salis. Between the Liefs of Courland (*Sea-shore-men*) and the Letts, the commerce is of the scantiest : intermarriages being rare ; and their respective pursuits and aptitudes different. In the way of physical conformation, bodily stamina, and energy of temperament, the balance is in favour of the fishermen. On the other hand, however, they are hard drinkers, and unscrupulous wreckers.

Small as is the number of these fragmentary Liefs, their language falls into two decided dialects, that of Pisen, and that of Kolken—not to mention the Lief of Liefland, in the strict and proper meaning of the term, with its twelve proprietors.

It is only by courtesy that the Liefs find a place in a work on nationalities ; so microscopically small is the portion of the earth's surface which they cover, and so numerically small is the amount of the population ; for of all those divisions or subdivisions of mankind in which the ethnologist delights, and for which no one else cares, the Lief is the smallest that Europe can supply. There is as small a one in Asia, and there may be smaller ones in America ; but in Europe there is nothing so fragmentary.

In *Livonia*, though the *Liefs*, who gave the name to the district, are now, in all probability, extinct, there is plenty of the Fins of the ordinary Estonian type. This is nearly that of the proper *Finlanders*, or the occupants of the Duchy of Finland ; so that what applies to the Estonian Fins applies to the Livonian also.

Estonia, like the other Baltic, or German, provinces of Russia, is largely Germanized. Like Courland and Liefland, it was conquered by the Knights of the Sword ; and, like the Lieflanders and the Courlanders, the native Fins were reduced to the condition of serfs. The serfs, however, who, in Courland, were almost exclusively Letts, and in Livonia were Letts and Fins in something like equal proportions, were, in Estonia, almost wholly Fin. Indeed, in the way of ethnology, Estonia begins on the river Salis; and, so doing, includes nearly all the northern half of Livonia.

The Fin element, then, is common to both provinces; being paramount in Estonia.

Its ordinary name is German; *Estonia* being but a Latin form of *Estland, i.e.,* the Eastern Land. Word for word, this coincides with the term *Æstyii* in Tacitus—word for word, but not place for place. The *Æstyii* of Tacitus lay between the Vistula and the Niemen, and were the ancestors of the true Prussians; as is inferred from the fact of the Amber Country being their occupancy. To the informants of Tacitus this was the *Eastern* end of the Baltic; the coast of which, after we pass Konigsberg, suddenly turns northwards. It was only in after times that *Estland* meant the parts along the Gulf of Finland, or the *extreme* East.

The name by which the Estonians designate themselves is *Rahwa*; and as -*ma*, in Estonian, means -*land*, the native name for Estland is *Marahwa*=*Rahwaland.*

Estonia, rather than Livonia, is the Land of the Rahwas merely because it is the most especially Rahwa—Rahwa purely and simply rather than Rahwa and Lett. Looking, however, to the *numbers* alone, *half* Livonia is more than *all* Estonia.

In Liefland, the Rahwas amount to 355,216
Estonia,   ,,   ,,   252,608
Vitepsk,   ,,   ,,   9,936
Pleskov (Pskov)   ,,   8,000
St. Petersburg,   ,,   7,736

633,496

Some of the purest blood in Europe is to be found amongst the southern, the eastern, and the central Rahwas; the admixture of foreign elements being the greatest on the northern and western frontiers. In the south, too, and the east, the greatest number of national characteristics presents itself; and that in the way of physiognomy, in the way of manners and customs, and in the way of language.

Whatever may be the case with the Ugrians of Asia, of

whom we know comparatively little, there is no doubt as to the musical and the poetical aptitudes of the Baltic Fins. Even the fragmentary Liefs are known to have songs of some sort. But in Estonia the quantity of national poetry increases, and its quality improves. In Finland proper, in the famous Kalevala, it will reach its height.

The Estonian instrument is the harp, of which the following short poem gives us the early history:

On the pathway sang the women;
On the pathway, on the roadway,
Bridesmaids singing in the village.

On the way to church I sang;
In the porch and in the church.

My step-sisters murdered me;
With a round stone like an egg;
With a sharp axe.

Whither did they take the maiden?
To the moor with the bright berries.
What grew out of her?
Then grew out of her a noble birch-tree,
And it shed a smell around it.

What came out of the birch-tree?
The birch-tree was made into a harp;
It was cut into a fiddle.

What made the frame of the harp?
It was made of the gills of a salmon,
Out of the hard teeth of a pike.

And what were the harp-strings made of?
Out of the hair of the beautiful bride,
Out of the locks of the chickie-biddy.

But where were the players on the harp,
The players of the harp in the hall?
Brother, dear brother,
Take the harp to the hall,
Lean it against the wainscot,
Put your thumb to it,
Put the tips of your fingers,

Strike sharp with the iron.
The spell of the strings of the brothers sounded
With the sorrows of the only harp,

As when Vierland's maidens weep—
The sorrows of the bridesmaids of Harland
Going forth from the house of the father,
Going forth from the house of the mother,
Going out to the house of the bridegroom,
Going out to the house of the husband.

With this harp did the native bards wander from place to place as the harvest-home or the wedding-feast might tempt them. There are none such now alive, the last having died in 1813. He had no fixed residence; but was known and welcomed, whithersoever he chose to roam, as the *wanna laulumies,* or the old singing-man.

Neuss calls the following a drinking-song. The bacchanalian element, however, holds but a subordinate position.

I drank ale and emptied the can,
Threw the staves in the wood,
Threw the hoops in the thicket,
Dashed them on the ground,
In the morning went to look for them,
The day after looked about.
A fine ash-tree had grown up,
A fine ash-tree, a broad wood.
A muskin on each twig,
A squirrel on each branch,
A singing-bird on each roost.

Wait, wait, wait, squirrel,
Stay still little bird,
Till I get my gun,
Till I clean its barrel.

From every twig I shot a muskin,
From every branch I shot a squirrel,
From every roost I shot a singing-bird.

The *opus magnum* which Neuss dignifies by the name of Epic is the following. Its repetitions are Homeric; but there is a reason for them. The song was danced to, and the figures recurred.

Then the war began to lower;
Russian soldiers rushed upon us,
Polish soldiers came and robbed us,
Saxon soldiers came and shot us.

Young and tender, I kept crying,
Kneeling mid the garden flowers.
Keep me, keep me, Lord of Harland.
Bring out your deep boats,
Till I get back to the house,
Till I find some merchant,
Till I find some one to save me,
Who will save me in the war.
At the front-door, at the back-door,
In the war, and in the slaughter,
In the war, and in the clutchings,
From the Cûrlanders,
From the Russians,
From the murderous knives
From the foemen's sword.

Then I went to beg my mother.
"Oh! my dear mother,
  Save me from the war."
"How can I save you?"
"You have got three aprons,
  One worked with gold,
  One worked with silver
  One with old brass.
Give the best for me,
Give the best for your only daughter."
Then straightway the mother answered,
"I'll not give them for my daughter,
  Not my aprons for my daughter;
Daughters there are here and there,
Here to-day, and gone to-morrow.
Aprons last your lifetime."

Then the war began to lower,
Russian soldiers rushed upon us,
Polish soldiers came and robbed us,
Saxon soldiers came and shot us.
Young and tender, I kept crying,
Kneeling mid the garden flowers.
Keep me, keep me, Lord of Harland.
Bring out your deep boats,
  Till I get back to the house, &c.
Then I went to beg my father.
"Oh! my dear Father,
  Save me from the war.
  From the front-door," &c.
"How can I save you?"
"You have got three bullocks,
  One has a horn of gold,
  The other a horn of silver,
  The other a horn of old brass.
Give the best for me.

Give the best for your only daughter."
Then straightway the father answered,
" I'll not give them for my daughter,
Not my bullocks for my daughter;
Daughters there are here and there,
Here to-day, and gone to-morrow.
Bullocks last your lifetime."

Then the war began to lower, &c.
Then I went to beg my brother.
" Oh! my dear brother,
Save me from the war," &c.
" How can I save you?"
" You have got three horses.
One, a horse with mane of gold;
One, a horse with mane of silver;
And the third, a mane of old brass;
Give the best for me,
Give it for your only sister."
Then straightway the brother answered,
" I'll not give it for my sister,
Not my horses, for my sister;
Sisters there are here and there,
Here to-day, and gone to-morrow;
Horses last a lifetime."

Then the war began to lower, &c.
Then I went to beg my sister.
" Oh! my sister, little sister,
Save me from the war, my sister!" &c.
" How can I save you?"
" Ah! my little sister,
You have three garlands;
One is like a garland of gold;
Another like a garland of silver,
The third is of old brass.
Give the best for me, my sister,
Give it for your only sister."
Then the sister answered straightway,
" I'll not give them for my sister,
Not my garlands for my sister;
Sisters there are here and there,
Sisters you can have for one moon;
Sisters you can have for two moons;
Garlands last your whole life long."

Then the war began to lower. &c.
" Lads of Vierland,
Noble fellows,
Save the maiden
From the soldiers," &c.
' How can we save you?"
" You have got three hats,

One is a hat of old brass;
One is a hat of new silver;
And the third, a hat of gold.
Give the best for me,
Give it for your only maiden."
"How long will a hat last?
Hats last only two days;
Maidens last a whole life long."

Sword-dance.

There was a maid, a young maid,
She took the herds to the homestead;
Found a chicken in the field,
Took the chicken home;
Out of the chicken came a man.
The maid was Salmi, Salmi the fair.

There came three wooers—
One, the Moon's son,
One, the Sun's son,
The third, the Star's son.
The handsome Moon's son came,
He came with fifty horses;
He came with sixty bold led-horses.
Then spoke Salmi from the corn-loft:
Crying out, from out the barn—
"No, no; not the Moon for me;
He has three duties:
First, he rises in the twilight,
Then he rises at the sunset,
Then he rises at the sinking."

The handsome Sun's son came,
He came with fifty horses;
He came with sixty bold led-horses.
Then spoke Salmi:
"No, no; not the Sun for me
The Sun has many duties:
The Sun sends hot beams,
Makes the fine weather,
Makes the harvest for the mowing,
Makes the rain come down in showers;
Sets the crops of oats a-growing,
Makes it sultry, makes it thunder;
Burning up the oats a-growing,
Kills the barley in the valleys;
In the sand beats down the linseed,
And the peas in all the furrows;
And the wheat behind the farm-yard,
And the flax along the forest."

The handsome Star's son came,
He came with fifty horses ;
He came with sixty bold led-horses.
Then Salmi spake from out the corn-loft ;
Took the Star's horse to the stable,
The roan to the stable,
Gave him his fill of oats,
Dressed him in fine linen,
Put a housing over him,
Let him close his eyes in silk,
Up to his hoofs in oats.
" Sit down, Star,
At the table
By the white-wall
On a bench of hornbeam
To the seasoned dishes,
Seasoned with pepper."
Then she took the Star to the chamber,
" Eat, Star ; drink, Star,
Live in pleasure."
But the Star drew his sword.
No eating, no drinking,
Send Salmi into the chamber.
Salmi spoke from out the corn-loft,
In the house behind the homestead .
" Dearest mate, and dearest bridegroom,
Give me time to grow :
Give me time to array myself.
Slowly does the fatherless one array herself;
Slowly does the motherless one array herself;
Slowly does the orphan array herself.
No mother to dress me,
No parents to clothe me ;
The mothers of the village must dress me,
The old women must clothe me.
The village gives cold comfort,
The people of an iron heart."

Of the war songs the number as well as the merit is higher
than it is in Lithuania.

Could I but die in the war,
Die in the war without sickness;
Go off with the shot of the enemy,
Without the weary pain,
Without the weakness of death,
Without the waste of sickness.
Better to fall asleep in the battle,
To fall before the banners,
To sell your life to the sword,
To the arrow from the cross-bow.

" No fight with sickness,
No slavery to sorrow ;
Sleepless on tho bed of pain.
Death in war has higher joy,
With tho wounds of your brothers,
When tho sister's eye weeps.
' Ah ! my brother, in the pride of life,
Has fallen in open war.' "

In the Governments of St. Petersburg and Novogorod the population becomes more exclusively Russian, and the fragments of a once continuous Finland, or Ugria, become less conspicuous.

Still there are traces of the older populations, and with that the definite characteristic of language.

The ground on which the great city of St. Petersburg stands belonged, at the accession of Peter the Great, to Sweden. But the Swedish dominion itself was foreign, and such Swedish elements as Ingria, or the present Government of St. Petersburg, contained were intrusive—so truly was it a continuation of Finland in the direction of Estonia, or of Estonia in that of Finland. Hence there is a Swedish as well as a Russian element in these parts.

Akin to the Rahwahs and, at the same time, akin to the Finlanders, yet different from both, are the *Vod* ; the Vod who are the true representatives of the aborigines of the Government of St. Petersburg ; the Vod who serve as samples for what the occupants were when all between Narva and Viborg was Ugrian. There are other Ugrians besides ; some from the northern frontier of Estonia, some from the southern parts of Finland ; but the true aborigines are these Vod—transitional in language, and possibly in many other less definite characteristics, between the Estonians Proper and the Finlanders of Finland.

These Vatlanders, or Watlanders, call themselves Vadjalaiset. In number they amount to something more than five thousand. They occupy certain small villages between Narva and Cronstadt in the Circles of Oranienbaum and Yamsburg. We may think of them, if we choose, as the Ugrians of Yamsburg ; inasmuch as they, doubtless, belong to the great Yam division of the Ugrian population, a division which contained the

aborigines not only of St. Petersburg but of Novogorod as well—
of St. Petersburg and Novogorod as well as much besides.
These it was with whom the Slavonians from the south came in
contact, upon whom they encroached, and by whom they were
resisted. By the end, however, of the thirteenth century the
Vod, at least, were quieted. The fort Koporie was, then, built
to overawe them. Add to this the influences of Christianity;
which the Russians introduced. In *Estonia* it was the Germans
who did so; so that, in *Estonia*, the creed, now Lutheran, was,
originally, Roman Catholic. In *Vodland*, however, it both was
and is the Christianity of the Greek Church.

Their language is called *Vais*. "*Tunnet pajattaa Vaiss*" =
"*Do you speak Vod?*" It is in the parishes of Kattila and
Soikina that it is spoken; and it was from an old woman of
Kattila that Lönrot first, and Ahlqvist afterwards, made a collec-
tion of Vod songs; an old woman who has since died (*i. e.* in
1856).

In the eleventh century one of the divisions of the ancient
Novogorod was called *Votskaia Patina* (*i. e.* the *Vod Fifth*),
just as, in the eyes of the old Norsemen, Northumberland was a
fifth part of England, or, as in Yorkshire, we talk of the *Trith-
ings* (Ridings). The Swedes took up this name (Russian as it
was), and in a document of King John III. (A.D. 1590) we find
that he makes his son "Prince of Finland, Carelia, *Wätzkij-
Pethin*, and Ingermanland," in Russia.

Upon the popular poetry of the Vod a flood of light has been
recently thrown by Ahlqvist; previous to whose inquiries, two
short fragments were the only known representatives of what is,
apparently, a rich literature in its way. The great storehouse, as
is so often the case, and as we have just stated, was the memory
of an old woman; the most important poem which it supplied
being a long wedding-song. More than a mere ode, it seems
to be adapted to the details of the chief preliminary ceremonies;
and it was, to some extent, an acted chorus—a true *prothala-
mium*. Too long to be given in full, it is sufficiently remarkable
in form to claim notice. Hence, the following extracts are simply
intended as a sketch of its general structure. The imagery is that
of the Estonian compositions in general, and the metre is Estonian
as well.

The opening :—

>Bathe—bathe, my brother !
>Bathe—bathe, my spark !
>Bathe in ten parts water—
>Wash in eight parts !
>Before the door stands father,
>Island-boots in hand,
>Fish-caps under arm.
>Before the door stands mother,
>Checked shirt in hand,
>Fish-caps under arm—

And so on, through the brothers and sisters, &c., until the bridegroom leaves the bath-room. Then—

>Hail ! in the wind of Yumala !
>Hail ! out of the bath !
>Hail ! fish after the cleaning !
>Take now Yumala for thy help,
>Take the dear Creator,
>The mother of God before her.

On entering the room :—

>Come, Yumala, and help—
>Come, Yumala, and help the boy !
>Help him, kind father,
>In treading across the threshold,
>Villagers, Christians,
>Step on each side ;
>Make way for my grouse,
>Make way for my blackberry.
>Father at the top of the table, &c.

>* * * * *

>Sorrow not, my dear brother,
>Fear not, my spur-wearer.
>Never is your coat other than comely,
>Never are the island-boots shabby,
>Never is your belt bad,
>Never your hat awry.
>Honey-drops spirt out
>From the golden girdle,
>From the chalk-white helm.
>Sorrow not, my dear brother :
>Fear not, my spur-wearer.
>Go not alone, my brother ;
>Go not by yourself, my fish :
>With thee goes a line of bridesfolk,
>A band of mates.
>With the Moon as bridegroom's father,
>At the head of the troop the Sun ;
>Thou, as the Sun's son, at the side,
>With the bride's train as stars ;

The sister brings words in her glove—
Songs in the pocket of her gown.
Sorrow not, my dear brother ;
Fear not, my spur-wearer ;
Thou art new stricken, my leaf !
Not cast away, my berry !

The bridegroom takes his seat under a figure of St. George.

Great kinsmen of my bird,
Noble men of a high house,
Help the well-beloved :
Part with words, and part with clothing.
Help him with copper,
Help him with gold.
In married life gold goes,
Gold coins melt away.
Sorrow not, my dearest brother,
Work shall be done in the house.
Your father is still alive :
My mother is still alive.
At the table sits the father,
At the cupboard the mother.
The father helps his kin ;
The mother sets the table.

The bridegroom now goes to fetch the bride.

Help now, Yumala !
Come, Creator,
With the Mother of God !
Come, Creator, on the Cross !
Saviour on the   .   .   .
Mark a cross, my dearest !
Knock at door, my little bear !
Knock at door carefully,
Stoop your face, my golden one !
On each side, my little fish !
The tree thou nearest,
Red shall it be ;
The hedge thou nearest,
Green shall it be, &c.
Villagers, children of Christ, &c.

On entering the house of the bride :—

Come into the room, brother !
Warm, my heart !
My brother comes to one whom he knows
Come to the ownership of the house :
Father at the end of the table ;
Make room for the apple of my eye,
A place for my own and only one, &c.

Then, to the bridegroom :—

> Hast key in girdle?
> Hast secret skill behind?
> Canst open the Butterburg—
> The white Church of the Vod?

And now, they ask for meat and drink.

> My brothers-in-law, lads of gold,
> My true kinsmen,
> Let not the cates spoil,
> Let not the meats cool ;
> I shall not spare the cates,
> Nor yet hoard the drink.
> My brothers-in-law, lads of gold,
> The beer warms you,
> The brandy lights you up :
> Vierland's brandy, good for drinking,
> Honey-beer from our own land.
> I tarry not at the brandy :
> The beer does not warm me.
> Work must be done in the house :
> The mother is still alive, &c.

The bridegroom sits down at the table.

> Sit thee down, my loved one ;
> Sit thee down, my only brother,
> At the foot of Yumala,
> Under the holy kerchief,
> Before the face of the Kind One !

Grace after meat :—

> Thanks and blessings
> For the meat and drink :
> I've been at many weddings—
> At eight in all :
> Never ate I such cates,
> Never drank I such liquors, &c.

To the bridegroom :—

> Hast key in girdle?
> Hast skill in pocket?
> Canst open the Butterburg—
> The white Church of the Vod?

To the host :—

> Dear brother-in-law, my golden one,
> It is not my brother
> That thou deceivest,

It is thy own brother—
Thy own sister.
Take a message to the maiden,
Let goosey know,
That the maiden weep not more.
Weeping wears the heart,
Tears hurt the eyes.

As the guests depart :—

Time to go—time to go,
The horses are neighing,
The nags are whinnying, &c.

The bride reaches the bridegroom's house :—

Brotherkin went out alone :
Back he comes with some one else,
Bringing the mother a helpmate, &c.

Greeting of the bride :—

Hail, young, dear maiden !
Hail, coming from the way !
Let me see my maiden !
Let me see her by the fire—
Let me see her by the light !
Black was she painted, my chicken,
Smoke-black was she painted.
Black are they who said it—
Smoke-black the sayers.
She was good, and she is good ;
Fair in her open sleeves,
Clean in her silken shirt,
Beautiful in her kirtle.
Dear maid—dear maiden,
As thou comest, so stay, &c.

The bride is taken to a well to look at the water :—

Go to the well, my maiden,
To look at the water ;
How it springs up
From the pebbly bottom,
From the sandy spring.

The presents being inspected and divided, the poem concludes
with—

Dearest maiden—only maiden,
As thou comest, so stay.
Try to be careful,
Try to be right clean.

Ingria, or *Ingermanland*, takes its name from the *Ingrikot*, or *Izhor*; the former being the native, the latter the Russian, name. The Ingrikot amount to eighteen thousand, all within the Government of St. Petersburg.

In A.D. 1623, the district of Agrepää was ceded by the Russians to the Swedes, and along with it two others, namely Yeskis and Savolax. It is believed that when this took place the ancestors of the *Savakot* and *Auramoiset*, two other Fin populations of Ingria, migrated into their present localities. The former amount to 42,979, the latter to 29,344.

Another variety of the Ugrian family, known by the name of *Tshúd*, now comes under notice. This is believed to have been the name by which the Slavonians designated certain nations which were other than Slavonic. Still, they do not seem to have called the Germans so; for them they call *Niemce*. Nor yet the Turks; who are *Tatars*. Where, then, the word *Tshúd* is used, it is used by a Slavonian, and is, probably, applied to a Ugrian. It is not known to the Ugrians themselves, and is anything but a complimentary designation. It is much such a word as *Barbarus* in Greek and Latin, only not applied so generally.

I cannot, however, find that *all* the Ugrians were called *Tshúd*. The Estonians are not. The Finlanders are not. It seems, then, as if the name were given more especially by the Russians of Novogorod to the Ugrians of their immediate frontier. At any rate, the Ugrians under notice are pre-eminently Tshúd, and as Sjögren connects them with the Vod, he occasionally allows himself to speak of the one as the Northern, the other as the Southern, Tshúd.

But now another name occurs. Vladimir, son of Yaroslav, marched with a mighty army out of Novogorod, against a population called *Yem*, or *Yam*, and conquered it. He lost, however, his horses through a murrain. After this, the Yam appear frequently in Russian history, and that as a sturdy, brave people. Two elaborate papers of Sjögren address themselves to the question—Who were the *Yam*? The answer is, that they were the ancestors of the present Tshúd of Olonets and Novogorod.

A.D. 1042.

17 *

The Tshúd have suffered much from encroachment; more than the Ugrians of St. Petersburg. Sometimes they lie in patches, oases, or islands. Sometimes they have other Ugrians in contact with them. They lie—some on the banks of Lake Onega, others in the Circle of Bielosersk. They lie in Novogorod, as well as in Olonets. When Sjögren described them, he carried their numbers as high as twenty-one thousand. An earlier table gives for—

The Government of Novogorod	. .	7,067
,, Olonets	. . .	8,560
		15,627

These Tshúds call their language *Luudin kieli Luudin tongue* or *speech*. How such a name as this *may have* originated I shall suggest in my notice of the *Lith*uanians; but without affirming that it *did* so originate.

Another name for a Fin fragment is "*Vesp.*" This can scarcely be other than the "*Ves*" which has already been stated to be the name for the language of the *Vod*.

"*Karelian*" is the name for a dialect, or co-ordinate division of the Fin of Finland. It may, possibly, include both the *Luudin kieli* and the *Vesp*. Of the Karelians more than a hundred thousand are believed to lie apart from their congeners, in—

The Government of Novogorod	.		27,076
,, ,,	St. Petersburg	.	3,660
,, ,,	Tver	. .	84,638
,, ,,	Yaroslav	. .	1,283
			116,657

Such are the more fragmentary and sporadic Fins of certain Russian Governments rather than the typical Fins of the Duchy of Finland.

Of this, those of the south-western districts and the parts between the water-shed and the sea, or the parts about *Tavastahus*, form the *Tavastrian* division.

Those beyond the water-shed, in the direction of Olonetz and Archangel, are classed as *Karelians*.

The northern part of the coast of the Gulf of Bothnia gives us a third name; and the Finlanders for this part are called *Quains (Kwæn)*. The Quains were the *Sitones* of Tacitus; as is shown by a curious misinterpretation. *Qvinna*, in Swedish, means a *woman;* so that *a kingdom of Qvains* may be mistaken for a *kingdom of queans*. Some one between the first observer and the direct or indirect informant of Tacitus fell into this mistake; the result being that the text of the "Germania" tells us that the Sitones are ruled by a woman, and that they must be despised accordingly. The blunder continues. Alfred writes about *Cwænland;* and Adam of Bremen of a *Terra Amazonum*. Who first, cunningly, hit upon this element of error I am unable to say. I can only say that it has been recognized as a likely one; and that few doubt the identity between the Quains and the Sitones.

The *Fenni*, as described by Tacitus, are amongst the rudest and filthiest of nations—without arms, without horses, without household gods—*non arma, non equi, non Penates*. They feed on herbs; they wear skins; they lie on the ground. Their arrows are tipped with bone ; and the women join in the chase with the men. They live in wattled huts ; but, withal, live happily—" *securi adversus homines, securi adversus Deos, rem difficilliman adsecuti sunt ut illis non voto quidem opus esset.*" That this applies to the *Laps* rather than the Finlanders has been maintained by the learned; and the fact of *Finmark* being the Norwegian name for *Lapland* is in favour of the view.

That the original Fin polity was of the simplest is an inference from such words as *kuningas, tuomari, valtakunta, esivalta, sakko, tori,* &c., which mean *king, judge, authority, power, fine, market,* &c., all of which are Swedish. So are the names of the commoner trades and employments : with the notable exception of *kanguri* and *seppa,* meaning *weaver* and *smith*. These are native ; as are the *rauta=iron, tekase=steel, vaske=copper, hopia=silver, hölmä=bog-iron*. The word for a feast was *drinking*. A maiden given in marriage was *sold*. There was a name for freemen and for slaves : a name for a village, and a name for a large assembly of houses at which was held a kind of court—*kyla* and *kenaja* respectively.

If we put all this together we shall take the description of the Fenni, as found in Tacitus, with reservation: treating them as a rude population, but as a population of which the culture, though low, differed from that of the Germans and the Sarmatians in degree rather than kind. Between the time of Tacitus and the first Swedish invasions there is an interval of nearly a thousand years. How far it was stationary or progressive during this period is uncertain.

What in the way of useful arts and national polity the Fins had of their own, and what they adapted from the Swedes, has just been noticed. They certainly had *not* the art of writing. Their poems are called *runot*: a word to which the Fin language attaches a long list of derivatives. In the opinion of some this makes it a Fin word. Others hold it to be simply the Norse *Rune*.

The first notices of the Tavastrian part of Finland, or the Finland of the present Duchy, are no earlier than those of Sweden, indeed, not quite so old; and the earliest historical notices of Sweden are no earlier than A.D. 826. When Harald, the king of Jutland, was baptized in that year at Mentz, Anskar, a monk of Corvey, accompanied him home; offered himself as a missionary for the *terra incognita* of Norway and Sweden; visited Birca, where he was favourably received by King Biörn; returned to Hamburg, of which city he was constituted archbishop; and died in 868. With the exception of his immediate successor, Rimbert, no one, for seventy years after his death, revisited Sweden; so that when Unne, Archbishop of Bremen, at the end of that time, reached Birca, the work of conversion had to begin *de novo*. The earliest notices, then, in Swedish history, belong to the times of these three missionaries; and it is remarkable that they give us an expedition of one king against Curland, and one of another, Eric Edmundson, against not only Curland, but also against Estonia, Finland, and Karelia. Eric Edmundson died A.D. 885.

Then we get for about the same time notices of the piracy on the part of the Fins along the Malar Sea, and the invasion by St. Eric, about 1160, of Finland, one of the objects of which was to convert the Finlanders. Geijer calls it a crusade; and he further suggests that he planted Swedish colonies in the country, and laid the foundation of its long connexion with Sweden. He was accompanied by St. Henry, the first bishop of Upsala, who was the earliest apostle of Finland, and who suffered death at the hands of the natives. To St. Eric is attributed the first Swedish settlement in Nyland. To the year 1187 is assigned the destruction of Sigtuna by Fin pirates; and in 1259 a Papal Bull was addressed to the kings of Sweden and Denmark, exhorting them to make a joint effort against the pirates, then formidable. About 1248, Earl Birger puts himself at the head of what Geijer again calls a Crusade against the same enemies, who, so far as they were ever converted, have now relapsed, practising horrible cruelties, and, in union with the Carelians and Estonians, ravaging the coasts of Sweden. In this, Birger was successful; moreover, he built the castle of Tavastaborg. This is in the reign of the Grand Duke Alexander Nevski, with whom Birger came into collision.

Whether the statement that, up to this time, the Southern Fins had been subject to Russia be true is uncertain. It is only certain that, after the foundation of Tavastaborg, the Swedes turned their arms against the Russians, who in the Papal letters of the time are massed-up with the Fins as relapsed Christians, against whom a crusade was to be directed. The attack, however, on the Russians miscarried.

About 1300, another Birger, or rather the regent, Thorkel Knutson, completed the conversion of the Western Fins. The Karelians, however, remained pagan and formidable, and were coerced accordingly. It was against them that the fortress of Viborg was founded; a fortress which served as a basis of operations against Russia as well as against Karelia. Even now the names which appear so prominently in the later history of Estonia and Livonia present themselves with the same details. The Swedes take Kexholm from the Russians in one campaign, and the Russians take it from the Swedes in another. That some of the Fins of these parts owe their Christianity to Russia rather than Sweden is likely; and the Russians claim the credit of having converted them, A.D. 1227. They may have done this, and, yet, have done it ineffectually; for the special charge that lay against the Fins was that there was nothing real in their numerous conversions. When an enemy threatened them, they embraced Christianity, and, when that enemy left them, they apostatized.

Under the Union, Finland was held as a feudal tenure, by either some member of the royal family, or some great officer of state—who sometimes affected a dangerous independence. It was always being attacked by Russia and not always effectively defended.

Under the descendants of Gustavus Vasa it was better held than administered : indeed, so long as Livonia and Estonia were Swedish, the material strength, as well as the strategic positions, was on the side of Sweden.

Except, then, on the frontier of Ingria, and in Eastern Karelia, the civilization and Christianity of Finland are from Sweden—from Sweden with its Roman alphabet, its Protestant- ism, and its literature. Nor, were the benefits one-sided. Hardy seamen and brave soldiers were always forthcoming from Finland.

It is the character of the early civilization and the Chris- tianity of the Fins that is now the main object for our consideration.

Agriculture extended itself from South to North, from Tavas- tria, across the watershed, to Karelia, and, in the North-East, to Lapland.

As early as A.D. 1360, twenty Laplanders and Finlanders, as having been baptized by a Swedish bishop in a great vat at Tornea.

As far south as the parts about Orivesi, on the northern frontier of Tavastaland, the signs of an early Lap occupancy present themselves in the shape of what the Swedes call The Lap Rings (*Lappringarne*); *i.e.* circles of stones which increase in number as we move northwards, and decrease southwards. The word "*Lap*" itself is, also, considered to mean a *boundary, end,* or *march.* An early Esthonian missionary mentions a "*provincia extrema Lappegunda,*" and in Finland itself we may read a *Lap* Lake, a *Lap* Mountain, a *Lap* Bay, a *Lap* Tower, a *Lap* Marsh, a *Lap* Cairn, a *Lap* Strand, and a *Lap* Dale. On the other hand the Laps say that they are descended from two brothers. A storm came on. The Swedes (Laps of Sweden) put up a board, and took shelter under it. The Laps took to a tent. Ever since it is in tents that the Laps have lived; while the Swedes have lived in houses.

Finland, itself, is, of course, a Swedish word, and, as such, foreign to the Fins. It is, however, current among them ; and, though it has not wholly superseded the native name *Suomelaiset*, it is in a fair way of doing so. It is certain that Fins may be found who do not know the meaning of this last denomination. It is much such a word as *Kymry* in Wales; national, very national, tolerably old, but not universally recognized.

The term "*Tavastrian*" has already been noticed. Its opposite is "*Karelian*." For this last the word *Zavolok, Zavolockian, Savolaxian,* or *Savolocensian* is a rough equivalent ; the word being Russian, and meaning *Tramontane*, or, more literally, *beyond the watershed*. In all the later works upon Fin archæology this difference between the Tavastrians and Karelians is strongly and minutely insisted on. It is possible that, at times, it is overdone. This, however, is a point upon which a foreigner should speak with unfeigned diffidence. For Tavastrian, *Ham* and *Yem* are occasional synonyms, the former being, in its fuller form, *Hämalaiset* ; the opposite to which is *Kainuluiset*. For the *Karelians*, however, of the north-west *Zavolockian* is, probably, the commoner name.

On the Russian frontier there is an infusion of Russian blood, and in the maritime towns a still larger one of Swedish. In Norway there is a Norwegian, and in Lapland a Lap, inter-mixture. In the centre, however, of the Duchy the blood must be some of the purest in Europe. Not that even there, it is, to a certainty, absolutely pure. All that can be said is that it has received no foreign elements for more than a thousand years. At an early period, however, the Laps extended further south. Such, at least, is the opinion of the most accomplished native historians ; and such seems to be the legitimate inference from more than one fact in language, in archæology, and in legend. Be this, however, as it may, the present Finlander, in his typical form, is the representative of a very pure stock.

By the Fin philologues, who, in other languages besides their own, are approved investigators, great stress is laid upon the difference of the Tavastrian and Karelian dialects, the former being the most cultivated, the latter the most widely diffused, of the two. Between the two, however, the class, of which the Vod, the Estonian, the Lief, the Tshúd, the Vesh, and the Krivonian are members, the division of which the Fin of the Duchy of Finland is represented, is spoken in Curland (as a fragment), in Estonia, and in the Governments of St. Petersburg, Novogorod, Tver, Olonetz, and Archangel. Nor is it till we come to Vologda and to Permia that we meet with the languages of the Ugrians of our next chapter.

Whatever the Fins may have taken from Sweden in the way of creed and civilization, their original character has been but slightly changed. The Fin physiognomy, the Fin temperament, the Fin language, and the remains of the original Fin heathendom still remain. Nor do they seem likely to give way to any exotic influences. They have been fostered and encouraged, rather than opposed, by Russia ; which has shown no little wisdom in not only abstaining from the attempt to transform the Fins into Muscovites, but has made palpable efforts to develop a Fin, in opposition to a Swedish, nationality. Nevertheless, in even the latest ethnographical map of the Grand Duchy, the whole of the south-western coast is marked as *Fin and Swedish.* In the interior, however. and in the north the Scandinavian element decreases : until, on the frontier of Karelia, even the Lutheran form of religion is infringed on by that of the Greek Church.

Of the Fin physiognomy it is enough to say that, in such systematic works as deal in definite classes with broad lines of demarcation between them, it is designated by the term *Mongolian* : in other words, it is compared with that of the Asiatics of Central Asia and Siberia rather than with that of the Europeans of Germany, France, Italy, or Greece.

In respect to temperament the Fin is reserved, stubborn, obstinate, and enduring, with agricultural and maritime aptitudes, and a capacity, at least, equal to his opportunities.

His language is soft, with a paucity of consonantal combinations, and a highly developed declension—its congeners being the Vod, the Estonian, the Lief, and (less closely) the Lap, the

Votiak, the Zirianian, the Ostiak, the Vogul, the Magyar, the Tsherimis, the Mordvin, the Samoyed, and the Yukahiri. But of the Fin as the representative of a great ethnological class more will be said as we proceed ; or, rather, more will show itself as population after population is treated as Fin or Ugrian—for *Ugrian* is the name which is most convenient for the class when we speak of it as a large and important *genus*.

That no small amount of heathendom underlies the imperfect Christianity of the Lithuanians has already been seen ; and it has also been seen that in Estonia the amount of it increases. In Finland it obtains its *maximum ;* many of the details being the same for each country. This, indeed, is what we expect from the similarity of the Fin and Estonian languages ; not to mention other ethnological characteristics. In Finland, however, everything connected with mythology and legend is of large and grand dimensions. The Estonian narratives, with their human character and their moderate length, when they re-appear in Finland have expanded themselves into Epics. The small shrines scattered here and there in honour of some obscure divinities assume, in Finland, the proportions of a Pantheon. The Microcosm becomes Macrocosmic ; and much of what is obscure, fragmentary, and (if taken by itself) unintelligible in the Estonian legends, grows clear and definite when illustrated by a Fin commentary.

In a preface to one of the earlier Fin translations of the Psalms, Bishop Agricola enumerates the heathen deities in whom, notwithstanding their nominal Christianity, the Finlanders of his time still believed in.

Ucko ciet pluvias, metuendaque fulgura vibrat,
　Rauna movet ventos, fulmine et ipsa minax.
Rongotheus vestit flavente siligine campos,
　Neve sit Agricolæ spes sua vana facit.
Hordea *Pellpeckus* cultis producit in arvis,
　Zythifer et genti creditur esse Deus.
Wirankannus agros viridi fecundat avena,
　Egres lina, fabas, rapaque pigra serit.
Kondus arat colles, atque ustis semina tesquis
　Credere, Sarmatica callidus arte, docet.
At curat pecudem *Kekri*, atque propagine læta
　Respondet votis, pastor avare tuis.
Hisis prosequitur tristeis urosque luposque,
　Nyrka sciurorum dirigit omne genus.
Hillavanus leporis saltus moderatur hiberni,
　Venator felix est *Tapionis* ope.

Retia lenta replet diversis piscibus *Achtes*,
  Lickio sed plantis arboribusque praeest.
Dejicit hinc *Turisas* infestos arcubus hosteis,
  Ilmarinesque idem regna quiete beat.
Cyclops *Krattus* opes veneranti donat alumno,
  Tontus pacatam reddit ubique domum.
Luna coloratur variato lumine *Rachki*;
  Praedaque fit *Kapeis* non vigilante Jove.
Prata bonus *Kalevas* viridanti gramine texit,
  Atque replet foeno rustica tecta novo.
Dulce viatori carmen facit *Eunemoines*,
  Quo tardae fallat taedia longa viae.

Now, in a poem published within the last thirty years, many of these names re-appear; so that the pagan element of the sixteenth century is the pagan element of the nineteenth also.

The *cultus* of *Jumala* (*Yumala*) is one of the great Ugrian characteristics. It is widely spread. It originated early. Languages, wherein the names of the minor and newer divinities are different, all agree in containing the root *Jum*—for the syllable *-la* is a derivational affix. Thus, in the Samoyed, the word is *Num*; the change from *y* to *n* being common. The Tsherimis form is *Juma*, the Zirianian *Jen* (from *yenm*, or *yeml*). The Estonian and Lap names are *Jummal* and *Jubmal* respectively.

We may talk, then, of the *Jumala-cultus* as being the chief *cultus* of the Ugrians. The meaning of the word is various. It denotes (1.) the Sky or Heavens; (2.) the God of the Sky or Heavens; (3.) God in general; the existing Finlanders who have been Christianized, using it in this third sense at the present moment, notwithstanding its relation to their old heathen mythology, just as we use the word *Hell* from the Goddess *Hela*.

Ukko bears a name with, apparently, a very definite signification. In the Magyar, *agg* means *old*. In Ostiak, *yig* does the same. In a secondary sense this latter word is *father*. Word for word, it is the *aga*, or *aka*, of the Turk dialects, wherein it has almost as many meanings as forms. All, however, imply seniority, and the respect which seniority demands. In Yakut it is *father*, in other languages *elder brother*, *uncle*, *grandfather*. In pursuance with this, Ukko is (as Lenqvist writes) *totius aulae celestis senior et praeses*; his designation being a title, or form of address rather than a true and proper personal name. It is only this, however, in its primary etymology. In practice, it is a true and proper personal name as well. If so, Ukko is not only Pater and Princeps, but Diespiter, Jupiter, or Zeus. Like Zeus, too, he is the God of Heaven.

> Ukko, who art in the heavens ;
> Ukko, father of the heavens;
> Ukko, in the clouds that rulest,
> And the clouds and breezes drivest ;
> Rule the clouds, and rule the heavens,—
> Rule the sky and rule it kindly;
> Send a cloud from east to westward,
> Send a cloud from north to southward,
> Send a cloud from west to eastward,
> From the south send clouds and showers—
> Clouds whose showers drop like honey, &c.

Tapio, of Tapio*la,* or Tapio-*land,* heads the list of the genii of the forest, presiding over the beasts, both of the chase and the homestead, more especially, however, those of the chase. Yet his apparel and harness are scarcely those of the hunter. His cap is made of the needles of the fir, his jacket of the lichens. His jacket fits tight, and his cap is like the mitre of a bishop ; at least it bears the same name, *hippa.* His beard is brown, and his neck is long, so that he is sometimes called *Knippana* (long-necked) on that account. But he has many names besides this ; or, at any rate, many circumlocutions under which he is invoked. He is the Lord of Tapiola; the Old Man of the Woods; the Elder of the Hills; the King of the Forest; the Master of the Waste ; and the like.

His more especial epithet is *tarkha,* that is, the *exact* or *careful;* for where need a man be careful and exact if not in hunting ?

He has a wife, a maid, and a son. The son is noticed first; because when he has been noticed the whole of the male part of Tapio's family is disposed of. Yet the family is a large one. It is large, but it is a family of daughters ; for the gods of the Fin forest are chiefly goddesses. The Fauni and Silvani are Dryads and Oreads. *Nyyrikki,* however, or *Pinneys,* is a son ; the son of Tapio ; son and heir-male ; well-shaped and comely, with a high cap on his head, like his father ; but no jacket of lichens on his body. He has a blue vest instead, and he bears himself nobly in it

When the ways are foul. and the bogs deep, Nyyrikki, or Pinneys, makes bridges or lays stepping-stones; or, this being done already, directs the feet of the wandering huntsman to where they are. He marks, too, the trees, and, so doing, shows which way is to be taken, which avoided. Tapio, the father, gives the game. Nyyrikki, the son, gets it pursued in safety.

The mother of Nyyrikki and his numerous sisters is *Miellikki*. She has many names besides; but Miellikki is, probably, the commonest. She is the hostess of the woods; the mistress of the court of Tapio; the queen of the woodland; the mother of the honeycomb – of which she is the consumer as well. One of her names is *Simanten*; *sima* meaning *honey*. A damsel of her train is named Honeymouth.

If things go but badly, she is an ugly old woman dressed in rags, and those rags dirty. But if game be abundant, she is loaded with golden ornaments; rings on her fingers, rings on her toes, rings on her wrists, rings on her ankles, and ear-rings; all of gold. Golden, too, is the band round her forehead; and of gold the wires and pins of her hair. But her eyebrows are adorned with pearls, and her stockings are blue and her garters red.

As are the garments, so is the dwelling; so, at least, according to Castrèn's interpretation, runs an obscure passage in the Kalevala. Lemminkainen sings that one day, when he was a-hunting, he saw three houses, one of wood, one of bone, one of stone. The mansion of stone was the residence of Tapio when he was free and liberal in sending game. When he was chary, he lived in the lodge of wood; and when an actual niggard, in the bone-house. He owned treasures; of which honey in abundance was the chief. The key of the storehouse was of gold, and his wife, or housekeeper, kept it on a ring by her side. For Tapio had a housekeeper as well as his Miellikki. This was *Tellervo*, or *Hillervo*. She had a round and full figure with golden hair, and dressed herself in a fine linen smock with ornamented edges. I call her housekeeper, because I am uncertain about her actual relation to Tapio; who may have been a polygamist. She is called Tapio's maid and the maiden of the woods. She is once, however, if not oftener, called Tapio's wife; and, occasionally, she is confused with Miellikki.

She has a name to herself. So has the good-natured *Tuulikki*. The rest of the children, or maids, of Tapio, are known only by their function, which is to look after the wild and the tame. Collectively, however, the female portion of them (which, with the exception of Nyyrikki, means the whole) is called *Luonnottaret*, or *Luonnon tyttärat*. One of these is more especially *Metsän piika*, or the wood-maiden, short in stature, fond of music, fond of honey. Indeed, this is the young woman who has already been named as Honeymouth. Her flute is *Sima-pilli*, or honey-flute. She wakes the milkers with this, by blowing it in their ears if they be too late of a morning.

The remembrance of *Kekri* is still to be found in some parts of Finland, where All Saints' Day bears his name. It is the time when much corn is thrashed, so that, probably, Kekri is the genius of harvest, or the threshing-floor.

Ahti is the god of the sea; *Vellamo* being his wife.

Towards the end of the last century these and other remains of the original heathenhood commanded the especial attention of Ganander and Porthan; the latter the founder of the present school of mythological investigators. Then followed Topelius, who gave the germs of a system by arranging the legends round their several subjects. He collected, for instance, all those which appertained to a fabulous individual named *Vainamoinen*. Lönröt went further, both in the collection of legendary poems and in their arrangement. The result is the *Kalevala*; a Fin Ossian with fair claims to authenticity. It grew into form gradually, and was the work of more investigators than one. It is a pagan poem in respect to its machinery, though not without allusions to Christianity. Towards the end, the names even of Herod and the Virgin Mary appear; but this is in a kind of appendix to the poem, rather than the poem itself.

The Kalevala is a series of rhapsodies; the word being used in that technical sense in which it appears in the numerous writings on the Homeric poems. It is in the language of the present time and in the metre of Longfellow's Hiawatha; or rather, Hiawatha is in the metre of the Kalevala. The heroes are Vainamoinen, Illmarinen, and Lemminkainen, whose actions (like those of Diomed or Ulysses in the Iliad), though separate are still capable of being connected in such a manner as to give unity to the poem in which they are exhibited. The scenes are, for the most part, in Kalevala and Pohiola. All three of the above-named agents agree in acting more or less in concert. They represent Kalevala as opposed to Pohiola. A sketch, however, of the details shall speak for itself.

It was for a space of thirty summers and thirty winters that Vainamoinen, the Ancient of Days, lay in the womb of his mother, and long seemed those thirty years to Vainamoinen. He asked the Sun and he asked the Moon to set him free, and he asked Charles's Wain; but neither the moon nor the sun nor the Wain of Charles heard him. So he freed himself. It was in the night that he was born, and he was born a smith. On the first morning he went to the smithy, and he forged himself a horse. It was as a straw; and he rode on its back to Vainogard and Kalevala. There was a Lap, and he squinted, and he had long borne a grudge against Vainamoinen. He had a bow and a quiverful of arrows, and he waited from morn till night, and from night till morn, for Vainamoinen by the waterside. It was on the waterside that he drew his bow upon him, and shot his arrows; though his mother, and his wife, and three men, and three spirits had said "Lap! Lap! shoot not Vainamoinen, for he is the son of thy father's sister." The first arrow flew too high. The second flew too low; but the third struck the horse of Vaina-moinen on the left shoulder. So Vainamoinen fell into the sea, and lay there six years. For six years he lay adrift, with the waters below him and the sky above him. He raised his head, and there came an island. Where he stretched his hand there came a promontory, where his feet touched the bottom there came a fishing-ground. There came, too, from another quarter, an eagle—an eagle from Turialand and from Lapland. It was a nest that the eagle wanted, and it was on Vainamoinen's knee that it was made: for the Ancient of Days had raised his knees above the water, and they were all rough and shaggy like an old withered turf. Of this the eagle made its nest, and laid in it six eggs—six golden eggs. But the seventh egg was of iron. Vainamoinen felt the warmth and drew his knees under the water. He shook them, and the eggs rolled off. They rolled on a sunken rock and broke, and the eagle that had laid them flew away.

The lower part of the egg became the earth; the upper part the sky: the white became the sun, the yelk the moon. The little pieces that were broken-off became the stars. But Vainamoinen still lay adrift on the waters.

There blew a storm from the south-west; and at the west there was a rolling of billows: and Vainamoinen drove and drove before the wind, drifting and drifting on the billows, until he came to Pohiola—Pohiola the Dark. He had a hundred bruises on his side, a thousand buffets on his body.

Louhi, the mistress of Pohiola, had just risen. She had lit her fire, and had swept her hearth, and she went out to listen. What was it she heard? It was not a child that cried. It was not a woman who was moaning. The moaning was of a bearded man: the crying that of a Uvantolainen. So Louhi, the toothless, took her raft and put out to sea. Vainamoinen was very wet; so he got on the raft and sat at the steerage, whilst Louhi, the toothless, plied the oars, and rowed him to Pohiola, where she gave him flesh and honey to eat, and ale to drink. " Moan no more, Vainamoinen; cry no more, Uvantolainen : but live for the remainder of your days in Pohiola." But Vainamoinen said, " It is better to drink water in your own country than to fill yourself with ale on the ground of a stranger." Then said Louhi, "What will you do for me if I send you home?" and Vainamoinen answered, "What is it you want?" Louhi said, "Sampo." To which Vainamoinen replied, "I cannot make Sampo myself; but I know who can." "What's his name?" said Louhi. "Illmarinen," said Vainamoinen. "Let him do it, and he shall marry my daughter." So Vainamoinen set himself on a sledge, and started to drive from Pohiola the Dark and from the dreary Sariola.

Then rose up the fair maid of Pohiola and drew on her red stockings, and let herself be seen by Vainamoinen : who asked her to go with him in his sledge. "Willingly," said the maiden, "if you will do two things—cut through a tile with a blunt knife, and halve an egg without leaving a mark."

This Vainamoinen did, but the maiden would not go into the sledge: "Make for me," said she, " a boat."

Vainamoinen had now to use his axe; and he used it for the sake of the maid with the red stockings in Pohiola. He chopped and chopped; but Lempo sat on the blade, and Pira on the head, and Hiisi on the handle; so that when he was striking his strongest stroke the axe glinted aside and hit him on the knee. The knee bled, and bled, and Vainamoinen was left a limping cripple. There was a spell to cure him; but he had forgot the most important words that belonged to it. All the rest he knew; but the working words he did not know.

However, there was some one who did; and him Vainamoinen went to seek. At the first house at which he knocked he heard the voice of a child; but the child told him that no one there knew anything about the spell. He was sent onward; but the old woman at the next house knew as little as the child. She sent him on to the next: in which there was an old man. With this old man ends the third canto, book, duan, or rune—for the name by which the divisions should be called is, to a great extent, arbitrary.

The fourth, which may easily be separated from the rest, is a dialogue between the old man who cures Vainamoinen and his patient. They talk, *inter alia*, of iron; and Vainamoinen talks to advantage. He does, however, nothing which bears upon the rest of the story, and the fifth canto begins with his journey homewards; or, rather, to the dwelling-place of Illmarinen. Vainamoinen gets into his sledge without help, and starts.

Upon getting home and meeting Illmarinen, he tells his adventures, and adds that in the land of Pohiola, there is a toothless old woman as mistress, who is named Louhi, a beautiful maiden who wears red stockings, and a great demand for Sampo. If Illmarinen can make Sampo, he can marry the fair girl with the scarlet stockings. Illmarinen, however, has no wish to marry, and, if he had, would not go to Pohiola for a wife.

Vainamoinen now brings forth a fir-tree out of the earth which grows, and grows, until it is so tall that Illmarinen believes that if he climb to the top of it he will touch the moon and Charles's Wain. So he swarms up it—backed, of course, by Vainamoinen. As soon as he is up high enough, Vainamoinen whistles for a wind, and the fir-tree is uprooted, and its upper half falls into the sea; and the lower half follows, and the whole drifts until it comes to Pohiola: upon which Illmarinen arrives, just as Vainamoinen had arrived before, and where he found just Vainamoinen's conditions of residence and marriage.

These are, that he should make Sampo, which he does. He fares, however, no better than Vainamoinen who did not; and the maid with the red stockings is as little the bride of Illmarinen as she was of Vainamoinen.

With Illmarinen's disappointment ends the fifth rune of the Kalevala; and from the negative character of its termination, as well as from the fact of both Vainamoinen and Illmarinen appearing in all the other runes, it is clear that the story is not ended. At the same time the portion which the first five runes deal with is sufficiently separate from the remainder to take the appearance of an independent story. It can be joined-on, or worked-in with the rest, or it can be cut-off, and kept-apart, just *ad libitum*. It is essentially *rhapsodic; i. e.* it is like a pattern in a piece of needle-work, or like a window in a perpendicular chapel. It can be kept to itself, or it can be worked-in as a part of something else.

With the sixth canto, a new story begins and a new character, Lemminkainen, comes upon the scene. Lemminkainen is the antipodes of Vainamoinen. Like Vainamoinen and Illmarinen, he is skilled in smith's work, in spells and the like. He is young and good-looking; whilst Vainamoinen is old and ill-favoured : yet, upon the whole, though successful with women, he is less successful than his old mate. The three, however, form a definite trio—Vainamoinen, Illmarinen, and Lemminkainen,—Lemminkainen, Illmarinen, and Vainamoinen.

Lemminkainen starts for Pohiola, but with no very definite reason; still less under any temptations on the part of either Vainamoinen or Illmarinen. In his journey, however, to Pohiola lies the connecting link between the sixth and the preceding cantos. We find, from an incidental notice in the sequel, that he was a married man who left a wife behind him. He delights in love-locks, and it is whilst he is brushing his hair that he declares his intention. His mother dissuades him: telling him that the Lap wizards will be too much for him. He does not much fear them. He has spells of his own which will match theirs—not to mention a strong coat-of-mail. " When the Laps kill Lemminkainen, blood will come out of that brush," said he, and started. The brush was carefully put by, and watched.

It is on a sledge that he starts : not without a large feeling of complacency at his future triumphs over the Lap wizards.

Another name for Lemminkainen is Kaukomieli ; though Lem minkainen is the commoner designation. He drives one day, two days, three days, stopping on the road, much as Illmarinen did, and asking for some one who can unharness and bait his horse. The first applications are made in vain ; however, he reaches Pohiola, and is received by Louhi, whom he approaches without disturbing the dogs—at any rate, without their barking. "Who are you that come here so boldly—and no dog barks ? "

"I've not come hither without wit and skill. Your wizards may do their worst."

So now a contest ensues, in which Lemminkainen overcomes all the Laps but one ; and him he deems unworthy to be called a rival.

"Why don't you try me ? " said the last old man of the weird company. To which Lemminkainen answers rudely, tell-ing him that it is not against the like of him that he measures himself.

He, of course, suffers for this : for the old man betakes himself to the river Tuoni (which is interpreted the River of Death), and waits for Vainamoinen : whose immediate business is with Louhi and her daughter, the maid of the scarlet hose.

"You can have my daughter," said Louhi, " if you can run down the Hiisi elk with snow-skates." So Vainamoinen puts on his snow-skates and runs down the elk, after a long and adventurous run. Who can run in snow-skates like the sons of Kaleva ?

"Now catch the Hiisi horse." The horse is caught.

"Now shoot the swan of Tuoni,"—the River of Death.

But the swan was not so easily shot as the horse and elk were caught. On the contrary, the quest brought Lemminkainen to his end : for it was to Tuoni that the old insulted wizard had betaken himself to wait for Lemminkainen, whom he kills in the water.

The mother and wife, who were left at home, now saw that the brush was bleeding ; and the eighth canto gives a description of the mother's search for her son. She reaches Tuoni, makes a rake, and rakes up the remains, and brings Lemminkainen to life.

The three next cantos deal entirely with Vainamoinen and Illmarinen without mentioning even the name of Lemminkainen. However, Pohiola and the mistress of Pohiola, and her daughter with red stockings, connect the story with what has gone before, and with what will follow. Vainamoinen will build himself a boat, so he takes his axe and walks to the wood and begins to fell an oak. But the oak says, " I shall do no good in a boat, there's a worm at my root, and there's a raven among my branches with blood on its beak, blood on its neck, and blood on its head." So Vainamoinen left the oak, and went on to the fir tree, and he would have made a good boat out of the fir tree if he had not forgotten the three words. He had finished the prow, and he had shaped the sides, but when he got to the stern the three words were wanting, and he could not think what they were. He met a herdsman, and the herdsman said, " You may get them out of the topknot of a swallow, or the shoulders of a goose, or the head of a swan." But, though Vainamoinen shot many hundreds of swans, geese, and swallows, he could not find the words. He then met another herdsman, who told him he would find them under the tongue of a reindeer, or under the lips of a white squirrel. But Vainamoinen killed hundreds of reindeer and thousands of squirrels without finding the words.

So he took counsel of his own thoughts, and said, " It is only in Tuoni and Manala that I shall find them," so he went one day, and he went two days, and on the third day he came to the river of Tuoni.

Vainamoinen.—"Daughter of Tuoni, bring out the boat."

Daughter of Tuoni.—"Not unless you tell me what brought you here."

Vainamoinen.—"Tuoni himself brought me here."

Daughter of Tuoni.—" I can tell when a man lies."

Vainamoinen.—" Iron brought me to Manala, steel brought me to Tuoni."

Daughter of Tuoni.—" I can tell when a man lies. If steel had brought you hither, blood would run from your clothes."

Vainamoinen.—" Fire brought me to Manala, flames to Tuoni."

Daughter of Tuoni.—" I can tell when a man lies. If fire had brought you to Tuoni, your clothes would be burnt."

Vainamoinen.—" Water brought me to Manala, water brought me to Tuoni."

Daughter of Tuoni.—"I can tell when a man lies. If water had brought you to Tuoni, your clothes would be dripping with wet."

After this answer Vainamoinen told the truth, and Tuoni's daughter ferried him over, gave him meat and drink, and left him asleep.

Now whilst he was sleeping, she netted a net of iron wire, and fastened it to a stone at the bottom, and drew it under the river and over the river, so that Vainamoinen should be caught in his sleep. But Vainamoinen, though very tired, slept lightly, and, when he knew what she had done, turned himself into a stone and lay at the bottom. However, the net caught him, when he turned himself into an eel, and slipped through the meshes.

It's not often that any one escapes from Tuoni and Manala.

So Vainamoinen went home, thinking and thinking about the Three Words, until he thought of Antero Vipunen, that old Kalava who had been dead for many years, and who could only be reached by going along a road made of the tips of needles, and the points of swords, and the edges of axes.

So he went to Illmarinen, and told him to make an iron shirt and a crowbar of iron, "for I am going to Antero Vipunen, the old Kaleva."

"Antero Vipunen has long been dead, and you won't get a word from him, nor yet half a word."

However Vainamoinen went his way, and travelled along the road made of the tips of needles, and the points of swords, and the edges of axes, until he came to where Antero Vipunen lay buried.

An aspen had grown from his shoulder, and a birch from his temples, and an alder from his jaw, and a willow from his breast, and a hornbeam from his forehead, and a fir from his teeth, and a larch from his foot.

The aspen tree that grew from Antero Vipunen's shoulder, and the birch from his temples, and the alder from his jaw, and the willow from his beard, and the hornbeam from his forehead, and the fir from his teeth, and the larch from his feet did Vainamoinen chop up and throw down. He, then, drove his crowbar through the mould into Antero Vipunen's mouth. Now Antero Vipunen could not swallow the crowbar, so he swallowed Vainamoinen instead. Vainamoinen is now in the stomach of Antero Vipunen, and bethinks himself of what he can do. He takes off his shirt, and out of the sleeves makes bellows, out of his breeches he makes the pipe, out of his stockings the mouth, uses his own knee as an anvil, his elbows for a hammer, and his little finger for tongs: and so sets to work in the bowels of Antero Vipunen, whereat the old Kalava breaks out in singing. He sings through nearly four hundred lines. He ends his song by spitting out Vainamoinen, who out of it has been lucky enough to pick the three words, and with these he returns to Illmarinen.

"Well, what has the good old man told you? has he told you how to build the boat?"

"That is just what he has done," said Vainamoinen, "and I'm now going to build it."

The boat is built, and Vainamoinen is on his way to Pohiola, thinking of Louhi and the maiden with the scarlet hose. On his way he sails by a promontory, and there he sees the maiden Anni.

Anni was Illmarinen's sister, and she was busy in the bucktub, washing her linen on the sea-shore. "What's that in the distance?" said she; "it can't be a flock of geese, nor yet a swarm of fish, nor yet a rock; it must be a boat, it must be Vainamoinen's." So she hailed the boat, and asked what the boatman wanted.

"I have come," said Vainamoinen, "to see how they catch salmon in Manela."

"I know when a man tells a lie," said Anni; "when my father and grandfather went to catch salmon, they went with nets and spears."

"I have come to see how they catch geese."

"I know when a man tells a lie," said Anni, "it was not in a boat like that, that my father and grandfather caught geese."

"Come with me in a boat," said Vainamoinen.

"If you'll tell no more lies I will," said Anni.

So Vainamoinen told Anni the truth, and Anni went and told it again to her brother Illmarinen.—Illmarinen, who, as we know from previous story, was himself a wooer for the fair maid of Pohiola. So Illmarinen proposed to accompany Vainamoinen, and Vainamoinen was fain to put up with his company. Before they started, Illmarinen provided himself with rich gifts of gold and silver, and it must be remembered he was the younger man. They both arrived at the same time, and when Louhi saw them it was the old Vainamoinen whom she would fain have chosen for her daughter, but the daughter chose for herself. Vainamoinen asked her to be his wife at once, and was at once refused. Illmarinen asked her also, and was told that she would live with him if he would do three things. There was a field full of snakes, and this field he must plough; there was a wood full of bears and wolves, and these he must muzzle; there was a pike in the river of Tuoni which he must catch without tackle. All this he did, and told Vainamoinen that he had done it, whereupon the old smith hung down his head, turned his back, went homewards, and said those words: "Sons of men, born and unborn, do anything before you do business with Illmarinen.

> " Never swim a match,
> Never lay a wager,
> Never woo a maiden,
> With Illmarinen the smith."

The story might now end, inasmuch as the three next cantos are devoted to a description of the marriage. The details, however, are sufficiently numerous, sufficiently important, and sufficiently original to form a poem by themselves. They stand between what proceeds and what follows them, but they give us neither a breach nor a continuity. The wedding is celebrated in Pohiola, and it is Louhi who provides both the beef and the beer. There is no lack of either, but, on the contrary, a superfluity of both. They have to kill an ox, but this ox is of such a vast size that they have to go far for the butcher. It reached from the Gulf of Finland to the Arctic Ocean, so that it must have overshadowed all Finland and all Karelia. It was broad enough to stand with one foot in Lapland and one in Siberia.

From the tip of one horn to the tip of the other a swift swallow might fly on a summer's day.

From the root of the tail to the tuft at the end a squirrel could run in a month, resting for one night half-way.

It was in Finland that the ox was calved, and it was fed in Karelia. The tail swished Tavastaland; the head touched Kemi: one foot was put-down in Olonets, another in Turialand; the third on the waterfall of Vuoksen, and the fourth in Lapland. The butcher who can kill it is not to be found.

Neither is it an easy matter to brew the ale. They can get the hops, and they can get the malt; but they can't get the yeast.

The daughter of Louhi is told to send out a squirrel, but the squirrel is sent out in vain. She then sends out a martin, but the martin returns without the yeast, or, at any rate, without the means of making the brewing work. At last they send out a little bird named Mihilainen, who flies over nine seas, and half-way over a tenth, brings back some honey, and the ale is brewed. But it works so quickly, that no one vat, nor any ten vats will hold it; nor can it be held at all unless certain songs are sung by the company which has to drink it. So they apply to all the skilful singers, and, amongst them, to the old trusty Vainamoinen; whose songs are effective. Meanwhile they take especial care not to ask the lively wicked Lemminkainen.

Lemminkainen, however, comes uninvited. There is a great feast, and, after a time, Illmarinen is ready to go with his bride, and the bride seems only too willing to go with him. Her mother blames her for this, and then she is too much the other way. However, at the end, they start, reach Illmarinen's country, and have another great feast, which is prepared by Illmarinen's mother.

More episodic than the most episodic of their predecessors are the two next cantos—the seventeenth and eighteenth. They begin with the names Ahti and Kauko, each meaning the same person, and each, as we see in the sequel, meaning Lemminkainen.

Ahti, however, Kauko, or Lemminkainen, who dwells on a promontory, is busy at the plough. No one has such quick ears as Ahti: so he hears what is going-on in Pohiola; hears the sounds of messages containing invitations to a feast; hears the sound of the preparations for the feast itself; hears the names of many guests; but fails to hear his own. So he mounts his horse, and goes home to his mother: "Mother, mother, make ready the meat, and warm the bath; I must eat and wash." So his mother made ready the meat and warmed the bath. " Mother, mother, bring out my harness."

"Whither wilt thou go? to the wood, or to the sea, or to hunt the elk?"

"Not to hunt the elk, nor yet to the sea, nor yet to the wood. There is a wedding-feast in Pohiola, and I am not bidden to it."

The mother now went far in her dissuasions, telling him of many dangers, but of three most especially. The first was the cataract of flame; the second was the island of fire in the middle of a fiery lake; the third was the snakes at the gates of Pohiola itself—gates which were of iron and which reached from the earth to the sky.

"I can overcome all this," said Lemminkainen.

"But there are other dangers besides."

"Never mind, give me my harness; I look upon him as a man who can draw an arrow to the head on Lemminkainen's bow."

"Be it so; but when you drink empty only half the can."

He started, and overcame the three difficulties; not, however, without much detail, both in the way of action and of dialogue, and reached Pohiola.

Lemminkainen. The bidden guest is welcome, but more welcome still the unbidden one.

Louhi. I am sorry to see you. The ale is still in the malt, the malt in the corn. The wheaten bread has yet to be baked; the meat to be boiled. It were better for you to have come a night sooner or a day later.

But Lemminkainen would both eat and drink, and one of Louhi's maidens was told to bring him ale. She brought it in a double-handled can. There was water at the top, dregs at the bottom, and venom and snakes in the middle. But Lemminkainen took a probe of iron from his pocket, put it in the beer, and brought up hundreds of worms and thousands of black snakes. " Give me better ale than this."

But Louhi called-up a heavy stream of water to overflow the room and drown Lemminkainen.

Then Lemminkainen called up an ox to drink up the water

Then Louhi called up a wolf to tear down the ox.

Then Lemminkainen called up a white hare for the wolf to eat instead of the ox.

Then Louhi called up a dog to kill the hare.

Then Lemminkainen called up a squirrel to get on the dog's tail.

Then Louhi proposed that they should measure swords. The Pohiola weapon was no bigger than a grain of corn, no longer than the line of dust under a finger-nail.

The fight indoors only spoilt the doorposts. So they went out and continued the battle. They laid down a cow-hide, and on that they fought. The champion of Pohiola could not so much as draw blood. Lemminkainen, however, cut off his enemy's head at the first blow.

A loud yell from Louhi now brought down upon Lemminkainen the whole host of Pohiola; whereon he thought it better to go away. He got on his horse, and he rode home to his mother, sad in spirit, and with his head hanging down.

"Is it from drinking? Is it women? Is it a horse?"

"It is no horse; no woman; no drink. Get ready some meal, and let me have butter enough for the first year, and swine's flesh enough for the second. There are swords whetting, and lances gleaming. I've killed a champion of Pohiola. Where, mother, can I hide?"

Mother. It is hard to hide. If you are a fir or a birch you may be cut down; if you are a cloudberry or a bilberry you may be picked; pike are not safe in the waters, nor bears in the wood.

Lemminkainen. Whither can I go? Swords are whetting, lances gleaming.

Mother. I know of one place, and one only; but if I tell you where it is you must swear a strong oath that neither for silver nor for gold you will go to the wars for ten summers. So the son swore the oath to the mother.

Then Lemminkainen pushed off his boat and went in search of the island. The maidens of the island welcomed him. There was not a town in the island, but what had ten houses. There was not a house in the island, but what had ten maidens. There was not a maiden in any house by the side of whom Lemminkainen did not sleep; not one in ten, two in a hundred, or three in a thousand. These were the only maids and wives of the island without a name whom Lemminkainen failed to please; indeed, there was only one with whom he failed.

From town to town went Lemminkainen until he came to a town where there were men as well as maids. At last he saw no house in which there were not three rooms, no room in which there were not three fighting-men, no fighting-man who was not either sharpening a sword or whetting an axe.

It is now time for the disappointed traveller to get back to his boat. But the boat was a heap of ashes.

He builds another and pushes off. The wind rises and, on the third day, he comes to an island.

The boat.- Why was I built? Ahti no more will go to the wars, neither for silver nor for gold; not for ten summers.

Ahti (*Lemminkainen*).—Do not grieve; you shall still see some battles. I *will* go to the war.

So Ahti girded himself up for the war, though he broke the strong oath he had sworn to his mother. "Who shall I get to stand by my side—another man, another sword?" He had heard of Tiero; so he gets Tiero as a companion.

The next rune I pass over *sicco pede*. Though, in Castrèn's analysis, connected with what follows, it has no necessary connection with any part of the story: being little more than a scene in the life of Kullervo an Estonian rather than a Fin hero.

The next, however, gives us our old friends.

Sorrow sat heavy on Ilmarinen. He wept much a-mornings, more at noon, most at night. He was always plying his hammer, and he sought for gold and silver in the sea. Thirty loads of wood did he heap up, burnt them into charcoal, and smelted with it both his silver and his gold. His bellows, too, were always blowing. The thralls blew at them, and were never weary: the hired workmen blew at them fierce and fast. It's a wife of silver and gold that Ilmarinen will make for himself.

But now the thralls blew lazily and the hirelings slowly: so that it is Ilmarinen himself who must blow. Once he blows. Twice he blows. Thrice he blows. He looks along the bellows into the ashes of the charcoal and sees a sword—fair to see, bad to use. Every day it kills one man; on some days two. The sight of such a sword gladdens the thralls, but grieves the master.

And now Ilmarinen stirs the fire with his sword, and throws in of gold a capful, and of silver a hatful. The thralls blow well, but it is Ilmarinen who must go on with the blowing. He blows once, twice, thrice; looks down the bellows; sees a horse—fair to see, bad to use. The thralls are glad, but the master sorry.

Another capful of gold; another hatful of silver; more blowing by the thralls; more by Ilmarinen. From this comes a yellow-haired maiden. It is now the thralls who grieve, and the master who is glad.

But she has neither mouth nor eyes. These, however, Ilmarinen can give her. But he cannot give her speech. Yet she is fair to view: and Ilmarinen takes her to his bed. Sparks flash from the gold: sparks from the silver. "For whom will such a wife as this do? The old Vainamoinen will suit her, and her he shall have for his life."

The first night the old Vainamoinen slept by the side of his bride. The next night he dressed himself in wool. He wore five—six folds of flannel, and two—three bearskins. For all this the bride froze him into ice. "Young men," said the old Vainamoinen, "never marry wives of silver and gold."

Meanwhile Ilmarinen with sunken head and cap on one side betook himself to Pohiola for a wife of flesh and blood; but the hostess of Pohiola only called him a blood-hound, an eater of raw flesh, and a drinker of warm blood. So he brought no wife thence; but twisted his mouth, hung his head, shook his beard, and went homewards, when he met Vainamoinen.

"What is the news from Pohiola?"

"There is good living in Pohiola, for in Pohiola you may find Sampo."

Vainamoinen. Let us go and get it.

Ilmarinen. It is hard to get: it lies in a rock of stone, in a hill of copper, with nine locks and nine bolts. Its roots stretch nine fathoms deep, one in the earth, one in the water, one on the brink of the sky.

Vainamoinen. For all its hills, and all its rocks, and all its bolts, and all its roots, we'll get it. Let us make a sword with a fiery blade for the dogs of Pohiola.

So Ilmarinen set about the sword. He laid the iron in the fire; the thralls worked at the bellows, the hired workmen blew with the bellows; the thralls blew without ceasing: the hired workmen blew quick; until Ilmarinen, looking among the coals, saw a sword. He made for it a hilt of gold and silver and said to himself, "this sword suits the bearer." After this, he put on a shirt of iron and a belt of steel, and said to himself, "the shirt and belt suit the bearer." And now came the time for starting; Vainamoinen said "Let us go by water." Ilmarinen said "Let us go by land."

Whilst they were debating, Vainamoinen heard the voice of a boat, of a boat bewailing to itself: "The house of the man is the longing of the maiden; the billows of the sea are the longings of the boats. They said when they made me that I should be sent out to the wars. Worse boats than I go thither and bring back with them more than a king would earn in six—more than a smith in seven—summers. I was built by Vainamoinen and here I rot, with the worst of the grubs of the field in my planks and the worst of the birds of the air in my masts. Better be a fir-tree in the forest."

Vainamoinen. If you are Vainamoinen's boat, you can free yourself from your moorings, and take to the sea, without the help of hands.

Boat. Without hands neither I nor my brother boats can take to the sea.

Vainamoinen. If I unmoor you, can you run without a steerer?

Boat. Neither I nor my brother boats can run without a steerer.

Vainamoinen. If you are helped by oars and there is wind in your sails can you take to the sea?

Boat. I can take to the sea if there be wind in my sails and if I be helped by oars.

So Vainamoinen unloosed the boat, and sang for a crew. On one side was a crew of fair maidens, on the other a crew of bold bachelors. Vainamoinen steered at first, but after him Ilmarinen; and, with Ilmarinen steering, the boat shot away like a swan, until it came to a promontory where Ahti was sitting, where Kanko was sitting. Now Ahti or Kanko was Lemminkainen, who, when he saw Vainamoinen and Ilmarinen, and heard they were after Sampo, joined in the search.

The old Vainamoinen steers and steers until he comes to a waterfall; and to the maiden of the waterfall he prays that she will let his boat force its way through the rock that lies before it. He prays, too, to Ukko to let him pass onward. However, the boat will not move on, and Vainamoinen must think what it is that stops it. It is not a stone, and it is not a sand-bank; it is a big pike, and the boat has run aground on its shoulders. Lemminkainen sticks at it, but only breaks his sword; Ilmarinen does the same. Vainamoinen, however, digs into the flesh of the fish. After lifting it into the boat, he cries out to his boatmates, "Who is the oldest man amongst you? for he must cut up the fish." But the boatmates cry out to both the men and the women, "Who's got cleaner hands than the fisherman himself? Let him cut up the fish."

So Vainamoinen cut up the fish and said, "What shall we do with his teeth?"

"What can we do with them?" said Ilmarinen, "they are bad at the best."

"A skilful smith," said Vainamoinen, "might make a harp of them; but where is the skilful smith?"

That was Vainamoinen himself. So he made a frame out of the fir-tree, and the teeth of the pike he made into pegs. However, a little thing was yet wanting—where shall they find a string? They found that in the tail of the horse of Hiisi. Now "play on it some old man," but no old man could play on it. "Play on it some young man," but no young man could play on it. Lemminkainen tried to play. Ilmarinen tried to play. Neither Ilmarinen nor Lemminkainen could play on it; so the old trusty Vainamoinen sends the harp to Pohiola, the *kantel* to Kalevala. The hostess of Pohiola plays, the lads of Pohiola play, the lasses play, the bachelors play, the married men play. None of them, however, can bring out a sweet sound; and the old man himself must play. So he washes his thumbs, and sits on the stone of glee, by the side of a silvery brook, on the top of a golden hill. And now the sounds flowed sweetly—the sounds from the teeth of the pike, the sounds from the tail of the horse of Hiisi. Not a beast in the forest but came to hear it, nor a bird in the air but it listened. The wolf awoke in its cave, and the bear danced on the heath; the whole band of Tapio came to hear the sound, and Tapio's wife, with her blue stockings and her red shoe-strings, came to hear it. Not a beast in the forest but came, not a bird in the air but it listened. The eagle flew down from the sky, the hawk from the cloud, the duck from the sea, and the swan from the river—all the little finches, thousands of larks, and tens of thousands of siskins. The maidens of the air came to hear it, and the sun and the moon listened. Not a living thing in the water but came to hear it; and the fishes with their six fins listened. The salmon came, and the pike came, and the dog-fish came with them; and by hundreds and by thousands came all the little fishes. Ahti, with his grey beard, came to hear it, and his wife, who had combed her golden hair with a silver brush, listened to the sound of Vainamoinen's harp.

No heroes were so stern of mood, and no women so tender-hearted, but they heard and wept. Young cried, old cried, the bachelors, and even the married men, cried; middle-age men, and youths, maidens, and little children all cried. At last Vaina-moinen cried himself, with tears as big as berries, and as number-less as the feathers of a swallow. They rolled from his cheek to his breast, from his breast to his knee, from his knee to his ankle, from his ankles to his feet. They wetted his five woollen jackets, his six golden belts, his seven blue shirts, and his eight flannel waistcoats. Down they rolled into the sea, and became pearls. "Who'll pick up my tears?" said Vainamoinen. No one picked up the tears of Vainamoinen. At last there came a blue duck, and the blue duck dived to the bottom of the sea, and brought up the tears of Vainamoinen.

    *   *   *   *   *   *   *   *   *

Vainamoinen was one, Ilmarinen another, Lemminkainen the third.

"What's the news?" said the hostess of Pohiola.

"We are come to take our share of Sampo," said Vainamoinen.

"You cannot part a minever, nor yet halve a squirrel," said the hostess of Pohiola.

So Vainamoinen began to play on his harp, and the men of Pohiola fell asleep. He went on playing, and the bolts of the doors were moved. So Ilmarinen rubbed them over with butter, and pushed back the locks, but he could not reach Sampo.

He took an ox with a hundred horns—a beast with a thousand heads, and he ploughed up the ground till Sampo came in sight.

The old Vainamoinen was one, Ilmarinen was another, and Lemminkainen was the third.

They put out their arms and laid hands on Sampo, and took it to the boat.

"I know where to take it to," said Vainamoinen.

"But why don't you sing?" said Lemminkainen

"It's too soon for that," said Vainamoinen.

The wind blew till it shook the boat, and the hostess of Pohiola awoke, and woke up her men. A thousand went to the oars, and a thousand set up the sails, and they all went after Vainamoinen. Lemminkainen ran up the mast, and Vainamoinen asked him what he saw. "I see hawks on the aspen-trees, and eagles on the birches."

"Don't tell lies," said Vainamoinen; "but look again."

"I see a cloud from the north, a storm from the north-west."

"Don't tell lies," said Vainamoinen; "look again."

"I see," said Lemminkainen, "the boats of Pohiola, with a hundred rudders, and a thousand oars; a hundred men whetting their swords, and a thousand men with their swords by their sides."

"Row, mates, row; row Ilmarinen; row Lemminkainen; row one, row all."

Vainamoinen took out his tinder-box and threw a bit of tinder over his left arm into the sea "Burn, tinder, burn; burn all the boats of Pohiola."

The hostess of Pohiola, the toothless old woman, now changed her shape. The oars became wings, the rudder became a tail, and she and her boat became an eagle.

"I come to halve Sampo," said Vainamoinen.

"I come to take the whole of it," said the hostess of Pohiola.

Ilmarinen cut at her three times with the sword, but could not wound so much as one of her claws. Lemminkainen cut at her too, but the hostess of Pohiola only said, "I pity your mother, to whom you promised that neither for silver nor gold would you go to the wars for ten summers."

Vainamoinen cut at her too, and he left of her claws no more than a little finger. Down dropt the men into the sea; a hundred from the wings of the eagle, a thousand from the tail, ten from each feather, as the squirrel falls from the branch of a fir-tree. Down plumped Louhi herself.

19

But she laid a finger on Sampo, and threw it into the sea. There it lies; and the wealth of the sea is Sampo. Only a few bits were cast upon the shore, and from these came ploughing and sowing, and the wealth of the earth. A little bit only did the hostess of Pohiola keep, and this she took home, but the rest of Sampo is missing in Pohiola, and lost to Lapland.

If a poem which consists in the narrative of an endless contest between two series of immortal beings, who never know when they are beaten, can be said to ever have a natural ending, the Kalevala, as far as the epic's conditions of a beginning, a middle, and an end are complied with, may now be said to have come to its close. Yet we are far from the termination of the book that bears that name. Castrèn, who (from the work which he has so well translated and which he has done so much to make known to the world at large) is our great authority, especially states that, where the contest between the powers represented by the hostess of Pohiola, and the powers represented by Vainamoinen, Ilmarinen, and Lemminkainen, comes to a conclusion, the true Kalevala ends. However, he carries it beyond the date of the event last noticed—*i. e.* the sinking of Sampo in the sea.

With the *sequelæ* to this the twenty-third canto begins, in which we may remark that none of the old heroes, except Vainamoinen, plays any conspicuous part—no conspicuous part in the first instance at least—that we get a new name (*Sampsa* Pellervoinen) whose Christian name (so to say) is wonderfully like *Sampo;* that we get more decidedly than heretofore into Ingria, and Estonia, rather than Finland Proper; and, finally, that a notable Christian element exhibits itself in the greater solemnity of some of the invocations and the use of the name Creator, which, though it has occasionally appeared in the previous runes, appears much more frequently in the forthcoming ones.

So the old trusty Vainamoinen picks up from the sea-shore some bits of Sampo, and takes them to Sampsa Pellervoinen, perhaps the Kullervo of a previous rune. "Sow and plough, and out of these will come wealth." So Sampsa Pellervoinen sowed and ploughed. Six sorts of seeds, seven kinds of fruit did he put in a squirrel-skin bag, and he sowed them until grass, and corn, and trees of all kind grew — some ten, some a hundred, some a thousand fold. One tree alone would not spring up—and that was God's tree, the oak.

He had prayed to Ukko. He had loosened the oxen of his plough. He had gone one night, two nights, three nights, and come back again, for as many days, to see whether the oak would grow.

At last it grew too much for his good. It hid its branches amongst the clouds and its top among the heavens. It shaded and over-shaded the earth. It kept off the light of the moon. It kept off the warmth of the sun. The old troubles of cold and darkness had come upon Vainamoinen, Ilmarinen, and Lemminkainen again; and it was the Hostess of Pohiola that was the contriver of the evil. "What can be done, if the oak cannot be cut down? Who can do it?" said Vainamoinen.

There came up a little man from the sea. He was (like the ox of the wedding-feast) not of the largest nor yet of the smallest. He was a span in length; and he was all clad in copper—copper his hat, copper his shoes, copper his gloves, copper everything.

So he whetted his axe. Five stones from Estland; six quern-stones; seven grinding-stones—with these he whetted it.

And he became a man—a big man. The small of his leg was a fathom; his knee-bone a fathom and a half; his hip three fathoms. One foot forward and he reached the strand. Another foot forward and he reached the field where stood the oak. One blow—sparks; two blows—sparks; three blows—the oak fell to the ground. Its twigs made arrows for the bowmen, and lucky was he who got for himself one of its leaves. Vainamoinen was glad. "Now let us plough and sow." What was sown grew, and Vainamoinen would fain have taken the light of the moon, and the warmth of the sun, and the seed of the field to Suomela.

But the Hostess of Pohiola had another arrow in her quiver; and she locked up the moon in a rock, and the sun in a hill.

"Do what ye can now with your ploughing and your sowing," said she. Besides this she sang songs that brought hail and snow, frost and rain, that charmed the birds of the air and the beasts of the field. Meanwhile, Vainamoinen prayed to Ukko.

But Louhiatar helped Louhi, and bore nine sons—ten sons; all at one birth. There was Fever, Gout, Colik, Ague, Plague,

19*

and their brethren. What can Vainamoinen do with these? The sons of Vainos die under a strange ailment. A sudden sickness takes the Luoto-folk. What can Vainamoinen do? He sits over his fire, makes a salve, and calls upon the Creator. "Is this a plague from the Creator, or is it a punishment?" This is very like what Antero Vipunen had said before, and not very unlike something in the Book of Kings.

He also called upon Kivatar, the mother of ailments, and having got all of them together, put them in a little pot, no bigger than the three fingers of a man, and pitched them into a hole in a rock. With this and with the salves he cast out the sicknesses that the songs of Louhi had raised up.

Still neither sun nor moon shone. So Vainamoinen bespoke Illmarinen (who now for the first time appears in these extraneous runes or cantos) and asked him to go up into the sky to look after these two great bodies and Charles's Wain. They went up and found a maid on a cloud. She kept watch over the fire; but a spark had got away and gone downwards to the earth.

Ilmarinen and Vainamoinen built a boat and went after it. Sampsa Pellervoinen steered and it was over Neva up which he steered them. There they met the oldest of women—the mother of mankind; from whom they learned that the spark had left Truris, Palvonen, Tuoni, and Manala and that it was in the Lake Aluejarvi that a perch had swam after, but a white-fish had swallowed, it. A salmon had swallowed the white-fish, a pike the salmon. So Vainamoinen made a net, and prayed, to Wellamo. The Sun's son came and helped them.

"Shall I pull my best, or pull only for what is wanted?"

"For what is wanted."

So they set the net, and took a huge draught of fishes; but the pike was not among them. Again they set it, and the pike was taken. In the belly of the pike they found the salmon; in the belly of the salmon the white-fish; in the belly of the white-fish a perch; in the belly of the perch a blue ball of twine; in the blue ball of twine the spark. But it was the gain of a loss. The spark blazed, and blazed—and burnt, and burnt, until all was well-nigh burnt up. Ilmarinen, however, was able to sing down the flames—the flames of Panu.

The sun shone not; neither did the moon: and there was sorrow in the hearts of men. The fish knew the burrows of the deep, and the eagle knew the flight of the bird, and the wind knew which way the goose flew; but when day, dawn, and night came in no man knew. The young thought and the men of the middle-age thought about the sun and the moon and Charles's Wain. So Vainamoinen went to the smithy (whether his or Ilmarinen's is not stated) and wrought at the forge, till the sweat ran from his brow, to make a new sun and a new moon out of silver and gold. And he made them: but they were of no more good than the wife of the same materials. They would neither shine with light, nor glow with warmth.

"I must hie to Pohiola."

On the third day he reached the waters of Pohiola.

"A boat!"

But no boat came. So he whistled for a wind, and a wind took him over.

"One foot from the stream to the strand," cried the crew. So Vainamoinen, with both his feet from the stream to the strand strode up.

The crew. Now to the halls of Pohiola!

Pohiola's warriors. What does the rascal want here?

Vainamoinen. The sun and the moon.

Pohiola's warriors. Measure swords, and let the longest strike the first blow.

Vainamoinen's sword was the longer by a barley-corn, by a straw's breadth; and after cleaving the skulls of the warriors of Pohiola, he went to let out the sun and the moon.

But there was a rock of iron with ten doors and ten locks. So he betook himself to Ilmarinen, and asked him to forge a grapple with three prongs, a dozen axes, and a load of keys. One day worked Ilmarinen—two days worked Ilmarinen. On the third day came a lark to him.

The lark. Hear me, Ilmarinen, smith! you are just a first-rate smith; a hammerer without a match.

Ilmarinen. I am this because I always look towards God as I forge and as I weld a lock for the wind and sky.

The lark. But what is it you are forging now?

Ilmarinen. A ring for the necks of the hated women of Pohiola.

So the Hostess of Pohiola flew away with a sad mind; and when the morning dawned came again to the smithy of Ilmarinen as a dove. " News! The sun has come out of its rock; the moon has got loose from the hill." So Ilmarinen looked up; and when he felt the sun glowing and the moon shining broke forth into singing, " Old, and trusty Vainamoinen, come and see the sun and the moon." So Vainamoinen came, and with his song to the sun, ends the twenty-seventh rune or canto.

* * * * * * * * *

With the song to the sun, Castrèn considers that the true Kalevala ends. In his translation, however, there are still five more runes; of which all that can be said in the way of connection and unity with what has preceded is that Vainamoinen appears in them.

Twenty-eighth rune.

Old trusty Vainamoinen says to himself, "I must kill a bear."

He says much besides this; but the further details of his speech are unimportant as parts of the Kalevala, except so far as they give us a great number of mythologic names—Mielikki, Tellervo (*K*ullervo and *P*ellervoinen we have had before) Ohto, Tapio, and Tapiola, or Tapio's land. With these we find the name of the Creator.

Twenty-ninth rune.

Old trusty Vainamoinen says to himself, " I must make a harp," &c., &c. Ahti, Wellamo, and Ilmarinen appear in this canto.

Thirtieth and thirty-first runes.

Old trusty Vainamoinen walks out and meets Joukahinen, who will not make way for him. They fight until Joukahinen's sister is promised by her brother to Vainamoinen. But the sister is recalcitrant; and the disappointment of the old trusty one is, among other details, the result.

Thirty-second rune.

This is, at one and the same time, very scriptural and very unscriptural. It is decidedly based upon the narrative of the birth of our Lord, and it is evidently successful in transforming it into something else. It can scarcely be translated without engendering the notion of a caricature; indeed, how can it be otherwise in a poem, when by the side of Marietta (Mary) and Herodes (Herod) we have Tapio and Pillti with other incongruities to match ?

With a few verses in the way of epilogue ends this remarkable poem consisting of nearly thirteen thousand lines.

Those who love to discover the symbolic in the material may make out of it the antagonism between good and evil, between summer and winter, between light and darkness, between the Laps and the Fins; between, in short, any two opposing elements of any possible dualism. Those, too, who love difficult investigations and uncertain conjectures may tax their ingenuity in trying to find out what was meant by Sampo. It was, to a great extent, a mystery to Vainamoinen and Ilmarinen themselves, who, though they made and stole it, got but little use out of it.

Some commentatators have thought it a talisman, some a mill, some this thing, some that. What it was, however, is doubtful. It was made out of a swan's feather, a fibre of wool, a grain of corn, and bits of a broken distaff; to which some accounts add the milk of a cow. It ground a grist of three measures, one for the house, one for sale, and one for the granary. What it did to help the plougher and the sower we have already seen.

More instructive, because more intelligible than the inner meaning of the story is its outer history; and it is one which the thousand-and-one still unborn commentators on the great Homeric poems will do well to attend to; especially with a view to its essentially rhapsodic character; *rhapsodic* being taken in its strict etymological sense and with a definite technical import. By the skilful welding together of several isolated poems into a single mass, the Kalevala has become what may be dignified by the name of Epic; to which, if we choose, we may prefix the terms *great* and *national*. Its dimensions justify the first, its language and locality the second of these respectable adjectives.

The Wollfian doctrine of the rhapsodic character of the Homeric poems, had the existing state of knowledge been sufficient for the criticism, would scarcely have been paradox. As it was, it dealt with the Iliad and the Odyssey as ordinary epics; comparing them only with those of Virgil, Tasso, Ariosto, Camoens, Ercilla, and Milton ; epics of which the single-handed authorship was a patent historical event, as clear as that of the authorship of Falconer's Shipwreck or Glover's Leonidas. The fact that was either not recognized or not promulgated was, the essentially rhapsodic character of *all* known poems belonging to that stage of civilization to which the Homeric compositions are referred. With the recognition of this, the method, as well as the details, of the criticism wants changing : and it is not so much a question whether the facts in the structure of two wonderful poems justify the hypothesis that they arose out of the agglutination of rhapsodies, but whether there is even a presumption against their having done so.

The merits of the Kalevala will of course be different in the eyes of its different readers. They have had, however, ample justice done to them in more quarters than one. The poem probably has been more praised than read, though the readers of it have been numerous, and the imitators not a few. Indeed, whatever may be its demerits, it is essentially a readable poem ; this is because, the narrative itself having enough of movement to stimulate the reader's attention, its strange tenor makes it impossible for him to guess what will come next ; whilst the metre is short and pleasant, the images clear, the play of fancy pleasing. From the number of repetitions the poem seems shorter than it is.

Of those who can read it with ease and pleasure in the original Fin, the number out of Finland is few. Neither does the present expositor belong to them, notwithstanding his criticism and his exposition. He can just spell his way through parts of it by the help of the Swedish translation of Castrèn ; but the recognized merits of this are so great that it may pass for a practical equivalent to the original. This is, in part, due to the author's skill, in part to the pre-eminent fitness of the Swedish language ; which, though less vocalic than the Fin, is far more so than the German.

We may substitute an illustration for a description, and—by a comparison which the reader anticipates—say that the Kalevala reads very like Longfellow's Hiawatha ; or, rather, that Hiawatha reads very like the Kalevala. When the newer poem of the two was first published a good deal was said about the resemblance ; and it may be added that something was left unsaid. That Hiawatha was in any respect a plagiarism from the Fin poem was one of the laxest of charges, though one that was made. The answer, on the other hand, that it was a collection of genuine Indian legends was anything but a sufficient one. That the Kalevala suggested the Hiawatha, no one who has read the two poems can doubt. The relation, however, between the two poems was this. It was as if, during the time of the sensation created by Macpherson's Ossian, some French poet had visited England, read Temora, and worked up some Breton legends into a poem with an Ossianic character; the form of the poem being suggested *aliunde,* the matter original ; the form being from Scotland, the matter from Brittany. There would have been no plagiarism, and there would have been no absolute originality, of which the most original poets know that there is less anywhere than the world imagines.

That Lönröt is no Macpherson, and that the Kalevala is far more of an ancient Fin poem than Ossian is an old Gaelic one is admitted by his countrymen, who, notwithstanding the bias that may be given to their criticism by their nationality, are, upon the whole, the best judges. It might not be so if the Fin language were as well-known to the learned men of Europe as the Latin and Greek, or even as the Slavonic ; but, as matters stand, their authority must stand for what it is worth—and something more. It has not been received without criticism. On the other hand, it must be remembered that, unlike Ossian, the Kalevala made its first appearance in the original tongue.

The Kalevala is essentially rhapsodic. Neither is it without its repetitions. Not to mention the re-appearance of certain words and certain formulæ, there is more than one narrative which seems to be (if not the *fac-simile*) the reflex of some other. The forging of the sun and moon out of silver and gold is, apparently, a recast of Ilmarinen's wife out of the same materials —or *vice versâ.*

The *inner meaning*—to use an expression which is in a fair way of passing into a hazy platitude, but one which is still convenient—will, probably, be a mystery to the end of time ; and the more we look to any single principle for its solution the further we shall be from it. The poem is *not* a uniform whole, nor is the evidence of its separate elements being referable to a single source, satisfactory. The conflict between light and darkness as a dualism of one sort, and the conflict between the Fins and the Laps as a dualism of another, may each be true to a certain extent. Neither, however, nor both combined, will cover the whole ground. Even Sampo itself, whatever we may make of it, will carry us but a short way. To the main elements of the poem there is much superadded, and of these additions the character is miscellaneous and heterogeneous. Individually, I look for some of its important constituents in the South rather than the North; among the Slavonians the Lithuanians, the Livonians, and the other occupants of the southern coast of the Baltic rather than in Lapland or even in Finland Proper.

A remark of Sjögren's upon the Zirianian mythology, or rather upon the Zirianian want of one, is, if not absolutely accurate, suggestive. It is to the effect that, instead of a vast mass of the original paganism underlying their present Christianity, as is the case of the Fins and Estonians, the Zirianians have but few remains of their ancient mythology. The fact, itself, though likely enough, is probably exaggerated, resting chiefly on our want of minute information on an obscure subject. Hence, we may reasonably expect, that when properly looked for, more will present itself than has hitherto been found. Be this as it may, the explanation suggested by Sjögren is, that in Finland Protestantism was a form of Christianity uncongenial to the Fin mind, and that, coming as it did before the Gospel had taken a thorough root in the country, it arrested rather than favoured the development of Christianity. Protestants are, of course, slow to believe that their own creed is not, at all times and under all circumstances, the best. If, however, they can get over such an obstacle as this, the suggestion under notice has a fair amount of facts to recommend it. The Fins took their Protestantism from Sweden, and, after once adopting it, held it with the resolute obstinacy in which their strength of character shows itself. But it could scarcely have come home to them as it came home to the countrymen of Luther, to the Swedes, or to the English; and it could scarcely have appealed to their intellect in the way that it appealed to the intellect in France, Poland, or Hungary.

It is easy to see that a poem like the Kalevala, is not without its political import. In almost every part of the Continent, there is what is called a language-question; and though there is less of one in Russia than in most other countries, there is still a language-question even in Russia. In Poland, this is notoriously the fact; whilst in Gallicia it is the Russian language itself which is aggrieved, the Russians under Austria being neither willing to learn German nor ready to subordinate their own form of the Slavonic to the Polish.

In Finland, the language-question is in its rudiments. Nevertheless, it is, to some extent, a question. The Swedish is, in Finland, the language of commerce and literature; and, until the Russian conquest of Finland, it was this without a rival. It has been the policy of Russia, however, to create a native feeling, *i. e.* a feeling for Finland and the true Fins as against Sweden and the mixed Swedes. The encouragement of the Fin languages and the native philologues has been one of the means for effecting this; and it would be well if all other steps towards similar objects were in an equally praiseworthy direction. Fin philology has now risen to the dignity of a separate study; and the Fin philologues form a special school of great merit. How far they are Russians rather than Swedes is another question.

How far is the whole country Russian? In the ethnographical map of the Grand Duchy, five colours represent five divisions of the population; (1.) the Karelian; (2.) the Tavastrian; (3.) the Quain; (4.) the Swede; (5.) the Fin and Swede mixed.

Of these, the Karelians cover by far the largest area. They cover all the inland districts and extend into the Governments of Olonets and Arkangel. Viborg, too, is allotted to them; though it has been suggested that, on the southern frontier, and within the Russian Governments of Novogorod and St. Petersburgh, a slight mixture of hypothesis connects itself with the term Karelian. Though spread over a vast surface, the Karelian population is thin and scanty.

The Tavastrian division belongs to the south-western parts of the Duchy; but it touches the Baltic only between 60° 30″ and 62° N. L.—there or thereabouts. This means that between the parts north of Abo and Tornea, the occupancy is that of the Quains.

North of Finland is Lapland, which seems originally to have reached much farther southward. As it is, the Laps lie, at present, mainly within the Arctic Circle; and that in three kingdoms—Norway, Sweden, and Russia. It is only the last two who call them *Laps*. The Norwegians name them *Fins*; and *Finmark*, which in Sweden is *Lapmark*, is their occupancy. "*Fin*," too, is the name by which they recognise them; though "*Sabma*," the "*Suom*," or the "*Suom-alaiset*" of Finland, is to be found in books as their true denomination. In Norway, however, I never found any of them who answered to the name. They simply said that they were "*Fins*."

It is in Russia that the Lap population is the scantiest, where it is spread over the largest area, where the intermixture of foreign blood is the greatest, and where the differences of dialect are the greatest and most numerous. East of Archangel the native population is wholly extinct, until we reach the River Mezen; and here the aborigines are not of the Lap stock, but of the Samoyed; and between the two the difference is far greater than that between the Laps and the Fins of Finland.

It is in this part of the Government of Archangel that the discontinuity of the original Fin area, except in the case of the Magyars of Hungary, is at its *maximum*. The Laps and Samoyeds originally must have been in contact with one another; but separated by the intrusion of *both* the Russians and the present Finlanders.

Another division is that into the Reindeer Laps and the Fishing Laps, a division which, in the main, is natural, though there are many who both take fish and breed reindeer.

The *Murmanzi*, as the Russians call them, are a mixed population of periodical migrants, some Karelians, some Laps. They collect in the parts about Onega and Kem, and make their way to Rasnavolok, which lies a few miles to the south of Kola. They then divide, one part moving east, the other west. On the west they come in contact with the Norwegians of Nordland and Finmark. I find in a work by Keilhau, who visited Spitzbergen, written many years before that of my present authority, Castrèn, that they are formidable competitors to the Norwegians: being equally skilful, and more self-denying. The eastern division fishes between Kola and Swiatoi Noss.

Some of the Murmans are capitalists in a small way; some hired labourers. The roughness of their justice may be measured by the following extracts from their code of laws.

1. He who brings no wood to the fire shall sit away from the fire.

2. He who makes bread-soup shall give way to him who makes fish-soup.

3. The woman shall give way to the man.

4. The child shall give way to the woman.

5. The hired labourer shall give way to the master.

6. The men of the house and the hired labourers shall take their seats according as they put a kettle on the fire.

That an annual inroad like that of the Murmans should influence the habits and language of the populations through which they pass is only what we expect: so that it is no wonder that we find numerous Russian and Karelian words in the Lap of the district. Neither is it wonderful that quarrels should arise. Hence, more than one locality takes its name from a fight—*e. g. Rütasaari*, or *Battle Island*; and *Torajärwi*, or *Battle Lake*. I should add that another interpretation has been given to this by better authorities than myself; and that the word meaning *Battle* has been supposed to have originated out of a conflict between the Laps and the intrusive Fins.

Of legend in the Lap district there is no lack. The first two of the following are noticed from the fact of their being neither more nor less than the tale of Ulysses and Polyp emus and of William Tell, respectively, as they appear on the very confines of the Arctic Circle.

(1.)

There was once a Karelian who had been taken by a giant, and was kept in a castle. The giant had only one eye: but he had flocks and herds. The night came, and the giant fell asleep. The Karelian put out his eye. The giant, who now could no longer see, sat at the door, and felt everything that went out. He had a great many sheep in the court-yard. The Karelian got under the belly of one of them, and escaped.

(2.)

There was a band of Karelians, and they set upon the village of Alajärvi, which they plundered. There was one old man whom they most particularly wished to punish. His son, who was only twelve years old, followed them, and threatened to shoot anyone who hurt his father. They then said that he should be set free on this condition : the son was to stand at one side, the father on the other side, of the river ; an apple was to be laid on the father's head, and the son was to split it with an arrow. The father said, " Raise one hand ; sink the other; for the water of the lake will draw the arrow." So he shot and split the apple.

The next has a theological aspect. A long time ago, there lived a Tadibi, whose name was Urier. He was a Tadibi of the Tadibis ; and the wisest of all wise men. He was a soothsayer of soothsayers. There had been no such master of the craft since or before. If any man lost a reindeer, who but Urier did he seek ? He had many reindeer of his own ; and had visited many countries. But he grew old, and perceived that all was vanity, and that the world was growing worse and worse. " The reindeer fall-off in numbers. The moss dies, or ceases to grow. The game decreases. There is nothing but avarice and deceit. I will live no longer in this wicked world : but will go up to heaven." So he told his two wives to get things ready for a journey, and to harness his reindeer. But he ordered that everything should be new : and that no single piece of old stuff was to be either used or packed-up. So they got themselves ready for the journey ; and harnessed the reindeer to a sledge. When all was prepared he mounted aloft, and drove through the air up into the sky. There were four male reindeer in each sledge—one sledge for Urier, one for his wives who followed. They had scarcely got half-way, when Urier's reindeer fell sick and could go no further. There was no need to tell him what had been done. He knew it. His second wife had not obeyed his orders, but had put the band of an old jacket in the harness. She had rather live on earth with her children, than go to heaven with her husband. So he let her go down. But the other went to heaven with him.

This is one version. Another carries both of the wives to heaven ; whence, after a time, Urier sends down a son to teach the Samoyeds on earth.

Again—a long time ago, there was an English Viking, and he used to sail every year to the Murman coast to take tribute. If no tribute were paid, he challenged the best fighting-man to single combat. He was stout, bold, and so skilful in all sorts of arms, that no one was able to conquer him, and the tribute was paid, year by year, for a long time. One summer, however, he came to the coast, and, as was his wont, asked for tribute. There was no one who dared meet him : except a small, weak man, who had never borne arms, and was so useless as a fighting-man, that he was made to cook the victuals. So the English Viking came and asked for tribute ; or, else, for a man who would fight him hand to hand. The poor, weak cook was the only one who dared to do so. He fought against him and won the battle: since which time no more tribute has b~en paid to any English Viking.

The Lap legends, according to Castrèn, are by no means of home growth. On the contrary, many are Russian. At any rate, they are, comparatively speaking, few and fragmentary, and are much less akin to those of Finland than are the legends and super- stitions of Estonia.

The Laps of Russian Lapland amount to about 1000.

CHAPTER XI.

The Permians and Zirianians.—The Votiaks.—The Volga Fins, the Tsherimis and Mordvins.—The Voguls and Ostiaks.—The Samoyeds.

THE *Permians* are the aborigines of the Government of Perm; the Zirianians of that of Vologda. Such, at least, is the rough view of them; though their limits are not exactly defined in the statement. There are Permians and Zirianians beyond these two Governments, and there are within the two Governments populations other than Permian and Zirianian.

The distinction, too, is political rather than ethnological; since the difference between the two populations is slight; neither do they themselves recognize it. They call themselves *Komimurt:* and speak dialects of the same language, which, though separated from the true Fin by the intrusion of the Russian, is closely allied to it—or, at least, is closer to it than are the Vogul, the Ostiak, the Samoyed, and the Lap.

The Permians have long been Christianized, and differ from the Russians much as a Welshman differs from an Englishman; in other words, their civilization is the same. They build and dress after the Russian fashion, work steadily at their mines, and are little more than the Fins of the far east. At the same time, they have fallen-off in numbers.

The *Zirianians* are somewhat less industrial than the Permians, being the occupants of the forest rather than a mining district. Still, in the south they are greatly Russianized. Beyond, however, the tree-line their character changes and their habits are more unsettled. Even in the south, they are hunters. In the parts about Obdorsk (for their area reaches the Arctic Sea) they meet the Ostiaks and the Samoyeds; and in the parts about Ishim there is a long line of Samoyed frontier, of which a considerable part is a debateable land. The following conversations between Castrèn and certain optimist Ziriananians illustrate the views of these outlying members of the more civilized divisions of the Fin family. "I believe in God—" said the interlocutor — "and I believe that nothing is done without his leave. The Zirianians have gotten many of the Samoyed reindeer: but it is by the will of God. The Devil has something to do with it; for the Devil has a hand in everything. You who are a Tartar do not believe this; but so it is. God made the earth in six days: but the Devil mixed poison with the juices of the plants, and put snakes in the grass. He put, too, the pike amongst the fishes. But God protected the fishes, and marked their heads with the sign of the cross. What God wills we must do. We have gotten the herds of the Samoyeds: but for the Samoyeds we have done great things. Before we came they offered sacrifices to trees, and knew no more than dogs and stone-foxes. We have taught them how to take fishes and hunt with guns. We were sent as teachers. It has pleased God to give us their herds, and they are our servants. When they become good Christians, God, in his mercy, will give them back their reindeer, and all will go well with them."

Another view was—that the ways of men are many: here and everywhere. There are bad men among the Zirianians, and good men among the Samoyeds. The bad Zirianians rob the good Samoyeds. But this is for their good. It is we who have the most to complain of. The wrongs to the Samoyeds were done long ago. They, now, break into our grounds and steal our reindeer. When they are all driven off the tundra there will be a good time.

Another. It is good for the Samoyeds that we take their reindeer. We make shammy leather, sell it to the Russians, and buy meal and wares. We make the most of the reindeer, and it is right that we should have them.

All this tells us that we have left the land of the horse and cow. In a Zirianian caravan, with which Castrèn travelled, there were one hundred and fifty sledges; in ten divisions of fifteen each. Each sledge had two reindeer, and was attached to the one before by a long rope; and each division had a man at the head in a light sledge drawn by three or four reindeer.

The early history of the Permians has long commanded attention.

20

It is well-known that in one of the earliest Arctic traders we have a notice of them. It is contained in the narrative of Other, which was taken and recorded by King Alfred; and which has come down to us in Alfred's own Anglo-Saxon. Other narratives give us the first account of Biarmaland; which, like Finmark or Norwegian Lapland, was the occupancy of a population of Fin blood ; but a population belonging to a more civilized division of the stock. Word for word *Biarmaland* is *Permia*. That these Permians and the Zirianians are exactly the descendants of the old Biarmalanders (notwithstanding the identity of name) is not quite certain. The presumption is in favour of their being so. At the same time many competent authorities look upon them as Proper Fins—Fins akin to those of the Government of Olonets and Arkangel, who, in the time of Alfred, had extended themselves to the Dwina and its mouth. Among these Biarmalanders, however, Other was afraid to trust himself; so that he did not land. Some of them, however, came aboard his ship, and held converse with them. Their language was sufficiently like that of the Fins to be understood.

The original extent of the Komimurt area has been investigated by Sjögren. In all inquiries of this kind the first step is an easy one. Take up a map, and pick out the local names which are other than Russian : they will be Ugrian, numerous or scanty— according to the particular district under notice. Then begin the difficulties. Are they Fin Proper, or Lap ? Are they Estonian, or Votiak ? Are they Zirianian, or only referable to some form of speech belonging to the class in which the Zirianian is contained ? *Oportet discentem credere;* in pursuance to which I give the approximate boundaries of the old Komimurt area as I find them. Northwards they approached to the Arctic Circle, probably by encroachment upon the Laplanders and Samoyeds. Eastwards they reached the Obi; much of the country which now belongs to the Voguls, having, originally, been Komimurt. Due south, the *situs* appears to have been much as it is at present, the exact details between the Permian and Votiak frontiers being unimportant. For the south-west, on the other hand, they are full of interest. In the Governments of Kostroma, Vladimir, Yaroslav, and (?) Tver, Sjögren finds traces of the original occupancy having been Komimurt; and, what is of more interest still, he suggests that Moscow was Komimurt also ; Moscow, which, according to

Zirianian account, became Russian in the following manner. A chief got leave to take as much land as he could compass with a cow's hide—we know the rest. It is the old, old story of Dido and the Numidians, of Hengist and the Britons, of the Saxons and the Thuringians, and, doubtless, of many others besides. It is noticed here, because it applies to Moscow, and because it is Zirianian.

The little town of Ustvymsk in the circle of Yarensk, with about 200 houses, is the centre to which we must trace the Christianity of Permia and Zirania: Utsvymsk the small and shrunken metropolis of the great Russian missionary Saint Stephanus. Here he is believed to have reduced the Permian language to writing, and, upon the Old Slavonic as a basis, to have formed the Permian alphabet. Of this, two or three imperfect representatives are extant. Of the matter which it embodied we have less. Three short inscriptions on stone and a fragment of fourteen letters in MS. are all that has yet been found—found, but scarcely deciphered and translated: indeed one of the inscriptions has been destroyed by fire.

A fragment of a translation of the liturgy of St. Chrysostom in Slavonic characters, represents the literature; the fate of the remainder being doubtful. Sanguine students indulge in the hope that, some day or other, it may be found. The credulous fear that it has been burnt, whilst the sceptical suggest that its original importance may have been exaggerated.

In the Government of Viatka, the *Votiaks* (or as they call themselves the Udmurt) stand in the same relation to the soil as the Permians do to that of Permia. And to the Permians they are near congeners; though I doubt whether the two languages are mutually intelligible. Like the Zirianians, they live in clearings of the forest: keep themselves more free from Russian intermixture than the other Ugrians: retain much of their original paganism—especially in the northern portion of their area. On the south they come in contact with the Bashkirs, and have, in a few instances, adopted Mahometanism. They are said to approach the true Fins very closely, both in temperament and in physical conformation.

A Votiak village contains from twenty to forty houses. It covers a clearance in the forest, the wood being left in its natural condition on the boundary. This isolates the Votiak villages, so

20*

that they lie as the old German ones did—with wastes and wood-lands between them. When the ground of a settlement has become exhausted by cropping, the occupants leave it and migrate elsewhere, sometimes making the old place over to other settlers. The house is of wood, scarcely different from that of the Russians; or rather the Russian house is like the Votiak—the style of build-ing being, in all probability, indigenous. The men dress like the Russians, the women only preserving the old costume. The ma-terial for their cap is the white bark of the birch-tree, with a band of blue linen round it, and adorned in the front with silver orna-ments—often coins. This fashion we shall find amongst the Tshuvashes—the fashion, I mean, of using pieces of money as decorations. Then there are streamers of white linen flowing and floating over the back and shoulders, with red fringes and em-broidery along the borders. This head-dress is the *aishon*. If a stranger sleep in the house, the *aishon* will be worn all night as well as all day, since it is decorous to keep the head covered, indecorous to let down the hair. The shirts and shifts, too, are more or less embroidered.

The tribunal organization, so characteristic of the Turk stock, appears in a modified form amongst the Votiaks, who are specially stated to retain their original division into tribes and families, and to give the names of these to their villages. Their noble families, however, are, for the most part, extinct.

The three populations that now follow live on the drainage of the Volga. All occupy, more or less, portions of the Govern-ments of Kazan. All come in contact with a Tartar population.

The first two are unequivocally Ugrian in language—whatever they may be in blood. The Tshuvash language, on the other hand, is held by some to be more Turk than Fin.

The most northern of these are the *Tsherimis*, amounting

In the Government of Viatka to . . .	75,450
——————————— Kazan	71,375
——————————— Permia . . .	7938
——————————— Nizhnigorod . .	4330
——————————— Kostroma . . .	3357
——————————— Orenburg . . .	2626
	165,076

Some of them are pure pagans; the majority being but imperfect and approximate Christians; retaining, under the surface of their later creed, most of the essentials of their original heathendom.

The *Tsherimis* have been more nomadic than they are at present; hunters, perhaps, rather than herdsmen, during the earliest period of their history. At present, however, they are agricultural, settled, and more or less industrial. Their villages are said to be smaller than those of the Votiaks and Tshuvash, and perhaps they are more sequestered. At the same time they are regular villages, with the village organization of a head-man or elder for the settlement of disputes and for their simple legislation. There are houses, too, which approach the Russian standard of comfort; with property on the part of the owners to match.

The great Votiak festival was that of the *Keremet;* and the *Keremet* also is the great Tsherimis one. It is at the time of the *Keremet* that there are meetings under the ordinance of a priest in the holier parts of the forest, when offerings of animals are made to the bad, of flowers to the good, demons. The following is a Tsherimis hymn:—

1. May God give health and happiness to him who offers a sacrifice!
2. To the children who come into the world, give, O Yuma, plenty of good things—gold, bread, cattle, and bees!
3. During the new year, make our bees to swarm and give much honey.
4. Bless our chase after birds and after beasts.
5. Give us our fill of gold and silver.
6. Make us, O Yuma, masters of all the treasures buried in the earth, all over the world!
7. Grant that, in our bargains, we may make three times the value of our goods.
8. Enable us to pay our tribute.
9. Grant that, at the beginning of the spring, our three sorts of cattle may find their ways back by three different paths, and that we may keep them from bears, from wolves, and from robbers.
10. Make our cows with calf.
11. Make our thin kine fatten for the good of our children.
12. Enable us with one hand to sell our barren cows, and with the other to take the money.
13. Send us, O Yuma, a true and trusty friend!
14. When we travel far, preserve us, O Yuma, from bad men, from sickness, from fools, from bad judges, and from lying tongues!
15. As the hop grows, and throws out his scent, so, O Yuma, grant that we may wax strong through goodness, and smell sweet from reason!

16. As the wax sparkles in burning, so let us, O Yuma, live in joy and health.

17. Let our existence be as calm and regular as the cells of a honeycomb.

18. Grant, O Yuma, that he who asks may obtain the object of his prayer !

When this prayer is finished, the head, heart, lungs, and liver are offered up to the deity to whom it is addressed ; another prayer being said by the officiating minister alone. Then they eat and pray again. This is kept on for three days. When all is over, the bones, entrails, and such parts of the sacrifices as have not been consumed, are burnt, the fire having never been allowed to go out during the whole festival.

Though he delights in the flesh of the horse, the Tsherimis abominates that of the hog ; and this even where his habits are unwarped by any influence from his Tartar neighbours.

The next name makes its first appearance in Jornandes ; who mentions the nation of the *Mordvins* as one of the tributaries to the great Hermanric. In Porphyrogeneta their land is called Mordia. It lay one day's journey from Russia ; ten from the country of the Petshinegs. The name again appears in Nestor.

In 1104, Yaroslav Swiatieslavitsh attacked the Mordvins, and was repulsed. Somewhat later a portion of them was reduced.

Containing, as it did, some of the most fertile tracts in Russia, the Mordvin country, *nimium vicina Cremonæ*, was one of the first which came under the dominion of the Mongols ; and when the Mongol Empire was broken up, the whole, or nearly the whole of it, became comprised in the Khanate of Kazan. When this became Russian, the Mordvins became Russian also : though, during the time of the Khans, they had, more than once, joined the Tsherimis and the Tartars in their contests against their encroaching neighbours : their chief weapon being the bow. They used it with the usual skill of nomads and huntsmen. But this is a character which has long been laid aside. The Russians themselves are no better agriculturists than the present Mordvins : who, like their neighbours, the Bashkirs, are, also, great bee-masters. The Russians themselves, except in a few districts where the original paganism still keeps its ground, are no better Christians. Indeed, except that there is no mining, and no nautical industry (deficiencies arising from the physical condition of their country, rather than from any want of aptitude on the part of the occupants), the present civilization of the Mordvins is on the high level of that of the Permians and the

Finlanders. The Russian language is generally understood; though the Mordvin is the more familiar one. Lastly, their numbers appear to be on the increase. The details in 1844 run thus :—

In the Government of	Penza . . .	106,025
————————	Simbirsk . . .	98,968
————————	Saratov . . .	78,060
————————	Samar	74,910
————————	Nizhnigorod . .	53,382
————————	Tambov . . .	48,491
————————	Kazan . . .	14,867
————————	Orenburg . . .	5,200
————————	Tauris	340
————————	Astrakan . . .	48
		480,241

In Tauris and Astrakan they are recent immigrants.

They fall into three divisions, the Ersad (? Ἄορσοι), the Moksha, and the Karatai; this last being, by far, the smallest.

The *Tshuvash*, if they differ from the Tartars in nothing else, differ in creed; being Christians rather than Mahometans. They amount

In the Government of	Kazan	to	300,091
————————	Simbirsk	—	84,714
————————	Samar	—	29,926
————————	Orenburg	—	8,352
————————	Saratov	—	6,852
————————	Viatka	—	17
			429,952

and are an increasing population. In Kazan, where they are the most numerous, their number nearly equals that of the Tartars; who amount to about 308,574. The names by which they designate themselves are Vereyal, Khirdeyal, and Vyres. The Tsherimis call them *Kurkmari* or *Hill-men*, the Mordvins *Wiedke*. *Tshuvash*, itself, I take for a Tartar word.

That the Tshuvash are Christians *rather* than Mahometans has just been stated—and it is all that can well be said.

Of the Ugrians, who are neither Magyar nor Fin, after the manner of the Finlanders of the Duchy of Finland, the Mordvins are the most important; indeed, since the time of Ivan the Terrible, there has been such an event as a Mordvin war, not one of formidable dimensions, but, nevertheless, one against a population which we scarcely expect would venture on a rebellion.

The *Voguls* are rude hunters, spread over a vast district, along the ridge of the Urals, amounting to about 900 in the Government of Perm, and to about 5000 in that of Tobolsk.

The Voguls, compared with any of the tribes that lie south of them, are a comfortless, undersized, ill-developed population; who, if they contrast favourably with the Lap and Samoyed, show to a disadvantage by the side of the Finlander or the Ziriauian. Their villages are small, and the size of the village gives a fair measure of the well-being of the population that occupies it. From four to eight cabins constitute a Vogul one, and these lie from ten to fifteen miles apart: the forest lying between—with few, or no, clearings. Game is the chief sustenance; and for the production of it the forest has to be kept wild. To this extent the Voguls are a hunter population; for it is only in the southern parts of their area that the signs of settled life are to be found.

A little tillage and a little cattle appear as we approach the Bashkir frontier, the Bashkir habits being partially adopted. The Bashkir, however, is, himself, but half agricultural.

The winter-hut of the Vogul is small, close, and smoky; the summer-cabin is made of the boughs and rind of the birch-tree. These are raised or pulled down, as the necessities of the chase require; as one locality must be exchanged for another.

The Vogul hunts on foot. He has no pastures for horses; and the boggy, woody tracts under his occupancy are ill adapted for the use of them. Even the dog is a rare companion. On the other hand, a few cows may constitute the property of one of the wealthier proprietors. The elk, however, is the chief beast for sustenance, and the sable for trade. The reindeer is less abundant; and it is in the skin of the elk, amongst ruminants, that their tribute of peltry is paid. The flesh is dried, not salted—cut into strips and dried in the open air, so that a kind of pemmican is made of it.

The Vogul uses the gun as well as the bow; and he is skilful in the contrivance of traps and pitfalls. He fishes, too, as well as hunts. For hunting, his best month is November; when the animals have their winter fur about them. Obdorsk, a factory rather than a town, is the Vogul's trading-town. Thither he resorts with his skins, berries, and such like small articles of barter.

Pallas (with, I believe, other observers) speaks to the fact of the Voguls wholly dispensing with the use of salt. Berries they have, but no vegetables. They chew the turpentine of the larch; but they use no salt, and enjoy good health notwithstanding. They are said to be healthy, but neither long-lived nor strong; and of all the Ugrians of the forest districts they have a physiognomy that most approaches the typical Mongol.

Success in hunting, is the chief object of the Vogul's prayers. To this end, the carved image of the god takes the form of the beast under pursuit, being sable-shaped, elk-shaped, or bear-shaped, according as the bear, the elk, or the sable is the more especial object.

Near a hunting-lodge on the Sosva is the rude image of an elk, carved by an unknown hand out of stone, an image of some antiquity. This the Voguls visit from considerable distances, and invoke its favour during their expeditions. Müller says that it is " rough-hewn out of stone." The analogy, however, of the Lap mythology makes it probable that it is a natural piece of rock, whereof the shape is elk-like enough to suggest the comparison. However this may be, offerings are made to it by its visitors.

Other figures are in the human form, and of these some are of metal, iron or copper. It is in certain holy places that they are to be found, fixed in the clefts of a rock or tree; raised on poles stuck in the ground—the ground being the most elevated spot about. On one of the numerous streams called *Shatanka* (*Satan's river*) is a holy cavern, on the floor of which are found bones, the remains of Vogul offerings—bones and rings of Russian workmanship, but of Vogul consecration

The Torom Saktaag bear a name allied to the name for priest, which is *Sakta*-taba. *Torom*, on the other hand, is the name of a god whose residence is in the sun or moon, a god whose name appears in all, or nearly all, of the other Ugrian mythologies. *Yelbola* is the name of the feast of *Torom*; probably the same word as the Finlandish *Yumala*, and the Lap *Yubmel*—and with the feast of Yelbola the Vogul year begins.

The *Ostiaks* of the Obi, the *true* Ostiaks (for the Samoyeds bear the name wrongly), are the nearest congeners of the Voguls; but are a much more important division of the Ugrian class. They extend along the Irtish and Obi from 56" to 67° N. L., Surgut, and Beresov being the chief towns of the true Ostiak district. Narym is only on the Ostiak frontier, and has Tartars and Samoyeds as well as Ostiaks in its neighbourhood: whilst Obdorsk is surrounded by Ostiaks, Samoyeds, and Zirianians. In 1838 the number of the Ostiaks was about 19,000.

That the division into tribes and sub-tribes prevails amongst the Ostiaks, as it did among the Samoyeds, and as it does with most (perhaps all) of the allied populations, is evident from the following list of the southern section of them.

The Dyenshtshitovski Division.

1. Turtas-mir	Turtass volost	117
2. Nasym-mir	Nasym volost	302
3. Num-mir	Upper Dyemyan volost	286
4. Tyapar-mir	Narym volost	443
5. Wodzh-itpa-mir	Tarkhan volost	701
6. Khunda-mir	Lesser Konda volost	828
7. Terek-mir, or Utkhar-mir	Tyemlashtshev volost	305
		2,982

The Surgut Division.

1. As-mir	Selyarov volost	134
2. Sodom-mir	Salym volost	826
3. Pyng-mir	Pym volost	166
4. As-torm-yogan-mir	Podgorodnaya volost	862
5. Entl-yogan-mir	Great Yugan volost	592
6. Ai-yogan-mir	Little Yugan volost	286
7. Torm-yogan-mir	Tri Yugan volost	297
8. Agan-mir	Agan volost	96
9. Vakh-mir	Vakh volost	706
10. Lung-pugotl-mir	Lumpokolsk volost	808
11. Saltik-mir	Saltikovsk volost	359
12. Pirtyi-mir	Pirtshinsk volost	860
		4,492

The Kondin Division.

1. Kodskiye Gorodki volost . . . 2,628
2. Podgoronaya volost 328
3. Sosva volost 968
4. Lyapin volost 1,585
5. Kasym volost 1,274

6,853

The Obdorsk Division.

1. Kunovat volost 1,630
2. Obdorsk volost 2,700

4,330

Broken and depressed as they are at the present time, the Voguls and Ostiaks have, apparently, had a history of some magnitude—a history and a nationality. All the researches concerning their origin point one way. All the researches upon their ethnology give them an honourable connection.

Allied to each other they have for their nearest kinsmen the Magyars of Hungary, like whom they seem to have cut their way to their present occupancies. As the Hungarians are traced northwards, the Voguls and Ostiaks are brought from the south, and it was at the expense of the nations on the way that they fixed themselves where they now are.

A few of their wars are known even in their main details. Thus, it was the Komimurt that the Voguls dispossessed; the Komimurt being, themselves, a conquering population. Of their encroachments upon the Samoyeds, as a measure of their prowess, less can be said to their credit. For their wars between one another there is plenty of miserable detail.

Of the Voguls and the Ostiaks each represents a broken nation, and each, perhaps, a degenerate one. The physical conditions of their country are worse than they were at first; and there is no proof that they have made up for the loss by an increased civilization.

The very reverse of this has befallen the Magyars. They outnumber all the other Ugrians put together They are European in civilization, and formidable from the strength and intensity of their nationality. Yet, thirty generations ago, there was little to choose between ancestors of the Esterhazys and Szhechenyis, and the ancestors of the present Turtasmir elders. The Obi, however, was the lot of one branch, the Danube and the Teiss of the other. The one came in contact with the Samoyeds and Zirianians, the other with the Germans and Poles.

The *Samoyeds* of the north-western division, or the Samoyeds of Europe, are called the *Yurak* Samoyeds by the Russians; by themselves *Kasova* (*Hasowaio*), or *Nyenets* = *men*. They extend into Asia as far as the Tas.

In Asia, those of the extreme East, between the Lower Yenisey and the Chatunga are called the *Avam*, or *Avamski* Samoyeds.

The Samoyeds of the Obi are improperly called *Ostiaks*. They are chiefly found on the Obi and its feeders, on the Tshulim, on the Ket, and even as far south as the Tym and the parts about Narym.

The *Mokasi*, on the Tas, and the *Karasin* on the Lower Yenisey are also Samoyeds—in language, if not in blood.

In the west, however, the Samoyed country begins in the parts about Mezen; and at Mezen European civilization ends. The town is small and insignificant. Still it is a Russian town, and has a tincture of Russian civilization. However, in the market-place and the street you meet with Samoyeds; who are brought thither by the love of brandy; for brandy is the curse of all the Samoyeds of the western portion of the area. Castrèn wanted a teacher; a man who could teach him his language. But no one who knew it would be paid in anything but brandy, and most of them were drunk already. There was one man whose sobriety could be relied on. He was sent from a distance, and with great pains. He came; and was drunk like the rest. A little has been done by the Government to arrest this annihilating vice of drinking: but the orders are ineffectively executed and drunkenness still prevails.

The whole district is a tundra, and it bears the name of the Bolshezemla Tundra; or the tundra of the Great Land. It reaches from Mezen to the Ural. The Petshora divides it. The western part has no general name in Russian, but the Samoyeds call it the Little Land. It falls into the Kanin and Timan divisions; the former being the more western of the two. The river Piosha, according to the Russian geography, the river Soba, according to that of the Samoyeds, divides them. When these two are taken together, the name of the first division, the Bolshezemla Tundra, between the Petshora and the Ural, forms a third of the whole district; the term being taken in a *restricted* sense.

There is another division. The Bolshezemla Tundra being taken in its *wider* sense, falls into three Volosts—the Pustosersk, the Ustsylm, and the Ishim Volosts: the first two of which lie north and west, the last south and east. The first two are nearly wholly Samoyed; but the Ishim Tundra is Samoyed and Zirianian as well: for the Zirianians have encroached on the Samoyeds and extended themselves as far as the mouth of the Obi; Obdorsk, though essentially a town of the Ostiaks, with whom we meet as soon as we cross the Ural, being visited by both Zirianians and Samoyeds.

Something has been done to introduce Christianity amongst the Samoyeds; though only lately; *i. e.* since 1830. And those who have adopted it have adopted it imperfectly; retaining almost all their old superstitions. The converts, indeed, who go so far as to invoke the Russian St. Nicolas when they are sick, look upon him as the magician Nikola rather than as the Christian saint.

The ordinary belief is in the *Tadibi* or medicine man, who has the power of interceding with the *Tadebsio*. The following is a Samoyed invocation.

Tadibi.

Come, come !
Spirits of Magic !
If you come to me,
I'll come to you ;
Wake up ! wake up !
Spirits of Magic !
I've come to you :
Awake from sleep !

Tadebsio.

Say why
Thou art come !
Why comest thou
To disturb our rest?

> There came to me
> A young Nients (*Samoyed*),
> This man here,
> Who vexes me much;
> His reindeer is gone;
> This is why
> I have come.

Of metrical compositions of this kind little can be said, especially when we compare them with such works as the Kalevala, or even the less ambitious poems of the Esthonians and the Vods. Of Samoyed legends, however, in prose there are several.

The language, whatever may be the blood of the men who use it, though spoken on the coast of the Arctic Ocean, is, also, spoken within the frontiers of China,* in the parts about Lake Ubsa. Then it is in contact with the Ostiak; and it is probable that both are *in situ*. As the Laps seem to have been driven northwards by the Finlanders, so seem the Samoyeds to have been pressed forward into a like inhospitable region by either the Turks, or some cognate Ugrian population stronger than themselves.

Of the Magyars of Hungary little need be said, except that their language has been, for more than a century, recognised as a member of the Ugrian class. This was indicated by the Swedish philologues of the last century, and the result of their enquiries was known to and promulgated by Gibbon. Since then, the doctrine has been expanded and confirmed; and not only do we know the general Fin affinities of the Magyar, but their special ones. The two languages of the family with which it is the most closely connected, are the Ostiak and Vogul; the Vogul more particularly. Now these are by no means the languages which are suggested by the geography. The Fin form of speech which reaches farthest south, and is, consequently, the least distant from Hungary, is the Morduin of Penza; and, after this, the Tsherimiss of Kazan and Viatka.

But it is not these with which the Magyar is most readily connected.

* Page 234.

This is as much as need be said about them; for the political importance of the Magyars belongs to a different division of our subject. The chief element in it is not so much the fact of their being Ugrian, or Fin, but that of their *not* being Slavonic.

CHAPTER XII.

Lithuania and the Lithuanic Family.—Prussians.—Yatshvings.—Lithuanians Proper.—Letts.

THERE are four divisions of the Lithuanian family—the Lithuanians proper, the Prussians, the Yatshvings, and the Letts. Of the first and last we have existing representatives. The Prussians and the Yatshvings have disappeared from history. In the strict sense, then, of the term, it is only for the district between the Vistula and the Niemen that the present Emperor of Germany is a King of Prussia; for it was the area between these two rivers that constituted the old Prussian domain; and the true Prussians are those of *East,* and not of *West,* Prussia; the men of the parts about Konigsberg, and not the men of the parts about Berlin. The East Prussians may, no doubt, at some early period, have had a line of country on the left bank of the Lower Vistula; but, so early as the time of King Alfred, the Vistula was held to be the boundary between the Slavonians and the Lithuanians, or, as the royal geographer calls them, the *Wends* and the *Wites.* But that in the thirteenth century the Prussian area began at the Vistula, and either reached or approached the Niemen, is certain; and equally certain is it that their language was a form of the Lithuanic. We know this, because it survived the independence of the nation; and a kind of catechism in it of the date of the Reformation has come down to us. Moreover, there is the account of, at least, one traveller who visited the country, and came in contact with the native Old Prussians. What proportion it bore to the rest he does not say. But he tells us that he heard them converse in their own mother tongue, and that he was present at a ceremony, which he describes, of a purely pagan character, a statement which we may readily believe; for the obstinacy with which the Lithuanians in general held to their original creed was a notable characteristic of the race. The name of one of their holy places was either * *Rome*, or something very like it.

The southern boundary of Prussia, or Pruthenia, was the river Ossa, which divided it from Polonia. Eastward, however, it is probable that the Lithuanic area extended farther south. The divisions of this Prussia when the whole country was made over to the Teutonic Knights and the Knights of the Sword were : —(1) *Culm* and *Lubau*, (2) *Pomerania*, (3) *Pogesania*, (4) *Warmia*, (5) *Nattangia*, (6) *Sambia*, (7) *Nadrovia*, (8) *Scalovia*, (9) *Sudovia*, (10) *Galindia*, (11, 12) " *Barthe* et *Plica Barthe*, quæ nunc *Major* et *Minor Bartha* vocatur, in qua Barthe vel Barthenses habitabant. Vix aliqua istarum nationum fuit, quæ non haberet ad bellum duo millia virorum equitum et multa millia pugnatorum.—Dusburg iii. 3." Nearly all these had their eponymus in the twelve sons of *Wudewut*; viz. :—*Litpho*, *Saimo*, *Sudro*, *Naidro*, *Scalowo*, *Natango*, *Bartho*, *Galindo*, *Warmo*, *Hoggo* (?), *Pomeszo*, *Chelmo*. The two traditionary founders of the nation were this *Wudewut* and *Brut*, or Bruten (Latin, *Brutenus*). Then the people made their priest, Wudewut, their king. The three great divinities were *Perkunos*, *Potrimpus*, and *Pikullos*. Perkunos was the God of Thunder, and his name may be found in the Lithuanic songs of the present time ; while, even in West Prussia, " *Pakul* " is the name for the Devil.

We know the physical character of these districts which constituted the Old, or original, Prussia, and that of their boundaries on the side of Poland. But the relations that the

---

* Fuit autem in medio nationis hujus perversæ, scilicet in Nadrovia, locus quidam dictus *Romow*, trahens nomen suum a *Roma*, in quo habitabat quidem dictus *Criwe*, quem colebant pro *Papa*. Quia secut dominus Papa regit universalem Ecclesiam fidelium, ita ad istius nutum seu mandatum non solum gentes predictæ, sed et Letowini et aliæ nationes Livoniæ terræ regebantur. *Dusburg*, iii. 5.

natives bore to the other members of the Lithuanian family
are uncertain.   Due attention has been paid to the scanty
remains of the language; and it is considered to be different
from ordinary Lithuanic, and still more so from the Lett.   It
is probable that in the first matter there is some exaggeration,
and that Prussia was little more than a westward extension of
the Lithuanic area, with a different name.

The first effect of the crusade against the Prussians was to
extend the sea coast of Germany, and, by Germanizing the
districts of the Lower Vistula, to interfere with the power of
Poland on the Baltic.   This encroachment was partially abated
by the recognition of a suzerainty on the side of Poland, which
afterwards placed that kingdom in unfavourable relations
with the Empire.   Eventually Poland lost all real power as a
maritime state.

*   *   *   *   *

If the Prussians have left a well-known name behind, it
is more than the Yatshvings have done, though, like the
Prussians, the Yatshvings were great warriors in their day.
At present, however, the name occurs in only the following
localities.

(1. 2.) There are two small villages on the left bank of
the Bobr, in the Circle of Bialostock, named *Yatvez Stara,*
and *Yatvez Nova,* or *Old* and *New Yatvez.*   The Prussian
maps give the form of *Jacwiz.*   Not far from these are the
Mogilki Yadzhvingovskie, or the *Yatshving Graves;* memorials,
in all probability, of one of the battles of the thirteenth
century.

(3. 4.) Two villages named *Yatvesk* lie on the right side of
the Niemen, in the Government of Vilna, and in the Circle of
Lila.   The environment here is Lithuanic.   With the villages
in Bialostock, it was Polish.   In Schubert's map, a distinction
is drawn between the two, and the one is called *Polish,* the
other *Russian,* Yatvesk.

(5.) Not far from these is a small population called *Yatveshai.*
Are these the *Yodvezhai* which Narbut places to the east of
Grodno, occupants of *Yatvez* Pol, or the *Yatshving* Field?   If

so, they are said to differ from their neighbours in habits, in dress, and in complexion, their skins and clothing being dark.

(6.) There is a village named Yatvesk about seven versts from Sswislotsch.

The history of the Yatshvings is also fragmentary, though at one time they were a formidable people. Their name commands attention, or rather the multiplicity of forms under which it is found. Nor is this to be wondered at. To say nothing about the extent to which the Lithuanian phonesis differs from the Latin and the German, the difference between the populations by which the Yatshving area was surrounded is alone sufficient to account for it. So many languages, so many *media :* so many *media*, so many chances of change. Then there are the differences of orthography ; *e. g.* the use of *t* for *c*, and *vice versâ.* Thunmann found the form *Jecwesin*, and, treating it as the accusative case of *Jecwesi*, made it a Fin gloss, the termination *-wesi* being Fin for *water*. He might, however, have found any amount of strange forms, *i. e.* Jacuitæ, Jatuitæ, Gzecwesii, Terra Gzecwesia, Gzetwintzitæ, Getwinziti, Getwezitæ, Jetwesen, Jazuingi, Jasuingi, Jacuingi, Jaczwingi, Jacwingi, Yatwyagi, Yatwyazhi, Yatwyagove, the latter forms being Russian. *Getæ*, too, and *Jazyges*, he might have found ; but, with these it would be doubtful whether he had a real name or a piece of ethnological speculation. It is only certain that forms like those given above are, by no means, uncommon. Little, however, has been written about them.

The Mithridates—whereof it may be said, by the bye, that the section on the Lithuanic is one of the most exceptionable parts of the whole—mentions them, in a cursory and perfunctory manner ; excusable, perhaps, from the fact of Language being the main object of the work, combined with that of the Yatshvings having left no specimens of their speech except a few proper names. It mentions them, however, after Thunmann and Slözer; treating them as Lithuanians. Winning, who is the only Englishman who has written at large upon the Prussians, never mentions the Yatshvings. Neither does Prichard. Amongst the Germans, Zeuss, whose work, though a Kosmos for fact, is an *ignis fatuus* for results, tells us more about them than any previous writer. Nevertheless, there is one standard monograph upon

21 *

them—one by Sjögren in the Transactions of the Imperial Academy of St. Petersburg; and it is this from which the following fragmentary notices are taken.

The place is the Polish, Prussian. and Lithuanian frontiers; the time the thirteenth century.

The town and fortress of Drohitshyn is stated by fair authorities to have been the metropolis of the Yatshvings in the plentitude of their power. This, however, is denied by Sjögren; who says that, as a general rule, it was in the hands of either the Russians or the Poles, and, for a short time, in those of the Teutonic Knights. The same able writer demurs to the statement of Dlugosz, who gives the year 1264 as the date of their final overthrow; not to say their extermination. Then, (as is said) Boleslas the Chaste, so utterly broke their power and dissolved their nationality, that, with the exception of a few peaceful labourers and some sick men, the whole population either made itself over to the conqueror, or mixed itself with the Lithuanians; and that to such a degree that "now the very name of Yatshving is no longer in existence." Mathias of Miechov's notice is, in the main, the same; except that instead of his saying that the name is extinct, he writes that it is *perrarum et paucis notum*. It is enough to believe that Boleslas' victory ejected them from Podlachia: inasmuch as, in 1282, along with a formidable body of Lithuanians, they attacked Lublin. To bring down their history somewhat lower, Kromer writes that in 1589 a few remains of them were said to survive the rest of their nations (*feruntur superesse*) in Russia and Lithuania, distinguished by their language from the Lithuanians and the Russians. We have seen that it can be carried farther down.

The centre of the stock was Podlachia, nearly coinciding with the present province of Bialostock: of which they appear to have held the whole. On the west they extended into Mazovia, of which they held only a part; the remainder being Polish. On the east a portion of Polesia was Yatshving; and here their frontagers were either pure Lithuanians, pure Russians, or a population of mixed blood. Finally, a part, at least, of the area usually assigned to the Old, or true, Prussians was Yatshving: namely, the *Sudauer* district. Now if this name be, word for word, *Sudeni*, and if it also represent the early population of the country, the Sudeni of Ptolemy were among the ancestors of the northern Yatshvings.

What they were remarkable for was their obstinate Paganism; and the extent to which every man's hand was held against them. Their only allies seem to have been the Cumanians and the Mongols. Notwithstanding all the allowance that must be made for the dark colours in which they are drawn, they were, evidently, a barbarous, though a brave, people. By 1300, however, they had ceased to be a nation.

The first campaign against them was undertaken by Conrad, duke of Mazovia, and Vassilko Romanovitsh, who, conjointly with his brother Daniel, was Duke of Halicz, or Gallicia. This was in 1246. The year after this, Conrad, and the year after that, Conrad's son and successor, died. This made Semovit duke: and, under him, the offensive alliance with the princes of Gallicia continued. There were battles in 1248 and 1251. Meanwhile, the Teutonic Knights, with their hands against every one, were fighting to-day against their old allies, and to-morrow in alliance with their old enemies. By 1254 Semovit has made over to them a sixth of the Yatshving territory—whatever that was. The part that was thus cut off from the rest seems to have lien in the Sudauer country. The next year the allied arms of the Mazovians and the Gallicians extorted tribute from another Yatshving district. In 1256, the Pope, Alexander IV., announces the voluntary conversion of a few of them; and makes them over to the protecting hands of the Bishop of Breslau and two of the Teutonic Knights. About the same time he enjoins a crusade against the remainder; including in his denunciations the Lithuanians.

And now the Mongols have reached Volhynia, Gallicia, and the frontiers of Lithuania and Poland; and Wasilko Romanovitsh is compelled to join them in the inroad upon the Lithuanians and the Yatshvings whose frontier has again to be encroached on. The great Lithuanian king, Mindog, gives a part of it to the Teutonic Knights.

In 1264 the Yatshvings attack Lublin, and we may suppose that their chief, Komat, is at their head; since that is the name of the Yatshving king who, a few months afterwards, is killed in the great battle (already alluded to) which was won by Boleslas, to the discomfiture, though not (as asserted) to the utter annihilation of the Yatshvings. The chiefs, Mintelä, Schurpja, Mudejko, and Pestilo, are still able to offer an ineffectual resistance to the Russian princes, Lew, Vladimir, and Mtsislav, in 1272. Soon afterwards, another chief, Skumand, heads their armies : and it is, probably, he who, after joining an heterogeneous army of Russians, Lithuanians, and Tatars in a murderous invasion of Poland, is attacked by the Grandmaster Mangold, defeated, and baptized. Skumand was the last of the Yatshvings whose name appears in history, and he was, perhaps, the first who died in his bed. This he did between 1280 and 1290.

*   *   *   *   *

Lithuania.—So low is the present condition of the small peasantry which now represents the Lithuanic name and language, that many of those who assume the immutable character of national aptitudes and national energies, are unwilling to believe that the original Lithuanians were formidable warriors, and ferocious conquerors ; so much so that they have taken refuge in the doctrine that, in the times of their historical importance, the Lithuanian leaders were no Lithuanians at all, but either Poles or Russians, or of mixed blood. From the details of their early history, and from the names of their heroes, I find myself unable to agree with this view ; I find that, anterior to the union with Poland, there is no evidence of any notable Polish influence ; and that, in respect to Russia, it was the Lithuanians who, in the way of domination, exerted full as much power as was brought to bear upon themselves. This, however, refers only to the earlier, and, I may add, to the darker and more obscure periods of their history.

In wars against the Letts and Courlanders, their own near congeners, the Lithuanians were generally victorious ; and it is the early historian of Liefland, Henry, himself a Lett, who writes that his countrymen were as lambs to wolves in respect to the Lithuanians. The analogy of the Yatshvings and the Old Prussians, points in the same direction. Between these and the Lithuanian there were border wars. There were also intestine wars between the different divisions of the Lithuanians themselves, especially in Samogitia, the typically Lithuanian part of Lithuania, both at the dawn of history, and at the present time.

Upon the Ugrians of their frontier the Lithuanians seem steadily to have encroached ; so much so that I doubt whether there is a single acre of Eastern Lithuania which was not originally Finn. This, however, is a point of general ethnology, upon which there is no need to enlarge ; neither is the fact very important. So many are in the habit of looking upon the Ugrians as one of the weaker divisions of mankind, that no amount of victories over them would prove much as to the prowess of the conqueror. Though I hold this view to be erroneous, I need scarcely stop to correct it. What I wish to suggest at present is the fact that, though now depressed, the Lithuanians were once bold warriors. The Germans, however, upon the whole, worsted them ; though not at once and easily. From West to East the encroachment of the Teutonic Knights and the Knights of the Swords was steadily successful. Yet it told more upon Courland and Livonia than upon Samogitia and Lithuania Proper. Besides which, it was backed by a mass of powerful dukedoms, principalities, and kingdoms ; not to say an empire and a pope. These wars of the Orders under notice were Crusades, though not in the technical sense of the term. They were Crusades like that against the Albigenses, and, perhaps, bloodier and more disgraceful ones. They were resisted, but not equally, or in all directions, and they were only partially complete. Though Courland and Livonia were, more or less, Germanized, and though, at the present time, they constitute the so-called German Governments of the Russian Empire, Lithuania and Samogitia are as they were always Russian or Polish, rather than Teutonic. Neither, in later times, did the Swedish influence extend far southwards.

The strength and courage of the Lithuanians themselves had much to do with this; yet it cannot be denied that the impracticable nature of their country had a large share in it.

It is hardly necessary for us to speculate upon the forces by which the Lithuanian nationality was broken up : inasmuch as it was never thoroughly consolidated. When we first meet with the name, the condition of the populations to which, in its

general sense, we have applied it, was that of a loose aggregate
of States; some of which might be more inclined to amalgamate
with their neighbours than others, and some of which had grown
larger than the others by the absorption of the smaller ones.
Besides which, there was an irregular chain of affinities and
intermarriages amongst the potentates. But this state of things
is the rule rather than the exception with all countries in their
infancy; and it no more applied to Lithuania in particular than
it did to the neighbouring countries of Poland and Russia;
where the Duke of Mazovia or Susdalia might, in one year, lead
an army against the Duke of Cujavia or Novogorod, and in
another marry his daughter or contract an offensive or a defensive alliance with him. It no more applied to Lithuania, in
particular, than it did to that heterogeneous mass of principalities which, under the name of Germany, has lately been consolidated into a unity. It no more applied to Lithuania, in
particular, than it did to England under the Heptarchy. Here
and elsewhere, as well as in Lithuania, there was only an incipient
consolidation. This, in the course of time, developed itself
into its full integrity, and out of it grew powerful kingdoms;
powerful because the union was complete. With the Lithuanians, however, this development was arrested, and the fusion
of Courlanders, Livonians, Samogitians, Yatshvings and Prussians into one, or even two, united empires never took place.
If, then, there be, at the present time, but little nationality to
lose, and if the little that there was be well-nigh lost, it is
because there was, from the very beginning, but little to keep.
There never was a time when Lithuania was at once consolidated
into a single kingdom and united to Poland.

In the eleventh and twelfth centuries the small principalities
seem to have been that of Lithuania Proper; that of Samogitia;
that of the Lett country. If these weakened the influence of
the Lithuanian name, the weakness was relative rather than
absolute. There were the same divisions elsewhere.

The reign of Ringold was nearly concurrent with that of
Batú. How far he wielded the whole power of Lithuania is as
difficult to ascertain as the real power of Egbert and some of
the early Anglo-Saxon kings. His power had, doubtless, risen

at the expense of several minor princes, whose discontent was a
source of weakness. The list, however, of the districts which he
ruled is a long one, and, if we take it literally, spreads over a
vast area. If Kurland were reduced by him he touched the
Baltic, and, if Tshernigov were also reduced, he must have
crossed the Dnieper. Indeed, all White Russia is assigned to
him. Grodno, Minsk, and Vilna were his most unequivocal
possessions.

The great battle of Mohilna was won by Ringold over the
Russians; another in Samogitia over the Teutonic knights.

Some of his conquests were given back to Russia by his
successor, Mindog.

Mindog, being murdered, was succeeded by his son Voyshelg.
But the succession of Voyshelg was disputed by Dovmont,
whose relations to Russia were of more importance than even
Mindog's. Dovmont, defeated in Lithuania, betook himself to
Pskov; which, whether Russian, Lithuanian, Fin, or a mixture
of the three, received him, converted him to Christianity,
and elected him Prince. His authority was supported by
Novogorod.

Meanwhile, Voyshelg had contracted an alliance with the
family of Daniel of Galicia; apparently by marrying his
daughter to Shvano, Daniel's younger son. His appanage was
Chelm and Gallicia. This, united with Lithuania, made him an
object of hate and dread to his elder brother Leo; by whose
contrivance Voyshelg was murdered and the union of Lithuania
and Galicia prevented. In this later principality Leo built
Leopol, or Lemberg.

The succession in Lithuania is now obscure. Troid, however,
was one of the successors of Voyshelg. But this is the date
of the consolidation of the Lithuanic power, and the time
when it became formidable to Russia.

Gedimin was the cotemporary of Uzbek, under whose suzerainty the duchy of Moscow took its imperial pre-eminence.
In this lay the nucleus of Great, or Moscovite, as opposed to
Little, or Kiovian, Russia. In Moscow, too, lay the starting-
point for the conquests which were effectively achieved by Ivan
the Terrible in Kazan and Astrakan.

Olgerd, a greater conqueror than any of his predecessors, succeeded to a divided inheritance. Of his brothers, one held Vilna, another Pinsk, a third, Kastuti, Troki. Of Olgerd's actions it is enough to say that the sack   Nov. 21, 1868. of Moscow was one of them.

Yagellon united Lithuania with Poland. Under Poland, Vitolt, the son of Kastuti, held as a fief a large part of Lithuania; Vitepsk on the north, Podolia on the south. Vitolt, too, it was who reduced that part of Smolensk which had been restored by Mindog.

This has been written in order to correct the notion that the Lithuanians are to be considered a warlike people, either mainly or exclusively, on the strength of their connection with Poland.

What follows are selected instances of the extent to which their union with Poland was a thoroughly inharmonious one. The first touches the question of religious creed.

It is a generally received opinion that the Polono-Lithuanic union introduced Christianity into Lithuania; and in Lithuania there was, and is at the present moment, abundance of Paganism. But the Christianity of the Poles meant the orthodoxy of the Western Church as opposed to the heresy of the Eastern.

*   *   *   *   *

Until the Frank conquest of the Eastern Empire, the metropolitan of Kiev was consecrated at Constantinople; afterwards at Nicæa; afterwards and again at Constantinople. The Lithuanic conquests completed what the Mongol had begun, and Russia was driven northwards; to Vladimir and to Moscow. But the Mahometan conquest of Constantinople affected Little Russia ecclesiastically even more than either the Lithuanic or the Mongol. The Emperor and the Patriarch offered any price for the aid of the West, and, as far as they were concerned, the imperfect and temporary union of the Greek Church with the Latin was the result.

Foremost among the suffragans of the Patriarch of Constantinople was Isidore, Archbishop of Kiev. He consented that Russia should do what was done by the Greeks. A pestilence broke out at Ferrara, and it was the Russians that most especially suffered by it.

From Ferrara the bishops moved to Florence, where the impracticability of the union became more and more apparent. The legation would have melted away if it could; but the Bishop of Heraclea and Mark of Ephesus, who had attempted flight, had been brought back. At Florence the four great points of difference were mooted, and, with the exception of Mark of Ephesus, the Greeks were unduly submissive; none more than Isidore of Kiev. He it was who drew up the treaty in which the temporal elements, the material conditions of the union, were embodied; viz., means for returning to Constantinople, promises of soldiers, and the like. He it was who strove to sell Russia to Constantinople. He it was who, on his return, was resisted and repudiated for his anti-national work.

As it was, the return of Isidore was the signal for an anti-patriarch; whilst, on the side of the Pope, it was followed by the institution of bishops *in partibus*. More than this, the glory of Kiev as the orthodox metropolis had been impaired. The spiritual authority had followed the temporal dignity.

With a Latin bishop at Kiev, Minsk became the seat of the Little Russian primacy; and the orthodox bishops, the voyvodes of Kiev, and the hetmans of the Kosaks, now became the chief actors in these agitated districts.

In 1569, the union between Poland and Lithuania, which, under the first Jagellons, was of the loosest, was drawn closer, and the three primary conditions on the part of the Little Russian provinces were :—

1. The integrity of the *Lithuanic* laws.
2.   ,,   ,,   *Russian* language.
3.   ,,   ,,   *Greek* creed.

Upon all these, however, encroachments were made; slight encroachments at first, a serious one after 1578. Then it was that Stephen Bathory, a brave soldier, and in some respects a good king, allowed a Jesuit college to be founded at Polotsk. The conflict that followed led to the ruin of Poland.

*   *   *   *   *

Our next illustration, then, is from a political, or national, view.

It was at the death of Sigismund I. that the Crown first became elective; and amongst the numerous bitter dissensions which took place during the interregnum, was one as to the place of the election. The Poles proposed Warsaw, the Lithuanians a village on the frontiers of Poland and Lithuania. The Poles carried the day. Nor was the question an unimportant one. It was an election to which neither deputies nor proxies were admitted. It was an election in which every noble was to meet his peers in person. In such a plan as this, distance is an important element; and when the third election came on the Lithuanians complained, and with probable justice, that in the first two the Poles had carried matters with an unduly high hand, and that the Grand Duchy had been but imperfectly represented. Next came the question as to the Dissidents; a term which included, among others, the members of the Greek Church—the Church which had an overwhelming majority in Lithuania. Finally, the Czar was one of the candidates: the candidate who had the support of Lithuania, and the candidate who lost.

As far as the Grand Duchy was concerned, full equality of vote was ensured to it; but there were Lithuanians both in Prussia and Cúrland, and from Prussia and Cúrland no noble was allowed to attend. Neither did those countries send deputies.

To Stephen Bathory Lithuania owed much, and acknowledged the debt. He founded the University of Vilna. He recovered Polotsk from the Russians, who had conquered it during the reign of Sigismund I., and conferred it as a fief upon the Duke of Cúrland. He cut his way still further northwards; even to Novogorod. In his Russian campaign he met with every sign of the truest attachment—not, however, from the Poles, but from the Lithuanians. In Vilna he inspired confidence; in Warsaw discontent and jealousy. And here, as the wars with the Kosaks of the Ukraine are approaching, I may remark that a great proportion of these formidable warriors, if not the majority, was of Lithuanian blood; a fact which must be remembered when we find the Lithuanians so often claiming an extension towards the south   After Stephen Bathory's death, they demand not only Livonia, but Volhynia and Podolia for the Grand Duchy, and insist upon their being incorporated with it. This is when Sigismind III. is elected; the Lithuanian candidate being the Czar. That Sigismund was the Crown Prince of Sweden, who, for the throne of Poland, embraced the Roman Catholic religion, has already been mentioned, and it may be added that he was an intolerant king; Lithuania being full of Greek Church Dissidents. During the reign of his successor, Ladislas VII., Lithuania was the base of a successful campaign against Russia, and in that of his. successor of an unsuccessful one. At the conclusion of the former, the Polish kingdom comprised Smolensko and Tshernigof, over which the Czar renounced all claims or pretension. At the conclusion of the latter, the Russians held possession of Semigallia, on the very frontier of Cúrland. This arose out of the alliance between the Kosaks and the Czar—the fortunes of Lithuania being connected with those of the Kosaks, with whom they were much more closely allied than with the Poles. After the death of Bogdan this became apparent. The eastern half of the Kosak country went to Russia, and even Vilna went with it. Podolia and Volhynia were won back; but the parts beyond the Dnieper never reverted to Poland. Under Michael there were fresh quarrels and factions. I cannot give the details of them; but it is a remarkable fact that, even under a leader like Sobieski, the fidelity of the Lithuanian portion of the army could never be depended on. Twice it traversed the plans of that soldier, by either desertion *en masse*, or by loud expressions of discontent. Indeed, in the campaign of 1672, there was actual mutiny—mutiny, however, which was too strong to be punished. Kaminiec had been taken, Podolia was reduced, Red Russia was overrun; Mahomet, in person, had invested Leopol; and by the peace of Budchaz the Ukraine and the suzerainty (such as it was) over the Kosaks had been ceded. Finally, tribute had been promised; but not paid. The Grand Vizier having renewed the war, Sobieski intended to fall upon two of the Turkish generals separately, and then to advance against Kaminiec or the main body of the army which the Sultan in person was expected to lead. The Lithuanians compelled him to reverse the order in which he had prepared to take the generals, and to begin with Hussein, who, with eighty thousand men, held Koczim, rather than with Caplan Pasha, who was advancing through Moldavia. Even against Hussein they marched unwillingly; and when they found him, Paz, the Lithuanian hetman, was with difficulty persuaded to co-operate. Koczim, however, was taken; only, however, to be retaken; for Michael died, and the election of Sobieski as king followed, remarkable for nothing more than for the unanimous opposition raised by the Lithuanians against the only man who could save Poland. The hetman Paz was his personal enemy; and it was not until he found his opposition useless that it was withdrawn. The king, however, was bound to pass one year in three in Lithuania, and to hold every third Diet at Grodno.

Still the army was as untrustworthy as before. Koczim taken, and retaken, had to be again taken; and one of the first acts of Sobieski's reign was an attempt to recover it. He was in a fair way of doing it, when Paz, with his Lithuanians, again deserted, leaving him to retreat before a fresh army of Ottomans and Tatars. The indignation, however, of his countrymen forced him to re-unite, and, unwillingly, to share in the glory of more than one victory. In the relief, however, of Vienna, the Lithuanian army took no share. The next important occasion on which there was room for any notable display of a Lithuanian feeling as opposed to a Polish, was when Charles XII. invaded Ingria, Estonia, and Livonia. At this time the Duchy was divided between two great factions; that of the Radzivils and that of the Sapiehas. At any rate, the Sapiehas held with Charles; but as the Polish feeling was, to a great extent, in the same direction (Augustus being considered a Saxon rather than a Polish king), I do not lay much stress on this. Then came the times of the Partition; when Lithuania became mainly Russian. But the Partitions will be considered when Poland comes under notice. Then the times of Napoleon; upon which we may pause.

In 1812 Vilna was the scene of a succession of intrigues; being, during April, May, and June, the residence of the Czar and his generals, and during July that of Napoleon. As the

Czar left, the Emperor entered. The intrigues, however, continued; though they fell into different hands, and were carried
on for different objects. Alexander had dazzled the people of
Vilna with the splendour of his entertainments, and pleased
them with the affability of his manners. The heads of the
Lithuanian nobility (I observe that all the names given by
Schlosser are *Polish*) had ribbons and stars conferred on them;
and deputies from Poland were received with honour. The
departure, however, of the Emperor and his staff was abrupt.
They left behind them a great part of their provisions and am-
munitions, and the administration of Lithuania fell into the
hands of the able agents of Napoleon. Although the pro-
visional government consisted of Poles, everything was directed
by Frenchmen. Bignon and Jomini first, and Hogendorp
afterwards, were at the head of the war department. The last,
by his rudeness, did much to estrange the Lithuanians; whose
country was now divided into four intendancies—Vilna, Grodno,
Minsk, and Bialystock, the intendants being Frenchmen. It
was during Napoleon's stay in Vilna that some of the more
important declarations concerning both the wishes of the Poles
and the intentions of the Emperor were made; these last being
regulated by the conditions through which the co-operation of
Austria was insured. To a deputation from Warsaw the
answer was that he—Napoleon—"saw, with pleasure, the
Poles full of enthusiasm for the resurrection of Poland; but
that it was not consistent with his policy publicly to declare
himself favourable to the restoration." The answer to the
speech containing this disheartening announcement—an answer
which had been prepared under the expectation of a favourable
promise—was never delivered; but another, put into the mouth
of the Voyood Vybicski, with, apparently, a touch or two of
Bignon's, was substituted for it. Let it merely be said that
"the kingdom of Poland exists, and sixteen millions of Poles
will sacrifice either life or fortune for emperors." However,
this was neither said explicitly, nor left unsaid. The Emperor
had duties of divers kinds to fulfil, and complicated interests
to reconcile. He could admire the enthusiasm of the Poles,
and sympathise in their denunciations of the Czar—but "I hold

the same language as I held from the beginning; and I should also add that I have guaranteed the Emperor of Austria the integrity of his dominions, and that I cannot authorise any scheme or any movement which would tend to trouble him in the peaceable possession of the Polish provinces which remain to him. Let Lithuania, Samogitia, Vitepsk, Polotsk, Mohilev, Volhynia, Podolia, and the Ukraine become animated with the spirit which has shown itself in Great Poland, and Providence will crown with success the sanctity of your cause." But no such demonstrations were made; and the retreat from Moscow ended the Napoleonic portion of Lithuanian history. If we remember this was delivered, and look to the names of the districts mentioned, the speech looks much more like a suggestion to the Lithuanians than a promise to the Poles.

CHAPTER XIII.

The Lithuanians Proper.—Their Poetry.—Their Fairy Tales.

WITH the single exception of the Esthonians, the Lithuanians are the most pagan of all the nations of civilized Europe : in other words, their superstitions are not only the most numerous, but they are the most redolent of Heathendom. Of the thousand-and-one songs which illustrate the simple modes of thought of the flax-dressers and foresters of their rude regions scarcely one is founded upon either a saintly legend or a Chris-tian sentiment. The Virgin is nowhere : the miracle nowhere : the saint nowhere. There are holy wells, and mysterious groves : but the tales connected with them are not of a holy character. There is superstition and there is religion ; but it is the super-stition which in Italy would invoke Neptune in a storm, and the religion which sees in the Sun and the Morning-star a God of Light and a Messenger of the Dawn rather than mere heavenly bodies. As little do the ballads savour of heroes, warriors, and robbers. For all that they tell us, there is no heroic, no predatory age in Lithuania. Of border feuds, and of bold moss-troopers, there is scarcely a word ; and scarcely a word about any ancient king or captain. Of the songs that show even the soldier-sentiment there are but few, and the antiquity of these is but low. They date back to the times of Frederic the Great or of Charles XII. at the very most. All the following are samples from Nesselmann :—

1.

1.
To-day we'll drink ale ;
To-morrow we'll march out
To the land of Hungary,

2.
Where there are rivers of wine,
Where there are golden apples,
And where the woods are orchards.

3.
And what shall we do there?
And what shall we do there,
In the land of Hungary ?

4.
We'll build us a city
With costly stones,
And windows of the Sun.

22

5.

And what shall we eat?
And what shall we eat,
In the land of Hungary?

6.

Tender chickens;
Pigeons roasted,
At the Sun's stove.

7.

And what shall we drink?
And what shall we drink,
In the land of Hungary?

8.

Milk, mead,
Double beer,
Red wine.

9.

And what shall we wear?
Short coats,
With gold buttons.

10.

And where shall we sleep?
On beds of silk,
And pillows of down.

11.

And who shall wait on us?
And who shall wait on us,
In the land of Hungary?

12.

The Daughters of the Gods,
With white hands,
And soft words.

13.

And when shall we come back?
And when shall we come back,
From the land of Hungary?

14.

When posts have buds,
When stones have leaves,
When trees grow on the sea.

2.

1.

To-day we will drink mead;
To-morrow we will march
Into the land of the Franks.

2.

There grows a green forest
In the land of the Franks—
In the land of the Franks.

3.

Through that green forest
Runs a clear stream—
Runs a clear stream.

4.

Over the clear stream
Is a bright bridge—
Is a bright bridge.

5.

Under the bright bridge
Swims a many-coloured fish—
Swims a many-coloured fish.

6.

He that shall catch the fish
Shall be king of Poland—
Shall be king of Poland.

7.

The Saxon shall catch it,
And he shall be king of Poland—
And he shall be king of Poland.

In all this the Lithuanian songs stand in strong contrast to those of the Servians, the Spaniards and the Scotch, and the Germans; in all of which the personal element and the adventure are prominent. But of the simple sentiment of rural life, they are full; and the imagery corresponds. Here and there, too, there is an approach to the apologue.

1.

The sparrow gave
A wedding feast for his daughter;
Dam dam dali dam,
A wedding feast for his daughter.

2.

Out of a grain of rye
He baked the bread;
Dam dam dali dam,
He baked the bread.

3.

Out of a grain of barley
He brewed the ale;
Dam dam dali dam,
He brewed the ale.

4.

And he called
All the birds;
Dam dam dali dam,
All the birds.

5.

The owl alone
Was not called;
Dam dam dali dam,
The owl alone.

6.

But the owl came
Uncalled;
Dam dam dali dam,
Uncalled.

7.

The owl set himself
At the end of the table;
Dam dam dali dam,
At the end of the table.

8.

The owl took
Crumbs of white bread;
Dam dam dali dam,
Crumbs of white bread.

9.

The sparrow asked
The owl to dance;
Dam dam dali dam,
The owl to dance.

10.

The sparrow trod on
The owl's toes;

3.

Dam dam dali dam,
The owl's toes.

11.

The sparrow picked out
The owl's eye,
Dam dam dali dam,
The owl's eye.

12.

The owl danced
Blind and lame;
Dam dam dali dam,
Blind and lame.

13.

The owl as judge
On the hedge;
Dam dam dali dam,
On the hedge.

14.

The owl's nest,
Is it not a palace?
Dam dam dali dam,
Is it not a palace?

15.

The owl's sons,
Are they not lords?
Dam dam dali dam,
Are they not lords?

16.

The owl's daughters,
Are they not ladies?
Dam dam dali dam,
Are they not ladies?

17.

The owl's head,
Is it not a skillet?
Dam dam dali dam?
Is it not a skillet?

18.

The owl's eyes,
Are they not bungholes?
Dam dam dali dam?
Are they not bungholes?

19.

The owl's beak,
Is it not a gun?
Dam dam dali dam,
Is it not a gun?

22 *

20.

The owl's feathers,
Are they not silk?
Dam dam dali dam,
Are they not silk?

21.

The owl's wings
Are they not posies?
Dam dam dali dam,
Are they not posies?

22.

The owl's feet,
Are they not harrows?
Dam dam dali dam,
Are they not harrows?

23.

The owl's tail
Is it not a besom?
Dam dam dali dam,
Is it not a besom?

4.

1.

The wolf, the wolfie,
The beast of the forest,
Goes out of the wood
Into the meadows,
Worries the calves,
And the foals:
Such is his work.

2.

The fox, the foxie,
The beast of the forest,
Creeps from the wood
Into the homestead,
Steals and bites
Cocks and geese:
Such is his work.

3.

The dog, the doggie,
The watcher of the house,
Barks and bites
The thief's toes,
Frightens old women,
And beggar-men:
Such is his work.

4.

4.

The flea, the fleaie,
Sucks the blood
At dawn of day,
To wake the maids,
To milk the cows:
Such is his work.

5.

The bee, the beeie,
The insect of the forest,
Hums on the heath,
Stings our fingers,
Ears, and face,
Gives us honey:
Such is his work.

6.

Oh! man, manikin,
Look at the bee,
Thou stingest
Our hearts, our hearties,
Give then comfort
To your brother:
Such is man's work.

More interesting than any of the preceding are those which convey allusions to the old mythology of the pagan period; or, to speak more strictly, those which represent that amount of Paganism which still exists—still exists, though overlaid and disguised by an imperfect Christianity. To Perkun, Perkuns, or Perkunos, was awarded either the first, or the second place in the Lithuanic Pantheon—his rival in power being Pikullos. The name of the latter, though not found in the collection from which the present specimens are taken, is, still, to be found elsewhere —as will be shown in the sequel.

5.

1.

"Sun, Daughter of God,
 Why so far goest thou ?
 Why so long waitest thou,
 From us departing ?"

2.

" Over seas, over hills,
 I have looked at the meadows,
 I have cheered the shepherds :
 Many are my gifts."

3.

" Sun, Daughter of God,
 Who, Morning and Evening,
 Lights your fire,
 Makes your bed ?"

4.

" The Morning-Star, the Evening-Star ;
 The Morning-Star for my fire,
 The Evening-Star for my bed :
 Many are my mates."

6.

1.

The Moon went with the Sun,
 In the early Spring ;
 The Sun got up early :
 The Moon went away from him.

2.

The Moon walked alone,
 Fell in love with the Morning-Star ;

Perkun, greatly angered,
 Stabbed her with a sword.

3.

Why wentest thou away from the Sun ?
 Why walk alone in the night ?
 Why fall in love with the Morning-
   Star ?
 Your heart is full of sorrow.

7.

1.

Yesterday, in the evening,
 My lamb got lost ;
 Who'll help to seek
 My only lamb ?

2.

I went to the Morning-Star ;
 The Morning-Star answered,
 " At the dawn of Day,
 I must light the Sun's fire."

3.

I went to the Evening-Star ;
 The Evening-Star answered,

" At the close of Day,
 I must make the Sun's bed."

4.

I went to the Moon ;
 And the Moon answered,
 " I have been stabbed by a sword :
 Sad is my countenance !"

5.

I went to the Sun ;
 The Sun answered,
 " For nine Days will I search,
 And on the tenth I won't leave off."

8.

1.

The Morning-Star gave a feast ;
 Perkun rode past the gate :
 He struck down a green oak-tree.

2.

The oak-tree, dripping with blood,
 Splashed my garment—
 Splashed my garland.

3.

The Sun's Daughter, weeping,
 Collected, for three years,
 The withered leaves.

4.

" Oh, where, my mother,
 Shall I wash my garments ?
 Where shall I wash out the blood ?"

5.

"Oh, my young daughter,
Go to the pond
Into which nine streams flow ! "

6.

" And where, my mother,
Shall I dry my clothes?
Where shall I dry them in the wind ?"

7.

" Oh, my young daughter,
In that green garden
Where nine rose-trees grow ! "

9.

1.

There sailed—there sailed
From the Russian town,
Two young fishermen.

2.

They cast—they cast
Their fine nets,
In the middle of the bay.

3.

They took—they took
The fishes of the sea,
With their fine nets.

4.

And they caught in their nets—
Oh, what a wonder !—
Two sea-calves.

5.

" Mate ! mate !
Friend ! friend !
What are these two fishes?"

6.

And the God of the Sea
Was angry with them :
A storm arose.

7.

" Oh, mate ! mate !
Friend ! friend !
Throw out the golden anchor ! "

8.

" Oh, mate ! mate !
Friend ! friend !
Run up to the top of the mast!

9.

" Perhaps you may see
The hills of the harbour ;
Perhaps a slender fir-tree."

10.

" I see no harbour—
I see no hills—
I see no slender fir-tree.

11.

" I can only see
My own dear maiden,
Walking in the fir-wood.

12.

" Black—black is her garland,
Yellow her curls,
Green her skirt.

13.

"I would if I could
Pull in two
The green skirt.

14.

" One half
I would keep in my locker ;
Of the other half I would make a flag."

Poems, however, of this kind are exceptional. The generality is of the same sort as those of Estonia; and to some extent, (allowing for a difference of imagery) of the Swiss and Tyrolese. But, as will be seen in the sequel, it is with that of those of

Estonia that the imagery most agrees. The horse, which is always called by its poetic name *zirgus* rather than by its ordinary name *arklys*, appears in almost all of them. It carries the lover to his sweet-heart, who is in a garden of rue and peonies, plucking lilies, and preparing wreaths. Or she is helping at the mowing; or pulling the flax; or, it may be, spinning in her mother's hut. The love-making, though an air of simple sentiment is flung around it, is of an ordinary kind; with a *modicum* of reserve and but little refinement. Allowing, however, for the practice of what the Germans call "love between the blankets," to which the Welsh give a grosser name—it is innocent withal. It is done prettily, to say the least; perhaps, poetically.

10.

1.

"Come hither, maiden!
Come hither, young one!
Let us talk sweet talk —
Let us dream dreams,
    Where the springs are the deepest—
    Where the love is the lovingest."

2.

"I cannot, young man—
I cannot, young man!
My mother will scold,
The old father will scold,
    If I go home late—
    If I go home late."

3.

"Then say, young maiden—
Then say, young one,
That two ducks flew to the spring,
And muddied the water."

4.

"It is not true, my daughter—
It is not true, my young one;
You talked with a young man—
You dreamed with a young man,
    Under the green,
    With sweet words."

11.

1.

"My daughter Simonene,
    Where did you get the boy?
Dam, dam, dali dam,
    Where did you get the boy?"

2.

"Mother—honoured mother,
    It came in a dream;
Dam, dam, dali dam,
    It came in a dream."

3.

"My daughter Simonene,
    And how will you cover him?
Dam, dam, dali dam,
    And how will you cover him?"

4.

"Mother—honoured mother,
    In the hood of my gown;
Dam, dam, dali dam,
    In the hood of my gown."

5.

"My daughter Simonene,
    And who will watch over him?
Dam, dam, dali dam,
    And who will watch over him?"

6.

"Mother—honoured mother,
    The daughters of God,
Dam, dam, dali dam,
    Will bear him on their hands."

7.

" My daughter Simouene,
  What will you lay him in ?
Dam, dam, dali dam,
  What will you lay him in ?"

8.

" Mother—honoured mother,
  In the shroud of the dew ;
Dam, dam, dali dam,
  In the shroud of the dew."

9.

" My daughter Simonene,
  Where will you rock him ?
Dam, dam, dali dam,
  Where will you rock him ?"

10.

" Mother—honoured mother,
  In the cradle of the Laima ;
Dam, dam, dali dam,
  In the cradle of the Laima."

11.

" My daughter Simonene,
  What will you feed him with ?
Dam, dam, dali dam,
  What will you feed him with ?"

12.

" Mother—honoured mother,
  With the white bread of the Sun ;
Dam, dam, dali dam,
  With the white bread of the Sun."

13.

" My daughter Simonene,
  Where will you send him ?
Dam, dam, dali dam,
  Where will you send him ?"

14.

" Mother—honoured mother,
  In the army of the Boyards ;
Dam, dam, dali dam,
  In the army of the Boyards."

15.

" My daughter Simonene,
  What will he be ?
Dam, dam, dali dam,
  What will he be ?"

16.

" Mother—honoured mother,
  He will be a Hetman ;
Dam, dam, dali dam,
  He will be a Hetman."

12.

1.

I went into the town of Tilsit—
Into the town of Tilsit, among the dragoons.

2.

There rode out one troop —there rode out another,
But there was not--there was not my young man.

3.

I went into Köningsberg—
Into Köningsberg, among the fine people.

4.

There walked out one company—there walked out another,
But there was not—there was not my young man.

5.

I went into Berlin,
Amongst the King's guards.

6.

There went out one company—there went out another,
But there was not—there was not my young man.

7.

I went into a green meadow—
Into a green meadow, among the mowers.

8.

I looked at one, I looked at the other,
But there was not—there was not my young man.

9.

I went on a high hill—
On a high hill, among the ploughers.

10.

I looked at one, and I looked at the other,
And there I set eyes on my young man.

13.

1.

And there flew a bright-coloured greenfinch
    Out of the garden,
And bespoke a many-coloured nightingale
    In the garden.
" Now, go away, you many-coloured greenfinch,
    From me ;
You will find other nightingales
    As good as I."
" No ! I have flown over a hundred gardens
    And one,
But never I have found nightingale
    Like you ! "

2.

And there rode a young courtier
    Out of the court,
And bespoke a young court lady,
    In the court.
" Now, go away, you young courtier,
    From me ;
You will find other court ladies
    As good as I."
" No ! I have ridden through ten courts
    And one,
But never found lady like you ! "

3.

And there rode a young villager
    Out of the village,
And bespoke a young maiden
    In the village.
" Now, go away, you young villager,
    From me ;

You will find other maidens
    As good as I."
" No ! I have ridden through ten villages
    And one,
And never found a maiden like you."

4.

And there rode a young townsman
    Out of the town,
And bespoke a young lady
    In the town.
" Now, go away, you young townsman,
    From me ;
You will find other young ladies
    As good as I."
" No ! I have ridden through ten towns
    And one,
And never found lady like you !"

Between the earliest of these and the latest there is but little
difference. The oldest song in Lithuanic belongs to the sixteenth century ; but it might have been composed yesterday ; as
hundreds like it are composed. Perhaps, we should say that the
Lithuanian songs *grow :* for they are anonymous, and, until lately,
all unwritten ; and in different parts of the country the same song
takes a different form or differs in length from its fellow. Thus
a few stanzas may be found in one village ; whereas another may
give it with addition upon addition. The longest, however, are short
—sonnets, so to say, in a metre different from that of the ordinary
sonneteer. The name for them is *Dainus ;* word for word, the
name of similar songs in Wallachia and Moldavia. The *gesme*
is the sacred song, the *dainus* the popular one. The *gesme* makes,
perhaps, a hundredth part of the whole collection ; the *dainus*
all the rest.

The fairies of Lithuania are the *Laumas*, of whom tale upon
tale is current. The Lauma haunts lonely places, and visits the
dwellings of men at night. It is a female, and is skilled in all
female employment. It can spin, weave, sew, work in the fields.
One thing, however, it can *not* do. It cannot begin a work, and it
cannot end one. It is not malicious, but only mischievous. It
steals and changes infants. A child of a Lauma is soon either
discovered or suspected. It has a big swollen head. It sometimes
lives to be ten years old, rarely twelve, never thirteen.

CHAPTER XIV.

The Letts.—The Baltic, or German Provinces of Russia: Estonia, Livonia, Cúrland.

THE contest between Russia and Sweden for Livonia took a definite form towards the end of the reign of Gustavus Vasa. For one of his intractable sons, John, a portion of Livonia was intended as an appanage; inasmuch as it was the dominant wish of the old king that the influence of Denmark in Esthonia should be abated; and, at this time, the Danes had just received the submission of Reval. Upon this the father writes :—" We would have you think, dear son, what detriment it would work to our affairs if the Danes should be our neighbours on this side, whether it would not be better to forestall than to be fore-stalled; to take the piece from the hound in time, than to be bitten by him—give us thy opinion hereupon."*

The Grand-master, then, was to be assisted by a loan from Sweden, for which the town of Reval was to be impignorated. But the power of the Grand-master and his Order was on the wane. Poland, the Empire, Denmark, and Sweden were ap-pealed to for defence against Russia; and in a multitude of applications there was room for intrigue, cross-purposes, fraud and dissimulation. Indeed, though the policy indicated in the letter just quoted is a sufficient explanation of Gustavus' conduct, it is not the only one. It is suggested by the historian of Sweden that it was not against Denmark alone that these precautions were taken. John had been intriguing in the same

* Letter of the King to Eric, December 8 and 10, 1558. From Gejer's His-tory of Sweden.

quarter, and with offers of nearly similar terms. He had connived at the piracies of Reval; he had given shelter in Finland to some of the pirates; and he was tendering a loan to the Grand-master as a security for a certain fortress. It was wise on the part of Gustavus to get the management of an affair like this into his own hands, instead of letting it fall into those of his unwary sons, who were making their arragements without his privity, though not without his knowledge. He had suspected, if not observed, something clandestine for some time, and had made a strong representation on the matter:—
"Seeing thou well knowest that Finland is not a separate dominion from Sweden, but that both are counted as members of one body, it becomes thee to undertake nothing which concerns the whole kingdom, unless he who is the true head of Sweden, with the estates of the realm, be consulted thereupon, and it be approved and confirmed by him and them, as thy bounden duty points out, and Sweden's law requires."

However, the machinations continued, though the completion of them was put off. Neither was the plan concocted amongst the brothers ever put into effect. The father, whom they had conspired to deceive, was on the edge of the grave; and when the grave closed over him a more than Theban enmity broke out between the sons.

On the accession of Eric, his brother John reminded him that a territory in Livonia had been promised to him; and that if this promise were fulfilled he would undertake the protection of Reval against the Russians under Ivan Vassiliewitch II. But Eric undertook the affair himself, and sent over an army which was received into the town. The nobles submitted to Swedish rule; and, after Eric had been crowned, their privileges were confirmed by the royal sanction given at Stockholm. The title, too, of Eric became "King of the Swedes, Goths, and Vandals, Lord of Livonia and Reval." A war was the result. It did not, however, break out at once; inasmuch as peace with Russia was preserved. This was because there was a common enemy in Poland. Cúrland, under Kettler, had become a Polish fief: and, of all the Powers of Europe, the one that was most feared and most suspected was Poland; whilst the Power that was strongest to oppose her was neither Russia nor the Empire, but Sweden.

And now our history is full of complications. Poland, with Cúrland as a fief; Russia pressing northwards or westwards from Novogorod and Moscow; and Denmark, with a powerful navy, are all fixing their attention upon Livonia and Estonia. In the family of Gustavus the counsels are divided; if counsel it may be called that has its origin in ambition, egotism, and jealousy, rather than in the judgment. John recommends a Polish alliance as against Russia: Eric allies himself with Russia as against Poland. When a Danish war breaks out, as it does a few years afterwards, the complications increase, and the extraordinary offers in the way of compromise suggest reflections upon the slightness of the causes upon which great effects may hang. It was proposed that the Swedish possessions in Livonia should be made over to the Empire, and held under the Empire, as a fief, by Denmark. It was proposed that the Danish prince, Magnus, should marry the Czar's niece, and put himself under Russian protection. This was done; and he bore, for a time, the title of King of Liefland: with Russia to back his pretensions. Afterwards, however, the contest is almost wholly between Sweden and Russia.

It was now incumbent upon Russia to make good her engagement to John: and an army invaded Estonia and Livonia. They left blood upon every footstep, and struck a terror in the hearts of all except the garrison of Reval. This held out for Sweden till the eleventh hour: when relief came. The Russian successes and the Russian cruelties had done much to weaken the Swedish dominion: but the disastrous quarrels within the Swedish army itself had done more. It was not an army of Swedes. There were German mercenaries in it, and there were Scotch mercenaries; for Scotch assistance was generally to be hired by the Swedes. Not on one occasion only, but on many, must we remember this when we have occasion to go into the minute ethnology of Scandinavia. In one of the mutinies as many as fifteen hundred Scots were cut down. But a Turkish war broke out, and Sweden was appealed to on both sides. This gave her an opportunity for retrieving her fortunes; and it was improved by the accession of a skilful officer to her ranks. Pontus de la Gardie was a Frenchman; but he served the Swedes better than they served themselves. He married a natural daughter of the King, and was appointed general against the Russians. He ejected them from Livonia; and followed them beyond the boundary. He took Narva, Kexholm, and all the fortresses in Ingria. The Swedes claim for their countrymen the award of comparative humanity in their dealings with the natives—but comparative humanity, when an invading army of Russians under such a king as Ivan Vassilie-vitsh is the standard, is but faint praise. The Russians were merciless: but they were then, as now, brave and obstinate. Their discipline then, as now, was such as to make them undergo any extremity rather than yield. It is Geijer, the Swedish historian, writes thus, and enlarges on it.

After the death of Stephen Bathory, the Crown of Poland became vacant, and Sigismund, the son of John, who had married Catherine, the last of the Yagellon princesses, and the sister of Bathory's widow, was elected against the powerful interest of the Archduke Maximilian. The difficulties that this introduced were of the gravest kind. His father was still alive, so that, though King of Poland, he was only Crown Prince of Sweden. The national religion of the Poles was Romanism. The Swedes were Protestants, though not, as yet, such strong and almost fanatic Protestants as they became under the great Gustavus. As Henry IV. was in respect to Navarre and France: so was Sigismund in respect to Sweden and Poland. The creed which was compatible with one crown was impossible for the other. The sacrifice which this involved, had it come to one, and had the King been free to determine it, would have been made in favour of Rome. We know, however, that no such sacrifice was required.

A.D. 1586.

The transactions that followed are characterized by anything but good faith on the part of Sigismund. The two Swedish diplomatists who had the most to do with the agreement guaranteed that that portion of Livonia which belonged to Sweden should be incorporated with Lithuania, and, as a part of Lithuania, be also incorporated with Poland. Had this been done, an arrangement too fortunate to occur in history would have been effected, and, with the exception of its Fin and German elements, the Duchy of Lithuania would have taken a truly Lithuanic augment. Poland, too, would have been strengthened on the Baltic, and the Russians permanently beaten-off from the coast of the Gulf of Finland. The act, however, of the councillors, Eric Sparre and Eric Brahe, was repudiated by their Government, and Sigismund, when he arrived in Poland, refused to confirm the cession; not absolutely and for ever, but until the death of his father, when, instead of being Crown Prince, he would be King. In this, the Poles, who seem to have been easily satisfied, acquiesced; and Sigismund was crowned at Cracow. The further details of this complicated arrangement belong to the civil history of Sweden, rather than to an ethnological notice of Livonia and Estonia; and, in the civil history of Sweden, they are of the greatest interest. It turned upon John and Sigismund whether Sweden was to have a king who was half a Romanist or a Gustavus Adolphus. Without, however, going into these details, we may state that, notwithstanding the claims of Sigismund as John's son, the successor to John was Charles; his brother; the youngest of the sons of Gustavus Vasa, and, with all his faults, the noblest.

Sigismund remained King of Poland; and, from Poland, maintained his pretensions: so that the war with Livonia devolved upon Charles IX.; in which he was more than merely unsuccessful. The battle of Kexholm seems to have been disgracefully lost against an inferior force. The men "ran, and let their backs be hacked like a flock of poultry fleeing before a small body, where they were four or five to one, and leaving us on the field." The horse that bore the king was killed under him, when a *Livonian* nobleman, Henry of Wrede, gave him his, and met his own death on foot. His widow and children were rewarded by manors in Finland. Livonia, however, remained Swedish; for Charles IX. was, on the whole, a successful guardian of the honour of his country. His immediate successors were this and more.

From the time when Eric, the son of Gustavus Vasa, wrote

himself " Lord of Reval and Livonia " to the peace
of Nystadt is one hundred and sixty years; during   A.D. 1721.
the whole of which time Livonia, Estonia, Ingria, and the
southern parts of Finland are little more than battle-fields for
Russia, Sweden, and Poland—for Russia and Sweden as the
principals, but for Poland as a subordinate; although not
always and only so. After the death of Kettler, Cúrland was a
fief of Poland's. A part, too, of Livonia was Polish; and,
perhaps, on the Lithuanian frontier, a part of Estonia as well.
At whatever time we take the history of this period the same
names appear and re-appear: the same towns being besieged,
with the same spots witnessing the same battles between the
same combatants. The cessions, too, of territory repeat themselves. Does Russia succeed in fighting her way towards the
locality of her present capital, and gaining a port on the Baltic,
it is certain parts of Ingria that are ceded to her by Sweden,
and when under a change of fortune she recedes, it is certain
parts of Ingria which Sweden takes back. The same is the
case on the northern side of the Gulf of Finland; in Finland
Proper and Karelia. It is the Government of Viborg and the
fortress of Kexholm that we meet and meet again—sometimes
Russian, sometimes Swedish, just as if it were their business to
be always changing hands. In like manner, Reval, Riga, and
Narva are always being besieged or relieved; so that Estonia
and Livonia are ever under the miseries of war. We must, for
most purposes, take them together; for though, in their
ethnology, they differ from one another more than Livonia and
Cúrland, Estonia being Fin rather than Lett, they agree in their
political history: both being more Swedish than Polish.

Upon the whole, Ingria was Russian; and, upon the whole,
there was a discontinuity in the area held by Sweden on the
two sides of the Gulf of Finland; a discontinuity which is
ethnological and religious as well as historical. Finland is Fin
and Protestant, and Estonia is Fin and Protestant; but Ingria,
or the Government of St. Petersburg, though there are fragments of a Fin population within its boundaries, is Russian in
language and Greek in creed. So it is at the present time,
from the fact of so vast a capital as St. Petersburg belonging to

it. But so it was, to a great extent, a hundred and fifty years before St. Petersburg was founded.

Charles XII., at the age of nineteen, has succeeded to the crown of Sweden, and the Elector of Saxony, the King of Denmark, and the Czar have entered into a league against him. They are to divide among them all his non-Swedish possessions. The Czar is Peter the Great; and the Elector of Saxony is also the King of Poland. We must distinguish between the two dignities. The Poles did so, and we must do the same. It was as Elector of Saxony that he joined the league against Charles. As King of Poland, he could do but little against him : for, however much the case of Sweden may have been a true partition, or however much it may be excused as having been nothing worse than an amputation or mutilation, and however much it may (from the fact of a king of Poland having been a party to it) wear the garb of a precedent that fell back upon its originators, it is nothing of the kind as far as regards Poland. It has nothing of the Nemesis (to use a hack platitude) about it. It was the achievement, in a small way, of the Elector of Saxony; and it was not achieved off hand. How Charles dissipated the thunder-cloud which had crowded together over his head, and which had begun to burst, is a matter for either the personal biographer or the historian of Sweden. He broke and scattered it for a time.

Peter, when it was first charged with its terrors, had, after the manner of all the Czars, a Turkish war on hand; of which he contrived to clear himself in time to move towards Estonia, when the Elector appeared before Riga; but only half harnessed for the campaign. This was at the head of a foreign army. Meanwhile, the factions of the country itself were to be utilized by the miserable Patkul, the Patkul who was afterwards betrayed by the Saxon Elector, and disgracefully murdered (tortured on the wheel) by Charles. Charles was a brave man, but a very relentless one. Paykull's fate as well as Patkul's disgraces him. Patkul, however, at the time when the Elector failed before Riga, failed himself. Neither the nobles nor the people answered his call : a fact which gives us one of the measures we have of the feeling of Livonia towards Sweden.

The Saxons withdrew from Riga. They then attempted Riga again. They withdrew again. Again, and for a third time, they attempted it, and withdrew; when peace was concluded with Denmark.

Estonia was as Livonia; harassed by the Czar, even as Livonia was harassed by the Elector. But the great Swedish victory at Narva checked this. After that Lithuania, or, at least, the Sapiehas, joined themselves to Charles; and the Elector of Brandenburgh, ambitious of becoming King of Prussia, made a fourth in the party of would-be partitioners. He, too, had something in Pomerania and Prussia to get out from the wreck of the Swedish domains in Germany.

Meanwhile, Charles was acting on the offensive in Cúrland; for Cúrland was a fief of Poland's, and with its Grand-duke married to the niece of Peter, prospectively, an annexation of Russia's. He took Dünamünde; passed the Dwina in the face of Russians, and pushed on for Poland. Peter, meanwhile, gathered together the fragments of the army that had been beaten at Narva, and taught them to conquer by a campaign in Estonia and Livonia. He looked to the possession of these as a secondary affair; Ingria and the southern parts of Finland being his immediate objects. These he eventually made his own; as he, also, made Livonia and Estonia. Before Ingria had become Russian, and before it was wrested from Sweden, he laid the foundations of St. Petersburg.

For dealing with such a pigmy as the Elector, and neglecting such a giant as the Czar, Charles has been blamed—perhaps rightly. But he judged for himself. " Be assured," he writes in one of his despatches, " if I could rely upon the word of King Augustus, I would immediately leave him in peace. But if peace were concluded and we marched into Russia, he would instantly accept Russian money and fall upon us in the rear, and then our affairs would be in a greater state of entanglement than at present. What Livonia suffers in the mean time may be made good by conferring privileges and acts of grace when God gives us peace."

And Livonia suffered. Lewenhaupt, whom Charles left in the country, did all that a great general could do; possibly more than the conqueror at Narva himself would have done. However, Pultava was lost; and, when the Peace of Nystadt was effected, Livonia and Estonia became Russian. So they are now. So they were during the whole interval. A few years afterwards Cúrland became Russian also.

It was the Peace of Nystadt which, following the death of Charles XII., was the result of the humiliations and defeats with which the latter half of his reign was clouded. It was the measure, too, of the weakness of Sweden.

A.D. 1721.

Nor was the dismemberment limited to Livonia. Cúrland, soon afterwards became Russian.

Cúrland was a conquest of the Crusaders of the thirteenth century; and, at first, was held by the Grand-master of the Order. After the Reformation it became Protestant : and the name of the first Duke was Ketteler, and it was upon his dynasty that the fortune of Cúrland turned. His family became extinct: and the Protestant succession came to an end. During its continuance Russia had grown stronger, Sweden weaker, Poland weaker—both weaker, but especially Sweden; Russia being, most especially, not only absolutely stronger, but stronger at the expense of the two.

Though Cúrland was independent of Sweden, it was not so of Poland. Poland held it as a fief. Now, the policy of Poland was to incorporate Cúrland as an integral part of the kingdom as soon as ever the line of Kettler had died out. It *did* die out; and then came tergiversations on both sides. But there was a strong hand to control them. During the wars between Charles XII. and Peter the Great concerning the nomination of the King of Poland, it was a mere matter of strategies that Cúrland should be either effectually defended by Poland, or occupied by Russia. The latter was the alternative. The Russians took possession, and kept it. So it was *de facto*. Considered *de jure*, the Poles were the more important party in the suit. They had, when the perpetuity of the line of Kettler was in doubt, recognized the secularization of the religious estates, and the change of spiritual bishops into temporal princes; and they had done this in favour of the Protestant duke on the condition that when the Protestant Succession

23 *

ceased, or that when his line came to an end, the relation of fief and suzerain should cease, and that Cúrland should be incorporated with Poland Whatever may have been the faults in Polish policy elsewhere, there is nothing here to which we can refuse our approbation. And the line *did* come to an end : and the last duke was a convert : and the last duke was child-less : and the last duke cared little about Cúrland. He apostatized from his creed and country, and his race became extinct : and the Poles were ready to take possession when the men who were the statesmen of Cúrland either repudiated or evaded the agreement. They called in a son of Augustus II., and offered to make him duke. He accepted the offer, and was acknowledged by both the Cúrlanders and the Poles—but not by the Russians. The Russians kept their troops in the duchy, and the troops forbid his installation. The details of their occupancy are of little importance. We need only remember that the dukes of Cúrland had intermarried with the Russian Royal Family; and add that the wife and widow of the last duke was a niece of Peter's : who afterwards became Anne the Czarina of all the Russias. No wonder that her hold on Cúrland was of the strongest. She had a favourite, Biren ; and this favourite she forced upon Cúrland, and enjoined the recognition of him on Augustus III. As King of Poland he mixed compliancy with resistance. He acknowledged Biren ; but he required certain formalities from him which implied the suzerainty of Poland. He held Cúrland, but held it as a fief of Poland. He was required to undergo certain formal proceedings at Warsaw. He did it, and was invested.

Now Biren was a favourite : and, in course of time, he was a disgraced favourite. He went to Siberia as an exile. He put in certain claims as Duke of Cúrland, and vassal of Poland. The Russian Government acknowledged each claim : and des-pised it. His suzerain exerted himself in his behalf ; and he exerted himself in vain. The time had come when Cúrland must take one Russian *nominee* in exchange for another. Prince Louis of Brunswick was put forward to replace Biren. But the revolution which replaced Anne by Elizabeth prevented him. There was a lull as to the question of succession.

Cúrland was in the meanwhile misgoverned; so far as anarchy, with all the disadvantages of bad government, can be called government. The orders, when they came at all, came from St. Petersburg. The men who enforced them were Russian soldiers; soldiers who had never evacuated the country. The men who conveyed them were Russian officials. All, in short, so far as it was anything, was Russian. The finance, such as it was, was managed by Russians; and the taxes were applied to the payment of Biren's personal debts to Russian creditors. Some of these were real; some usuriously exaggerated; some wholly unreal. However, the Cúrland taxes went to St. Petersburg. In 1754, the King of Poland, whose claims had to some extent been recognized by Elizabeth, had allowed a deputation to apply for Biren's liberation. But the Empress never met it. All that was not Russia was anarchy.

The duke, who had been refused by Russia, and who had been acknowledged by both the Poles and Cúrlanders, was Count Maurice of Saxony, afterwards famous in the military history of France. He was a natural son of Augustus II. The candidate now put forward, was a legitimate son of Augustus III. He satisfied Elizabeth, who was pleased to announce to Augustus III. that he might be invested. The Polish King and the Polish Senate agreed to him: but the Grand Duke, afterwards Peter III., objected. His *nominee* was a prince of the Holstein family: a fact which directs our attention towards Denmark. Even Catherine—even she, though Biren was Anne's, her predecessor's, favourite, supported him. But Biren misgoverned Cúrland, and it became a Russian province.

CHAPTER XV.

Populations neither Turk nor Fin.—Of Northern Asia.—Mongols.—Tungusians.
—Yeniseians.—Jukahiri.—Koriaks and Kamtshatkans.—Aino or Kurilian
Islanders.—Aleutians.—The Independent Tshuktshi.—The Eskimo.—Cau-
casus and Transcaucasia.—Shamil.

I. The chief members of the great *Mongol* family in Russia
are the Buriats, six Kalka tribes, and the Kalmuks. The
Buriat area begins in the parts about Nizhni Udinsk, to the
east of the Lena, and extends to the country of the Khorin
and Barguzin tribes (both of which it includes) beyond Lake
Baikal. It is bounded on the south by the Chinese frontier,
beyond which few or no Buriats are to be found; the Mongols
of the northern parts of China and Mongolia, in the proper
sense of the term, being Kalkas.

Of these Kalka tribes, six, either wholly or partially, are
to be found within the Russian territory. These are the
Dzongol, the Ashe-khabat, the Tabang-gut, the Sartol, the
Atagan, and the Katshagan.

The Buriats amount to about one hundred and ninety
thousand souls; some few being Mahometans, some Christians,
some Shamanists, the majority Bhuddists.

II. The word *Tongús*, used in the sense which it bears in the
present work, is strictly ethnological. There is a general name
wanted for a population in Northern Asia, which falls into
numerous and important divisions and sub-divisions; and this
is it. To some of the tribes to which the term applies it would
doubtless be intelligible; whilst others, such as the Mantshus,
would, in all probability, repudiate it with indignation. The
word, however, is useful, and it is used by the Russians both

in scientific works and in ordinary language. The most western of the populations to which it applies are occupants of the Lower Tunguska; some of whom (perhaps all) call themselves *Orotshong,* and some of whom (perhaps all) are called by others *Tshapodzhir;* a word which is sufficiently conspicuous on most maps. For the Tungús at large there is not only no general name, but nothing that approaches one. Different tribes designate themselves differently. *Donki,* which I submit is, word for word, *Tongús,* is one name; *beye,* meaning the same, another. The Mantshus call *all* the tribes beyond the confines of Mantshuria, and not the Tshapodzhirs alone, *Orotshong.* Other names indicate geographical localities. Thus the *Lamuts* are the men of the sea-coast. Meanwhile another division arises from their habits; these being determined from the domestic animal employed.

The *Horse* Tungús are those of the southern and western portions of the area; these being most akin to the Buriat in their habits and civilization. The *Reindeer* Tungús are those of the north, where they come in contact with the Koriak. The *Lamut* Tungús are met with as we approach the neck of the Peninsular of Kamtshatka. The *Forest* and *Steppe* Tungús, along with the Tungús who go on foot, are either sub-divisions or cross-divisions.

All the members of this class belong to either Russia or China, those of China being the Mantshus of Mantshuria. The Mantshurians, as a body, are perhaps somewhat ruder than the Mongols, and the Russian Tungús somewhat ruder than the Mantshus. As a rule, they are Shamanists, and imperfect converts to Christianity, rather than Buddhists. I am not aware that there is either much Mahometanism or many remains of the old Persian Fire-worship amongst them. With populations that have no general name, we can scarcely expect any wide diffusion of any nationality. Add to this that the land they live in is, in some parts, within the Arctic Circle, and that it extends over an enormous area. The valley of the Amur is the most favoured portion of the Tongús country, and it is here that the first signs of the Tongús civilization appear to have developed themselves.

Two populations may now be taken together; not because they are specially allied to each other (which they are not), but because they are so very small and fragmentary.

III. In all the works anterior to the publication of the *Asia Polyglotta*, certain small tribes on the Yenisey were called *Ostiak*. As they differed, however, in language from the true Ostiaks, Klaproth called them *Yeniseians*. Castrèn calls the northern branch of them "*Yeniseian Ostiaks*," the southern "*Kot.*"

The northern Yeniseians lie between 60° and 66° N.L. A few lie on the river Ket. Still, the Yenisey is their proper river. They call themselves *Könniyung*. The *Denka*, if they still exist, have lost their language.

Between these and their congeners on the south lie some degrees of latitude; so that nothing Yeniseian (in the ethnological sense of the term) is to be found before we reach the parts about Abakansk. And here, so great has been either the absorption or the annihilation of their nation that the number of individuals who, at the present time, speak the original language, falls short of a dozen. They are the Kot of Castrèn.

IV. The *Jukahiri* also are nearly extinct. Those, however, who survive, occupy the lower part of the rivers Kolyma and Indidzhirka. The pressure upon them seems to have been exerted on every side; by the Yakuts, by the Koriaks, and by the Tungús. From the likeness which their language bears to the Samoyed, I infer that their area extended eastward. The name of the extinct tribes are Omoki, Shelagi, Tshuvantsi, &c. "The fires on the hearths of the Omoki were once as numerous as the stars in the sky." So runs the belief in the country which they once occupied.

The few Jukahiri who remain are said to be well-built men. There is, however, no population of which less is known; though, to the ethnologist, it is one of great interest—inasmuch as its language, with Fin affinities on the one side, has American ones on the other.

V. The Koriaks occupy the northern parts of the Peninsula of Kamtshatka and the districts about Okhotsk; being greatly Russianized. They are either Shamanists or imperfect Christians. The nearer they are to the town of Okhotsk, the more they are Russianized. They drive dogs, and, in most points, resemble the Kamtshadales, who belong to the same stock; though Klaproth has, over-hastily, separated the two languages.

The contrast between the Koriak and Tungús physiognomy is generally insisted on—the Koriak skull being less round and the Koriak features less flat than those of the Tungús. On the contrary, its likeness to that of the Americans of the extreme north-west, especially the Loucheux, has been indicated.

The Koriaks fall into two primary divisions, the *Nomads* and the *Villagers*—the first being the owners of large flocks of reindeer, which they follow from spot to spot as the season or the scanty vegetation directs. Of the sub-divisions of these we know but little. Of the Village, Stationary, or Settled tribes we know more. They occupy five different districts, separate from each other—so that it is no wonder that their language falls into just so many well-marked dialects.

VI. *Aino* is the name of the inhabitants of the Kurile islands and the peninsula of Sakalin. A few, too, are (or were) to be found at the extremity of Kamtshatka. Some members of this small family are subject to China; some to Japan; some (as is implied by the fact of their being mentioned here) to Russia.

Those Aino of the island of Sakalin who are Russian subjects occupy the northern part of the southern third of the island.

They dress in dog-skins, seal-skins, fish-skins, Japanese cottons; and (either deservedly or undeservedly) have been praised by some observers for their cleanliness. They weave, spin, and make a sort of cloth from the bark of the willow. They build large storehouses, keep bears, and dig for the roots of a yellow lily and the angelica—but are no husbandmen.

At the autumnal feast of the Omsia a bear is killed, and eaten.

They poison their arrows, and sell such miserables as they can kidnap to the Tungús of the Amur.

According to a Japanese account, the method of barter among the Aino is that of the Western Africans, as described by Herodotus; as well as that of certain tribes in Vera Paz and elsewhere. The Santans (this is the Japanese name for the people of the Lower Amur) place their wares on the shore and retire. The Aino then advance and replace them by an equivalent in furs.

Of the Kurile *Islands,* the most northern, Samshu, is the smallest; and it is the occupancy of the Russian American Fur Company. Such natives as still remain without being Russianized must be few. Every notice of the Aino mentions them as a population which is fast dying out.

In the Aleutian islands, where the ethnological affinities are with the Eskimo on the one side, and the North American Indians on the other, the extinction of the language is, I believe, absolute; and so, likewise, that of the pure-blooded natives,—though of mixed blood, Aleutian and Russian, there is much—much, also, in the island of Sitka, now, along with the rest of Russian America, made over to the United States. Where the native population of this large area is not Eskimo, it is Athabaskan. But is now no longer Russian.

On the other side of Behring's Straits, and in the northeastern extremity of Asia, there is a small population of the Koriak family, which, of all those of Northern Asia, stands alone in the honourable position of a nation, which is still free from the rule of the Czar. It is the *Independent Tshuktshi* that give their name to *Tshuktshy Noss,* or the *Tshuktshi* Promontory. Their language belongs to the Koriak class; and the drainage of the Anadyr is their more especial area. Along the sea-coast a new population presents itself; but it is not indigenous to Asia. The *Namollos* of the coast on each side of the Anadyr are Eskimos, congeners to those of the Arctic parts of the New World, of Labrador, and of Greenland.

* * * * *

Such are the families of the north and north-east; and it is with China and the United States, rather than with any European power, that their frontiers come in contact. With the division that now presents itself the case is different. In *Caucasus* and *Transcaucasia,* the boundary is on the side of Persia and Turkey.

So far as such a thing as a natural boundary against an ambitious and intrusive Power can have any existence at all, there is a natural boundary against both the Russians and the Turks in the impracticable range of the Caucasus. It is a boundary on both sides; on the northern side towards Siberia, and on the southern towards Persia and Asia Minor. But natural boundaries are material, whilst the spirit of expansion and aggression is moral; and between the two powers there is no commensuration. It is only to a very slight extent that Caucasus has ever been a barrier. On the south it has been encroached on by the Persians; on the north by the Tatars first, and by the Russians afterwards.

(*a*.) In Caucasus itself the four primary ethnological divisions, according to their languages, are as follows:—

1. *Apkhazes*, or Apkhazians, and *Circassians*; the former on the side of the Black Sea, the latter on land and in the direction of the Caspian. The Kuban is the river that more especially belongs to this class.

2. In the centre, about Vladikaukas, the *Iron*, or *Ossetes*.

3. East of them the *Tshetsh*, or Tshetsentz. In many of the maps we find this small district marked as Tshetshenia.

4. The *Lesgians*, also on the side of the Caspian. This is the Lesgistan, Daghestan, or Avaria of the maps. Shamil was a Lesgian.

(*b*.) Of the *Georgians*, in the ethnological sense of the term, if we begin with the sub-divisions of the class, there are as many as eleven sections.

1. The *Georgians* Proper, of the Province of Kartueli, and the parts about Tiflis; called by the Russians Grusinians.

2, 3, 4. The *Imeretians*, *Mingrelians*, and *Gurians*; like the Georgians of Kartueli, civilized and Christian, and either actual Russian subjects or recognizing the suzerainty of the Czar.

5, 6. The *Pshav*, to the number of 5,700, and the *Khevsur* to the number of 5,500, in the mountains between Georgia and the Tshetsh country; probably, more or less, Tshetsh in blood.

8, 9, 10. The Suans, or Suanetians, that follow the line of the sea-coast south of Apkhazes; the rudest of the group.

11. The *Laz*, or *Lazes*, belong to Asia Minor rather than to

Caucasus Proper; Mahometans in creed, and, in their political relations, are subject to Turkey.

This arrangement is geographical, and it runs from north-east to south-west; the Apkhazes being the nearest to the Crimea, the Georgians and Lesgians to Persia; but for the political ethnology of Caucasus, more of our information must be got from maps than from books.

Of the *Apkhazes* and *Circassians*, the history begins as early as the time of Peter the Great; and that—as we expect *à priori*—from the fact of their being the most northern of the mountaineers, and, as such, the frontagers of the Tatars of both Astrakan and the Crimea.

Of *Georgia*, and the allied districts, the history is from an earlier time; the frontier here being Armenia and Persia. The wars between Persia and the Porte have already been noticed. Of these the most important was the one made after the Peace of Passarovitz, where the alliance was that of the Sultan and the Czar. It was a very disastrous war for Turkey; for what could result from it but a quarrel?

Of the three minor divisions of the interior, *Ironistan* is the smallest; the most Russian, and as such, the least known as a fighting country; the most Christian, or, rather, the least Mahometan and Pagan; and, finally, the least Caucasian—this meaning that, from their language, the Iron have been considered to belong to the same ethnological class as the Persians—*i.e.* Indo-European, Arian, Aryan, or whatever else we may choose to call or to spell the denomination. It is probable that, in the way of creed, they may belong to the same mixed group to which the Yezids and the Druzes and others have been assigned. Iliyas, or Elisha, is their chief prophet, or saint, and along with him the Holy St. Gregory. They occupy the parts on each side of the military road, or the parts of Vladikaukaz, between the great mountains Elburg and Kasbeg; and this may account for their Russianism. They fall into only two or three divisions.

On the east of these lies *Tshetshenia*, or the land of the Tshetsh, Tshetshentz, Mizhdzhedzhi, Ingush, or Kisteti. Neither are the divisions, in language or dialect, of these numerous: indeed the class is a small one. They lie east of the Iron, and, being occupants of a small area, nowhere touch the Caspian. Of all the mountaineers these are, probably, the most free from foreign influences; and, being this, they seem to retain the most of their original paganism. As fighting-men they are less conspicuous than either the Lesgians or the Circassians; though with the former they seem to be the most connected.

The third of these groups, which lie between the central district of Ironistan and the Caspian, gives us the Lesgians, or men of Daghestan; also called, though the two names do not absolutely coincide, Avaria. These are the numerous tribes and sub-tribes of which Shamil is the representative hero; Shamil, the Abd-al-Kader of the Caucasus, and the great personification of their heroism—of this and something more. His real life is a mystery; but what I find about it I will lay before the reader, who may probably agree with me in seeing in it, if not exactly a mythical element, a religious one, or, at any rate, a special instance of fanaticism. I take the account as I find it in Haxthausen, who takes it as he has found it in Caucasia, and rates it at what it may be worth in the way of real history. The merits he probably puts low; though, of course, there is an historical element in it somewhere, and to some extent. What the narrative is worth lies in its value as a fact in the history of belief or opinion—mainly this; but, at the same time, something more.

Of the *Lesgians* the great hero is Shamil. In 1823 the Kasi-kumuk and Kurali districts formed the Khanate of Arslan Khan, who either acknowledged the Czar as his suzerain or was on friendly terms with Russia. At any rate he was, so to say, Russianized. The second in authority to him was the Mullah Mohammed, the Kadi of the Khanate of Jaraih. A small village in Kuri was his residence, and the Mosque at Jaraih is, at the present time, the object of veneration to every Murid in Eastern Caucasus. Here the Mullah Mohammed taught and officiated; blind from intensity of study, ascetic, and incorruptible. For little beyond the quiet virtues suggested by these epithets was the Mullah Mohammed famous until the year 1823.

Another Mohammed then comes in contact with him, a Kazi

Mohammed from Bokhara, and sits at his feet as disciple, admirer, and friend. There was no one who so valued the Mullah as Kazi Mohammed, and the Mullah had no disciple, even amongst his own countrymen of Daghestan, whom he loved like Kazi. But the time came for Kazi to go away. He departed, however, only to return after a short absence. And his return was a mystery. He was still the disciple and the admirer, but he was an altered man. He had a secret. Would he tell it to the Mullah? Would the Mullah go with him into Shirvan and drink wisdom from the lips of Hadji Ismael of Kundomir? The Mullah would. So the two friends went, and when they reached the garden of Hadji Ismael they found him cutting off the young twigs of the mulberry-trees to feed his silk-worms with. Shocked at his impiety (injuries to mulberry-trees being prominent among the *mala prohibita* of the Koran), they expressed their pain and wonder. Could so good a man be wilfully disobedient? Could so wise a one be foolishly improvident?

Now mark the wisdom of Hadji Ismael, and admire the manner in which he taught his hearers that rules and ordinances were to be obeyed or neglected according to the circumstances with which they might come in contact. " In Arabia," said he, " where the mulberry is scarce, and the climate dry, and where the Koran was written for Arabians, to feed the silk-worm with a young branch would, doubtless, be a crime. But in Shirvan, where the trees are numerous and the twigs grow freely, changes of circumstances change the interpretation of the rule." In this way his visitors were taught to look to the spirit rather than the letter of enactments, and were prepared to hear more from so enlightened a teacher.

They went home instructed. After which a good deal is heard about the Mullah, a very little about the Kazi; and about Hadji Ismael, the Mohametan rationalist of Kundomir in Shirvan—nothing at all. There was a war at this time between Persia and Russia, and many men believed that he was simply an agent from Persia.

Whether true or not as a phenomenon in the region of facts, this belief is an absolute truth in the history of opinions; and,

as it is chiefly through opinion that facts act, it must be dealt
with as it comes; just like any other fact or no-fact upon the
opinions concerning which men may act. That he was what
he was supposed to be is very likely. The little we know
favours the view. The Mullah was a quiet man till Kazi came,
and Kazi came from Bokhara, which is more Persian than
Turk; Turk in its dynasty, but Persian in language, intellect,
and the nationality of the people in general. The Hadji was
found on Persian ground, and he talked like a Persian about
mulberry-trees. As for the apologue, it is one of a numerous
family.

It is not the parts on the immediate frontier of Lesgistan that
best illustrate the peculiar character of the Lesgians. There is
heroic courage and strong patriotism throughout the whole
range of the mountains; but in Lesgistan there is a religious
element as well, and that of a kind which has but little affinity
with the creed of either the Turk or the Tatar. We best
understand this when we consider that Lesgistan, or Dagistan,
is on the Persian frontier; for the province of Shirvan on the
south is Persian. Then runs the line of the Persian language
as opposed to those of Georgia and Armenia along the southern
coast of the Caspian, as far as the Turcoman country on the
east. Here it was that in the time of the Crusades lay the
original occupancies along with the chief forts and fastnesses of
a sect upon which we have already written—that of the Ismaeli
or Assassins. We know the most about the working of their
terrible faith in Syria; but we also know that in the north of
Syria was its metropolis. As the creed still holds its ground
in Persia, and even in India, I submit that it was the basis of
the philosophy or theology of Hadji Ismael of Kundomir.

We have seen that, either rightly or wrongly, Hadji Ismael
was considered to be a Persian spy.

We may now add that, at least as early as 1785, the creed of
which Ismael is now the expositor was either introduced into
this part of Caucasus or revived—probably the latter.

The great propagator of the Muridism of 1785 appeared at
first as Dervish Mohammed, but continued his mission as
Sheikh Mansúr. A war between Turkey and Persia was going

on when he first showed himself, and, like Hadji Ismael, he was considered to be a spy—a Turkish one.

In each case there is a war, a suspected spy, and a reasonable suspicion.

One of the Kazi Mullah's youthful disciples was named Shamil. He is described as moody, wayward, impulsive, and pre-eminently open to religious impressions. Whether this temperament was the cause or the effect of his attachment to Kazi Mullah is unknown. However, " *Muridism* " was the creed of which both were the apostles.

The general character of Muridism is Persian. It is not a sect. It is rather a political organization with a religious stimulus as the moving power. It is, so to say, a revival; but a revival of a catholic and unsectarian character. It is an ecclesiastical revival; a revival as opposed to a secular decay. It is a protest against the political Erastianism of the representative of the Kalif ; with a general appeal to the Mahometan world, and a special one to the nationality of the Caucasian mountaineers. But it begins in the most Persian part of Caucasus ; and that during a war between Persia and Russia.

Let the distinction between the Sunnites and the Shiites be merged into the great question of the independence of Mahometanism as a religion. The higher Powers, the Sultans and Shahs, have backslided. They treat the Christian potentates as friends, equals, nay, even as superiors. Let the faithful at large take back what the kings of the earth have surrendered ; and let the Church with its Mullahs represent the people. Above all, let the Murids obey their teachers and leaders to the strictest letter of the most perilous commands, even to certain and immediate death. With a clear comprehension of this element in their fanaticism we may see our way to some of the events in the career of Shamil, the Aristomenes of Dagistan, both in respect to his heroism and to the wonderful character of his escapes. His primary ones were three in number.

On the 18th of October, 1832, Himri was invested by an overwhelming army of Russians. Shamil, then a Murid under Kazi Mullah, helped to defend it. Almost every man was left dead, Kazi Mullah being one of them. Shamil, like the rest, fought heroically; and for two years was never heard of At the end of that time he showed himself, and, by simply doing so, congregated a body of enthusiasts around him. All, however, that the most knowing among them knew was that, at the taking of Gumri, he received three wounds. Where had he been in the interval ? Some say in Russia ; where he had accepted service, taken offence, and become a patriot after being a renegade. Some say in a cave. Some say among the dead, being actually killed, but raised to life in order to be the saviour of his country. One of these stories is about as likely as the other ; or rather, the first has been disproved, the second is unlikely, the last impossible. Shamil himself encouraged the mystery. As facts, these are nothing. As measures of what was believed to be believed they are not without their value.

In 1834, the attack of Gamsag Beg on the Khan of Avaria was avenged. The massacre, of which Khunsag was the locality, was general. Two only escaped it. Of these Shamil was one.

Up to this time he was a simple Murid. When Gamsag Beg died there was disorder, anarchy, and despair, among the Lesgians. No one was the universally-acknowledged captain. Tashav Hadji was the nearest approach to one. In 1837, however, Tashav Hadji recognized the ascendency of Shamil, and withdrew in his favour.

Ten years afterwards there was the storming of a fort—Akulko —in the Tshetsh country. It was an action in which the desperate courage of the Tshetshents (whose fame for the defence of Caucasus has been unduly eclipsed by that of the Lesgians and Circassians) showed itself in both sexes. The women stood on a ledge of rock to roll down stones on the assailants, until they were, themselves, cast down from the height—themselves and the children. There was one pinnacle higher than the rest. Upon this the last remnant of the defenders had taken refuge. It was believed by the Russians that Shamil was among them. They had only to keep guard, and either starve or take him. At the dead of night a Lesgian let himself down by a rope – cunningly and stealthily, but only to be taken by the guard. Another followed : and he was taken also. The third, knowing the fate of the others, descended. He wore the dress by which Shamil was known to the Russians, and was (as he meant to be) captured. A few days afterwards, Shamil had a band of Murids about him in another part of the country.

It was no part of his policy to let his countrymen know how he escaped. He cultivated mystery. We do not know the dates, places, and occasions of his speeches; but the following is a sample of what is believed to have been his oratory :—

"Do not believe that God favours the greatest number! God is on the side of good men, and these are always less numerous than the godless. Look around you, and you will everywhere find a confirmation of what I say. Are there not fewer roses than weeds? Is there not more dirt than pearls, more vermin than useful animals? Is not gold rarer than the ignoble metals? And are we not much nobler than gold and roses, than pearls and horses, and every useful animal put together? All the treasures of the world are transitory, while eternal life is promised us.

"But if there are more weeds than roses, shall we then, instead of rooting out the former, wait till they have quite overgrown and choked the noble flowers? and if our enemies are more numerous than we, is it wise for us to suffer ourselves to be caught in their nets?

"Do not say our enemies have taken Tcherkay, besieged Achulko, and conquered all Avaria! If the lightning strike a tree, do all the other trees bow their heads before it? do they fall down through fear of being also struck? O ye of little faith, follow the example given you by the trees of the forest, which would put you to shame if they had tongues and could speak. And if a fruit is devoured by worms, do the other fruits also rot through fear of being attacked in the same way?

"Do not alarm yourselves because the infidels increase so quickly, and continually send fresh warriors to the battle-field, in the place of those whom we have destroyed, for I tell you, that a thousand poisonous fungi spring out of the earth before a single good tree reaches maturity. I am the root of the tree of liberty : my Murids are the trunk, and you are the branches. But do you believe that the rottenness of one branch must entail the destruction of the entire tree? God will lop off the rotten branches, and cast them into the eternal fire. Return, therefore, penitently, and enrol yourselves among the number of those who fight for our faith, and you will gain my favour, and I will be your protector.

"But if you persist in giving more belief to the seductive speeches of the Christian dogs than to my exhortations, then I will carry out what Kazi Mullah formerly threatened you with. My bands will burst upon your souls like a thunder cloud, and obtain by force what you refuse to friendly persuasion. I will wade in blood. Desolation and terror shall follow me ; for what the power of eloquence cannot obtain, must be required by the edge of the sword."

If Muridism began in Mahometan rationalism, it ended in Mahometan Puritanism ; and, at the present time, even when Shamil is living easily at St. Petersburg, and when Daghestan is, with the exception of a few outbreaks, a Russian province, the Mahometanism that prevails has an ascetic, rather than a transcendental, character. Both, however, were potent *stimuli;* and under Shamil they had their full sway. The whole of Lesgistan was divided into departments—Naibdoms. When the spirit flagged, Shamil (according to Russian accounts) burnt the villages that the Russians spared, and the Russians spared but little.

After a long contest numbers and organization prevailed. The last stronghold of the Lesgians was Ghunib.

In general aspect, Ghunib does not materially differ from many mountains in its neighbourhood. Some of these are even more escarped, but they want other advantages which Ghunib possesses. It is an isolated oval rock of lime-stone, rising in precipitous and almost inaccessible terraces, between three and four thousand feet from the valleys surrounding it. At one end—I will call it the north, for though, perhaps, it is not strictly so, it will make my description more simple—at the north end, then, the inclination is more gradual, and the Russians have here completed an excellent road as far as a plateau eleven hundred feet above the Kari-Koi-Soo, which runs at its foot, and are preparing to erect upon this a fortress, with hospital, store-houses, &c., and a house for General Lazaroff, the Commander-in-Chief of Daghestan. Above this, again, is a steep range of rocks, and, through a long gully in the middle of these, a zig-zag road leads to the top of the mountain. The extreme length of it is stated to be six versts, the extreme breadth four; but it has not been measured, and I believe it to be one-third more. The Tartar aoul, not far from the north end, has been ascertained to be 4920 feet above the sea; thence there is a continual rise to the south end, which is 7742 feet. The top of the mountain is not a plain surface, as I should have imagined from below, but very much hollowed out, in shape like a shell, the aoul lying in the bottom, and is diversified with rocks and valleys. What constitutes the prime excellence of Ghunib as a natural fortress is, that it is not only so escarped as to be, except at the north end, practically inaccessible, if held by even a moderate force; but that it con-tains abundantly within itself, everything necessary for the provision of its garrison for an indefinite time. The soil is fertile, and produces, where it is cultivated, fine crops of corn; the rest is covered with long thick grass, upon which the Russian captors found three hundred horses and six thousand sheep at pasture. It is watered by two streams which, rising in the high ground, join near the aoul; they find an exit to the west, where they pour over the rocks down to the valley below, and nourish the fruit-trees and gardens of Hindak. One little rivulet runs into the gully at the north end, and forms a singular waterfall: it comes to the abrupt edge of a cleft in the rock with sufficient force to clear it in a bound, and falls from the opposite side of the cleft to a great depth in a shower of spray, a veritable Staubbach.

On the mountain itself are a very few trees, only one small clump of birches; but fuel abounds in the neighbourhood. Coal, of a fine quality, is plentiful; but, unfortunately, it lies between strata of such hard rock, as not to pay for the working. On the other hand, large fields exist of an inferior kind, mixed with earth, which require little labour to utilize, and which afford the fuel that is generally burned. Capital turf, too, abounds in the district.

No natives are now allowed to live upon the mountain, and the aoul is already falling into decay. The house which Schamyl occupied is the only one kept in repair, and is used as a hospital. It was clean and in good order. One room

was filled by Tatar invalids from the neighbourhood, who, even in bed, wore
their shaggy caps upon their shaven heads. The kindness shown to them is
only one instance of the conciliating treatment which I everywhere observed
to be pursued by the Russians towards the inhabitants of the country.

Such was the last stronghold of the Eastern Caucasus.
There were but four hundred men and two cannons to defend it.
But the place, as has been seen, was a natural fortification ; and
it had been improved by art. Three walls had been drawn
across the gully at the north end. This was considered the only
passage by which an entrance could be made. The ground about
was rocky, so that the progress of the Russians in the way of
regular approaches was slow.

These were abandoned for a general attack. There were twelve
thousand Russians against the four hundred Lesgians. But, at
the head of the Lesgians, was Shamil. There were some among
his soldiers who had devoted themselves to death in battle.
There were some renegades from the Russian armies who had no
hopes but in victory. There was not a man whose heart mis-
gave him. There was not a woman who was not prepared to
fight and die by his side—as many of them actually did.

The place was stormed : and on the surrender of Shamil the
war in Eastern Caucasus ended. " On the walls of one of the
reception rooms, in the palace of the Viceroy at Tiflis, beside
glittering trophies of arms, is hung up the plain leathern saddle,
in which he rode to a conquest of which he might well be proud,
for it terminated a long, weary contest, in which Russia had not
always the advantage. In a large plaster map, in the same
room, where the whole chain of the Caucasus is shown in relief,
a gilded spot marks the summit of Ghunib."*

Such is the hero of Lesgistan. As a nation the *Circassians*
have been the more formidable enemy to Russia, and an older
one : and, what is more, they have also been to some extent
either her subject or her vassals. On some Circassian districts
the Czar has something like a legitimate claim ; over others a
plausible one ; but for the rest nothing beyond a violent and
forced interpretation of certain treaties with Turkey, and thus
it is beyond doubt that, so far as the Sultan has conceded any
part of Circassia or Apkhazia to Russia, he has given what was
not his to give.

* Marshall ; Vacation Tourists and Notes of Travel for 1862.

CHAPTER XVI.

Rise and progres of the Russian Empire.—Early piracy.—Probable Russians.
—The name Rôs.—The early historical period.—Conquests of Vladimir
the Great, and his successors, in the direction of the Baltic.—Conquests
of Ivan IV. the Terrible.—Peter the Great.—The Czarinas Anne and
Catherine.—Conquest of the Crimea.—Incorporation of Lithuania.—
Conquest of Finland.—The Treaty of Vienna.

THE germ of the great Russian empire in the fifth and sixth
centuries seems to have been the present Russian governments
of Kiev, Podolia (in part), Pultava, Kharkov, and parts of
Tshernigov, Ekaterinoslav, and Kherson; all on ground now
Little Russian.   Add to these, on the east, the Ruthenian or
Rusniak part of Gallicia, or the district of which Leopol (Lemberg) as opposed to Cracow, is the capital town.   In the older
maps it presents itself as *Lodomiria, i.e. Vladimiria,* from
Vladimir the Great, who conquered it; but I think it was
Russian as it is now, in language, before his time.   This belongs
to the division called *Red* Russia; and to it we may, probably,
add part of Volhynia.   But beyond this, the original Fin or
Ugrian area may have extended on the north, and the Lithuanian on the north-west.   East of this there were probably
Turks in Ekaterinoslav and Kherson, and Poles in the parts
about Cracow.   On the south were the mountainous frontiers,
formed by the natural boundary of the Carpathians; of Hungary westwards, and of Moldavia eastwards.   Beyond this a
is the result of conquest.

How early this began is uncertain ; nor is it certain as to the
time when we first meet with the Russians.   This is because it
is not necessary that their first inroads upon non-Russian districts were made under that name.   For instance, the following
notice suggests a Russian invasion ; but without giving us the
name " *Russ*,"—not, at least, in the first instance.

As early as the sixth century, in the reign of Tiberius, we
have seen how the whole of Macedonia and Greece was Slavonized : and until the latter part of the eighth century we
have no name for the populations which effected the change
less general than " *Slaveni.*"   However, before A.D. 800 we
get more than one for certain special members of the Slavonic
denomination.   Nevertheless, it must not be concealed that the
evidence of this is other than cotemporary.   With this premise,
we may state that in a Greek legend which Zeuss ascribes to
the eighth (or at the latest to the ninth) century concerning
Bishop John, who lived in the latter part of the preceding one,
appear two remarkable names—those of the *Dragovitæ* and the
Sagudatæ as Slavonians in Macedonia.   The farther we follow
these, though the evidence is later, the more we become justified in making them—not decided and undoubted Russians (for
they may have been more or less, Lithuanic or Fin), but—invaders from territory that is afterwards Russian ; and that from
parts as far from Macedonia as Minsk, Grodno, Smolensk, and
Polotsk, on the west, and the country about Moscow on the
east.   They descend upon the Greeks of Macedonia in boats
made out of a single tree (*monoxyla*), which implies the navigation of a river ; *i.e.*, the Dnieper more especially, and, to a
less extent, the Don.   The *Dragovitæ*, who as *Dregoviczi* are
noticed by Nestor in their own proper district, are assigned to
the middle and upper parts of the Dnieper; indeed, so far
north as Polotsk.   The *Sagudatæ* (in the later writers *Sugodatæ*)
are the people of *Sougdaia*.   Zeuss suggests that this should be
Sugdalia; but whether it is or is not, he identifies it as a name
with *Suzdalia*, the district around Moscow.   In later allusions
to the same invasion we find the additional name *Galazi*, and
Smoleni= Galacz and *Smolensko*—also *Krivanitæ*, or *Krivonians*,
a population assigned by Nestor to the parts about Smolensko

—probably Fins. Finally, in Constantine Porphyrogeneta, within a century after the first notice, they are called "*confederates of the Russ*"—ὑπο πακτου τῶν Ῥῶς.

This appearance of the word "*Rhōs*," or "*Russ*," as an indeclinable noun, though not quite the earliest that presents itself, is nearly so. There is one instance, at least, earlier by about half a century, and there is, earlier still, the adjective ῥυσιος. The name is, from any point of view, an important one; but up to the middle of the tenth century it is, also, an ambiguous one. And it is this to an important extent in the history of opinion. It is probable that a majority of nine out of ten takes this term in, what, at first sight, looks like a *non-natural* sense; for the current doctrine is to the effect that all the early history of Russia, even to the very foundation of the empire, is to be assigned to the *Swedes*, and not to the *Russians*; in other words, that up to a certain time, Ῥῶς is to be translated "*Swede*."

Strange as this paradox may appear, there is no doubt as to its existence. It is naturally the dominant belief in Scandinavia; but it is also the dominant one in Russia itself. Still, there is a minority against it, and to this the present writer belongs. The whole question is a complicated one; but the view which, in my mind, best helps us to account for the confusion is, when put in its most general form, the following :— viz., that the Byzantine writers of the time, who knew the Slavonians well, knew them only by that name, and did *not* know that the men who called themselves, and were called by others, Ῥῶς were, with a difference which is now put at its proper value but which was then greatly exaggerated, Slavonic also. I do not say that this view will explain everything. I only submit that it indicates the right line of our criticism. That there was a great intermixture of Swedes and Russians along the whole line from Kiev to Novogorod, as well as in each of those towns is certain.

That there are hard facts to be got rid of, I by no means deny; especially that in connection with *the cataracts of the Dnieper*. These, at the end of the tenth century have *two* names, one *Slavonic* (Σκλαβινιστὶ), another *Russian* (Ῥωσιστὶ),

and of these the most undoubted is that of the *fifth* of the falls
and rapids—βουλνηπράχ in *Slavonic;* βαρυφόρος in *Russian*
('Ρῶσιστὶ). Now, the first, in the Slavonic forms of speech
in general, is *Volny prag=wave-stream;* the second, word for
word, the Norse *Vorenförs.** Beyond all doubt the so-called
Russian name is not only a Swedish one, but that of the greatest
and the best known water-fall in Norway at the present
moment. I have laid this instance before the reader, because
I consider it the hardest one to account for. Still, I think,
that the hypothesis just suggested covers it.

If this can be explained, all the rest are comparatively easy;
for it has already been stated that the mixture of the two
denominations is real; and the later the date the greater.is the
evidence of its reality.

The measure of the extent to which Russia had made her way
northwards is to be found in the later dates of her connection
with Sweden. In the reign of Vladimir, according to Geijer,
about A.D. 980, that great king took certain Varangians into
his service; apparently with the consent of Eric the Conqueror,
who was then King of Sweden. Vladimir, when they had done
what he wanted, instead of sending them home, passed them on
to Constantinople, with a request to the Emperor not to allow
them to return. With this, probably, began the employment
in Contstantinople of the Varangians as an Imperial body-
guard. We know of no earlier definite instance of the north-
men thus treated; but it is probable that the so-called Ρῶς, who
under Theophilus, more than a hundred years before, were got
rid of by being sent over to Louis I., the Emperor of Germany
were unwelcome guests of the same kind. But be this as it
may, the result of the grant of the Varangians was a marriage
between Jaroslaf, the son of Vladimir, and a daughter (Geijer does
not give her name) of the Swedish king. There was, certainly,
a political element in this; inasmuch as the Swedish princess—
name unknown—was originally meant to be bride of Olaf of
Norway, who married her sister instead; though not with the
goodwill of her father. Then, some years afterwards, A.D.
1101, when Inge, King of Sweden, concludes a war with Magnus

---

* The Russo-Greek Β is pronounced as V.

Barefoot, King of Norway, Eric Eiegod of Denmark being a party to the treaty, one of Inge's daughters marries Magnus, and another a *Russian* Archduke. Then, when the lines of Stenkil and Swerker become extinct, we have at the head of the dynasty of the Folkungers, as names of the first two kings of Sweden, Waldemar (Vladimir) and Ladulas (Ladislas), both Slavonic—the first Russian, the second Polish.

At the end of the period, or in the time of the Folkungers, "*the King of Sweden*" meant what it does now, *i.e.*, a king of both Sweden and Gothland. In the time of Vladimir it meant a king of *Sweden*—and *not* one of Gothland, which was, then, a pagan and semi-independent country. Russia, however, as a conquering nation, was from the time of Vladimir a Christian nation as well. But it may be objected to this that, instead of the Russians pressing northwards, the Swedes may have pressed southwards, and that the contact between the two is thus to be explained. I find, however, no evidence of it beyond the confusion already noticed. About 1250 the Swedish are defeated by Alexander Nevski, on Russian territory; but, this is in Finland, *i.e.* north of the gulf so called.

    *   *   *   *   *

Later than the time when Ῥῶς is supposed to mean "*Swede*" or "*Swedish*," and when it begins to bear its present sense (about the middle of the tenth century), we get well-recognized historical notices of an attack of Constantinople under *Igor*; which is, possibly, a Swedish name. Another under *Sviatislaf*, who, as we have already seen, was killed under the orders of the Petshineg king *Kour*, is, undoubtedly, Russian. His grandson is Vladimir I., the Great, a Christianized, semi-civilized, and undeniable Russian. This is towards the end of the tenth century.

Vladimir was both a great conqueror and a politic contriver of alliances; the measure of his success in this respect being his own marriage with a daughter of the Emperor's. We now hear but little of Novogorod; for Kiev now is, exclusively, the representative town of Russia—*Little* Russia, as opposed to *Great* Russia, or Moscovy. This last has yet to be called into existence. *Red* Russia, too, is part of the Russia of Vladimir.

This means the eastern part of Gallicia, or the parts about Lemberg (Leopol), rather than the parts about Cracov. These last are Polish; but, of the eastern division which belonged to Vladimir the language is even now Russian. It is not the policy of Austria to draw attention to this district. The maps, however, anterior to the partition of Poland, present us with its older name, *Lodomiria, i.e. Vladimiria.*

Lodomiria represents *Red*, Kiev, *Little* Russia; and in these two divisions we have the Russia of Vladimir.

Black Russia (Minsk and Grodno), and *White* Russia (Mohilev and Smolensko), lie northwards.

As a conqueror, Vladimir did the most in the direction of Poland; and this was, probably, the one in which conquest was the most difficult. It is likely that the Poles encroached upon Russia, rather than that Russia encroached upon Poland. That Eastern Gallicia was and is Ruthenian or Rusniak, has already been stated; and, as it was subsequently reconquered by either the Princes of Gallicia or the Poles, it is not likely that the Russian, which is the present language of the district, is of recent origin. Indeed, besides Lodomiria, a part of Volhynia, and the district of Chelm (a part of the Kingdom of Poland) is still in the same category, *i.e.* still Rusniak, Ruthenian, or Red Russian. Northward, or in the direction of Novogorod, Vladimir, at the very least, kept the way to the Baltic open; and from some Fin populations, if not from the Lithuanians as well, he is said to have taken tribute. On the west he chastized the Tatars, and in Hungary and Rumania the Petshinegs. As against those, and still more as against the Bulgarians, he fought as the ally of the Emperor rather than as ruler of the Russians. Hence it was in the direction of Poland on the west, and of the Letts and Swedes in the direction of the Baltic, that Vladimir most especially influenced the future of Russia.

From a line drawn between Kiev and Novogorod, the subsequent expansion of the Russian empire lay *east*ward, *i.e.* the additions to it were made at the expense of the Fin populations of the present governments of Orel, Kaluga, Tula, Moscow, Vladimir, Tambov, Penza, Tver, and others, rather than in those of

Minsk or Grodno (*Black* Russia), or Mohilev, and Smolensko (*White* Russia), wherein the population was either wholly or largely Lithuanian. These, of course, came to be Russian in time ; but, in the beginning, it was almost exclusively at the expense of the Fins, or Ugrians, that the whole of *Great* or Moscovite Russia was established.

The governments of Moscow, Vladimir, Nishni-Novogorod, Jaroslaf, and Kostroma were Fin.

In Kazan, Penza, Simbirsk, Savatov, and Astrakhan, Tatary or the Turk districts, began ; and of these it is not easy to say what parts were or were not Russian before the thirteenth century. By 1250, however, the great Mongol inroads had reduced Russia to the state of a vassal and tributary dukedom ; so that for more than three centuries, except in the remote districts of the governments of Archangel and Vologda, there was little opportunity for territorial development.

Then came the reign of Ivan IV., and the two great and complete conquests of the Khanates of Kazan and Astrakhan. along with a part of Siberia; also of the Don Kosak district in the fourth Khanate, or that of the Crimea.

Unlike Kazan and Astrakhan, the country of the Crimean Tatars, was a Mongol province, with an Ottoman suzerain. But the conquest of it under Mahomet II. was an exceptional one. It was not conducted by the Sultan in person, but by his Vizier Ahmed Keduk. It was more against the Genoese of Kaffa than against the peninsula as a whole; for the elements of the peninsula were inordinately heterogeneous—Genoese, Germans in the remains of the old Goths (Gothi Tetraxitæ), Karaite Jews (whose history seems to be connected with that of the Khazars), Khazars proper, Petshinegs, and Khersonites, or Greeks of the old Imperial town of Kherson, who may have represented the descendants of the Hellenic subjects of the Kings of Bosphorus; with differences in the way of pure, and cross-divisions in the way of mixed, blood to any extent. But, from first to last, it was, politically and dynastically, a part of the great Mongol Empire. Yet its geographical conformation and its very civilization isolated it. It was never, from first to last, purely

Imperial. It was never, till the time of Catherine the Great of Russia, either purely Russian or purely Ottoman. It never professed perfect independence; and when, a little before its final annexation to Russia, it was made over to the Czarina as its suzerain, the condition was that its Khans should be chosen from the family of Tshingiz-Khan, or Temudjin. It was during a disputed succession between one of these Temudjinian Khans that Mahomet II. was called in. This victory was an easy one; but it was only over the Genoese town of Kaffa. On the one side it shows that the navy of the Ottomans was superior to that of the Genoese; on the other it gives us the measure of either the weakness or the supineness of the Mongols. The most important fact connected with it is this, that from the time of Mahomet II. to the time of Catherine the Great, it suited the Turks of the Crimean Khanate to act just as they chose against the Russians as an independent power; and then to claim the protection of their Ottoman suzerain whenever they were in danger of retribution. It was so in the sixteenth century, and so in the eighteenth—so throughout. Of all the Ottoman conquests, that of the Crimea is the one that has done the most to disintegrate the Ottoman Empire, and eventually has proved the pre-eminent *damnosa hereditas* of the Porte.

From this point of view we may give the *disjecta membra* of its subsequent history.

Thirty-one years after the death of Mahomet II., his grandson, Selim I., the rebellious son of Bajazet II., took refuge in the Crimea, of which the Khan was his father-in-law. With an army which was half Tatar, he crossed the Dnieper on the ice, and, within thirty miles of Constantinople, was met by the Aga of the Janissaries, who conducted him in triumph to the capital. Here he forced his father to abdicate in his favour. The Khans, as we learn from this, have intermarried with their conquerors within two generations from the conquest. Bajazet II., the father of Selim, had complained to the Tatar Khan of the arrogance of the Russian Ambassador. Such is the continuity of the relations between the suzerain and the vassal.

Under the great Solyman I. the Tatars seem to have been

quiet; but under his son Selim II., we have the first notice of the first Ottoman *war* against Russia; and we have seen that it was probably a defensive one on the part of the Porte. And we have also seen that, *inter alia*, the Khan had sacked Moscow.

Under the second Selim's successor, Amurath III., there is a Persian war, or rather a continuation of another *damnosa hereditas*, viz. the conquests of Selim I. in Persia and Armenia. And now the Crimean Tatars assist the Ottomans; herein giving, if it were needful, an instance of the ease with which the so-called natural boundary of the Caucasus is over-stepped. They cross it at once; and, so doing, help the Ottomans efficiently. But before the end of the war they rebel; and the head of their Khan is sent to Constantinople as a trophy. In this campaign the so-called barrier was twice either traversed or turned. The Tatars who assisted the Porte made their way along the side of the Caspian. The Pasha who sent the head of the Khan as a trophy cut his way from Georgia to the Kuban through the most impracticable part of the mountains.

Again, in the reign of Achmet I., and in the very first year of the first Czar of the Romanoff family, the Kosaks crossed the Black Sea and sacked Sinope. A.D. 1613.

Twenty-eight years after, 1641, in the disgraceful reign of Ibrahim, the town of Azov is in the possession of the Kosaks of the Don. It had been so for four years; and the Kosaks of this *Don* were now the subjects of the Czar. The first expedition from Constantinople is repelled. By the second the Russians are driven out; but it is not before they have sacked and burnt the city that they are constrained to evacuate it. The Czar has simply to ignore them, or rather to persuade the Sultan that they are vagabond outlaws beyond his control, and that he cannot command, and will not attempt to coerce them. He is prepared to pay his usual tribute to the Sultan, and hopes that this is sufficient. This, though it satisfies the Sultan suzerain, by no means pleases the vassal Khan, who continues the war. In the campaign of 1646, the Tatars sell 3,000 Russian captives at Perecop, and send 400 prisoners and 800 heads to Constantinople. But the Sultan forbids the continuance of the war. Nevertheless, in 1648, the Tatars carry away of Russian and Polish slaves as many as 40,000. This latter number, we may reasonably hope, is exaggerated. But, be this as it may, the impotence of the Sultan to restrain his contumacious vassals is made manifest. Both sovereigns seem to be in honest earnest. But the Khan Islam Ghirai can afford to show his contempt of both, and that at the expense of Poland as well as of Russia.

It is in vain that the Sultan insists upon their emancipation. The Khan of the Crimea simply accuses Russia of connivance, and states that, unless checked, she will seize Bessarabia and Moldavia. This is his answer to an embassy from his suzerain. Upon this point he is probably in the right; for it is not the language of one Khan only, but of all with whom the several Sultans take counsel. Nor did the Russians put much trust in the commands of the suzerain to his vassal. No two contiguous powers better understood the impossibility of anything like friendly relations between them. It is now that the term Kosak becomes ambiguous. The word is a Turkish one; and so is *"Hetman,"* the title of their chief or captain.

By 1667, however, they are divided between Russia and Poland. The Zaporog Kosaks, or those beyond the Falls of the Dnieper, decline to be made over to the Poles; and in 1672 they appeal to the Porte. Then follows the war under the Vizierate of Ahmed Kiuprili, in the reign of Mahomet IV.; when Alexis, the father of Peter the Great, is the Czar, and Sobieski is the King of Poland. It is the first of a series for which the general character is that they are not so much the results of individual quarrels between Russia and the Tatars (in which the Porte was generally involved against its will), as wars between the two great imperial powers as principals. The time has gone by when the Crimean Khanate is the only focus of hostilities.

Poland, Sweden, and Austria are now elements in the development of the Russo-Turkish system of chronic hostility; and in the background lie the more distant states of western Europe, and the doctrine of the Balance of Power. This is well established by the time of Charles VI. in Austria, Louis XIV. in France, Charles XII. in Sweden, William III. in England, and Mustapha II. in Turkey.

In a short war under Solyman II., the Porte has the best of it, and it is to Achmet Ghirai, the Khan of the Crimea, that the success is mainly due.

Under Peter the Great, the pressing want on the part of Russia, was a port on the sea of Azov.   If the Tatar Khan gave a pretext, and provoked a quarrel, well and good.   If not, a *casus belli* must be either found or made.   The Swedish war interfered with this.   Nevertheless, there *was* a war, and the Czar *did* appropriate certain parts of the Crimean Khanate, and a valuable sea-board was acquired for Russia.   But by the Compact of the Pruth, A.D. 1711, all, or nearly all of these important acquisitions had to be restored, though it was not till 1714, and until the western powers had exerted pressure upon the Czar, that the full effects of the compact were recognized by Russia ; and then, even up to the very last, the voice of the Khan of the Crimea, Devlet Ghirai, was for a continuation of the war ; and had it not been for a rupture with Austria, such might have been the case.   As it was the Peace of Passarovitz, in 1718, in which the representatives of England and Holland, as mediatory states, took a part, effected, so far as Europe was concerned, something like an armistice.   Nevertheless, there was a hostile feeling on the part of England and Austria against Russia, and of this the Porte had the advantage.   By a treaty made in 1720, the Czar and the Sultan become the best of friends ; and by 1723 they have agreed to unite in the dismemberment and partition of Persia.   In this nefarious project originates a complicated series of disasters to the Porte. The compact enabled Russia, now acting with the Khan of the Crimea, to conduct an army through the whole range of the Eastern Caucasus, and finally led to the conquest of Georgia, and to plausible claims upon parts of Lesgistan and Circassia ; and we know, now, what has followed from this. It was under the influence of almost judicial blindness that, in this ill-omened campaign, Turkey should allow Russia to effect, as an ally, would she could scarcely have effected as an enemy.

The actual beginning of the end of the Crimean Khanate dates from the accession of the Czarina Anne. In her reign are the terrible campaigns of her Generals Lasky and Münnich; the former either wholly or mainly in the Crimea, the latter in both the Crimea and Bessarabia. This, too, is the date of the so-called Oriental Project, *i.e.* the restoration of the Roman Empire in a Greek capital, under a Moscovite ruler, Czar or Czarina as the case may be.

The Treaty of Belgrade, 1739, is followed by nearly thirty years of peace. Then comes the time not only of Catherine the Great in Russia, but of Frederic the Great in Prussia; and a higher, a subtler, and a more iniquitous policy is introduced into the history of more countries than one; a policy by which the gainers are Russia, Prussia, and Austria; the losers, Poland and the Porte. By 1771 the Crimea is declared independent of Turkey; by 1783 it is a part and parcel of the Russian empire.

Now come, almost concurrently with the conquest of the Crimea, the three instalments by which Lithuania became Russian. By the first partition of Poland, Russia took Polotsk and Vitepsk; by the second, Mohilev and Minsk; by the third, the remainder of Lithuania.

Six great additions of territory; three from the fragments of the great Mongol empire, and three from the dismemberment of Poland; the first, Turk; and the second, Lithuanian. These are the earliest notable additions to the vast domain now under notice.

The next is about half a century later, and in a different direction, and made at the expense of a different potentate.

In 1806 the Emperor Alexander, at war with France, had promised to do his utmost that the Prussian dominions should not lose even a single village. In 1807 he signed away one-half of Prussia in favour of Napoleon, and added a portion of the remainder to his own empire. All that had been done by Frederic the Great was undone, and Prussia was reduced to nearly the boundaries that existed before the First Partition of Poland; and the parts of that kingdom which had since become Prussian were made over to the King of Saxony. The city of

Dantzic was made independent. Such was the effect of the treaty, or rather treaties, of Tilsit, one of which, between France and Russia, was signed on the 7th, and another, between France and Prussia, on the 9th, of July 1807.

By this famous treaty it was agreed between Napoleon and Alexander that Russia should be free to conquer Finland, and that Denmark should be compelled to join in the confederacy against England. The articles which contained these conditions were secret, or meant to be so. A copy, however, or a trustworthy notice of their contents, found its way to the British Government. The power as well as the inclination of Denmark to uphold her neutrality was more than doubtful; and, with laudable decision, it was determined to demand that her fleet should be put into the hands of England. Less than this it would have been foolish to have asked. The demand, however, was one which no high-spirited nation could have complied with; and the bombardment of Copenhagen, under Lord Cathcart and Admiral Gambier, was the result.

It was to England that the Swedes looked for assistance; and, to some degree, that assistance was forthcoming. But the King, Gustavus Adolphus II., in every way unfit for the crisis, and a strange mixture of heroism and vacillation, made co-operation impossible. The expedition of Sir John Moore ended unsuccessfully. The ten thousand men under his command found that there were no adequate preparations for even the defence of Sweden, much less the invasion of Denmark and the relief of Finland. Upon the former plan there could scarcely have been a second opinion; upon the latter there were fair grounds for a difference. That Sir John Moore's instructions were to help in the defence of Sweden, and not to seek an enemy off Swedish ground, is probable; whilst it is transparently clear that from offensive operations against Denmark, which no one, perhaps, but the king himself had contemplated, he did wisely in abstaining. Whether Finland should have been left to its fate is another question. The English troops were wanted elsewhere, and the differences of opinion between Gustavus and Sir John Moore took an extreme form. The English general left in hasty and undignified manner; and the army was withdrawn for services in the Peninsula, which ended in the retreat from Corunna. Of the king's impracticability sufficient proof was given in the sequel. He brought his kingdom to the very verge of ruin and was forced to abdicate. The line of Vasa ended with his successor, and Bernadotte became King of Sweden under the name of Carl Johann.

Meanwhile the conquest of Finland was going on. That it was effected is not to be wondered at. The wonder is that it was effected in a single campaign. Charges were brought against the Russians for having tendered, and against the Swedish generals for having received, bribes: but charges of the kind were common on both sides of the Baltic. The special evidence that touches the question most nearly is the fact that, by the terms of the capitulation of Sweaborg, the Russians engaged to make good certain deficiencies in the military accounts. How far an arrangement of this extremely suspicious kind admits of a second interpretation is best known to military men. The imputation of having received bribes is indignantly repudiated by the Swedes, and that of having offered them by the Russians. *Valeant quantum.* The surrender of Sweaborg implies a deficiency of some kind. That, after the campaign, several Swedish officers entered into the service of Russia is another fact in the same direction—though one of less weight than the other. The officers were ordered to retire whenever the enemy was superior, and never to risk a doubtful battle. These were the orders of the king. They were not those that would have been issued by the great Gustavus, or by either of the Charleses. They were orders, however, that the circumstances appeared to have justified; and they were orders which were not always acted on.

The six strategic points in Finland are Sweaborg, Abo, and Vasa, on the sea; Tavastahus, Kuopio, and Uleaborg inland—the last in the extreme north, the former the most important The campaign began in January, 1808, and ended in the same year.

On the entering of Finland, the commander, Count Boux-hoevden, issued the following proclamation; artfully worded, and (it is believed) not wholly uneffective.

It is with the utmost concern his Imperial Majesty, my most gracious master, finds himself necessitated to order his troops under my command to enter your country, good friends and inhabitants of Swedish Finland. His Imperial Majesty feels the more concerned to be obliged to take this step, to which he is compelled by the transactions which have taken place in Sweden, as he still bears in mind the generous and friendly sentiments which the Fius displayed towards Russia in the last war, when the Swedish king engaged in an invasion of Finland, in a manner equally unexpected and unwarrantable. His present Swedish Majesty, far from joining his Imperial Majesty in his exertions to restore the tranquillity of Europe, which alone can be effected by the coalition, which so fortunately has been formed by the most powerful States, has, on the contrary, formed a closer alliance with the enemy of tranquillity and peace, whose oppressive system and unwarrantable conduct towards his Imperial Majesty, and his nearest ally, his Imperial Majesty cannot by any means look upon with indifference. It is on this ground, in addition to what his Majesty owes to the security of his own dominions, that he finds himself necessitated to take your country under his own protection, in order to reserve to himself due satisfaction, in case his Swedish Majesty should persist in his design not to accept the just conditions of peace which have been tendered to him by his French Majesty, through the mediation of his Imperial Russian Majesty, in order to restore the blessings of peace, which are at all times the principal object of his Imperial Majesty's attention. Good friends, and men of Finland, remain in quiet and fear nought; we do not come to you as enemies, but as friends and protectors, to render you more prosperous and happy, and to avert from you the calamities which, if war should become indispensable, must necessarily befall you. Do not allow yourselves to be seduced to take to arms or to treat in a hostile manner the troops who are committed to my orders; should any one offend against this admonition, he must impute to himself the consequences of his conduct; while, on the other hand, those who meet his Imperial Majesty's paternal care for the welfare of this country, may rest assured of his powerful favour and protection. And as it is his Imperial Majesty's will, that all affairs should pursue their usual course, and be managed according to your ancient laws and customs, which are to remain undisturbed as long as his troops remain in your country, all officers, both civil and military, are herewith directed to conform themselves thereto, provided that no bad use be made of this indulgence contrary to the good of the country. Prompt payment shall be made for all provisions and refreshments required for the troops; and in order that you may be still more convinced of his Majesty's paternal solicitude for your welfare he has ordered several magazines to be formed, in addition to those which are already established, out of which the most indigent inhabitants shall be supplied with necessaries in common with his Majesty's troops. Should circumstances arise to require an amicable discussion and deliberation, in that case you are directed to send your deputies, chosen in the usual manner, to Abo, in order to deliberate upon the subject, and adopt such measures as the welfare of the country shall require. It is his Imperial Majesty's pleasure, that from this moment Finland shall be considered and treated in the same manner as other conquered provinces of the Russian

25 *

empire, which now enjoy happiness and peace under the mild government of his Imperial Majesty, and remain in full possession of the freedom of religion and worship, as well as of all its ancient rights and privileges. The taxes payable to the crown remain in substance unaltered, and the pay of the public officers of every description continues likewise on its ancient footing.

One division crossed the Kymene, and entered the province of Tavastahus; the other invaded the Savolax. Both moved northwards, with a *minimum* resistance. Sweaborg, which was treated as an island rather than as a fortification of the main land, was left in the rear as the Russian army under Bouxhoevden moved northwards. Abo was abandoned without a blow, and within the first month of the campaign both Southern and Central Finland had been reduced. The Aland Isles, which were afterwards recaptured, submitted on the first summons.

The first serious engagement cost about one thousand on both sides, when the Russians were driven from the ground; but, as they regained it after the retreat of the Swedes, they call the victory a doubtful one. A Swedish orator compared it to Mantineia and Marengo. In this, notwithstanding the standing orders to proceed with caution, the Swedes acted on the offensive; and the improvement in the spirit of the army that was developed by the movement justified their boldness.

The greatest battle was that of Orovais. The Swedish generals, Adlerkreutz and Vegesack, had the advantage of the Russian general in position, and considered that their victory was easy. They swept down from their advantageous occupancy of some heights that overlooked his army, and, in a few minutes, routed more than seven thousand of the Russian Light Infantry. The Russians fled before them, and there was a body of Swedes in reserve. The only hopes of Kamensky were in four battalions which were pushing on from Vasa. They arrived in time; and a few words of encouragement did the work. The Swedes were defeated, and Orovais was taken. The battle had lasted fourteen hours; and both the Swedes and Russians had shot away their last cartridge. Night and the exhaustion of the Russians favoured the retreat of the Swedes. This was the great battle of the Campaign; and, as a measure of its comparatively small dimensions, the loss on both sides was about two thousand men. The military historian whom I follow—a Russian—calls it a complete massacre: but massacres of two thousand men which had to the subjugation of a country as large as France are small things in the way of great victories.

After this Kuopio and Uleaborg were taken, and Marshal Klingsporr concluded an armistice, and left the army for the capital. He was an old man and an ailing one; and he hoped, by representations made in person, to persuade the king that the recovery of Finland was impossible. Part, too, of his army had been driven back beyond the Arctic Circle, and he hoped for leave to be allowed to let it fall back upon Sweden. His command devolved upon General Klercker, and his reception in Sweden was favourable. Still, the king was immovable. He only sent fresh troops into Finland without a corresponding commissariat and with the knowledge that the country could not keep them. There was a short armistice; and then the capture of a few subordinate, though, apparently, strong positions by the Russians. The Russian general waived some advantages which, if it had not been for the armistice, he might have taken. For all practical purposes, however, Finland was lost.

The year was closing, and Napoleon was at Erfurth. The war was determined by England still to continue. The King of Sweden thought only of his next campaign. His revenue was wholly inadequate, and the English subsidy covered but one-third of the outlay. The English soldiers were wanted for Spain, and the Ministry had no confidence in Gustavus. Sir J. Moore had been sent to defend Sweden, not to protect Finland; still less to attack Denmark. Gustavus had insisted on the recall of the English Minister, and yet was asking for a fresh subsidy. He was on the point of laying an embargo on the numerous vessels then in the Swedish ports, and it was only the strong reclamations of his subjects that stopped his mad design. No other ally but England then remained. Nor would he condescend to constitutional measures. Nothing would induce him to call a States' General. His will and the patriotism of the Swedes were to be enough. Of the feelings of the Finlanders I have not the knowledge which enables me to speak. It seems to have been put to as low an item on either side. There was an extraordinary contribution and a fresh levy: and spring was waited for. The Russians were now in the far north, and nothing was expected from them except through their fleet. But the month of January was unusually cold, and the ice made it possible for the Russians to treat it as solid ground. Charles XII. had crossed the Belt, and the Russians determined on crossing the Gulf of Bothnia. An attack on the part of the Danes was also arranged : they also passing on the ice. But the ice of the Sound broke up. Knorring had orders to reconquer the Alands and he did it; *viâ* the ice. Barclay de Tolli, with about five thousand men, crossed from Vasa to Umea, where the Swedes had their depôts and reserves. The passage to the Alands was made in March. A long train of sledges with provisions, fuel, and brandy, started with the army. The islands between had been evacuated and devastated. The king, who had lived in Aland, and had believed that the Alanders, whom he had promised never to abandon, would stand by him as long as he stood by them, had directed that the island must be defended; and this order was one of the last of his reign. During the passage, which was effected with little difficulty, he was deposed: and his uncle, a man advanced in years, appointed Regent. The Russians then crossed from Aland to the continent.

Within a few days of the passage for Aland Barclay de Tolli crossed for Umea. On the fourth day he reached a lighthouse in the mid-channel. Ten days afterwards he attacked Umea. Meanwhile the Emperor Alexander was in Finland comporting himself with politic affability. The main points of the cession were settled. It was only on the Alands that there was a doubt. A little to prevent the settlement was done by the appearance of some Swedish and English vessels in the Gulf of Bothnia, and a little to promote it by the appearance of a Danish and Norwegian army on the frontier. The new king signalized the beginning of his reign by some notable activities : the fruit of which was an advantage gained over the Russians at Ratan. It failed, however, to lower the claims of the Czar. The Alands followed Finland, and Finland went to Alexander.

The campaign by which it was reduced was pre-eminently a bloodless one. Of the feeling manifested by the parties most concerned, the Finlanders themselves, I have no satisfactory evidence. The honesty of the Swedish commanders I am not prepared to defend. The surrender of Sweaborg was, to say the least, suspicious. The fact of all the extraordinary successes of the Russians having been effected against stone walls rather than facing bodies of men drawn up in battle array, is also suspicious. Measured by their successes and sieges, the career of the Russians is glorious. Measured by their successes in the open field, it is scarcely creditable. Creditable, however, to the hardihood of both nations is their tolerance of the rigors of a hard winter in a climate like that of Finland; and the bold passage of the Gulf of Bothnia over the ice surpasses that of Charles XII. over the Belt.

On the conduct of England the less said the better. The orders should have gone beyond the mere defence of the soil of Sweden; especially when it was known that the Danish attack had failed, and that the Russians could afford so small a portion of the forces as they actually employed in the invasion. The *real* cause of the quarrel was the compact between France and Russia; and if the English predilections of Sweden had not given a colourable occasion, some other pretext would have been found. Still, the *ostensible* cause of hostilities was the adherence of Sweden to the English alliance after the bombardment of Copenhagen, and the consequent dereliction of her duties as one of the conservators of the Baltic, in keeping up her friendly relations with us, after the practical demolition of the Danish fleet. Of the two acts (one of commission and the other of omission), the latter, in the mind of the present writer, is the one which lies the heaviest upon us.

I conclude with the following extract from the Russian Declaration of War, dated February 20, 1808:—

"But the question here was, the checking of those aggressions which England had commenced and by which all Europe was disturbed. The Emperor demanded from the King of Sweden a co-operation founded on treaties, but his Swedish Majesty answered, by proposing to delay the execution of the treaty to another period, and by troubling himself with opening the Dutch ports for England,—in a word, with rendering himself of service to that England, against which the measures of defence ought to have been taken. It would be difficult to find a more striking proof of partiality on the part of the King of Sweden towards Great Britain, than this which he has here given.

"His Imperial Majesty, therefore, cannot allow the relations of Sweden towards Russia to remain any longer in a state of uncertainty. He cannot give his consent to such a neutrality. His Swedish Majesty, therefore, being no longer doubtful, nothing remained for his Imperial Majesty but to resort to those means which Providence has placed in his hands, for no other purpose, except that of giving protection and safety to his dominions; and he has deemed it right to notify this intention to the King of Sweden, and to all Europe. Having thus acquitted himself of that duty which the safety of his dominions requires, his Imperial Majesty is ready to change the measures he is about to take to measures of precaution only, if the King of Sweden will, without delay, join Russia and Denmark in shutting up the Baltic against England until the conclusion of a maritime peace."

Valeat quantum. The real reason for the invasion of Finland was the proximity of the Swedish frontier to the Russian capital; and, according to the ordinary rules of political morality, it was a sufficient one.

Soon after the annexation circumstances changed. The good understanding between France and Russia came to an end; the overthrow of Napoleon followed; and, at the Congress of Vienna, Sweden had to be strengthened—though not at the expense of Russia. So, to make matters smooth, Denmark took Lauenburg and lost Norway; Sweden took Norway; and Finland remained with Russia.

*   *   *   *   *

The Treaty of Vienna gives us the next notable accesion to the domain of the Czar, viz., the kingdom of Poland—of Poland pure and simple; Poland without Gallicia, which, ethnologically, is half Russian; and Poland without Lithuania, which was only Polish as Ireland is English. These have been already assigned to Austria and Russia respectively, by the three partitions; while the kingdom of Poland, since the campaigns of Jena and Eylau, has been Saxon, *i.e.* handed over to Saxony by Napoleon, and, as such, made an integral portion of the vast system of kings, vassal kingdoms, and constrained alliances at the disposal of that great conqueror. This is as much as need be said at present; inasmuch as the subject of the following chapter is the order and character of those vast additions by which the Russia of Vladimir the Great attained its existing dimensions; how far the several conquests were honest or dishonest, being a reserved question; a question, moreover, involving another, viz., the extent to which the undeniable blameworthiness of some of them is to be attached to Russia as a simply insatiable conqueror, or more equitably (perhaps more charitably) divided between others; or, in some cases, attributable to circumstances or the chapter of accidents. The *modicum*, however, that can be written in this way, will not be written in the spirit of either a partisan or an apologist.

It must be clear that, by this time, there can be but little assurance against future augmentation for any of the minor Powers, such as they are, on Russia's immediate frontier. One by one they have either been annihilated, or crippled—the Kiptshak or Mongolian Turks of Asia, Sweden, Poland, the Porte, Caucasus and Transcausia, Turkestan, and even, to some degree, Chi . T..e intangible, immaterial, and uncertain Balance of Power is now the only check; and this is at the present time on its trial.

Since the Treaty of Vienna, the great landmarks have, in the main, stood as they were in 1816. But there have, nevertheless, been important extensions of frontier. The beginning of the end (if it be the end) of Russian aggression on the side of Rumania began before the Treaty of Kainairdji, and it has ended, perhaps, better than could be expected, in the annexation of only a part of Bessarabia. The indentations that have been made on the Chinese frontier, though considerable, are not, at present, invested with much interest; the footing that Russia got in North America was the fair reward of honourable exploration, and is now no longer Russian. But in Caucasus and Transcaucasia, in the mountain range itself, in Persia, Armenia, and elsewhere, in what used to be called Independent and Chinese Tartary, the incorporated additaments are of serious magnitude.

Those of Caucasus and Transcaucasia, undoubtedly, date from the suicidal allowance between the Porte and Russia, after the Treaty of Passarovitz. Between the two Powers that agreed to the dismemberment of Persia, differences arose before the first campaign was over, and the time came when the subsequent doubts as to the respective claims of the two invaders had to be settled; and then the position of Russia, as the adjudicator, was that of the lion in the fable. We know the result of it. It has carried the Russians over the whole of Caucasus itself, has given them great indentations on the

Persian frontier, has made them the actual possessors of all Georgia, a great part of Armenia, and in both countries has put them in the plausible position of the defenders of a Christian population against a Mahometan.

What is going on at present in Turkestan is a question for the able authorities in the Indian service; and one which the present writer only indicates. The little that his space and information allow him to write on Armenia will be found in the concluding chapter.

CHAPTER XVII.

The Decline of the Ottoman Empire.—After Mahomet II. too large for prac-
tical Administration.—Mahomet II.'s Conquest of the Crimea.—Selim I.'s
Conquests in Armenia, Persia, Syria, Egypt.—Soliman I., the Barbary
Regencies.—No permanent Impression made on Germany.—Injurious
Effects of the Ottoman Attacks upon Persia.—Natural Antagonism on the
part of Russia.—Peter the Great as an Enemy; and less formidable than
Anne and Catherine.—Value of Sweden as an Element in the Balance of
Power of Poland.—Decline of the Influence of both.—The subsequent
conditional integrity of the Ottoman Empire.—Retrospect.

UP to the time of Mahomet II. the Ottoman history is a series
of successful campaigns and decisive battles; and that, in certain particular instances, over really formidable enemies. It
was not, however, until the domain of the Western Church
was attacked, that there was any opposition which conquerors,
like the Seljukian Turks, could consider formidable; neither,
from first to last, except so far as Hungary involved Austria,
was there any prolonged contest on equal terms, with any of
the states of the German family, or, with the exception of
Venice, with any of the Latin.

Nor was the territory to which Mahomet II. succeeded of
any extraordinary magnitude. It was in proportion to the
dimensions and importance of the capital, but nothing more.

This implies that it is not until the time of Mahomet II.
that the Ottoman Empire shows any sign of being too vast, too
irregular in its outline, or too heterogeneous in its ethnology
to be fairly or even well administered. Neither was the conquest of it an over-hasty one. Between the accession of
Orchan in 1326 to that of Mahomet II. in 1451, more than a
century had intervened, and though five out of his six predecessors were active warriors, one, Mahomet I., was, for a
sultan, a man of peace. The others were certainly warlike; but
it is only in Bajazet I. that we see the arrogance of the conven-

tional tyrant of the East. But be this as it may, there are no symptoms, hitherto, of the Ottoman Empire being likely to sink under its own magnitude. Of making conquest for the mere pleasure of conquering, and of extending the empire for the mere sake of being proud of its magnitude, the six first Sultans may be acquitted.

It is not so easy to say this of Mahomet II. He would have been unwise in neglecting to make himself absolutely safe of a supremacy in the Black Sea and the Sea of Azov; but of all the relations of the Porte, those of the Khan of the Crimea have, without scarcely a redeeming character, being from first to last detrimental—we may almost say ruinous. The Khan, however, was a vassal rather than a subject, and the administration of his Khanate belonged to him rather than to the Sultan. The other conquests of Mahomet differed but little from those of his predecessors; being, in the reduction of the islands, a completion of the conquests of Albania and Greece, that of Trebizond a completion of that of Asia Minor.

The next great conqueror was Mahomet's grandson, Selim I.; and he added the two provinces of Syria and Egypt; the latter an outlying district in the way of geography, and, of all provinces, one that it was the most difficult to govern from a distance. Syria was less difficult of retention; but, both—and the difference is important—were not Turkish, but Arabian. Selim's conquests on the east, in Armenia and Persia, were those of a religious persecutor.

For the invasion of both Syria and Egypt he had ample provocation. It began in the time of his father, Bajazet II.; but Bajazet, like Mahomet I., was one who preferred peace to war. However, even in his we get the beginning of the Turkish navy; and, what is more, we get in the first hostile collision between the Ottomans and the hitherto unattacked kingdoms of Western Europe. This is the time of Ferdinand and Isabella in Spain, and the expulsion of the last remains of the Arabian Mahometans from that peninsula. Such help as Bajazet could give to his co-religionists of Grenada he gave, by sending a fleet under Kemal Reis, the first of a series of great admirals, to ravage the southern coast of Spain.

When Egypt becomes a Turkish province, it leads to the extension of Turkish influence, and something more than a nominal suzerainty over the Barbary States of Tunis, Tripoli, and Algiers. It suits the corsair captains of these states to sail under the Turkish flag; and it suits the Sultan to make admirable use of them. But in proportion as piracy in the Mediterranean is abated, the value of their help decreases, and their vassalage to the Turk becomes more and more nominal; or, *vice versâ*, the more the Ottoman power diminishes the more the piracy is abated. We can scarcely say when the Barbary provinces began to be Turkish; nor, with the exception of Algiers, which in our own time has been, in the French phrase, *relieved* from the tyranny of the Turks, when they will, to a certain extent, cease to be so.

In the reign, however, of Solyman I. they were important elements in the Ottoman power; especially after his conquest of Rhodes. But the great territorial addition made by Solyman was that of Hungary.

So far as an alliance with one of the kings of Western Europe abates the proverbially Asiatic character of the Ottoman Turks, and so far as it does this subtracts something from this barbarity, Solyman I. was a European; for it was the alliance with the Ottomans of Francis I. against the Emperor Charles V. that scandalized Europe in the reign of those two kings. But the fighting in the first instance was in Hungary, on the field of Mohacz, in which Louis, the last King of Hungary, was slain. The question of his successor led to a war with Austria; and of this the great event was the first siege of Vienna, A.D. 1529, three years after the death of Louis. This the Sultan was compelled to desist from; but farther than the walls of Vienna, and against Austria, and, *à fortiori*, against the rest of Germany, as opposed to Hungary, the Ottomans have never been successful.

Under Selim II. Cyprus is conquered, and after a war of twenty years, between the reigns of Ibrahim and Achmet, Candia; these two being the ultimate and penultimate European conquests of Turkey. The Morea in 1688 was lost to, and in 1715 recovered from, Venice. Two years after the reduction of Cyprus is fought the battle of Lepanto. It ought, perhaps, to have been followed by the expulsion of the Turks from Cyprus. It might, perhaps, have been followed by an immediate attack upon Constantinople. But it was the first defeat by sea that the Ottomans sustained. By land they have, as yet, been uniformily victorious; and, by land, they will yet be victorious again,—in Hungary, and in the battle of Cerestes, under Mahomet III., in 1596.

The hostility between the Porte and Austria has now become chronic; and the result of it is, in 1664 the signal defeat of St. Gothard. It was fought on the banks of the Raab, on Hungarian soil, but the battle was won by Germans under an Italian general, Montecuculi. Much is written about the uniform superiority of both the Turkish navy and the Turkish army, from the uniform character of their victories, both by sea and land, over all enemies, up to the time of the two great battles of Lepanto and St. Gothard; and such is the truth. But it is scarcely the whole truth. The truer way of putting the statement is to say, that so long as they had to fight against Asiatics, South Slavonians, Albanians, Arabs, and Greeks, the Ottomans won an uninterrupted series of victories; but that as soon as they came in contact with either Spain or Germany they were defeated. They are again defeated by Louis of Baden at Salankeman; and again at Zenta, in 1697, by Prince Eugene of Savoy. Two years afterwards, in the last year of the seventeenth century, follows the Treaty of Carlowitz. This gives us the date from which, to use a familiar expression, the importance of Turkey "*becomes diplomatic.*" She has still, however, sufficient strength to complete her last conquest, that of Candia; and still sufficient to cope with Venice single-handed. The great General Morosini, who had to cede Candia, re-establishes his high reputation by the conquest of the Morea; but this, between the Treaties of the Pruth and Passavoritz, the Ottomans re-conquer. Still, too, has the Porte strength enough to be a formidable enemy to Persia. This she was steadily and perseveringly, from the reign of Selim I. to that of Achmet III., whose suicidal alliance with Peter the Great, against her, has already been noticed.

Such is the sketch of the order and general character of the Ottoman conquests. Upon that of her institutions I abstain from enlarging. We know the general character of them ; and we know that they are bad. Two abatements in respect to them, and I know of no third, may be made. It was, perhaps, when the Porte was strong, well for states, which were bones of contention between two rival enemies, to be under a government which could keep them to herself ; and it was well, perhaps, when there were two forms of Christianity on the same area, to be under a rule that was contemptuously indifferent to both. But this is no apology for Turkey. It is rather an incrimination of others. It is, however, as much as can be said.

* * * * *

We now pass to the chief details of her gradual dismemberment ; and these are of two kinds, those due to

  1. National and religious revolts ; and

  2. Revolts of Pashas.

To the first belong—1, *Servia*; 2 and 3, *Greece*, and *Rumania*.

To the second—*Egypt*.

The Russian conquest of the Crimea has been already noticed ; and that of Algeria by the French can scarcely, from the looseness of its connection, be considered a dismemberment ; indeed, that of Egypt is only a partial one.

I. SERVIA.—For the movements which chiefly led to the independent position in which Servia now stands the year 1787 is a convenient date. Events like those which then took place had taken place before. There had been wars in which Austria had been successful ; wars in which the Servians had fought on the Austrian side ; wars which had made over to Austria parts of Bosnia and even of Servia itself. There were wars and there were treaties ; but of these treaties and these wars the main results were remarkable for their negative character. What Austria gained in one settlement she lost by another ; while the Servians, who knew what it was to be transferred from Turkish rule to Austrian, knew equally well the converse process which transferred them from Austrian to Turkish. They changed hands ; but at every change they anticipated a return to the

original *status*. The peace most favourable to Austria was that
of Passarovitz. But the treaty of Belgrade was in favour of
Turkey. It restored the important fortress of Belgrade itself.
Then came a peace of nearly thirty years. Then the war
which, ending with the Treaty of Kainardzhi, cost the Porte
Crim-Tatary.

In the war which commenced in 1787, and which was conducted against the united forces of Russia and Austria, the
troops of the last-named Power had not only entered Servia,
and made it, to a great extent, the seat of war, but had been
well received and actively assisted by the Servians. A body of
Servian volunteers had attached itself to the Austrians, and,
under more than one native officer, had rendered more than
ordinary service. No wonder, then, that when, by the Treaty
of Sistova, the fortresses in the occupation of Austria were
evacuated, the military bearing and acquired skill of the
hitherto despised rayas should have provoked wonder, not
unmixed with suspicious apprehensions, on the part of the
Ottomans ; their discipline being the more readily appreciated
inasmuch as it was the introduction of European tactics at
which the energetic Sultan, along with his best ministers and
officers, was more especially labouring. Here, then, they had
soldiers, after the fashion of Western Europe, ready formed.
That they were Christians was the bitter matter of regret.
" Neighbours ! what have you made our rayas ?" was the exclamation of a Turkish officer to an Austrian, when the latter
paraded, out of one of the restored fortresses, a body of Servians,
as well accoutred and as likely-looking soldiers as his own
Germans or Hungarians. Regiments of this kind are not
easily disbanded ; especially when the land they live in is poor
and rugged, and when the language has a mild name for *robber*.
Klephth, in Greece, is *heyduk* in Servia ; and of heyduks there
was an inordinate proportion after the Treaty of Sistova.

The reform of the Turkish army had a definite, though indirect, bearing upon the changes in the temper and discipline
of the Servians. The power of the janissaries had to be broken ;
but it was by no means easy to break it. Insubordinate in
most districts, these Prætorians were pre-eminently insub-

ordinate in Servia. The mode of recruiting them by means of the tribute of Christian children had long passed away. So had the necessity of their remaining unmarried. As soon as the service became remunerative, the men who derived advantage from it kept it for their own offspring, and became the fathers of the sons to whom it was transmitted. The tendency to remain in the districts in which they were garrisoned had set in. The habit, in time of peace, of pursuing some civil occupation or trade had grown up. The captaincies were becoming hereditary. In some cases the captains usurped titles beyond their rank. That under such conditions they should be insolent and oppressive to Christians and civilians is what we expect. In Servia they had encroached upon the rights and even the property of the spahis, or those soldiers whose service was rendered as a feudal obligation. The lands which the Servian spahis held on this tenure the janissaries threatened to take for themselves; and on one occasion as many as fifteen spahis were murdered by their co-religionists and fellow-soldiers. At the head of the janissaries of Belgrade was Deli Achmet. The Sultan and the Minister of War knew him only as their Aga. He designated himself as the Dey.

To coerce these unruly troops Abu Bekir was sent as Pasha to Belgrade with more than ordinary powers. His first act was the treacherous murder of Deli Achmet. The Pasha of Viddin, the formidable Paswan Oglu, was then in a state of inchoate, if not actual, rebellion; and with Paswan Oglu the soldiers of the murdered Aga found a ready welcome. His own troops were a heterogeneous mixture of heyduks and adventurers, Christian as well as Mahometan. Of these, Kridzhali as they were called, the rebel janissaries doubled the strength. At the head of these mixed companies Paswan Oglu invaded Servia, and took Tshernets, Kraiova, and Nicopolis, before his career was notably checked.

Of the government of the Pasha Abu Bekir the Servians had nothing to complain. That of his successor Hadzhi Mustafa was remembered with gratitude, as shown by his hypocoristic cognomen, *Srbska Maika=Servia's Mother*. Such services as the rayas were free to render, they rendered; and with their aid the career of Paswan and his myrmidons was checked. But

> Non tali auxilio nec defensoribus istis
> Est opus——

though not exactly the cry, was the sentiment in Constantinople. To reduce the Faithful by the help of the Infidel was an abomination in the eyes of the extreme, and even the moderate, Mahometans. " If such are the terms on which the janissaries are to be coerced, re-admit them." This was the gist of the new order of the Sultan.

It is in this revolution of Servia, and just at this time, that the difference between the two most important elements in the Ottoman army exhibits itself in its extreme form. The organization of the Janissaries and that of the Spahis was essentially different. The former were paid soldiers, the trained and converted descendants of Christians, upon whom was levied the tribute of a thousand children annually; who were converted into Mahometans, soldiers, and, to some extent, Ottomans. This institution was the older one. The Spahis were the holders of fiefs, of which each holder was bound to supply a certain contingent of fighting-men. The Janissaries had been partially got rid of; but now they are re-admitted.

Re-admitted, they took the power in their own hands. Four of their Agas they ennobled by the title of Dey, and allotted a district to each. The onslaught upon the rights of the spahis was continued. Ali Vidaitsh of Bosnia supported the aggressors. The humbler prayers of the rayas were now supported by the more influential remonstrances of the spahis; indeed, the lot of the spahis was a hard one. Whatever may have been their value on the field of battle in conjunction with the janissaries and against a common foe, they were wholly unequal to a struggle with the janissaries themselves. Neither did the Sultan sufficiently strengthen them. His threat, however, to the janissaries was one pregnant with consequences. " It is a grievous thing," he proclaimed, " for true believers to fight against each other.'

Soldiers of another nation and another creed shall oe sent against you." The threatened usurpers interpreted this to mean the Servians: and upon a massacre, sufficiently effective to make such assistance impossible, they at once decided. The onslaught took place in February, 1804.

The details of the beginning of a massacre, when the attack is made by the armed upon the unarmed, much as they may shock, do little in the way of instructing, us. They are numerous, and, all the world over, they are alike. Few difficulties have to be surmounted. Hence they are the measure of little except the cunning of the contrivers and the obduracy of the perpetrators. What really both affects and instructs us is the resistance.

Even in revolutions the most important characteristics are few in number, and, generally, of one kind. When fairly set a-going revolts present a remarkable sameness of aspect—the same courage, both active and passive, often rising into heroism, often sinking into brutal ferocity; the same horrible cruelties; too often the same contempt for the most solemn engagements; unity and unanimity when the pressure of the common enemy is heavy; discord and faction when that pressure is lightened; interminable jealousies and factions; exceptional treacheries; acts of sordid selfishness; foreign intervention; ingratitude and repudiation. That the spirit of liberty for which this, with the like, is the price, redeems the crimes and follies of individuals, is true; but in all this, except so far as they differ in degree, the best and the worst revolutions agree in the general character of their details. This is my excuse for not going into the minutiæ of the Servian struggle for independence. One revolution is already contained in this volume; and others will have to be noticed. But, like a war in an enemy's country which an unscrupulous commander makes self-sustained, a revolution, when once fairly afloat, propagates itself. The first step towards it is the important one. This separates it from the previous state of things. And the inaugurator is the hero. This is the man whose courage is of the rarest kind, and for the work to be done, the most valuable and indispensable. The man who—to use an expression, of which the origin is in our nursery fables and its application in the history of Scotland—first dares to *bell the cat* is the man whose name, when known, should never be left without its record and its honour. He is in political, what the leader of a forlorn hope is in military, history. He is rarely a blameless character; for the blameless character may turn the left cheek to the smiter of the right. He is not always wise in council ; not always absolutely unexceptionable in his motives, good, bad, or indifferent. However, he has the one quality of revolutionary daring which the hero of a hundred battles may admire.

For such a man Servia had not long to wait. Some twenty of his countrymen (we know the names of fourteen knezes and priests) may have been put to death before Kara George began the liberation of his country with a signal act of stern resolulution, but one which his subsequent life showed to be in strict harmony with his character.

Kara George, *Czerny* George, *Black* George—they all mean the same; the first name being Turkish, the second Servian. I have chosen the Turkish adjective, not because it is, theoretically, the best, but because it sounds best.

Kara George had served during the Austrian war against the Turks. When the war was over, he seems to be what in Cumberland would be called a statesman or yeoman farmer. But his herds consisted of hogs—the common cattle of Servia. He bred and dealt in them. It is mere disparagement to call him a swineherd or a hog-jobber. Yet we can hardly call him a farmer or a merchant. He was essentially a man of the middle class; and, even before his elevation, a man of influence in his district.

He had completed a bargain, and was driving his swine to the place of delivery, accompanied by his father, when he saw a gang of janissaries in pursuit of him. For the younger man an escape was doubtful; for the older impossible. For whichever was taken a cruel death was the only certainty. Kara George saw this at once, and shot his father on the spot. After this he completed his escape.

It was across the Save that he fled, and on the bank or in the stream of that river he left the dead body of his father. It is in the rugged district of Shumadia that he is next found.

Shumadia, in the north of Servia, may be called the cradle of the revolution. It lies as a broad watershed between the lower courses of the Drin and the Morava. On each side lie the valleys of those two streams and their feeders, each feeder with its valley. The largest of these is that of the Kolubara. In Upper Servia, the valleys are both narrower and more complex; the country more truly mountainous; the towns and villages smaller.

In Shumadia, the revolution was organized. There met the first triumvirate; Kara George, Yanko Katitsh, and Vasso Tsharopitsh. Katitsh had served against Paswan Oglu. The brother of Tsharopitsh had been one of the first victims of the massacre. They determined upon a general resistance. The apportionment of the country to the organizers of the different districts was an easy matter. So definite were the natural boundaries, that it may be said to have allotted itself. Nor were the men wanting to the place. For the districts beyond the Kolubara there were Yakob Nenadovitsh, a knez; Luka Lazarovitsh, a priest; and Kyurtshia, a heyduk: for the Upper Morava, Milenko, and Peter Theodorovitsh. These had the chief voice in the election of their leader, director, chief, general, or dictator. The first offer was made to Glavash, who had degenerated from a herdsman into a heyduk. His wife had lamented the falling-off. "We are all heyduks in times like these," was the husband's answer. In the council, however, he admitted that his profession was a drawback, and stated that a heyduk was not the proper leader of the Servians. Then the choice fell on a knez (local magistrate, esquire, country-gentleman), Theodore Oratshi. "The fit man," said Oratshi, "is Kara George;" and as Oratshi was known to mean what he said, the votes went to Kara George. For the third time unfitness was pleaded. "I am too hot in temper. If offended, I strike at once."

"This is what we want; a man with a will. We are an unruly set. The strongest hand is the best for us."

To this effect spoke the meeting and Kara George was named the leader. The character he gave himself was a true one: though only as far as it goes. That he was a kindly man when his angry fits were not upon him is just possible. The kindliness, however, with which he has been invested is of a doubtful kind. With the description that he gave of himself and with his father's blood (whatever may have been the necessity for shedding it) on his hands, a little tenderness goes a long way 'When a man seems very bad it is easy to say that the appearances are worse than the reality.

He was severe, to say the least. When his power and responsibilities were at their height, his brother scandalized the cause by an aggravated case of seduction—not, perhaps, the first that was charged against him. Him, Kara George ordered to be hung. The mother he forbade to wear mourning. That he enforced his order by clapping a live bee-hive over her head is only a floating report—perhaps a false one. True or false, however, it shows that Kara George had the credit of doing strange things.

The third of those sacrifices which Kara George had the evil hap to make of men who, under ordinary circumstances, would have been pre-eminently safe, was that of the knez to whom he owed his dictatorship. Before Kara George's dictatorship was over, orders had been given for Oratshi to be cut-down. "May God punish him who gave cause for this quarrel," was his reflection on it.

Still, of purely gratuitous cruelty, no charge lies against Kara George. Nor yet any of perfidy or dissimulation. Neither was he warped from the simplicity of his original habits by the possession of power. Perhaps, in the plenitude of his power he was too ostentatiously simple. His first title was that of Commander: afterwards that of Highest Ruler.

And now the war against the Deys became organized; and, as the beginning of the Servian struggle was one of those strange conflicts which take the form of a triangular duel, it will be given in detail. There were three belligerents; indeed, in some sense, there were three parties. Two were certainly principals; the janissaries and the rayas. The representatives of the central government and the spahis were prepared to put down the former without admitting the latter to the full dignity of allies; though as allies, in the first instance, they were ready and willing to use them. Even the alliances were ambiguous, equivocal, and two-sided; as we may see from the example of the first of them.

Gushanz Ali joined the contest with a considerable body of kridzhalis. He was not disinclined to the Servians, not hostile to the rayas. He was a Mahometan. However, he fought on the side of Mahometanism and the Turks in either case. But he was not met more than half way by the Servians—if so much. The fewer Turks they had among them the better; a principle which gives us a measure of their confidence in themselves.

Ali Vidaitsh, also, of Bosnia, intermeddled, or tried to do so; and it was during his interference that the first blood was shed.

Then, the Servians undertake three sieges at once; that of Passarovitz by Milenko, that of Schabacz by Nenadovitsh, and that of Belgrade by Kara George. The results are favourable; and the Janissaries, by a revolting mixture of perfidy and audacity are driven out of Servia. Still, are there intestine quarrels, and there are foul murders of Servian leaders among themselves. However, in the beginning of 1805, a legation returns from St. Petersburg, with promises that any reasonable application to the Porte shall have the support of Russia. The Servians demand, amongst other things, the withdrawal of all Turks from the garrisons; in which none but Servian soldiers are to be admitted. The deputies are arrested, and the Pasha of Nish is ordered to disarm the rayas. Then comes the great event of the campaign. An army under Hadji Bey, from the East, and another consisting of forty thousand men, under the Pasha of Scutari, are ordered to march upon the Servians and crush the rebellion at once. The actions now assume magnitude and their results become decisive. By an attack with a far inferior force, in which he was ably supported by Katitsh, Kara George, with desperate boldness and unsurpassed rapidity, fell upon the two divisions in detail and won the first of two great victories. The second follows soon after; and then the capture of Belgrade. By the campaign of 1806, the Turks were driven beyond the Drin.

The practical independence of the country is now, for a time, established. It has a constitution; with Kara George at the head of the executive. The Turks have full employment elsewhere. But in 1810 hostilities recommence, and the success is on the side of the Ottomans. Faction, too, sets in; and Dobrinjaz accuses Kara George of affecting a dictatorship. The treaty of Bucharest leaves the Servians with the following amount of encouragement, viz. (secured by the eighth article) an amnesty, the right of administering their own internal

government, and a moderate amount of impost, which was to
be paid directly to the Porte instead of being farmed to con-
tractors :—" though it was impossible to doubt that the Sublime
Porte would, according to its principles, act with gentleness
and magnanimity to the Servians as a people that had long been
under its dominion.   Still, it was deemed just, in consideration
of the part taken by the Servians in the war, to come to a
solemn agreement respecting their security."

But the continuation of the insurrection is less marked with
success than its beginning; for the mediation suggested by
Russia has no immediate effect, and the contest continues.

The campaign of 1813 was in favour of the Ottomans, the
last of the patriots who held out with any notable effect being
Veliko.   He was cut in two by a cannon-ball while giving orders
on the battlements of Negotin.   Like Kyurtshia, a heyduk, he
had served his country better than more respectable men.
Unlike Kyurtshia, he fell on the field of battle, and, unlike
Kyurtshia, at a time when he could ill be spared.   Never was
the prospect more discouraging.   Except in the eyes of Veliko
himself, it was hopeless.   The Shumadia alone was unreduced ;
and of the heroes of the Shumadia, the first organizers of the
revolt, two were dead and one was untrue.   As the danger
increased, the energy of Kara George had fallen-off.   He was
seen but rarely; in the council or on the battle-field, never.
He was more with the Russian Consul than with anyone else.
During the whole of his government he had neither affected
display, nor indulged in luxury.   But money he was believed
to have saved; and money he loved.   He had probably buried
what he had amassed.

On the 1st of October, however, he appeared in the camp on
the Morava.   On the 2nd, the Turks had crossed the river, and
were advancing with a force apparently overwhelming.   In
1806 Kara George took no pains to count his enemy, and it
was against greater odds than this that his first victory had
been won.   But now, as if panic-stricken, he took flight : not
with his army, for that he abandoned, but with his secretary
and three others, Ncoloba, Leonti, and Philippovitsh.

Such was the degeneration of the great liberator, and such the beginning of his end.

We must account for this mysterious conduct of the liberator as we can; and without further evidence, it is as uncharitable as it is repugnant to brand him as either a coward or traitor. He seems to have felt himself distrusted by his countrymen. He knew that the man who supplanted, superseded, and eventually got him shot, Milosch Obrenovitsh, the founder of the present dynasty, was his enemy. Before Kara George's appearance at the Council, he had been almost exclusively in contact with the chief officials of Russia, and it is probable that these men had persuaded him that Russia could do more for his country than he could by himself. Russia certainly did something, and eventually much. The Czar prevailed on the Sultan to recognize Milosch Obrenonovitsh as, under the Porte, their administrator and prince; to enlarge his powers, and make Servia itself, to a great extent, autonomous. What was done in this direction was confirmed by the Treaty of Bucharest, extended by that of Akkerman, and subsequently extended farther, until Servia became what it is now. The Servians have now got, by one means or another, what ought to content them; but the present generation is not a generation of men like Kara George and his rough but brave coadjutors; though much more pretentious.

*   *   *   *   *

II. RUMANIA.—The insurrectionary movement in the Danubian Principalities was later than that in Servia; neither was it wholly for Rumanian emancipation. It was rather the beginning of a Greek revolution, originating on Rumanian soil.

A.D. 1391. It was under Bayazet I. that Valachia was conquered by the Ottomans; and of the Ottoman Empire it has been the least disturbed portion. Occasionally invaded by Poland, often occupied by Russia, it has, nevertheless, changed masters, only for a time, and in part.

The first hospodars were the native princes; but when Prince Kantemir of Moldavia revolted to Russia, the principle of nomination was changed, and Greeks were appointed instead of

Rumanyos. The Phanariot period, so called from the Phanar, or Greek quarter of Constantinople, ended in 1826; and the system of natives holding office for seven years, and being re-eligible, lasted until a few years ago, when the two hospodariats were united, or rather united themselves.

It was in the Danubian Principalities that the Greek Revolution broke out. It was in Yassi, Galacz, and Bucharest, that the secret societies had their more important centres. And for this there was a reason. The Turkish war with Russia had grown out of a Valachian disturbance, the deposition of one of the hospodars; and in no country were the Russian pretensions to interference in the religious and national questions of the Christians under the Porte earlier displayed, more definitely put into action, or better (up to a certain point) understood—than in the Principalities. The extent to which Russia limited her benevolent interpositions to her furtherance of her own ulterior views, and the readiness with which, when unnecessary, the *protégée* was abandoned, had yet to be learned. Again, the Danubian Principalities were on the Russian frontier. They were the outworks of the Ottoman Empire; almost a Debateable Land.

With Greeks, too, they swarmed; for with Greece, the Phanariot hospodars had made the Rumanyos familiar. Subtract, however, the revolutionary elements administered by Greece and Russia, and little enough remains. The hospodars were Greeks, supported by regiments of Albanians and Bulgarians. The boyards, when rich, were ostentatious and self-seeking; affecting the habits of that part of the Russian nobility which most affected those of the French. When poor they were ignorant and narrow-minded. The people were, if not actual serfs, in a condition nearly approaching serfage. The whole trade was sacrificed to the monopolies by which the hospodars enriched themselves and the members of the monied interest with whom they came most immediately in contact. Of such intellectual activity as familiarity with manufacturing processes and the congregation of artizans and masters in large masses engenders, they had nothing.

On elements of this kind did the first promoters of the Greek

Revolution work; but instead of a Kara George, or a Milosch, they had the contemptible Alexander Hypsilantes, the son of the ex-hospodar.

He crossed the Pruth. Two namesakes, though of different families, Micael Soutzos in Moldavia and Alexander in Valachia, were the hospodars; both members of the secret society —the Philike Hetairia. One lesson that the Russians and Greeks succeeded in teaching the Valachians was to believe in neither Greece nor Russia. But before the blunders of Hypsilantes had brought matters to a crisis, the Emperor Alexander had, in giving them to understand that he was no friend to revolutionary movements, repudiated the use of his name. One man, and one man only, of native blood, did the Principalities supply to the cause—Theodore Vladimiresco; and him the Greeks brand as a traitor; though Finlay reasonably remarks that, had a Valachian written the history of the Revolution, and had it become a Rumanyo one, Vladimiresco might have been a hero.

Even as far as it went, the war was like the one in Servia, at its beginning, a triple duel. The Greeks had their own view; the Rumanyos theirs; the Turks one adverse to both. Vladimiresco's was the amelioration of the condition of his own country. No wonder that, between Turk force and Geeck fraud, he failed and fell. However, he, and he alone, represents his country.

He soon detected the utter incapability of Hypsilantes. So did Savas, a Greek. Both distrusted him. Each hated and distrusted one another. Yet they intrigued with Hypsilantes; whilst, at the same time, they intrigued with the Pashas. It was Little Valachia that Savas occupied. His intrigues being suspected, an order was issued by Hypsilantes for his arrest. A copy of one of his letters to the secretary of the Pasha of Guirgevo was shown by Hypsilantes to Georgaki, who undertook to arrest him. Hypsilantes, who was himself meditating the abandonment of his followers, reproached him with treachery. Vladimiresco replied that he had served his country better than his accusers, and that he was thrown upon his correspondence with the enemy by the necessity of counteracting the treachery of Savas. Hypsilantes pretended to pardon him, and two days afterwards pardoned the men who murdered him.

In Moldavia, after the Czar's repudiation of the Revolution became known, and after the battle of Skuleni, the Sultan's authority was soon re-established. In Valachia it was re-established after the brave but hopeless stand made by Georgaki and Pharmaki at Seko.

This rebellion in Rumania is but loosely and interruptedly with the present independence of the two Principalities. Nevertheless, it was the beginning of the movement towards it; and, what is much more important, it, when quashed in Rumania, extended itself to Greece; for between Greece and the Danubian Principalities the connection had long been of the closest. In Greece, too, the necessity of a revolution was the greatest, and, moreover, Greece was less under the immediate supervision of the Czar. It was gradually, and somewhat slowly, that the two separate principalities of Vallachia and Moldavia became the present kingdom of Rumania. The oppression that they suffered from was, for Turkish provinces, moderate; though this means but little. In some respect their dependency on the Porte was an advantage to them. " If the revolution under Ypsilantes and his associates was, as far as Rumania is concerned, abortive, its subsequent history has made it a favoured and a fortunate country. Nevertheless, a rich soil, which less than most others has been devastated by invasions, with a drainage which might make it as productive as Lombardy, has failed to enrich its population. And that population is a large one. The good or bad government of the Danubian Principalities affects nearly four millions of Rumanyos.

"Their true policy, now that they have obtained practical independence along with the union between Moldavia and Valachia, is intense selfishness of the narrowest and most provincial kind. The temptations to launch into cosmopolitanism are great. The Rumanyo language is that of Transylvania and the Bukovina; but to sympathize with these is to come in contact with Austria. They want no protection so long as they keep within the law; which in the union of the hospodariats they have violated with advantage. To give Russia no opportunity for interference ; to turn a deaf ear to Greek intrigues ; to forget that they were ever connected with Hungary ; to keep out Propaganda Romanists, the forerunners of French interposition ; to live within the law as far as regards Turkey ; to either violate or alter it as regards their own boyards ; to make roads, irrigate fields, grow grain and prosper accordingly.

*   *   *   *   *

III. GREECE.—Such should have been the policy of Rumania.

But the insurrection on the Danube was the signal for a struggle rather than the struggle itself. In Greece, the 6th of April was the day fixed for what, by a mild euphemism, we may call the outbreak of the revolution. Outbreaks, however, of revolutions fixed for a day named by the committee of a secret society are very like what a cynic might call a Sicilian Vesper,— except that they are spread over a longer time. This is the interpretation of the following passage from Finlay:—"In the month of April, 1821, a Mussulman population, amounting to upwards of twenty thousand souls, was living, dispersed in Greece, and employed in agriculture. Before two months had elapsed the greater part was slain—men, women, and children were murdered without mercy or remorse. Old men still point to heaps of stones, and tell the traveller ' There stood the pyrgos (tower) of Ali Aga, and there we slew him, his harem, and his slaves ;' and the old man walks calmly on to plough the fields which once belonged to Ali Aga, without a thought that any vengeful fury can attend his path.

"The crime was a nation's crime, and whatever perturbations it may produce must be in a nation's conscience, as the deeds by which it can be expiated must be the acts of a nation."

These are statements which the writer himself must hope are exaggerated. Yet who has corrected them? The two months were not months of battle, except so far as the small combats with surprised garrisons deserve that name. It was not till afterwards that the struggle with the regular troops began.

Such the report. The evidence of it lies in the details, which are, of course, imperfect. Enough, however, is known of them to give a rough view of the penalty which overtakes vicious governments and intolerable oppression. It was in the Morea and the neighbourhood of Patras that the Hetærists held the meeting at

Vostitza, and, as they heard little about the movements February.
in Valachia, they counselled delay. Let the Archbishop
of Arta, who is at Pisa, and let Ypsilantes, who is, or ought to be,
at Bucharest, be consulted.   Let the Turks who, to say the least,
have grown suspicious, be deceived.   Let the people wait till after
the 6th.   But the people were less patient than the majority
of the committee which would guide them.   On the 25th of
March three Turkish couriers were waylaid and killed at Agridha.
The next day were killed eight Albanian collectors of the haratch.
The leader of the men who killed them increased his band to
three hundred, and at Bersova killed twenty and disarmed forty
Mussulmans—like the haratch collectors, Albanians.   On the
2nd of April many Turks were murdered at different places.   On
the 3rd, the fort of Kalavryta which the Turks, (on hearing of
a special act of violence contemplated, but not carried into
effect against Seid Aga of Lalla,) had made into a kind of barri-
cade, surrendered on terms; and three hundred soldiers fell into
the hands of the Greeks.   Half of these are considered to have
been put to death by the following August.   On the same day
Kalamata was besieged, and on the 4th it surrendered.   The
prisoners were distributed among the conquerors as domestic slaves.
Before the year was out "the moon had devoured them."   The
Varduniot Albanians, when they heard of the outbreak at
Kalamata, in passing through Mistra, on their way to Tripolitza,
spread the alarm among the Turks of that district, who tried to
escape to Tripolitza or Monemvasia.   About five thousand out
of nineteen thousand of these are supposed to have been either
surprised or killed on the way.   Meanwhile in the parts about
Patras regular fighting had begun.

I have given these details as I find them in Finlay; partly
because such details are the elements of our generalities, and partly
because they give us approximate numbers, dates, and places.
They are the details of a fortnight in the Morea only, and,
details of which the narrative has come down to us.   Allow for
what is unrecorded, and take fourteen days in the Morea as
a sample of fourteen days elsewhere and the picture gets
distinctness.

From the smaller let us go to the greater details. The first victory
won by the Greeks, on anything deserving the name of a battle-field,

was at Valtetzi, one of the positions for blockading Tripolitza. About five thousand Turks and three thousand Greeks were engaged; and of the latter one hundred and fifty, of the former four hundred, were killed. The first fortress that capitulated was Monemvasia; the second, Navarin; the third, Tripolitza—all in August. The general character of these and the other sieges was the same. The Turks had neglected all adequate preparation. The Greeks blockaded the towns and trusted to famine—to famine and treachery. The general rule seems to have been for some of the Greek captains to tamper with some of the Albanian portions of the garrison; to drive private bargains with some of the wealthier Turks; to regulate the energy of the attack according to the amount of money or jewels that they could extort from the possessors of them without being obliged to either share it with the common soldier as prize-money or to pay a portion of it into the national treasury. At Monemvasia there was a further complication. Demetrius Ypsilantes insisted on the surrender being made in his name. The Peloponnesian Senate overruled this piece of presumption, and decided that it should be given up to the Greek Government. Still, the three towns were taken; and broken faith and bloodshed attended the taking of each. At Monemvasia it was merely the murder of several Turks. At Navarin it was a general massacre of men, women, and children—women cut down with sabres, and deliberately shot; children dashed against the rocks, or hurled into the sea. After this the conquerors quarrelled among themselves about the booty.

The fraud, the bad faith, the intestine quarrels, the separate capitulation of Tripolitza were those of Navarin, only on a larger scale. The system of separate bargains attained here its completeness, and Greek women entered the city to persuade Turkish women to save their lives and honour, by giving up their jewels. One Bobolina, the widow of a Spetziot shipowner, was the great agent in these patriotic pieces of rapacity. Meanwhile, the chiefs drove bargains with the Turks or Mahometan Albanians of their old neighbourhoods, until the soldiers, more than suspicious of their double-dealing, determined upon storming the town as the only means of getting their own in the way of plunder. The Albanians took care of themselves and got away free; but the Turks were massacred. Two thousand of them, chiefly women and children, twenty-four hours after the town had been taken, and when the hot blood of the besiegers had had time to cool, were deliberately led to a ravine, and, one and all, murdered. This is Finlay's notice. Gordon puts the number of Turks killed during the whole siege at eight thousand. It is safe to say that not half of these died a soldier's death. The affair at Valtetzi will not account for an eighth of them; nor does it appear that the famine had actually reached that point when death by hundreds takes place from it.

The revolution continued as it began; and the Constitution of Epidaurus and the Presidency of Mavrocordata were its results. Then events took a turn, and Greece was in a fair way of being reconquered. The change began in 1823, and it was not until the battle of Navarino, which is only another name for foreign intervention, that anything like definite success attends the Greek cause. The details of the interval are, upon the whole, discreditable to the insurgents. The spirit of the people was the same; the contempt of danger; the hatred of the Turks; the resolution to be free. But the faults of the individual leaders become both more prominent and more dangerous; and the selfishness of individual bodies is more and more disgraceful. Above all, the absolute inability, on the part of anyone who had a chance of appropriating money, to resist the temptation of diverting funds intended for the service of the country at large, to his own individual advantage, becomes sadly apparent. During this interval the famous Greek loan was contracted; and as a pendant to it two civil wars broke out.

The great scene of undeserved calamity was Chios. A favoured island, it was comparatively beyond the influence which had elsewhere goaded the Greeks into rebellion. But it was not allowed to be left alone. A Samian, of the name of Lycurgus, undertook to revolutionize it: landed with an inadequate force; behaved as in a hostile country; and inflicted many of the miseries of war on the wealthy and peaceful population before the real conflict with the Turks had begun. The garrison, previously strengthened, was reinforced. A strong body of Turkish troops was landed. A decided superiority of power was exhibited, Lycurgus made his escape, leaving the Chiots, unwillingly connected with the revolution, to their fate. Had they been the first instigators they could scarcely have been treated with greater severity; and severity, in Turkish warfare, means revolting and inhuman cruelty. That the massacre, after it had lasted some days, was partially checked by the captain-pasha must be recorded in his favour. That the Greeks had been the first to stain their hands with the blood of unarmed prisoners is true as against the Samiots under Lycurgus. That the revolt of Chios may have appeared to the Sultan pre-eminently un-called for and gratuitous is likely. But it is beyond doubt, that of all the actors in the revolution, the Chiots were those who, for the smallest provocation, suffered the most. In the number of those who were massacred, and in the greater number of those who were sold as slaves, there is exaggeration; but in one monastery three, in another two, thousand were either cut to pieces or burnt with the building; whilst, as measures of cold-blooded cruelty, between seventy and eighty hostages, previously taken as securities against the revolt, were executed. Finlay, though he treats the high number of forty thousand Chiots either murdered or enslaved as an exaggeration, considers that in the January of '22 the population of the island was one hundred thou-sand, in August thirty thousand; of which only twenty thousand are accounted for as having escaped. Let the margin be what it may the penalty paid by the miserable islanders for the folly, crime, and cowardice of the Greeks under Lycurgus, was of the bloodiest.

In one respect, however, it was productive of good. The severity of the Sultan defeated its own end. Of all the events which directed the attention of Western Europe towards the affairs of Greece the massacres of Chios were, by far, the most important. It was this which most especially appealed to the common feeling of humanity; this that most strongly excited the indignation of all Christian nations; this that first taught statesmen that such a thing as a war of extermination was not impossibly contemplated; and that when this was the case, the principle of non-intervention should give way to the natural instincts and impulses of humanity.

The event which was the most ominous to Greece, and which, if Greece could by any means be welded into a unity, was most likely to have abolished all minor factions, was the reconciliation between the Sultan and Mahomet Ali. Mahomet Ali undertook the reduction of the Morea. Besides this, the conquest of the islands and of Northern Greece was undertaken from Constanti-nople. A victory gained by the orthodox Tosks over the Roman Catholic Mirdits opened the campaign. Then came the disgrace-ful pillage of Skiathos and Skopelos, Greek islands, by the Greek fugitives. Reshid Pasha had driven the armatoli of Olympus out of Thessaly. They took refuge on the two islands just named, and pillaged them as if they had been parts of an enemy's country. Then there were naval actions; one of which was followed by a violation of the neutrality of the Ionian Islands—neither for the first nor the second time. Then came the first instalment of the Greek loan, which put a stop to the first of the two civil wars. This was the result of the enmity between the parties of Kolettes and Konduriotes on the one side, and of Kolokotrones on the other; the former being in office, the latter, perhaps unjustly, excluded from it. His sons held Nauplia. However, one of the first payments out of the loan prevailed upon him to evacuate it, and the wounds of the first civil war were healed. It had lasted about nine months. The same son of the same patriot appears in the second, in which he was killed. This was between the ministerialists (if we may call them so) and the party of Zaimes and Landos—Zaimes, whom Lord Byron pronounced to be the one honest man with whom he had come in contact. Yet he was not honest enough to be quiet during a time when union was strength and disunion was weakness.

Such was the anarchy on land. By sea the navies of Hydra and Spetzas were either inactive or mischievous. The ship-owners jobbed, and palmed off crazy vessels for sound ones, the payment being made out of the loan. The men did nothing unless when paid in advance. When united with the Psariots and the Kasiots they quarrelled about plunder and fought. They quarrelled, indeed, with the Psariots because they had set a bad example by serving before they had received their pay. So Kasos and Psara were sacked by the Turks. With opponents at war with one another it was no hard matter for an able commander like Ibrahim Pasha to overrun the Morea; easy, too, it was for Reshid and Kosreff Pashas to reconquer the greater part of northern and western Greece. Missolonghi was taken after an obstinate—a heroic—resistance. The chief warriors in these events were Kolokotrones, who was generally defeated; Odysseus, who turned traitor and joined the Turks; and the admiral Miaoulis, who, whether successful or unsuccessful, was always brave, vigilant, prudent, and thoroughly patriotic.   In '26, Athens, after a long siege and many ineffectual attempts to relieve it, was finally retaken.

All this is so like a reconquest that when we take the main events of these four years in succession, the battle of Navarino looks like a simple act of violence on the part of the Western Powers.   A rebellion has broken out.   The Sultan has put it down.   He must now be compelled to yield to it.   Greece is nearly as much his own as it was in 1820; and the revolution begins afresh.   Such is the view of the prominently conspicuous events above noticed.   But this view—a view which charges England, France, and Russia with a most gratuitous piece of intervention—is only the superficial one.   The battle of Navarino was merely the conclusion of a long series of interferences, which ran concurrently with the events just alluded to, through, at least, the same years.   Remonstrance had followed remonstrance; suggestion, suggestion; and the affairs of Greece had been matters for the three cabinets ever since the end of 1822.

The division of continental Greece into three hospodariats, with native hospodars, whose subordinate officers should be natives chosen by the Sultan; with the Ægean Islands as a separate Government, directly under the Porte, but with guarantees for good administration; and a municipal system on the principles of that of Chios, Hydra, and Psara; one or all—this was the Russian plan.   It was meant to paralyze the revolutionary principle, to keep up a feeling of hostility (for the Turks were to garrison the fortresses), and to put Russia in the position of a protector; and it was well contrived for the purpose.   Nor was that purpose concealed.   *Paralyser l'influence des revolutionaires dans toute la Greece*, is part of a sentence in the notification of the proposal. To this, however, England objected; England, with Canning as Prime Minister.   To him the Greeks had addressed a protest against the Russian plan, and an answer to this was addressed direct to the Greeks themselves; *pro tanto*, an approximate acknowledgment of them as an independent Power.   But he said, also, that England and Turkey were friendly Powers.   Philellenism, at this time, was strong in England.   Money had been subscribed.

27 *

The famous Greek loan was being contracted.   The neutrality of the Ionian Islands was all on one side.   The English ambassador at Constantinople, Lord Strangford, had both the authority and the will to urge the claims of Greece as strongly as the temper of the Sultan would allow.   That Sultan, however, was Mahmud, who remonstrated in his turn.   Colonel Stanhope was ordered home.   The Lord High Commissioner of the Ionian Islands prohibited, by proclamation, the deposit of arms and ammunition intended for Greece.   But the policy of Mr. Canning was known, and there was no secret as to the Philellenic feelings of the British Commodore in the Mediterranean.   To a document empowering England to treat with the Sultan for _{August 25, 1825.} the independence of Greece, with an authority which had as yet been entrusted to neither any other Power nor to England before, the signatures of the most influential men of Greece were attached. By a subsequent decree this was interpreted to mean the Sultan's suzerainty and a fixed tribute.   On this, in a modified form, Russia soon afterwards agreed to act in union _{April, 1826.} with England.   Then came the fruits of the Holy Alliance as they showed themselves in '26 ; especially the occupation of Spain by French troops, and the counter-movement of English troops into Portugal : the act by which _{December, 1826.} England and the Holy Alliance were brought to the extreme points of their divergence.   They went no further ; and in '27, France joined the two ; so that the Treaty of _{July.} London was effected for the special pacification of Greece.   Internal independence, Turkish suzerainty, and an armistice pending the negotiations—this was the gist of it.   Notified to both belligerents, the armistice was accepted by the Greeks, rejected by the Turks.

The navies kept the sea; and on the 29th of September, Hastings gained an important victory over the Turks at Salona ; which Ibrahim Pasha, who was off Navarino when he heard of it, interpreted as a violation of the armistice—and that rightly ; as far, at least, as he, as a belligerent, was concerned.   Whether it were or not, the Turks were not bound by it.   He sent, therefore, a squadron against Hastings, which Sir Edward Codrington sent back.   It joined the main body of the fleet, and, with it, lay at anchor at Navarino.   Partly for the sake of the harbour ; partly to keep the Egyptian fleet from active operations against the Greeks, the allied admirals determined to do the same. We know the result the annihilation of the Turkish navy. The land, however, was still held by Ibrahim, the son of Mehemet Ali, and it was not till the 28th of July, 1828, that the French undertook to clear the Morea of the Turks; and this they did effectively. This being done the conclusion of the Greek revolution is mainly a matter for the diplomatists of France, England, and Russia; and when it has been settled that emancipated Hellas is to have a king, the question arises as to where one is to be found. We know that the search was eventually successful; but this, along with the events which followed, is scarcely a part of the history of the Ottomans.

   *   *   *   *   *

The loss to the Porte of Egypt is by no means so absolute as those of Servia, Greece, and Rumania. And it is due to a rebellion of another kind—a rebellion of a pasha rather than either a population or a sect. Of these revolts the class is a large one, for to some extent, at some time or other, almost every province in the empire has affected independence. The characteristic of the Egyptian revolt is that of its having been successful. In its origin, it was one of two, for, in the first instance, the connection between Syria and Egypt is so close that we expect that their history will be that of a single rebellion throughout. The event, however, is different. The two provinces hold together for some time; but by 1839, it is determined that, though Egypt is to be comparatively independent, Syria is to remain as it was. The chief details of the interval have already been indicated.

Of the countries which, without achieving independence, gave the most trouble to the Porte, Anatolia, under the Sultans of the early and middle period, was the most persevering, and the most uncertain in the outbreaks of its discontent. This, however, was less the result of bad government, of which these Asiatics were not very intolerant, than of their Koniarid, or Karamanian, rather than Ottoman nationality. In Syria, the revolts, though frequent, were partial, *i.e.* Druse or Maronite, &c., rather than Syrian as a whole. In Arabia, during the latter half of the last century, the Wahabite insurrection was one that took root in a religious reform rather than in any political grievance.   Of the rebellious pashas of the time of the Servian and the Greek revolutions, by far the most formidable was the noted Ali Pasha, of Albania; but it is doubtful whether any one, or any of two, of these would have been attended with serious injury to the Porte had they taken place at different times.

*   *   *   *   *

We may now turn from our notice of the decline and fall of the Ottoman to that of the rise and progress of the Moscovite Empire.

The wars before the time of Vladimir I., were rather acts of bold piracy on a great scale, than actual invasions of territory with the view of permanent conquest; through this they became under Vladimir and his successors.   Those in the direction of the Danube, the Don, and the Vistula against Tatars, Lithuanians, and Poles, were quite as likely to have been defensive as the contrary; though on this point our information is deficient. Those, however, in the direction of the Baltic and the Arctic Ocean are of a different character.   The whole area was Fin, or Ugrian; and as a family of mankind the Fins pass for one of the weaker ones.   They are this to some extent; but their distance from the centre of civilization has quite as much to do with their comparative inability to defend themselves as any physical inferiority.   Conquest spreads along the lines where there is the least resistance; and it is along these that Russia, in the first instance, cut its way northwards.

I have not, as has been already stated, gone into the question of the original country of the Russians, or attempted to fix the exact part of the old Slavonic area from which the first ancestors of the present conquerors are derived.   On the contrary I have merely given the approximate area from which the present Russians began their career of conquest, in the eighth or ninth century.   It was only in their movements northwards that they wholly succeeded in forming a vast dukedom, and that at the expense of the Fins.   The evidence of this is internal rather than historical.   That it was a Fin, or Ugrian, area upon which they first encroached, is generally admitted; the only question being the extent to which it extended southwards. At the present moment we find remains of the different Fin dialects as far south as the Governments of Perza, Tambov, and Simbirsk—at least. In Kursk the population is said to be of the Fin type; but here the evidence of language is wanting. In the central districts—Orel, Tula, Tshernigov, Vladimir, etc.,—the Slavonization of the country appears to be complete. But on each side of this district there seems to have been Fins and Lithuanians on the west, with Fins and Tatars on the east. Moreover, on each side of this area there seems to have been two roads to Novorogod; and these, I think, were originally lines of trade rather than conquest— the western one along the Fin and Lithuanic frontier, the eastern (probably that of the Khazars) along the Fin and Tatar frontier. At any rate, when history begins, we have a notice of two routes—the one by which the Swedes came in such close contact with the Russians as to be called 'Ρῶς; the other, the one suggested by Constantine Porphyrogeneta, who writes that *Mordia, i.e.* the present Government of Penza, was twelve days journey from the Don Kosak country. The confusion of the name Russ and Swede has been already noticed.

The Mongol conquests arrest the career of the Russians; and emperil—indeed, for a time, suspend—her independence. Hence, the two conquests of Ivan the Terrible may almost be called Wars of Liberation. And now it becomes clear that the conquest of Siberia is only a matter of degree; for Yermak the Kosak has begun it. But this is after the fashion of an American backwoodsman or a Hudson's Bay trader, rather than that of an ambitious emperor. In like manner, the final reduction of the Crimea is only one of time and opportunity. There was always a reasonable pretext for war. In the first instance, it is for one of reprisals and retaliation; but, when the Porte becomes weaker, it cannot but change its character. It is not in human nature for a vast country like Russia, with towns and a trade both in the south and in the latitude of the Baltic, to be satisfied with a single port at Archangel; and, with one enemy between them and the Euxine, and another between them and the Baltic, to neglect opportunities, perhaps, to solicit provocation. There must, under such circumstances, come a time when they will carry out their advantages to the utmost.   Neither Sweden nor the Crimean Tatars were powers which willingly left a neighbour without a pretext for war, or which, themselves, gave or expected much quarter when defeated. It is probable that the conquest of Crimea was the best service that was ever done by one enemy to another; for it was a vassal state that was always compromising its suzerain.

Siberia led sooner or later to wars with China and Turkestan; and how greatly the action of the Crimean Khan, by the passage across the Caucasus, as an ally of the Sultan in the Russo-Turkish alliance against Persia, prepared the way of the future conquest of his own territory, and for still greater annexations in Transcaucasia we have seen. So much for the four Khanates.

Nearly at the same time as the Crimea, the annexation of Lithuania began; but it is not with the Crimea that its history is connected. On the contrary, it is with Poland; indeed, though of Poland proper, Lithuania was no more an integral part, than Ireland is of England, and the little that has to be said about it is deferred until the most important of all the questions concerning the political morality or immorality of Russia—that of the Partitions of Poland—comes under notice. That Russia took to itself all Lithuania by her compacts with Austria and Prussia between the years 1763 and 1793 is certain; but the appropriation of any part of Poland itself is no earlier than 1815.   This must be remembered, viz., that it was by the Treaty of Vienna (and not before) that Poland proper was made over to Russia. What she got by the so-called Partitions was Lithuania.

*   *   *   *

The question of Partitions is important; and of these that of Poland is the most notorious instance. Hence the two subjects will be considered together; and that in detail, and from the beginning, i.e. from the time when the succession became *elective*.

At the choice of the first *elective* king, the Marshall, whose high office it was to proclaim him, was a Protestant; the candidate who was chosen was a Romanist—Henry of Valois, afterwards Henry III. of France. In this we have a measure of the power of the Dissidents on one side, and of the Romanists on the other. But the Christians of the Greek Church were strong enough to take care of themselves, even in Poland; while in Lithuania they formed the majority, and in Polish Russia nearly the whole population. But the new ruler abandoned his crown, and ran away from his kingdom. The Voyvode of Transylvania, Stephen Bathory, who succeeded him, though a good king in other respects, did more than any of his predecessors to make over his kingdom to the Jesuits. Then came, as the fruits of absenteeism on the part of the great landowners, the Kosak insurrection, in which Russia, the Porte, and Poland, were, to a great extent, at war with one another; and then the deposition of Micael Koributh, and the reign of Sobieski, great as a soldier, but, like Bathory, priest-ridden, and queen-ridden. Then came the time of Charles XII. and Peter the Great, and the antagonism between Stanislas Leczinski as the *nomine* of the first, and of Augustus Frederic, Elector of Saxony, of the second. The whole period up to this time has been one of trouble; and of this the two great causes have been the dissensions arising out of the elective principle, and the evil of religious discord; each stimulating, exaggerating, and with other minor motives acting and re-acting on one another.

After the death of John III., Sobieski, the anarchy was at its height, and the difficulty of anything like agreement in the election of a successor led to an interregnum, in which no one played a more flagitious part than Sobieski's widow. It ended, however, in the union of the two crowns under Frederic Augustus I., the Elector of Saxony.

In 1733, Frederic Augustus died, and an outburst of faction followed his death. The Diet passed a resolution that no one but a Piast should be eligible; and this meant the restoration of Charles's *nominé*. Both Austria and Russia supported the King of Saxony, and so did many Poles. France, however, promised assistance to Leczinski, for he was now the father-in-law of Louis XV., who married his daughter in 1723, the year in which he attained his majority. Louis was a bad husband;

but it suited him to support Leczinski's claim to the Polish crown. Frederic Augustus II., the son of the late king, was upheld by Russia; and the opposition of France died out. Indeed, though the Porte had let Russia understand that she was prepared to undertake a war for the independence and integrity of the kingdom of Poland, and that she left the Poles free to choose their own king, little came of her opposition. This, however, was before the Treaty of Belgrade, the one which was the most specially honourable to Turkey, as it concluded a war against Austria and Russia combined. After this, and for nearly thirty years after the death of Frederic Augustus I., there is peace between the Sultan and the Czar.

Then came the election, again under Russian influence, of Stanislas Augustus (Poniatovski); and again a Turco-Russian war; and again French intrigues; for Louis XV. was still alive, and had formed "*The Family Compact*" with the sovereigns of Spain, Naples, and Parma. The effective assistance that France gave the Porte in the war that now followed, amounted to little more than the Confederacy of Bar, and the result was, what France intrigued for—the interference of Turkey, who would willingly have been at peace with all Europe. But the Russians overstepped the boundaries of the Crimean Khan, in their pursuit of Polish detachments, who seem to have thought this the best way of embroiling the Porte itself with Russia; in which they were only too successful. The worst of these inroads was one over the Bessarabian frontier, when the town of Balta was savagely burnt by the Russians. At Constantinople the campaign was in a state of preparation; but the Tatar Khan Ghirai, lost no time in avenging it. His raid upon Russian territory, the one of which we have the fullest accounts; and, as such, passes for the most formidable one. Nevertheless, it is, certainly, only one out of scores. No one, more than Crim Ghirai, involved the Porte in irreconcilable hostility with Russia; and none more than he suggested to that empire the doctrine of "*Delenda est Carthago*." And the destruction soon came. Except when Crim Ghirai commanded, the Turks were beaten; and even Austria became jealous of Russia; and contemplated an alliance with Turkey. And here (earlier than

Russia), the Turkish legate suggested that Poland might either be divided between the Porte and Austria, or the Emperor of Austria might put whom he chose on the Polish throne. However, Austria prefers to act with Russia. In Poland itself anarchy continues, and opportunities present themselves which no good man would seize, and few ambitious men overlook. That Frederic suggested the dismemberment is likely. Catherine never pretended to be shocked by it. Austria had the choice of three lines of action. She could stand aloof and see the thing done; but to keep her hands from doing it; she could either single-handed, or with alliances, oppose it. She could acquiesce in it, and share the spoil. And this is what she did.

In the Partition of 1773 she took Gallicia; Prussia, certain German, or Germanizing districts on the Pomeranian and Brandenburgh frontier; Russia, Politsk, Vitepsk, Mohilev, and Polish Livonia.

In that of 1792, Austria took nothing; Prussia, Thorn. Dantzig, and the remainder of Great Poland, and a part of Little Poland ; Russia about half Lithuania, and half Volhynia.

In that of 1793, Russia took the remainder of Lithuania, and Prussia the remainder of Poland. But foreign interference began long before this; at least as early as the Thirty Years' War.

The great Gustavus Adolphus himself was by no means either purely chivalrous, or a purely Protestant champion. What he wanted was a footing in Germany, and when he undertook to defend Pomerania, he made a hard bargain, and he knew that he made it. Neither was he, elsewhere, deficient in calculation. For all this, the Swedish history, of which he and Charles XII. are extreme types, is a chivalrous history in the way of an approximation—an approximation only. Except that the Protestants would have persecuted the Catholics, instead of the Catholics persecuting the Protestants, and that the Sapiehas would have overridden the Oginskis instead of the Oginskis overriding the Sapiehas, the power of Charles XII. might wax or wane without either hurting or helping Poland. His influence on the affairs of that divided country was that of an ambitious foreigner; that of the Czar was no more. The same intrigues that brought Russia, Prussia, and Austria together, might have brought together Sweden, Prussia, and Turkey, or any three members of any combination; under the policy of whom the same internal dissensions might have been fostered, the same real improvements neglected, the same intolerance exhibited, and the same mutilations undergone. Indeed, till the battle of Pultova, Sweden, rather than Russia, is the great foreign enemy.

Sigismund III., when Crown Prince of Sweden, had been elected to the throne of Poland; but the throne of Poland required a Roman Catholic king, that of Sweden a Lutheran. Hence, the Crown of Sweden was absolutely impossible to the Swedish Crown Prince; and, as this was in the time of Gustavus Adolphus, the complication was not likely to be got over. Sigismund, then, never reigned in Sweden, though two of his sons were kings of Poland; but not in direct succession. Sigismund's *immediate* successor was a tolerant and energetic ruler, who died without issue; and whose death was followed by an interregnum. When this came to an end the candidates for the Crown were the Czar Alexis, the father of Peter the Great; the Voivode of Transylvania, Ragotski; and two sons of Sigismund, Swedes in blood and politics, both ecclesiastics, and both desirous of obtaining from the Pope a dispensation which should allow them to marry. The one was the Bishop, who afterwards reigned as John III.; the other was John Casimir, who was also suitor to Sigismund's widow. He was a Cardinal: but had resigned his high office for a higher one; for it was upon him that the election fell. This is that Cardinal King whom Mazeppa, in his youth, according to Byron, served as a page.

> John Casimir; I was his page
> Six summers in my early age.
> A learned monarch sure was he,
> And most unlike your Majesty:
> Who made no war, and did not gain
> New realms to lose them back again.
> And, save debates in Warsaw's Diet,
> He ruled in most unseemly quiet.
> Not that he had no cares to vex;
> He loved the Muses and the sex, &c.

He certainly did this, and that not wisely. For it was an intrigue with his Chancellor's wife which made the last drop of his troubles run over, and helped, *inter alia*, to bring upon him a war with Sweden. When the king of that country died, and the Crown from which John Casimir, as a Roman Catholic King of Poland, was debarred, became vacant, the injured husband fled to Sweden, and returned with the Swedish king at the head of an army. Meanwhile, the terrible war of the Kosaks under Bogdan was going on. Bogdan, who had previously conquered Gallicia, was now retreating—but with his face to the foe. Forty thousand Poles attacked him, and were cut to pieces. Kaminiec was then invested: and, in one of the obscure actions connected with this part of the campaign, his son was killed. The father now applied to the Czar, and offered to become his vassal if two hundred thousand Russians were poured into Lithuania. After some real or affected hesitation, Alexis accepted his proposal, and overran Smolensko, Mohilev, Vitepsk, Polotsk, Severia, and Semigallia.

It was at this juncture that the King of Sweden landed in Pomerania. The Greek Catholics had joined the Czar; the Protestants flocked to Charles; the Anabaptists and the extreme Dissidents had long ago crowded the tents of Bogdan. First at Warsaw, then at Cracow, then at Leopol did Charles show himself at the head of a victorious and ever-swelling army: the King of Poland having fled to Silesia. Then it was that a partition was proposed. The Elector of Bradenburg was to have an accession on the side of Prussia. Ragotski, the Voivode of Transylvania, was to have another portion. Russia had already a strong grip on Lithuania. The fact itself was determined on; and the name "*Partition*" was given to it in a speech by Lubomirski when denouncing it in the Diet.

Still it failed of effect. Holland, the Empire, and Denmark interposed. The Elector of Brandenburg himself either ceased to press, or opposed it. Europe, indeed, may be said to have forbidden it; the most effective of the Powers who then prevented what, in 1772, France and England could *not* prevent, being Denmark. Sweden was invaded; and the Elector of Brandenburg was released from doing homage for his fiefs in

Pomerania. He also had Lauenburg and Butov granted him. All claims on the part of John Casimir on the Swedish crown were renounced and the greater part of Livonia was ceded. The peace of Oliva, A.D. 1660, was the result : a peace which most especially promised religious toleration to the Dissidents. How its conditions in this respect were kept is another question. They were scandalously violated.

Hinc illæ lacrymæ.—Charles XII. was a worse enemy to Poland than Peter the Great. It is the common habit, however, to make him the scape-goat; and it is not uncommon to go farther. The Russian Archdukes, when Constantinople was Roman (or Greek), contracted marriages with the Imperial Family, and, partly on the strength of this, and partly from the Greek form of their Christianity, they got to consider themselves, more or less, Greek in their political predilections; and, by the time of Peter, the Greeks had made political capital out of the notion. They certainly went more than half-way to encourage the scheme of a Christian insurrection in case of any Russian war against Turkey; and Peter certainly thanked them for their civility ; perhaps stimulated it. But I fail to find that he thought much about Constantinople as a goal. What he thought about most especially was the immediate work he had for the time being ; and, because he did so, he generally succeeded in effecting it. His one absorbing thought was the possession of Azov : and if he dreamed of anything in the vista beyond, it was the Persian Gulf, rather than the Bosphorus. His alliance with the Porte against Persia *may* have been made with this view. In an attack, however, upon Constantinople he *must* have reckoned on the opposition of Austria; and it was not until the time of his successors, the Czarinas, that this standing antagonism was converted into a conspiracy. It was under the weak and vain Anne, and the proud and profligate Catherine, that the " Oriental Project " took form, and, if it did not originate in Greece, it was the Greeks who most especially stimulated it. The conquest of the Crimea made it easier, indeed without it it was well-nigh impossible. But, except so far as it was a stepping-stone to further encroachments, it was, if rightly interpreted, a benefit to the Porte. But it is scarcely one that we can expect will be appreciated; and it is certainly one that was not intended.

And now, closely connected with this, comes the well-known triple conspiracy, of the two empires and the new kingdom of Prussia. All three are now in harmony with each other, and the Partition of Poland goes on slowly but surely to a first, a second, and a third division; then to the presentation of the Prussian share of it to the King of Saxony by Napoleon; and, finally, to the transfer from Saxony to Russia at the Congress of Vienna.

There are Partitions and Partitions. You may take a part of certain extraneous and heterogeneous territories. Or you may distribute among your confederates the very heart and body of the nation; this last being the worst form of spoliation. For the former a majority of the transferred population may be thankful. By the latter, except in the case of a mixed population, a persecuted creed, or an oppressed class of Helots, there is no benefit to anyone. The first Partitions of Poland were of the former kind; and it is probable that both the Germans taken into Prussia, and the Lithuanians who were Russianized, were more than satisfied by the transfer. The fate of the true Polish parts was different. Austria took, in the first instance, Gallicia; but this was only partly Polish. Prussia annexed Posen. The remainder was given to Saxony by Napoleon, and to Russia by the Congress of Vienna. All this, from first to last, is bad; but the *odium* is distributed. The characteristic of Russia was at the time of the Partition her vile policy of opposing the reforms that might have led to independence, and upholding as a friend to Poland, the abuses that kept her weak. After the Treaty of Vienna the systematic perseverance with which she reduced, or strove to reduce, the kingdom to a province has been the chief charge against her.

With that of Poland as an example, it is by no means strange that Partitions are, generally and often justly, condemned. But so long as we have International Treaties, Guarantees, Congresses, and the whole apparatus connected with the Balance of Power, there is always a Partition in the prospect; a Partition in which unambitious states may inevitably find them-

selves partaking. It is a danger to which no nation is more liable
than our own; for what can be done if the Ottoman can neither
be improved nor upheld? Each power has to look at its own
interests; and however much it would be satisfied if the *status
quo* could be kept up for an indefinite period, must act, more or
less, according to the action of others. A necessary Partition
is a necessary evil; but the action of a single dishonest power
may bring it on prematurely. Then comes incrimination; and
the charge of having joined in a partition becomes odious. It
is one, however, that we must avoid as long as we can. But the
possibility of its being forced upon us must be recognized.

        *   *   *   *

The Ottoman Empire is now, in respect to administration,
almost entirely limited to Asia Minor. Here it is only partially that we meet with Greeks; while the Slavonic element is
almost wholly absent. Still there is a decided, and a very
important Christian element.

Armenia and Georgia are the two Christian populations of
Asia Minor. The former is exclusively so. In Georgia, however, the Lazes are Mahometan. The Georgian Christians are
under Russia.

The Armenian nationality has no exact analogue, unless
that of the Jews. There is a district called Armenian under the
Ottomans. There is a district so called under Persia. There
is a district so called under Russia. But neither under the
Czar, the Shah, nor the Sultan, is there an exclusively Armenian
country. It is, indeed, doubtful whether there is any large
district anywhere in which the majority of the population is,
according to the tests of language and creed, decidedly Armenian. There is always a concurrent population. In Erivan
this is made to constitute one-half; and it would be difficult to
find any province in which the Armenian is more prevalent
than this. With few exceptions, this concurrent population is
always Mahometan; and, except in Russia, dominant and privileged. With few exceptions it is either Turk or Persian;
Turk of the Tatar, Persian of the Kurd, branch. Nor is this
mixture of recent origin. That the language has held up
against this intrusion of foreign elements is due to the influence

of its letters and its Christian literature. At the same time, it is much in the position of the Hebrew. Just as there are few, if any, Jews, who are not compelled by the circumstances of their residence to learn some second language, which, in many cases, becomes, for all the purposes of common life, their true vernacular, so there are few, if any, Armenians, who are not bilingual; speaking Turkish, or Persian, or Hindostani, as the case may be.

Under such a stress of circumstances, the strongest advocate for the principle of nationality can scarcely recognize an Armenian kingdom, an Armenian confederacy, an Armenian republic. It has all the difficulties which would attend an attempt to reconstruct a national Judea, combined with others peculiar to itself. There is no Holy Land to the Armenian; no Jerusalem. In Etshmiadzhin is the seat of the Patriarch; and in Ararat the centre of the numberless traditions and beliefs. But the true analogue to a Palestine is wanting. On the other hand, the number of Armenians occupant of the soil of Armenia is greater than that of the Jews of the valley of the Jordan. Their occupancy, however, is larger.

Moreover, under such circumstances, few can see the extension of the Russian empire in the direction of Armenia with much regret; except, of course, when he looks from a point of view exclusively political. That history supplies many instances where the transfer of a Christian community from the rule of the Sultan to that of a sovereign of its own creed has been followed by complaints and regrets is true; and it is true that cynical writers have often contrasted the manner in which the Christians of one denomination have persecuted the Christians of another with the tolerance granted by certain Mahometan rulers. But truer than either is the fact that such cases have been exceptional, and that the practice of Mahometan toleration has never been either permanent or complete. It has, at best, been but a lucky accident. The present writer, perhaps, falls into an opposite error; for he believes that, for any long period of time, the worst Christian government is, for Christians, better than the best Mahometan.

This remark, however, is subject to one important qualification. In order for the general statement to hold good, it is necessary that the Christianity should be homogeneous; in other words, that the whole of the population so transferred should be of one religious denomination, sect, or church; all Greek or all Roman Catholic. When there is a division with any approach to equality, it is better for the Mahometan dominion to be retained. In all Mahometan countries Christians of different sects are more hostile to each other than they are to the infidel. If left free, they interfere with each other more than they would have been interfered with if left under infidel control.

With the populations now under notice, the rule of Russia has been a gain. It has certainly been powerful enough to protect them; and even where it has oppressed them, the oppression has arisen out of the vices of the administration rather than out of any permanent cause of suffering. That these have been great is only too true. That the Armenians, as a body, are not unwilling instruments to the ambition of Russia is well known, and it would be strange if it were otherwise. It is the Russian church which is the nearest to their own. It is Russia which is their natural protector against Mahometanism. The few that are in political relations with other countries are not enough to make any notable exception. In Venice there are Armenians under Austria; but there are no Turks in Venetia. In India there are Armenians under England; and of these it may be said that they are English in the way that those of Asia Minor are Russian.

The Armenian districts of Russia are Armenian and Persian rather than Armenian and Turk. The Armenians here are numerous in Shirvan. In Sheki they have been calculated as nine out of forty thousand; in Karabagh, as twenty to sixty thousand. Gandzha is Tatar and Armenian. In Erivan there may be an Armenian majority. If so it has been caused by immigrants rather than the original population. Of Nakhitshevan they are calculated at one third.

Akhalzik and Akhalkhaliku, like Lazistan, is Georgian rather than Armenian.

Though much may be said in the way of regret or con-
demnation about the actual emigration from the Armenian
districts of Turkey to those of Russia, it must be remembered
that the diminution of a population is widely different from a
loss of territory. The emigrants to Russia may and *do* return;
though this implies faultiness on the part of Russia rather than
any merits on that of the Porte. That in Asia Minor the
Armenians are the most important population is beyond
doubt. It is also the one that is the most exposed to annoyance.
The fiscal and religious disqualifications under which they
labour are those of the Christians in general. The one, and it
is one that they share with their co-religionists in Mesopotamia,
is the vicinity to the predatory tribes of the frontier—the Kurds,
the scourge of the Christians from the Georgian frontier to the
Syrian desert; and, along the frontier of the Desert, the Arabs.
Nor is the mere unprotectedness of the Christians in these parts
the sole element of their suffering. They are bought and sold
by their nominal protector; whilst the Mahometan officials of the
frontiers connive at their spoliations, and, in many cases, take a
per-centage of the spoil. The remedy for this—of all contemplated reforms the most important, and the first in order of time
that is called for—is easier on the south than on the east, or
easier against the Arab marauders than the Kurds; for the Kurds
are only partially subjects of the Porte. Some tribes are under
Persia; some are either Persian or Turk; and some are tributaries to both. The coercion of these predatory bands is, in
itself, no difficult matter. It is an office for which the Albanian
portion of the Ottoman army is pre-eminently fit; indeed it is
work for which the Arnaut seems made and predestined. But
before his services can be assured there is an indispensable
condition. He must be paid; liberally and regularly, if
possible; but regularly at all events. And so it is throughout;
one reform implies a previous one, and the whole series of
necessary alterations is one of a more or less relative and
conditional character throughout. But this is what we must
begin with.

LONDON :
PRINTED BY W. H. ALLEN AND CO.

028

www.ingramcontent.com/pod-product-compliance
Lightning Source LLC
Chambersburg PA
CBHW031058110726
47900CB00003B/978